Information Services for Innovative Organizations

Library and Information Science

Consulting Editor: *Harold Borko*
Graduate School of Library and Information Science
University of California, Los Angeles

Harold Borko and Charles L. Bernier
Abstracting Concepts and Methods

F. W. Lancaster
Toward Paperless Information Systems

H. S. Heaps
Information Retrieval: Computational and Theoretical Aspects

Harold Borko and Charles L. Bernier
Indexing Concepts and Methods

Gerald Jahoda and Judith Schiek Braunagel
The Librarian and Reference Queries: A Systematic Approach

Charles H. Busha and Stephen P. Harter
Research Methods in Librarianship: Techniques and Interpretation

Diana M. Thomas, Ann T. Hinckley, and Elizabeth R. Eisenbach
The Effective Reference Librarian

G. Edward Evans
Management Techniques for Librarians, Second Edition

Jessica L. Milstead
Subject Access Systems: Alternatives in Design

Dagobert Soergel
Information Storage and Retrieval: A Systems Approach

Stephen P. Harter
Online Information Retrieval: Concepts, Prinicples, and Techniques

Timothy C. Craven
String Indexing

The list of books continues at the end of the volume.

Information Services for Innovative Organizations

Carmel Maguire
School of Information, Library and Archives Studies
University of New South Wales
Kensington, New South Wales, Australia

Edward J. Kazlauskas
School of Education
University of Southern California
Los Angeles, California

Anthony D. Weir
Canberra, Australia

Academic Press
A Division of Harcourt Brace & Company
San Diego New York Boston London Sydney Tokyo Toronto

This book is printed on acid-free paper. ♾

Academic Press, Inc.
525 B Street, Suite 1900, San Diego, California 92101-4495

United Kingdom Edition published by
Academic Press Limited
24–28 Oval Road, London NW1 7DX

Library of Congress Cataloging-in-Publication Data

Maguire, Carmel.
Information services for innovative organization / Carmel Maguire, Edward J. Kazlauskas, Anthony D. Weir.
p. cm. -- (Library and information science)
Includes bibliographical references and index.
ISBN 0-12-465030-9
1. Business information services. I. Kazlauskas, Edward John. II. Weir, Anthony D. III. Title. IV. Series: Library and information science (New York, N.Y.)
HF54.5.M34 1994
658.4'038--dc20 93-38540
CIP

PRINTED IN THE UNITED STATES OF AMERICA
94 95 96 97 98 99 BC 9 8 7 6 5 4 3 2 1

Contents

Preface xi

1
The Importance of Innovation and Information

1.1 What Is Innovation? 2
1.2 Why Is Innovation Important? 5
1.2.1 Historical and Economic Perspectives 5
1.2.2 Political Perspective 8
1.2.3 Management Perspective 10
1.3 How Does Innovation Happen? 12
1.3.1 Models of the Innovation Process 13
1.4 What Is Information? 19
1.5 Information in the Economy 22
1.5.1 Prices as Information Carriers 22
1.5.2 The Information Economy 24
1.5.3 The Information Society 27
1.6 Connecting Innovation and Information 30
References 31

2
The Process of Innovation

2.1 The Idea of a System 36
2.2 Inputs or Sources for Innovation 41
2.2.1 Demand and Supply 41
2.2.2 Structure, Size, and Life Cycle 44
2.2.3 Economic Expectations 46

2.3 Processing or Managing Innovation 47
2.3.1 Picking up the Signals 47
2.3.2 Designing the Strategies 55
2.4 Innovation Outputs 60
2.5 Feedback in the Innovation System 62
2.6 The Environment of Innovation 64
References 67

3
Information Services: Fundamental Issues

3.1 Definitions and Distinctions 72
3.1.1 Information Systems and Information Technology 72
3.1.2 Information Sources, Resources, and Services 76
3.1.3 Information Markets and Invisible Assets 82
3.1.3.1 Efficiencies and Deficiencies 82
3.1.3.2 Ownership Issues 86
3.1.3.3 Public Good and Private Enterprise 87
3.1.3.4 Invisible Assets 90
3.1.4 Organizations as Information Systems 92
3.2 The Digital Environment 95
3.2.1 Convergence and Diversity 95
3.2.2 Effects on Information Specialities and Specialists 100
3.2.3 Effects on Management Strategies in Organizations 107
3.2.4 Effects on Information Products and Services 115
3.3 The Value of Information Services 121
3.3.1 Judgment of Value 121
3.3.2 Perspectives and Criteria 126
3.3.3 Demonstrations of Value 131
References 135

4
Information Sources for Innovation

4.1 Introduction 142
4.2 Categorizing Sources of Information 143
4.3 Categories of Information Sources 146
4.4 Internal Sources 149
4.4.1 Internal Peers 149

4.4.2 New Employees 149
4.4.3 Internally Generated Data and Reports 150
4.5 External Sources 154
4.5.1 Peers and the Importance of Informal Sources 155
4.5.2 Meetings, Seminars, Conferences, Study Missions 158
4.5.3 Publications 160
4.5.3.1 Patents 162
4.5.4 Electronic Information Services 164
4.6 Information Providers in Organizations 168
4.6.1 Librarians and Information Professionals 169
4.6.2 Competitor Intelligence Personnel 171
4.6.3 Marketing Personnel 174
4.6.4 Other Providers of Information 175
4.7 Case Examples of Information Resource Systems for Innovation 176
4.7.1 NASA 176
4.7.2 Other Systems 183
4.8 Organizations to Promote Innovation 184
4.8.1 Organizations for Innovation—Information Provider Organizations 185
4.8.2 Organizations for Innovation—Program Providers 185
4.9 Advisory Services 186
References 188

5

Information Technologies and Their Use

5.1 Introduction 194
5.2 Computer Hardware and Software 195
5.2.1 The Rise of the Personal Computer 199
5.2.2 Mass Storage Developments 202
5.2.3 Output and Input Devices 204
5.2.4 Operating Systems 206
5.2.5 The User Interface 209
5.2.6 Computer Languages 211
5.2.7 Application Software 213
5.3 Networking and Telecommunications 219
5.3.1 Local Area Networks 219
5.3.2 Facsimile Transmission 222

5.3.3 Wide Area Networks 223
5.3.3.1 WAN Performance 226
5.3.3.2 Protocols 227
5.3.3.3 Media 228
5.3.4 Public Networks 230
5.4 Harnessing Information Technology for Use 235
5.4.1 Technology and Human Behavior 236
5.4.2 Systems Analysis and Costing 242
5.4.3 Management Information Systems and Decision Support Systems 245
5.4.4 Information Resource Management 248
5.5 Trends 248
5.5.1 Infotrends 249
5.5.2 The Interplay of Three Trends: Entropy, Technostress, and Outsourcing 252
5.5.3 Standards for Information Transfer 254
5.5.4 End-User Computing 256
References 259

6

Information Services as Supporters and Exemplars of Innovation

6.1 Innovation as a Phenomenon 265
6.1.1 Why All Organizations Need to Innovate 265
6.1.2 Why Information Services Need to Innovate 266
6.1.3 Major Features of Innovation as a Phenomenon 267
6.2 Organizations as Information Processing Systems 271
6.2.1 Key Information Flows 271
6.2.2 How Information Services Facilitate Information Flows for Innovation 273
6.2.3 Some General Propositions about Organizations as Information Processing Systems 277
6.2.4 Effects of Technological Change on Information Services 280
6.2.5 Information-User Behavior 284
6.3 Principles for the Design of Information Services 286
6.3.1 Flexibility and Multifaceting 286
6.3.2 Competition and Collaboration 289
6.3.3 Intermediary Roles 292
6.3.4 Monitoring 295

6.3.5 Focus on Clients and Marketing 296
6.3.6 Constant Innovation 297
6.4 Strategies for the Promotion of Innovation 298
6.4.1 Promotion of Innovation in Information Services 298
6.4.2 Promotion of Innovation by Information Services 302
6.5 Conclusion 304
References 304

Index 307

Preface

Innovation is managed change. In this sense there is nothing new about it. Ideas about the beginnings of cultures may be based on divine revelation, traditional story, or scientific hypotheses. However based, all the myths postulate response to change as the beginning of things. The challenged organisms range from amoeba through wolf cubs to human beings, and those which prove best able to adapt to changed circumstances prevail.

At least since the early part of this century it has been recognized that capitalist societies depend on continuing innovation. More recently the collapse of the planned economies of Eastern Europe and the Soviet Union has demonstrated that no society can be immune to change and that the entrepreneurial approach seems the only one capable of increasing resources and opportunities at anything like the rate required to cope with world populations.

Innovation does not only refer to change based on advances in scientific and technological knowledge. Nor is it confined to changes in products and processes. Innovations in services are also important and often lucrative, and so are innovations in management. In fact many would argue that social innovations, within organizations and in the broader society, are the most important of all. These are the changes in attitudes, practices, and relationships that have to occur for any innovation, technical or otherwise, to be successful. It may be argued, for example, that recycling and the accompanying attitude changes will make more difference to United States society than any breakthrough in technology or advance in scientific knowledge.

Society's preoccupation with innovation, especially in industry and business, is reflected in the literature. In the past twenty years the steady stream of writings on innovation has turned into a raging torrent. There are books, journal articles, research reports, conference proceedings, papers from government and nongovernment commissions of inquiry, as well as courses of instruction at all levels and in all media, television features and audio productions. All urge innovation as a global good in the interest of economic productivity and many also see in it hope of ecological repair.

By no means do all the writings about innovation emanate from economists. Many of the writers are management consultants, and many others represent disciplines and interests as diverse as human communications, sociology of knowledge, engineering, science and technology policy, history of ideas, organization theory, technology transfer, and research management.

That there is a connection between innovation and information is obvious. News of new ways of doing things, of new forms of demand, and of new opportunities generally has to be encoded in messages of some kind and communicated. Empirical studies have repeatedly found that in more prosperous enterprises there is greater awareness of information and greater ability to manage it. There is also strong evidence that the quality, both of an organization's activities in the gathering and analysis of information and of the store of the information which it possesses, is reflected in the commercial success of its innovations. Information superiority has also been claimed to give nations as well as individual firms competitive advantage.

All organizations process information. They gather information from the environment, they generate much more in their own operations and they return some of that to the environment, whatever the products they make or the processes or services they perform. Information services may be parts of organizations, or independent service organizations, which aim to provide the information which would not necessarily reach individuals or organizations in the natural course of their operations, but which is nevertheless relevant to their objectives and may even be important for their survival.

There is an extensive literature on how to organize information services. These works are mainly about the organization and management of libraries, with a smaller literature on how to manage publishing enterprises and bookshops, and a yet smaller but growing segment on how to create, manage, and distribute electronic information services. A useful body of knowledge has also been gleaned from research in librarianship, information science, and communications about the information usage characteristics of various industrial, professional, demographic, and ethnic groups.

None of these works seeks explicitly to associate information services with the particular requirements of organizations which are focused on innovation. This book seeks to fill this gap in the literature. It is intended to provide a sound basis for the design and management of information services which will (1) give decision makers more help in the management of change; (2) make corporate decision makers more aware of information as an asset and of information management as a strategy for improved innovation decisions; and (3) make information service providers potential sources of innovation for organizations of all kinds.

This book has been designed specifically to serve the needs of students of information services management, in schools of library and information science and in business information studies courses in schools of management. It is also intended for practitioners—librarians and other managers—who provide information services in business, industry, and government, either from within or as external consultants and contractors. This book also aims to assist those managers of computer and communications facilities whose opportunities for innovation will increasingly include the provision of information services. Digitization of information is erasing distinctions in the means, the places, and the occupations through which different types of information are handled. Already some university computer center managers find themselves networking CD-ROMs on campus, not necessarily unwillingly but perhaps unwittingly, becoming information service providers. This role will also become increasingly part of that played by the telephone companies in the United States and telecommunications companies everywhere.

This exploration of the connection between information services and innovation is built on the following plan. The introductory chapter examines the concept of innovation, and briefly indicates the importance of innovation to the nation and to the organization, whether it is a commercial firm, a professional association, or a public service institution. Preliminary examination of the innovation process reveals its dependency on information. Information and related concepts are defined, and indications are given of the pervasive nature of information-related activities in today's society.

Chapter 2 goes more deeply into the nature of innovation as a process. In so doing it categorizes more closely the kinds of information required for innovation, and places these requirements in the broader context of corporate planning. For an organization to be consistently successful at innovation, and thereby to survive in today's rapidly changing social and business environment, good information is only one of many requirements. The reasons why some organizations are better at innovation than others begin to emerge as helpful models of the process are analyzed.

It emerges from that analysis that one of the requirements of an appropriate corporate strategy is an information strategy. Chapter 3 looks generally at how information services, both in-house and external, fit into the information strategy of an innovative organization, and at times help shape it. The effects of digital information on both information specialists and information products and services are examined in some depth. The chapter also looks at evidence of the value of information services and how their value in an organization has been calculated.

Chapter 4 categorizes the information sources that are available, and gives many examples of each and how they have been applied in the innovation process. Emphasis is placed on the variety of sources available—personal, impersonal, formal and informal, individual and corporate—as well as on the circumstances and environments in which they appear to be most effective in the transmission and translation of information to useful knowledge.

In recent years, information technology has made possible a dramatic transformation in information services, which has yet to be fully appreciated or implemented. Chapter 5 reviews the nature of each of the relevant technologies and follows up on how the technologies can be integrated with each other and with human capability and work habits to produce useable and useful information systems.

Chapter 6 brings these threads together. The general reasons why all organizations need to innovate are summarized along with the particular reasons that apply to information services. A series of propositions is presented, derived from study of innovation as a phenomenon, of effects of technological change on information services, and of information user behavior. The propositions are then synthesized into a set of design and management principles for information services that contribute effectively to the innovation process. Strategies are also proposed by which information services may both exploit the sources of innovation available to them and act as sources of innovation for the organizations which they serve.

The authors hope that, like all successful innovations, their book will find wide acceptance and attract many imitators.

The authors' families, friends, and colleagues have assisted them in many ways. Particular acknowledgment is recorded of the encouragement and assistance received from Dr. Patricia Willard as Head of the School of Information, Library and Archives Studies at the University of New South Wales; Dr. Robert M. Hayes, Dean Emeritus of the Graduate School of Library and Information Science at the University of California, Los Angeles; and the Australian Department of Industry, Technology and Regional Development, especially through Mr. Mike Perri and Mr. Neville Hurst. The authors' special thanks are also due to Mr. Ron Iehl, California State University Northridge, for his library reference assistance; and Ms. Merilyn J. Bryce for her assistance in correcting proofs.

Carmel Maguire
Edward J. Kazlauskas
Anthony D. Weir

1

The Importance of Innovation and Information

A nation's competitiveness depends on the capacity of its industry to innovate and upgrade.

—M. Porter, The Competitive Advantage of Nations, p.73. Reprinted by permission of the *Harvard Business Review*. Excerpt from "The Competitive Advantage of Nations" by Michael E. Porter (March-April 1990). Copyright © 1990 by the President and Fellows of Harvard College; all rights reserved.

If Australians of the next century are to inhabit a prosperous nation and a clean and safe world, we today must grasp the challenge of gaining control of the processes of scientific and technological innovation and ensure that we receive benefit, not disadvantage from change.

—R. J. Hawke, then Prime Minister of Australia in speech to Parliament, 8 May 1989.

[Successful companies] believe that managing innovations is the key to sustaining high levels of performance for their shareholders. They assume that the innovators, the attackers, will ultimately have the advantage . . . that as risky as innovation is, not innovating is even riskier.

—R. N. Foster, *Innovation: The Attacker's Advantage,* p. 30. Copyright © 1986 by McKinsey & Co., Inc. Reprinted by permission of Simon & Schuster, Inc.

Capitalism . . . is by nature a form or method of economic change and not only never is but never can be stationary . . . The fundamental impulse that sets and keeps the capitalist engine in motion comes from the new consumers' goods, the new methods of production or transportation, the new markets, the new forms of industrial organization that capitalist enterprise creates.

—Joseph Schumpeter, *Capitalism, Socialism and Democracy,* p. 82.

Chapter Synopsis

The preceding quotations suggest that innovation is important for industrial prosperity and therefore for national well-being. But what exactly is innovation, why is it important, and what are the processes that promote it? This chapter opens with an exploration of the meaning of innovation and proceeds to an explanation of its importance in modern societies. The focus is on innovation in all organizations, whether they operate in business, industry, government, or as public service institutions. In order to amplify understanding, some of the models of the innovation process that have been proposed are discussed. These models all establish the role of information flow as a key component of the innovation process. This view prompts a discussion of information and its economic importance, as well as of the connections between innovation and information.

The rest of the book then proceeds to look in more detail at the process of innovation and at how the relevant information can be identified, acquired by, and transferred within and through the innovating organization.

1.1 What Is Innovation?

The word *innovation* derives from the Latin *innovare,* meaning to renew or alter. The senses of both the "introduction of novelties" and of "something new introduced" go back to the sixteenth century, according to the *Oxford English Dictionary* (OED) (1989, pp. 997–998). Another sense as "a political revolution, a rebellion or insurrection" seems not to have survived the eighteenth century.

The OED also offers a meaning for innovation, which it describes as "in commercial usage," namely, "the action of introducing a new product into the market; a product newly brought on to the market." The first cited usage of this meaning is from Schumpeter (1939, v.1). This is probably the dominant meaning in popular understanding today, but it is useful to widen this definition to cover developments other than new products. Thus, innovation is also a change in processes so that old products are made in new ways. The novelties brought about by innovation may be in services or in the systems of management and marketing by which products and services are brought into being and distributed. Thus, in a broader sense again, innovation is not confined to the manufacturers or distributors of products and services in the commercial sector. Organizations in all three levels of government, legislative, executive, and judiciary, in education, health care, and all branches of the not-for-profit sector also need to innovate to meet changing conditions and even to anticipate them.

In order to attain a perspective broad enough for the study of innovation in all these environments, it is also necessary to recognize that the introduction of novelties is possible without anything we would identify as *invention* and that invention, does not necessarily induce innovation. It is also useful to make a distinction between *invention* as the discovery of a new idea, and *innovation* as the putting of that idea into commercial or organizational practice for the first time. To decouple invention from innovation is not easy and for good reason. Much of the glamor that surrounds this century's advances in scientific research derives from widely publicized scientific and technological "breakthroughs" which have resulted in advanced products and services. The fallacy that invention is necessary and sufficient for innovation is reinforced by the media and by writers, readers, and viewers who find breakthroughs to be the best stories.

The discovery of antibiotics is a good example. In 1928 a British chemist, Alexander Fleming, discovered that penicillin, a mold that had hitherto been regarded as simply a nuisance in growing laboratory cultures, killed bacteria. This was undoubtedly an important and dramatic event, at least in retrospect. Its development into an innovation, let alone a benefit to humanity, did not begin until 1938 when other scientists at the University of Oxford worked on the substance. By 1941 they had refined it to the stage where human trials could be carried out. It became an innovation only when the Pfizer Company brought it to market. Popular belief is not only that penicillin drugs followed fast on Fleming's discovery, but that their development was motivated by a desire to apply them in treating the sick and wounded of World War II. Ronayne (1984, p. 62) quotes the explicit denial by Ernest Chain, one of the Oxford researchers, that he and his colleagues were in any way motivated by patriotism when they began their work. Chain is in fact adamant that the possibility of a practical use for penicillin in clinical medicine never entered the heads of the group when they commenced work on it. But breakthrough legends remain powerful.

The nonlegendary aspects of the penicillin story illustrate the two-way relationship of social change and innovation. Penicillin would not have been rushed into field use without the demands for such a substance stimulated by the mass infection of war wounds in World War II. And it had the expected technical effect. What could not have been predicted was the social effect. Widespread use of penicillin and related compounds, by rendering almost harmless many of the infections of childhood and thus reducing mortality, has been an influence in lowering birth rates in developed countries.

In this book we take the broad view of innovation as a total process, not necessarily based on science, technology, or invention. A new idea brought into commercial practice need not be technological to be of economic and social value. Innovation can be organizational or social in nature.

For example, the nineteenth century innovations of the mass-circulation newspaper and of payment by installments have had profound effects on society. Recycling may prove to be one of the most powerful influences in changing United States society in the last decade of the twentieth century. Innovations can be in products, processes or services, and in the management theories and practices by which all three are controlled in organizations and distributed in markets. In organizations, as in society generally, innovations have to be articulated by their originators or champions and described so that others can understand and support them. To have significant impact, innovations need to be diffused throughout the organization or society and even into other organizations or societies. Obviously then, communication is an important aspect of innovation, and what is communicated is information about the potential or proposed innovation.

Drucker (1985) characterized innovation as "the art that endows resources with a new capacity to create wealth" (p. 30), and to this he added the corollary "Equally whatever changes the wealth-producing potential of already existing resources constitutes innovation" (p. 31).

Kingston (1977) takes a particularly broad view of innovation. He not only distinguishes invention (the discovery of a new idea) from innovation, but also places both in a spectrum of human activity that ranges from the artist (whose vision is mainly inwards) to the trader (who is mainly concerned with manipulating objects in the real world, rather than with ideas). Artistic activity is concerned with the artist's personal vision of the world, but it seeks to make the world of the imagination accessible to others. (If this world of the imagination is so personal that it cannot be communicated to others, then the artist is at the end of the spectrum: a dreamer rather than an artist). The artist seeks and makes a different world, but the inventor sees the possibility of some new relationship between aspects of the existing world; the innovator makes this relationship a reality. Towards the other end of the spectrum, the trader deals only slightly in ideas: but sees that the world can be changed, albeit slightly, by moving existing goods from one place to another, for the trader's financial gain. The entrepreneur brings the worldliness of the trader to the ideas of the inventor in Kingston's spectrum, a diagram of which is reproduced as Figure 1.1. This may serve as a useful reminder of all the players in the theater of human creativity, some of whom, especially the artists and traders, will receive little further attention in this book.

Another aspect of the definition of innovation as a broad social phenomenon is that its novelty does not have to be absolute. This concept is very neatly caught in the definition by Rogers (1983) whereby innovation is "an idea, practice, or object that is perceived as new by an individual or another unit of adoption" (p. xviii).

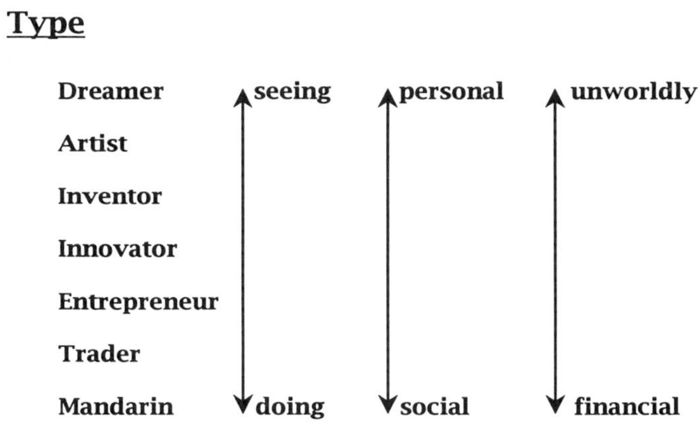

Figure 1.1
A spectrum of human activity from the "artist" to the "trader" (Adapted from Kingston, 1977).

Bringing these ideas together, in this book we adopt the definition that

innovation is the application in any organization of ideas new to it, whether they are embodied in products, processes, services, or in the systems of management and marketing through which the organization operates.

1.2 Why is Innovation Important?

1.2.1 Historical and Economic Perspectives

The successive cycles of economic growth and recession over at least the last 200 years have been the subject of much economic analysis. In particular, Kondratiev in the 1920s pointed to a series of "long waves" separated by about 50 years, starting with what is usually called the Industrial Revolution, that is, the transformation of the British textile industry in the late eighteenth century. Schumpeter (1943) was the first to associate these cycles with innovation. He pointed out that all were associated with radical new technologies. Each long wave starts with a major technological innovation (such as the steam engine). This new technology then diffuses through an industry and is continually improved in practice. The process of adoption and incremental innovations has historically often taken decades. Associated with this process are major organizational innovations. The move to work in factories was one of them. There is also, of course, substantial investment and economic activity generally.

As Rothwell and Zegweld (1985) point out, "To be sure, Schumpeter stressed the uniqueness of each cycle, pointing to such important exogenous factors as wars and harvest failures; nevertheless the most important feature was innovation, and Schumpeter spoke explicitly of technological revolutions being the driving force of economic growth" (p. 28).

Not all agree that the revolutions that drive the economy have to be technological, and some of these views are discussed in Chapter 2 on the process of innovation. There is no dispute, however, that in the process of innovation, diffusion is all important, and it is a social process, as indeed is the process that leads to the first adoption of new technology or of new ideas in services or management. But the benefits associated with an innovation accrue to the economy as a whole only when the new technology or technique is widely taken up. Diffusion then is a very important process, and obviously the diffusion of an innovation requires the diffusion of information about it.

In time, the innovation acquires so many riders on what Rothwell and Zegweld (1985) call "the entrepreneurial bandwagon" (p. 28) that the market becomes saturated and profit margins fall. Competition kills off some of the producers, leading to unemployment and recession as the suppliers and other associated industries decline in parallel. An example often quoted is the collapse of the British railway boom in the 1850s. But while this is occurring, according to Schumpeterian theory, a new wave of innovations will be occurring in the "process of Creative Destruction," which is the capitalist system as described by Schumpeter (1943, p. 83).

Schumpeter's view that innovation is the driving force for economic growth was eagerly seized on in Japan (Prestowitz, 1988), but at least until recently rather neglected in the West, where economic debate is considered by some to have centered on arcane questions of fiscal and monetary policy in the increasingly unrealistic model of a technologically static society. The orthodoxy in economics has been that technical and institutional change is an exogenous variable, somehow external to the economy rather than central to its performance. Arguments that seek to refute this static view have been advanced by some economists, especially by Christopher Freeman (1982) and others at the Science Policy Research Unit at the University of Sussex in the United Kingdom. Their ideas are presented at length in Dosi *et al.* (1988) and more accessibly for the student in Clark (1985).

Essentially, these economists have sought a new economic theory capable of incorporating technical and institutional change into the mainstream of economic analysis and policy-making. In this approach they have regarded technical change as fundamental in shaping the patterns of transformation in the economy, pointed to dynamic adjustment mechanisms that involve changes both technical and institutional, and paid attention to the socio-institutional framework which always influences the processes of change. Much of their effort has been focused on the large picture of change in relation to economic cycles, national systems of innovation, and international technology transfer.

A related microeconomic perspective on innovation has also been much discussed in the economic and policy literature. Here the focus is on innovation as a means of raising productivity and efficiency at the level of the firm. The idea is that improvements in process efficiency mean more product can be produced more cheaply, and thus raise the economic competitiveness of the firm, and ultimately of the nation. *Productivity* is a term that may be used loosely and generally, almost as a synonym for *prosperity,* but which has a more precise meaning in economics as a measurement of output in relation to input. In the United States the measurement quoted for productivity tends to be the workers' hourly output as measured by the Bureau of Labor Statistics.

In this narrow sense productivity is obviously focused on manufacturing output and has been deemed an inappropriate measure for today's economy. As Schlefer (1989) points out, "Productivity statistics do the worst job at assessing the most innovative sectors of the economy." He proceeds to the following example: "When USX produces another ingot of steel, that is duly tabulated. When an innovative software package is developed, that cannot be adequately measured. This flaw is fatal since innovation is the lifeblood of capitalism" (p. 34). Kelly and Wyckoff (1989) see productivity measurement as misleading in the service sector. They explain:

> Unlike manufacturing industries, the services generate an output that is extremely difficult to measure, so in some service industries such as banking, government statisticians estimate output by looking at the number of employee hours in a particular year. The more workers, the higher the output is presumed to be. The problem is that labor productivity in the service sector, as in other industries, is typically calculated by dividing total output by the total number of hours needed to generate it. Since the number of hours has already been used to estimate the amount of output in the first place, this puts hours in both the numerator and the denominator of the ratio, canceling one another out. The result is that productivity increases are eliminated by definition (pp. 56–57).

This is not an isolated expression of concern since the report of the MIT Commission (1989) identified the need for the United States to forge the idea of a new industrial paradigm which will reflect a fundamentally different productive system.

At the base of arguments about productivity are differences of belief about the nature of capitalist enterprise. Among economists, these are often acted out between supply-siders (Friedmanites) and liberals (Keynesians), but in current debates both sides seem to suggest similar remedies in which more managerial innovation and better motivation of workers are important ingredients.

1.2.2 Political Perspective

The First and Second World Wars brought to popular and political attention the power of technology. In the popular mind the association of science and technology with new things, good and bad, was strengthened. In World War II especially, the harnessing of scientific effort to produce war-winning products, ranging from pencillin to radar to the atomic bomb, greatly impressed politicians. After the war, they continued to pour money into scientific research (notably into nuclear power and aerospace) in the belief that science could likewise produce "the answers" to peacetime problems too. In his account of the relationship of science to government, Ronayne (1984) quotes Vannevar Bush, who was science adviser to several United States presidents and countless legislative and other inquiries. Bush (1960) wrote:

> Basic [pure] research leads to new knowledge. It provides scientific capital. It creates the fund from which the practical applications of knowledge must be drawn. New products and new processes are founded on new principles and new conceptions which, in turn, are painstakingly developed by research in the purest realms of science (p. 19).

As Ronayne (1984) remarks, "This excerpt illustrates what is now known as the linear model of innovation, a view of innovation that assumes it to be the product of prior research undertaken without thought of any practical application" (pp. 23–24). More discussion of the linear and other models of innovation will be entered in section 1.3 of this chapter. Suffice it to add here that the linear model was rather soon disputed in the period after World War II. Challenges came from empirical research on the diffusion of innovations and defense of it came from political necessity. Governments voting large amounts of funds to research had at least to assert that the moneys were directed towards the scientific and technological solution of their electors' problems. Then as now, political speeches justifying expenditure on scientific research (such as the quotation from an Australian Prime Minister at the opening of this chapter) relied explicitly or implicitly on the linear model of innovation.

When the realization came that more government spending on research and development (or R & D, as it swiftly came to be called after World War II) did not necessarily lead to greater innovation, governments began to consider the coupling between their science policies and their industry policies. By 1981, policies had progressed to the point where Rothwell and Zegweld were able to publish *Industrial Innovation and Public Policy,* in which they compared the "national innovation policies" of a range of Organisation for Economic Co-operation and Development (OECD) countries (Rothwell and Zegweld, 1981). In general, these policies comprised a range of measures called "science and technology policy" and another range called "industry policy." Government science and technology policies are those dealing with regulation of the ability to appropriate economic benefit from technology, such as the patent system, education—especially science education and technical training at all levels—and with the promotion of basic and applied research within the scientific and technological infrastructure. Industry policy on the other hand is that dealing with such things as taxation policy, investment grants, tariff policy, and industrial restructuring. More recently, the OECD itself began publication of a series of national reviews of innovation policy, to complement its previous reviews of science and technology policy. Innovation policies for France (Organisation for Economic Co-operation and Development, 1987a) and Ireland (Organisation for Economic Co-operation and Development, 1987b) are two examples. Discussion of the operation of such policies is pursued in Chapter 2.

It should be noted here that, although not often expressed in these terms, large social innovations have come about as a result of the experiences of war. The introduction of universal suffrage after the First World War is one example. Denial of the right to vote to women who had driven ambulances on the battlefields proved politically untenable even in societies notable for their conservatism on the subject prior to the war. The political climate for the extension of the welfare state, especially in the United Kingdom, after the Second World War can also at least in part be attributed to the leveling experiences of war.

There is abundant evidence that governments in all industrialized capitalist countries, at least since the beginning of the 1980s, have recognized the importance of innovation. Perhaps the most famous statements of this recognition are the successive "Visions for the future" published by Japan's Ministry of International Trade and Industry (MITI) (1980a,b, for example). These are expressions of the national consensus as to the fields in which innovative effort should be concentrated. The internationalization of trade and industry, including the opening of Eastern European markets, has led policymakers to the view that for their economies not to fall behind, their industries have to be world competitive—in particular, they have to keep up with the pace of world innovation (Porter, 1990a). Despite the scorn of many economists for countries and industries that are perceived as hiding behind tariff barriers, the amount of protection that is helpful to innovation at a national level remains moot, like so many of the topics of economic debate.

There is however general recognition that the innovative capacity of a nation is built on the innovative capacities of the firms and organizations within it. Hence there is also recognition of the importance of management as a factor in innovation.

1.2.3 Management Perspective

Innovation is important to an individual firm for much the same reason it is important to a nation. Without it, the firm is left to wither behind its rivals. The basic reason for this is a microcosm of the long economic cycle described previously, namely the product life cycle, which is illustrated in Figure 1.2.

Consider the introduction of, say, a new model of automobile. This

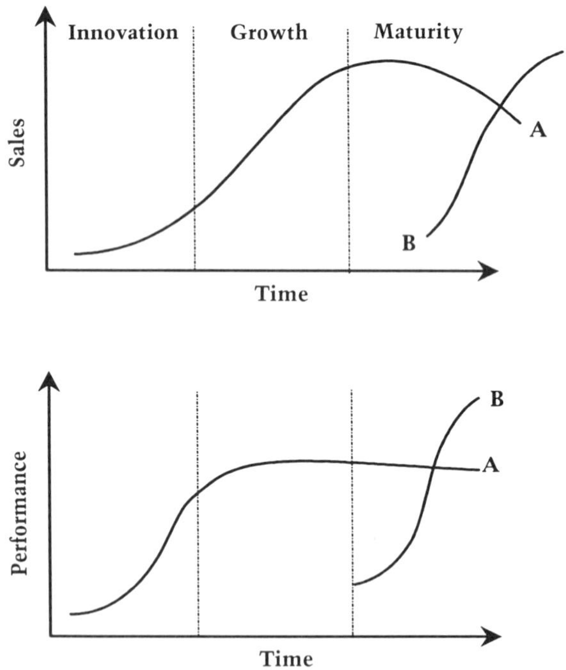

Figure 1.2
The product life cycle. The phases of innovation, growth, and maturity on the diagram refer to product A. Note the likelihood that a new rival, product B, will supercede product A (Adapted from Freeman, 1982).

might include some radical technological innovation (such as a radically new motor design). This is the innovative phase: sales start to grow from a low base. The technology will probably still have faults in the first form in which it is introduced. The motor may, for example, be unreliable in cold weather. The maker refines the product by incremental innovation, which, for example, makes the motor more reliable, adds different body styling options, and so on. Sales grow and performance improves. This is the growth phase of the cycle. At the end of it, the technology is mature; performance has reached the best that the design can produce without fresh radical innovation.

In a capitalist economy, there are many competitors who at the very least can imitate the design without incurring the development costs of the original producer, and thereby make a similar product cheaper. Other competitors are likely to respond by introducing new technology to produce innovations of their own, which produce superior performance to that possible from the now mature technology. Either way, sales of the mature producer fall off, and that manufacturer has to innovate afresh to stay in business (see Table 1.1). The story of the consequences of Henry Ford's refusal to recognize the maturity and even obsolescence of the Model T technology is well told in Hughes (1989).

The cycle is modified in a controlled economy. A mature design can remain in production unchanged and sales continue steadily. Consider, for example, East Germany before 1989 and the history of the Trabant motorcar. The Trabant, which produced large emissions and little power, continued in production in the former East Germany for nearly twenty years. Trabants were abandoned in the thousands when the collapse of the Berlin

Table 1.1
Reasons for Introducing New Products

Reasons	Score[a] mean	Standard deviation
1. Need to meet customers' changing needs	7.55	2.54
2. Need new products to meet financial goals	7.13	2.66
3. Need to be seen by customers as innovative	7.06	2.48
4. Current product range shows little growth	5.94	2.90
5. Availability of technological and research and development breakthroughs	5.58	2.97
6. Need to match competitor's new products	5.36	2.73
7. Changing availability and costs of raw materials	4.24	2.95
8. Government legislation is forcing us into new products	2.96	2.53

Source: Results from a survey of 140 Australian industrial companies by Link (1987).
[a]10 = very important; 1 = not very important.

Wall in 1989 allowed East Germans to access the West German cars, which (because of continuous competition) were more comfortable, more fuel efficient, more capacious, less polluting, and not much more expensive. In these circumstances the Trabant factory was soon put out of business.

The time frame of the product cycle varies. The life of a technology may vary from decades in basic or so-called smokestack industries such as steel-making, to a few months in some areas of "high technology," such as computers. Some areas of low technological intensity have short cycles, such as children's fad toys or ladies fashions, both of which have high marketing intensity. (In these areas the innovation lies in the concept and the way it is presented, rather than in the technology.)

Another controversy among economists, engineers, scientists and policy makers has centered on whether, to be successful, innovation needs to be the result of "technology push" or "market pull." Mowery and Rosenberg (1979) did great service by demonstrating that the results of some of the early and ambitious empirical studies addressing this question had been determined more by their prior assumptions than by evidence. The answer both in theory and practice is explored in the following section, and the special aspects of technological and market information as inputs to the innovation system are pursued in Chapter 2.

1.3 How Does Innovation Happen?

A review of theoretical and empirical studies of the innovation process reported between 1984 and 1988 has been completed by the Centre for Technology and Social Change of the University of Wollongong (Centre for Technology and Social Change, 1988) Although this review concentrates on technological innovation in industry, many of its conclusions apply more widely. One of the review's general insights is that

> innovation is centrally an organisational and managerial issue because innovations are produced within organisations that transform "knowledge." Thus the relationship between the nature and structure and values of an organisation and the innovations produced is a useful focus for analysis, and hence for the development of operational policies by managers and governments (p. 10).

This book adopts the approach to innovation as a process affecting and affected by all the characteristics of the organization. The Australian review also gives timely reminder of the variety that is also characteristic of the innovation process. "The sources of innovation vary across industries and across time; there is no general model. As a corollary, there is no ideal model of a science-industry relationship" (Centre for Technology and Social Change, 1988, p. 10).

1.3.1 Models of the Innovation Process

The search for an ideal model of the process of innovation may be unavailing but it is also unabating, and there is something to be learned from all of those propounded. Useful insight into the innovation process can be gained from each of the following simplified models, although all of them oversimplify and show only one or two faces of the multifaceted innovation "jewel." They all bring out the essential role of information transfer among the various parties involved.

Of great historical importance is the linear, science-push model of technological innovation, already referred to (pp. 8–9) and presented in diagrammatic form in Figure 1.3. In this model, as has already been briefly described in the previous section, new scientific knowledge (that is, new information) is taken up by engineers and applied scientists, who use it as the basis for new products and processes, which then go to the marketing departments of organizations who commercialize the knowledge. This model was widely used by scientists in the 1950s and 1960s to argue, often successfully, for more money for their research. The model implies that more research will inevitably lead to more salable products and thus greater prosperity for all. Embodying some of the results of the research into new products is not successful if no one wants to buy them, or at least not at the price at which they can be produced. Then the commercialization is unsuccessful, and the prosperity fails to follow, because the innovation has been a market failure.

While many references describe the linear model as discredited, the importance of basic science to modern technology and successful innovation cannot be so lightly dismissed. As Ronayne (1984) points out, "The sources

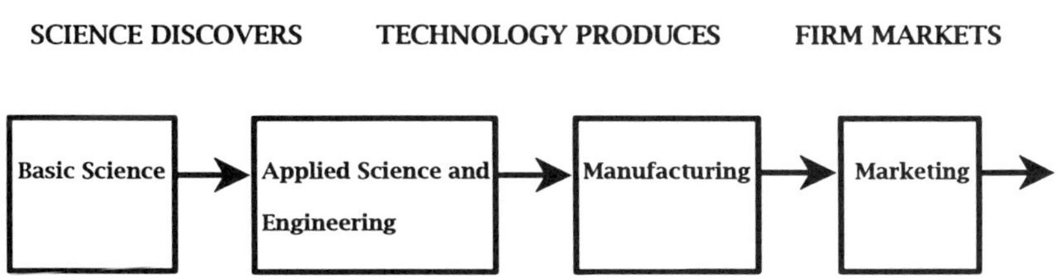

Figure 1.3
The science push linear model of innovation (Adapted from Rothwell and Zegveld, 1985).

of invention and innovation are scattered, numerous and varied and any description of the innovative process which assumes that this process always starts with basic research is simply wrong. Some innovations clearly do have such a starting point, however, and in allowing basic research to be neglected, as it would be if left entirely to the private sector according to the market failure theory, governments would be taking a conscious decision to forgo the sorts of public benefits that have in the past arisen from basic research" (pp. 65–66).

Much attention has been given to the conscious decisions that have to be made in organizations seeking to introduce technological innovation. The salient features of this work have been built into the model designed by Roberts and Frohman (1978), which is reproduced as Figure 1.4. As E. B. Roberts (1988, p. 13) points out in a later article, this model emphasizes two main generalizations: the first is that innovation is a multistage process, with differing requirements at different stages; and the second is that technical innovation primarily occurs through technical efforts carried out within an organization but requires heavy interaction with the external technological as well as market environment. It is important to note that a central ingredient in these generalizations is information. As E. B. Roberts (1988) has emphasized, "Proactive search for technical and market inputs, as well as receptivity to information sensed from external sources, are critical aspects of technology-based innovation" (p. 13).

Another model that features information is presented by Tyler (1981) as a conceptual illustration of the role of information in the production process. It is shown in Figure 1.5. Tyler sees information inputs as an integral part of a productive economic unit. Information input affects the information-handling component of the units, for example, information on price and supply availability. Information input also affects the manufacturing component; examples include employees' knowledge of a process or manufacturing properties, such as specific chemicals.

Rosenbloom's framework (Figure 1.6) also identifies information as a component in technological change. As a preliminary step, information from the environment is gathered. The environmental component can include, for example, technological and marketing information. Additional information gathering also occurs during the process of innovation when innovative ideas are generated. (Rosenbloom, 1978).

Rothwell (1983) presents an interactive model of innovation (shown in Figure 1.7). Rothwell emphasizes the connections among factors inside and outside the innovating organization. The model brings out the fact that the process of innovation represents the influence of technological capabilities and market needs within the framework of the innovating firm (Rothwell and Zegveld, 1985). The model shows a complex net of communication

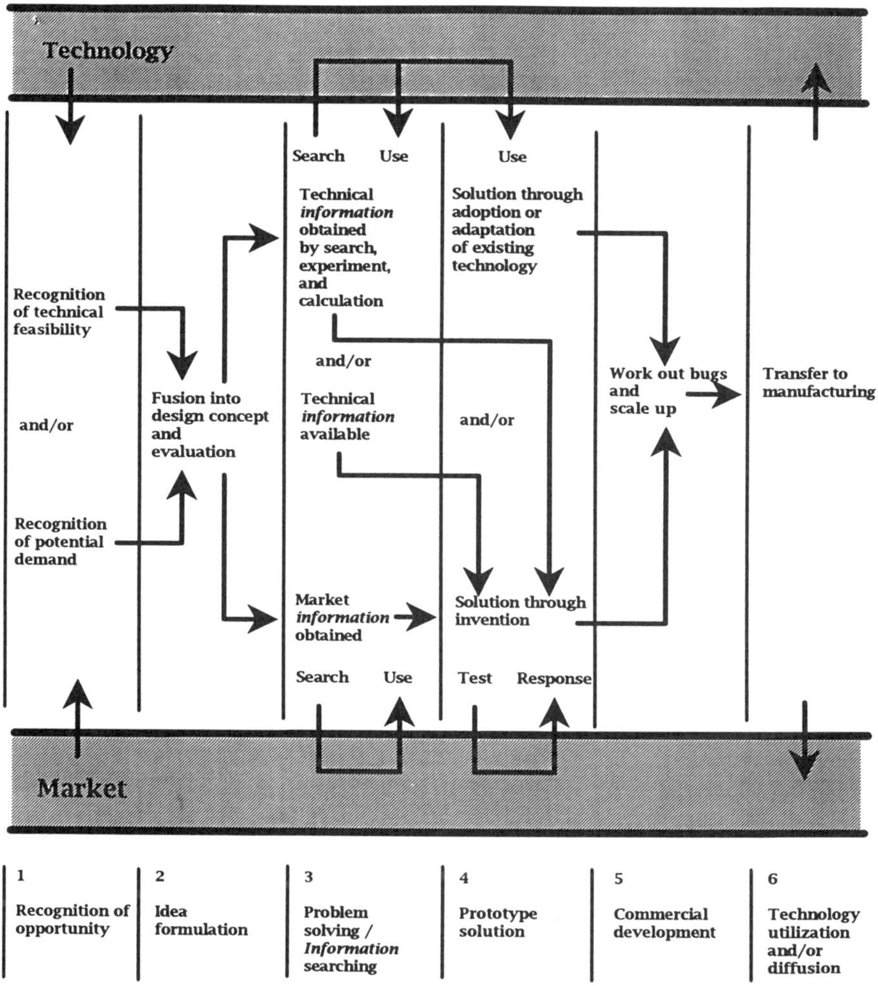

Figure 1.4
Roberts' multistage model of innovation. Note the frequent feedback loops (not all shown) and the drawing from the various information pools. From stage 1 to stage 6 may take several years (source: Roberts and Frohman, 1978, p. 32).

paths that move into, out of, and within the organization, bringing together the various in-house functions and linking the firm to the broader scientific and technological community and to the marketplace. Even if the innovator is a single person, rather than a substantial organization, he or she cannot operate in isolation.

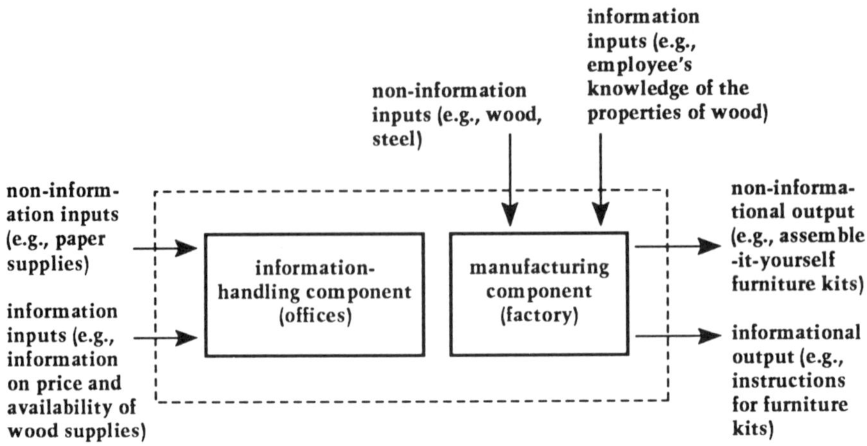

Figure 1.5
The role of information in the production process: a conceptual illustration (Adapted from Tyler, 1981, p. 11).

Rothwell's model has many similarities with the "fusion" model proposed by Ichimura *et al.* (1986) and shown in Figure 1.8. The model's main feature is that the results of various information inputs are fused into innovative ideas, hence the term "fusion" model. These information-based inputs can include market information, such as current economic conditions and politics; the results of users' needs assessment, whereby the perceived needs of a customer group are identified; technology assessment, whereby the

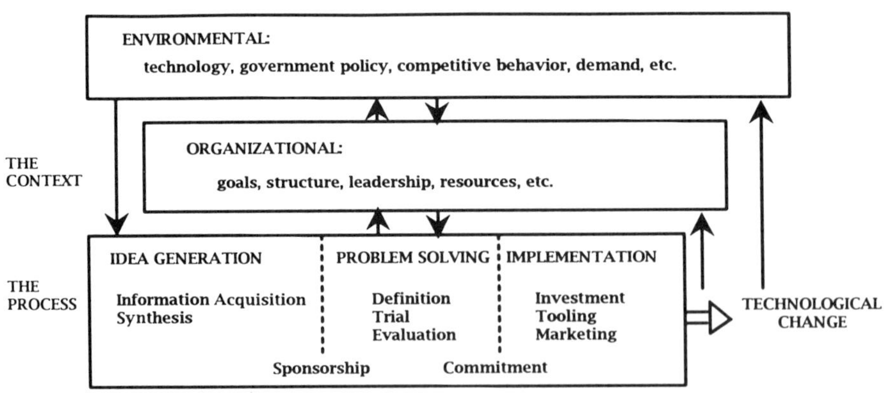

Figure 1.6
Rosenbloom's framework for technological change (source: Rosenbloom, 1978, p. 227).

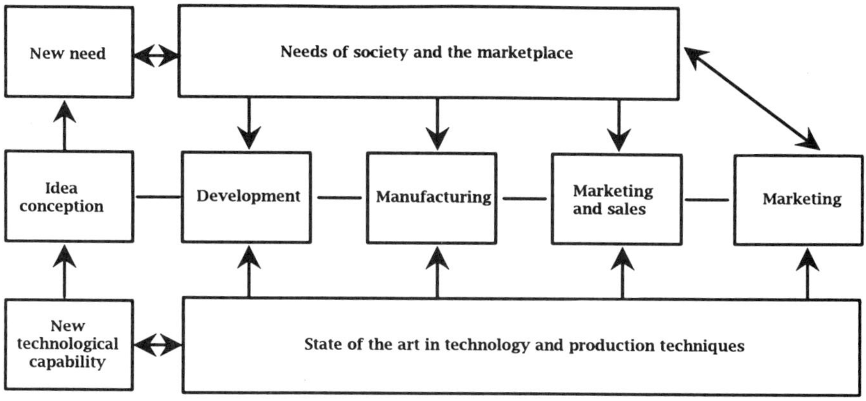

Figure 1.7
Interactive model of the innovation process (source: Rothwell, 1983).

technological possibility of the innovation is identified; and engineering information, about, for example, equipment, parts, and materials.

Brown and Karagozoglu (1989) present a systems model in which information flows are a component. Their model is shown in Figure 1.9. They state that information, or more precisely information flows, are of two types: "(1) information that exists outside the boundaries of an organization and enters the organization through 'boundary-spanners,' such as technological and market gatekeepers; and (2) internally circulating information, which feeds the process of innovation throughout its stages" (p. 12). They also present an illustration of the changing nature of information input during the different stages of the innovation process. For example, during idea generation they maintain that there should be increased flows of both internal and external information; during the problem solving stage there need to be information flows that integrate the various function areas. In addition, they claim that characteristics of information flow will vary depending on the nature of the innovation. Radically new products require considerable external information flow on the technology, whereas incrementally developed new products require increased internal information flow and an emphasis on external marketing information.

The systems approach adopted by Brown and Karagozoglu (1989) provides a powerful method for addressing the complexity of the interrelated elements that make up the innovation process, and a systems model is used in Chapter 2 in further exploration of the operation of information and information services within it. The importance of information and information flows (or communication) in the process has already been established.

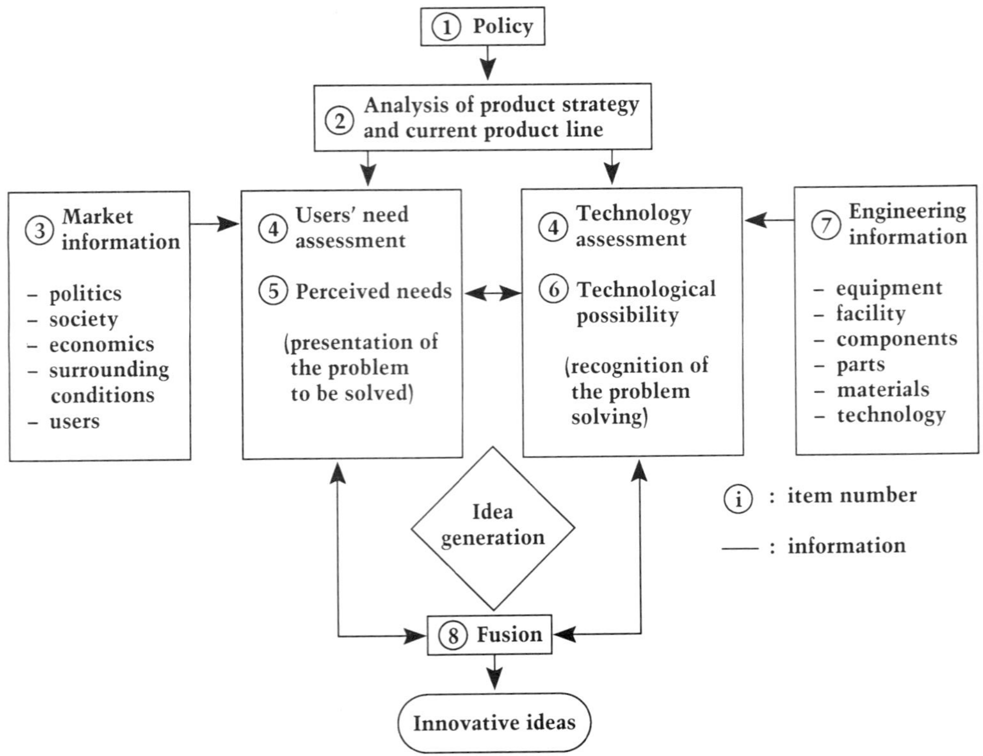

Figure 1.8
Fusion model for developing new products. The arrows indicate flow of information (source: Ichimura, Muramatsu, and Ishii, 1986, p. 133).

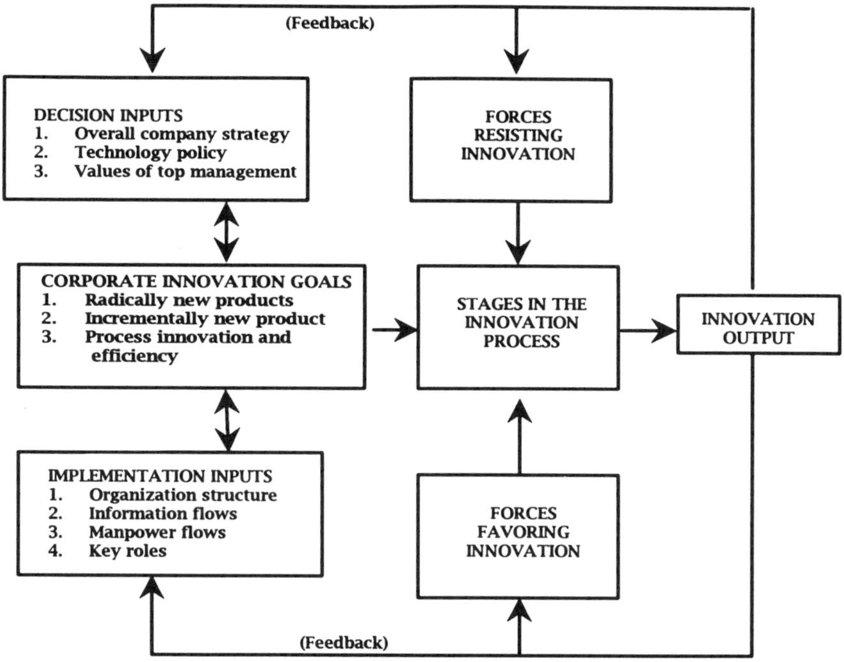

Figure 1.9
Brown and Karagozoglu's systems model of technological innovation. (Source: Brown and Karagozoglu, p. 12. Copyright © 1989 IEEE.)

1.4 What Is Information?

So information is important in innovation, but what do we mean by information? The *Economist* (16 June 1990, p. 19) notes that one of the ironies of the "information revolution" is that so few of those involved can give any definition of what information is. The problem is not new. Maguire and Kench (1984) pointed to the confusions that arise from differing concepts of what constitutes information, and especially to the difficulties in measuring it.

This book uses a broad, operational definition that includes in the concept of *information* the content of communicated messages of all kinds. In particular, information comprises all the messages containing data, theories, background, ideas, opinions, and so on, whether these messages are delivered through person-to-person exchanges, face to face, or through communications devices, at conferences or meetings, or through a whole range of different media, including journals, books, data sheets, patents, pictures, databases, and so on, regardless of whether such information is derived from sources inside or outside any particular group or organization. We note that information does not have to be in the form of words—it can include pictures, sound, music, dance, gesture, and so on.

Ideally, we would also like our concept of information to embrace all the meanings and all the senders and receivers of messages who impart meaning to them. The folly of trying to divorce knowledge from the "knowers" has been amply demonstrated in the information retrieval literature, dating at least back to Fairthorne (1954), and particularly in the communications literature that has taken into consideration some of the failures of technology transfer to developing countries (Dervin, 1980). We therefore want the definition of information also to encompass "the process of becoming informed" which is the phrase used by Buckland (1988, p. 115) The understanding of information as process will be pursued particularly in Chapter 3 of this work where the ideas of Zuboff (1988) on the "informating" as distinct from automating of organizations are pursued in relation to the effects of the digitization of information systems.

At the same time, in trying to exchange information about information, some distinctions can be useful if arbitrary, for example, distinctions between information, knowledge, and data. Though the dividing lines are quickly blurred in practice, the usual hierarchy is that the term *data* refers to isolated items that build up into information, which in turn contributes to knowledge. For example, a single letter of the alphabet ("a") could be an item of data. Letters can be built up into a sentence (such as this), which conveys information—in this case information about linguistics. The reader in turn assimilates the information thus conveyed into her or his personal knowledge of linguistics—which is everything that the person knows about language.

Thus, in this sense, one can never communicate the totality of one's knowledge, but only pieces of information drawn from it. Machlup (1980) suggests that it might therefore be useful to differentiate "stocks of knowledge" from "flows of information," but this verbal distinction is seldom observed and would be difficult to sustain. Some parts of knowledge can even be communicated without language as such, not only in gesture but in observation and imitation, as when an apprentice craftsman learns by example from a master the feel of how to shape a piece.

As we use the term here, knowledge is primarily personal—the totality of what a person knows—and comprises many forms, including knowledge of, knowledge about, knowledge how to, knowledge in words, and knowledge without words (visual, tactile, etc.), to quote a few from the wide-ranging discussion in volume 1 of Machlup's treatise (1980) on the subject. But by an important extension, one can, like the law, think of a corporate body as a kind of person, and thus we speak of the knowledge possessed by an organization, which is much more than the information written in its files, but includes also its culture, the way in which people interact within the organization, knowledge about the contacts they use to gain information from outside, and so on.

Thus we have a hierarchy—data, information, knowledge—in which each category assimilates and organizes the "lower" ones. An even more assimilated and personalized form than knowledge is wisdom. It is important for both organizations and individuals not to put all their effort into gathering information without assimilating it into knowledge, or better, into wisdom. Aimless data gathering is a waste of resources. As T. S. Eliot (1934) regretfully put it:

> Where is the wisdom we have lost in knowledge? Where is the knowledge we have lost in information? (p. 7).

Major themes of this book are the needs and means for turning into useful flows of information the stocks of knowledge in libraries and information centers and in the people who manage them.

Shannon (1949) introduced the technical concept of "information content" as a means of measuring information conveyed. He had in mind information as communicated down a channel such as a telephone line, and he was able to give a precise mathematical measure of the extent to which the message received reduced the uncertainty of the receiver; in essence, did it tell the receiver anything not already known? A message that conveys nothing new to the receiver has zero information content in this sense. The more it tells the receiver that was not already known, the greater is its information content.

Many information scientists have tried to apply Shannon's Law to the design of information retrieval systems. But the rationality of a communication line is not reflected in human communication. It can, for instance, be very interesting to be told something that you already know, depending on who tells you (the source or the sender), and how they tell you (the channel), and the environment (context) in which the communication takes place. Did the source not know you knew? Did they want you to know they knew? These are not necessarily silly questions in the sociopolitical environments in which innovation occurs or fails to occur.

Much of this book is concerned with methods and means of conveying information. We shall often refer to *information systems,* which we define as the means of capturing, storing, and channeling information. An information system uses information technology, whether high or low, to record, store, and pass on messages into the organizational system into which it fits. An *information service,* on the other hand, is a specialized organization or department of an organization thats major function is to capture, store, and transmit information to people, departments, or organizations outside the information service. The information it handles may originate inside or outside the parent organization. It may be brought into the organization on demand or in anticipation of demand. It may arrive fortuitously. An important part of the service is to select what looks to be relevant to the clients and potential clients from the wealth of information available. Examples of information services include libraries and public databases. Many other organizations, such as computer centers in universities, include information services. In some sense banks, insurance companies, parliaments, courts of law, and administrative departments of government are also information services. These are among the organizations classified by Engelbrecht (1985) as in the primary information sector. The distinction we would make is that unlike libraries, information centers, and public database providers, these institutions do not exist primarily for the supply of information. They rather collect, store, manipulate, and distribute it for the purpose of increasing wealth, lessening risk, making and administering laws, and so on.

In information services as in all human undertakings there is plenty of scope for innovation, and the influences on its success are similar to those in other organizations.

1.5 Information in the Economy

In this book, we shall concentrate on the importance of information services in helping organizations achieve innovation. The connection between information and innovation makes information important for the economy, but the importance of information for the workings of the economy and society generally is much deeper than this. It has been widely declared that today we live in an "information economy," and indeed an "information society." In this section, therefore, we briefly review the meanings of these concepts and their applicability to modern societies.

1.5.1 Prices as Information Carriers

Economists have long recognized the importance of information to the working of capitalist society, although they have not always presented it in these terms. Consider, for example, the classical concept, enunciated by Adam Smith in *Wealth of Nations* in 1776, by which the "invisible hand" of the market efficiently allocates resources in the interests of the nation as a whole. Information flow is the lifeblood of this invisible hand, because without it there would be no markets. Buyers would not even know who the sellers were, where they were to be found, or how their prices compared. Moreover, as explicitly recognized by von Hayek (1937), Arrow (1984), and others, the price of a product in a capitalist society embodies a wealth of information about the abundance or scarcity of the product and the factors that go into making it, such as labor, raw materials, and so on. (For detailed references, see Lamberton, 1983.) Indeed, to a classical "free market" economist, price contains essentially all the information needed to allocate resources. For example, if fuel becomes scarce, its price rises and this flows through to the prices of end products in proportion to the amount of fuel needed to produce each. Prompted by this price signal, consumer purchases of products strongly dependent on fuel decline, and the price equilibrates at a new level, reflecting the change in supply and demand.

This beautiful theory is marred in practice by the fact that, for many products, consumers are not perfectly informed. In particular they are not often able to compare a full range of sellers' prices. Shopping around (that is, gathering information on prices on offer) is often seen as more bother than it is worth. There is a "transaction cost" in finding the information, as the jargon puts it, and so consumers often settle for what they find first rather than for the best value. Thus inefficient producers are not necessarily driven out of the market on price alone. Worse, as Galbraith (1969) has emphasized, the markets in many products are dominated by a few sellers who control the market; they can charge what they like, so that information about factor costs is not conveyed by prices of end products. In effect, producers are able to keep this information to themselves, along with information about their profits. Occasionally, antitrust commissions and the like ferret out the information, at considerable cost, and try to ensure that its benefits flow to consumers. Nevertheless, in general, the price mechanism works remarkably well in conveying needed information from one sector of the economy to another. In centrally planned economies, by contrast, information about factor costs and resource inputs is jealously guarded by the central planners. Not even in theory does price convey the needed information. As a result, supply and demand are chronically mismatched.

That "knowledge is power" was itself common knowledge when Sir Francis Bacon penned the phrase some four hundred years ago. Inside information, that is, information available only to a select few, can often be of great value. For example, Nathan Rothschild made a substantial profit in the financial markets of the day by being the first in Britain to know the result of the Battle of Waterloo. Unlike most people in the City, as the financial district of London has long been known, Rothschild was confident that Napoleon would be defeated and had lent his bank's backing to the war effort. That he was the first to know the outcome of the battle was no accident; being very well aware of the value of information, he had a special carrier pigeon service and fast sailing boats organized to ensure that he was the first to get the news (Encyclopaedia Britannica, 1911).

1.5.2 The Information Economy

This century has seen a great transformation in the resources devoted to knowledge and information. Drucker (1969) pointed out that "from an economy of goods, which America was as recently as World War II, we have changed into a knowledge economy." He saw as fatuous the tendency of economists to continue to classify the knowledge industries as services, because "Knowledge has actually become the 'primary' industry, the industry that supplies to the economy the essential and central resource of production." In Drucker's view, "The economic history of the last hundred years in the advanced and developed countries could be called 'from agriculture to knowledge'" (pp. 247–248).

The principal manifestation of this trend is in the composition of the work force. Porat (1977) divided the United States labor force into four sectors, agriculture, industry, services, and information, and he used this framework to present his aggregation of the United States labor force, 1860–1980 (Porat, 1977), which is reproduced as Figure 1.10.

Figure 1.10 shows not only the dramatic decline in the percentage of the population employed in agriculture but the sharp decline in industrial employment from 1960, accompanied by a less steep rise of employment in the service industries in the same period. The spectacular change over the 120 years is the proportion of the labor force engaged in information occupations. Table 1.2 indicates that this transition has occurred in all developed economies; it is by no means confined to the United States.

This information sector of the economy provides soft or intangible services, and its common element is the processing of symbols and/or symbolic objects. Information activities include teaching, research, office work, public service, all forms of communication and the media, photography, postal service, telecommunications, book publishing, printing, banking, insurance, libraries, creative arts, data processing, computer software, accountancy, law, social work, management, advertising, the church, trades unions, and parliaments. The symbols used are words, sounds, images, and numbers, or symbolic objects that represent tangibles (e.g., money, checks, letters). The tools of trade used by information workers include voices, pens, telephones, typewriters, computer keyboards, calculators, microphones, cameras, microscopes, and tape recorders.

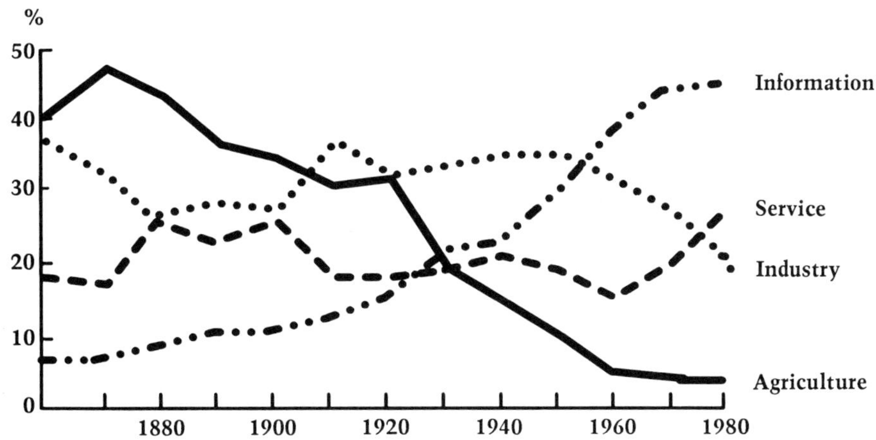

Figure 1.10
Four-section aggregation of the United States work force by percentage, 1860–1980. Median estimates of the information workers were used (source: Porat, 1977, p. 121).

Table 1.2
The Contribution of the Primary Information Sector to GDP and Workforce

Country	Year	% GDP[a]	% Total work force
		ASEAN[b]	
Indonesia	1975	10.6	6.0
Malaysia	1975	14.3	11.0
Philippines		12.0	5.7
Singapore	1976	26.0	26.0
Thailand	1975	9.9	9.0
		Pacific	
Fiji	1976	16.72	17.02
New Zealand	1972	14.6	12.00
Papua New Guinea	1972	12.96	13.00
		OECD[c]	
U.S.	1976	24	41
W. Germany	1975	17	27
Japan	1975	19	24
Australia	1977	19	17
U.K.	1975	22	33
France	1976	19	28

Source: Data collected from Jussawalla *et al.* (1988), p. 41, from various country studies.
[a]GDP, gross domestic product.
[b]ASEAN, Association of SouthEast Asian Nations.
[c]OECD, Organisation for Economic Co-operation and Development.

Information-based employment increased rapidly until the 1970s, and there were predictions that computer-based technology would reduce employment, in particular in those industries that were not dependent on physical presence or particular locations to effect transactions (e.g., airline bookings, banking, data processing). No such reduction seems to have occurred. In a report commissioned by the National Academy of Sciences, the National Academy of Engineering, and the Institute of Medicine, Hirschhorn (1988) explains:

> The empirical evidence suggests overall that computers have not replaced workers or destroyed jobs; if anything, they have created jobs. In the first phase of automation, despite extensive back-office automation, the number of clerks, typists, secretaries, and bookkeepers grew, while in the second phase the fast-growing business and professional services sector is also among the most computer intensive. Similarly, the data suggests that small firms that contribute a disproportionate number of new jobs have also capitalized their workers with computing power at a faster rate than large firms (p. 400).

Hirschhorn (1988) does not, however, deny that computers pose employment problems, notably in the changing skills required and the changing career ladders. In considering Figure 1.10, it is also necessary to note that the distinction between occupations classed as information and those classed as service is (at the boundaries) one of degree. Information occupations are those where the workers are primarily engaged in the manipulation of symbols, either at a high intellectual content (such as authors and students) or at a more routine level (such as bank tellers). As services generally are increasingly dependent on the rapid collection and processing of information, whether in tourist bookings or supermarket sales, tangible services take on more of the characteristics of information services.

Hirschhorn (1988) observes another movement between sectors. He writes that:

> The service and goods sectors are converging. While services are industrialized—service companies are capitalizing their workers while applying cost accounting and productivity measures inherited from the manufacturing world—manufacturing systems become increasingly like services. The convergence of the two and the new relationship between them are the best indicators of the emerging postindustrial economy (p. 380).

Little public fanfare has accompanied the rise of the information sector to be the largest employer in the United States, and close to it in all developed countries. Much less attention is being paid to the subtle changes in the nature of employment that are behind the convergence of sectors noted in Hirschborn's quote. Politicians, economists, and citizens generally tend to adhere to the image of industry as manufacturing industry and of the typical worker as a factory hand. This notion, after all, goes back to the roots of

Western industrial society and the blue-collar worker has traditionally been the inspiration, entrepreneur, and beneficiary of various innovations in organized labor since the late nineteenth century. However outdated, this view of industry as manufacturing industry is also reflected in the conventional classifications of firms and occupations, such as the standard industry classification (SIC). This is part of the problem of productivity measurement on which complaints by Schlefer (1989) and by Kelly and Wyckoff (1989) have been registered (see page 7, this text).

The first economist to examine systematically the size of the information sector was Fritz Machlup (1962), and he confessed that he was surprised at how large it turned out to be. It has also been calculated that in terms of productivity the information sector makes a contribution to wealth commensurate with its size. Table 1.2, based on Jussawalla, *et al.* (1988), shows that the income earned by the information sector as a proportion of gross domestic product is, in most countries, roughly proportional to the work force in that sector, that is, greater than 30%.

The conclusion is unavoidable that a modern economy is an information economy. As a result, a new speciality has arisen within economics, the economics of information. Fritz Machlup and Jacob Marschak are recognized as its pioneers and among its notable exponents are Arrow (1984), Boulding (1966), and Lamberton (1971). Proponents of this approach emphasize the factors that distinguish information as an economic commodity: for example, information remains with the seller even after the buyer has taken possession, and that the buyer cannot be allowed to know what the information is before purchase. They also affirm that structural change in organizations to improve the communication process is one of the keys to increased productivity.

This is consistent with the approach of this book, and the antecedents of this view go back to the classic study by Burns and Stalker (1961). Their study indicated the need for organic rather than mechanistic structures and flexibility in communication patterns in organizations that were able to adopt the new technology of electronics into their engineering activities. The question of the economic value of information, and other economic aspects such as information markets, are addressed again in Chapter 3.

1.5.3 The Information Society

But what kinds of information are being exchanged in this information economy, and who controls their flow? If the possession of information is indeed central to economic and social power, then these are key questions for society.

For example, a democracy cannot function properly if the citizens are un-informed about the issues of the day and the quality of the candidates for office. If, for example, one person controls over half of the newspapers in a country, there is a great danger that views contrary to those of that owner will not get a fair hearing. As James Madison (1910) wrote in the early days of the United States:

> A popular Government, without popular information, or the means of acquiring it, is but a Prologue to a Farce or a Tragedy; or, perhaps both. Knowledge will forever govern ignorance: And a people who mean to be their own Governors must arm themselves with the power which knowledge gives (p.103).

The sheer volume of scientific information has been estimated to have doubled every five years for at least the past two decades. In order to keep up, scientists have tended to become more and more specialized. Such fragmentation of knowledge, which is by no means confined to science, gives great difficulty to governments, who have to balance, for example, environmental and economic policies based on widely different assumptions, values, and backgrounds.

That a large fraction of the work force is occupied in generating new information, aided by the new information technology, contributes to what is frequently described as an information explosion, which because of its cumulative effects, might more accurately be described as an information avalanche. There is so much information around that how to sift and pull together the portions of it required for a particular purpose, in other words, to transform information into knowledge, is a central problem for all who seek to guide society. As Macdonald (1983) puts it:

> What has been ignored in the euphoria surrounding the declining production cost of information is the consumption cost of the information produced. Resources are required to use information, and the more information produced, the more resources are required. An obvious example would be the time taken to read, digest, and decide what to do with the information on a computer printout. More subtle would be the cost of making a better decision when half a dozen alternatives are increased to several thousand, or when the sheer quantity of information exceeds even short-term retention capacity and blurs the distinction between relevant and irrelevant (p.34).

The "natural" response when confronted with too much information is to do without. Or, as Calvin Mooers more elegantly expressed it in the law which bears his name, "an information retrieval system will tend not to be used whenever it is more painful and troublesome for a customer to have information than for him not to have it" (Mooers, 1960, p. 204). At the level of mass communication Wilbur Schramm (1954) set out his "fraction of selection," which was a function of the expected reward over the anticipated effort. Some years later Schramm (1971) remarked that

> The reservation I have about this idea, however, is that it implies a rationality that does not really bulk large in the process of selection. Much selection must be accidental: a person "just happens" to be where he can attend to a given message. Much is impulsive. On the other hand, over the years a person tends to seek the kinds of communication that have rewarded him in the past (p. 33).

There is a good deal that is accidental in the human selection of messages from all media. The danger of excessive rationality in the models of human information processing behavior that underlie some information retrieval systems is a theme taken up again in Chapter 6. Fortunately, however, some of the information technology that has caused the overload of available information can be used to select and sort from the information available, as we describe in Chapter 5. There is also much to be learned from the so-called human factors or "human-computer interface" research, which is dealt with in Chapters 5 and 6.

Information and communications link together diverse aspects of our society in ways that have not always seemed so significant in the past. In this sense, today's society is an information society. A range of social, economic, and political issues arise from these interconnections: issues ranging from economic growth, citizen's rights, to national sovereignty, and fields ranging from telecommunications infrastructure, legal measures, media, scientific and technical information, libraries, and education.

The breadth and importance of these issues for a modern society have suggested to governments with an interventionist philosophy and to liberal economists the need for a "national information policy," to give a framework for developments in each area. So far as we are aware, no country as yet has such a policy. One of the boldest attempts at creation of one was the initiative in Australia in the 1980s led by then minister of science, Barry Jones. In addition to being a politician, Jones is also a scholar, widely known for his erudition and the author of an influential book about the information society, *Sleepers Wake!* (Jones, 1982, 1990)

It says something about the fragmentation of knowledge and of power that the national information policy proposed by Jones (Department of Science, 1985) was not adopted by the Australian government of the day, largely because of the failure of the various government departments to agree on what information is, let alone on which aspects of it "belonged" to which department. Whether these departments were concerned with telecommunications policy, development of the computer industry, regulation of financial institutions, or publication of government reports, they seemed able to agree on only one thing, namely that any stated government policy, even in the form of mild guidelines, would be a threat to their ability to carry out the rest of government policy (Jones, 1987). One may readily extrapolate from this experience the lack of consensus likely to be encountered among the many and varied interests vested in the community at large.

It may however be pointed out that all countries in fact have information policies, represented by the totality of their decisions on information-related issues, however inconsistent, incoherent, and unstable these may be. Readers may also find interesting the information policy experience of government at the global level found in the history of UNESCO's attempts to introduce a "new information order." (K. H. Roberts, 1988)

1.6
Connecting Innovation and Information

This introductory chapter has brought out some of the obvious connections between innovation and information. In summary, innovation is based on new ideas, including new combinations of old ideas, the utility of which is tested with applications of many kinds of information. Empirical studies, going back at least to Carter and Williams (1957), have repeatedly found that in more prosperous enterprises there is greater awareness of information and greater ability to manage it. Sweeney (1989) reports that "empirical evidence strongly indicates that it is the quality of the information activities and of the information possessed by a firm which makes its innovations commercially successful and give it the competitive edge" (p. 1). Michael E. Porter (1990) makes a similarly forthright statement in *The Competitive Advantage of Nations,* where he writes:

> Information plays a large role in the process of innovation—information that is not sought or available to competitors, or information available to others that is interpreted in new ways. Sometimes it results from sheer investment in market research or R & D. It is striking, though, how often innovators are those firms that are simply looking in the right place, unencumbered by or unconcerned with conventional wisdom (p. 48).

Takeup of the empirical work on innovation in organizations was slow, and many of the earlier findings were rediscovered in the 1980s in a spate of bestsellers, such as Peters and Waterman (1982), Kanter (1984), Hilmer (1985), Peters (1987), and Waterman (1987). These kinds of books are frequently written by management consultants whose experience in many firms in many industries reinforces the earlier studies. Another spate of writings endorsing innovation and suggesting methods for its achievement has resulted from the study of Japanese firms and business practice. Much of the work on innovation in business and industry remains anecdotal. As Richard S. Rosenbloom of Harvard remarked in the introduction to *Research on Technological Innovation, Management and Policy,* vol. 1, "In this field, the development of scientific knowledge, usable and otherwise, is limited by a paucity of theory and a profusion of concepts" (Rosenbloom, 1983, p. x).

Useful guides to this literature on the innovation process are available in Rothwell and Zegveld (1985) and the Centre for Technology and Social Change (1988). There is also, of course, an extensive literature, directed mainly at students of librarianship, on the theory and practice of information services management. But none of these works make explicit connections with the particular requirements of innovation-oriented organizations.

Some research into the behavior of managers, notably by Mintzberg (1973) and some investigations by information scientists, librarians, and communications researchers, which are often referred to as "user studies," have looked at the kinds of information sought and used by scientists, research managers, and many professional, ethnic, and other community groups. There is also a subset of studies of the use made of various libraries and other information services. Findings from many of these studies will be referred to in this book and their cumulated wisdom included in the principles adduced in Chapter 6. Although most of these studies have aimed to assess the usefulness of information services and identify gaps therein, they have not often dealt, except incidentally, with the broader issues of innovation and information.

As befits their systems approach, Brown and Karagozoglu (1989) are careful to point out that "despite their importance, information flows are not the sine qua non for innovation" (p. 12). At the same time, it may well be that existing knowledge about the transfer of information in organizations and about the collection, storage, and redistribution of information through information services can be used to lessen some of the uncertainties of the innovation process. That process is the subject of Chapter 2.

References

Arrow, K. (1984). *Collected papers, vol. 4, The economics of information.* Oxford, Blackwell.

Boulding, K. (1966). The economics of knowledge and the knowledge of economics. *American Economic Review 56,* 1–13.

Brown, W. B. and N. Karagozoglu, (1989). A systems model of technological innovation. *IEEE Transactions on Engineering Management 36,* 11–16.

Buckland, M. K. (1988). Library services in theory and context (second ed.). Oxford, Pergamon.

Burns, T., and G. M. Stalker, (1961). *The management of innovation.* London, Tavistock.

Bush, V. (1960). *Science, the endless frontier.* Washington, National Science Foundation.

Carter, C. F., and B. R. Williams, (1957). *Industry and technical progress.* Oxford, Oxford University Press.

Centre for Technology and Social Change. (1988). *Innovation for the 1990s: new challenges for technology policy and strategy.* (by D. Scott-Kemmis, T. Darling, and R. Johnston). Canberra, Australia, Department of Industry Technology and Commerce.

Clark, N. (1985). *The political economy of science and technology.* Oxford, Blackwell.

Department of Science. (1985). *A national information policy for Australia: discussion paper.* Canberra.

Dervin, B. (1980). Communication gaps and inequities: moving toward a reconceptualization. *Progress in Communication Sciences 2,* 73–112.

Dosi, G., C. Freeman, R. Nelson, G. Silverberg, and L. Soete, eds., (1988). *Technical change and economic theory.* London, Pinter.

Drucker, P. F. (1969). *The age of discontinuity: Guidelines to our changing society.* London, Heinemann.

Drucker, P.F. (1985). *Innovation and entrepreneurship: practice and principles.* London, Heinemann.

Eliot, T. S. (1934). *The rock: a pageant play.* New York, Harcourt and Brace.

Encyclopaedia Britannica. (1911). Rothschild. *In Encyclopaedia britannica* (10th ed.) *23,* p. 758.

Engelbrecht, H. J. (1985). An exposition of the information sector approach with special reference to Australia. *Prometheus 3,* 370–386.

Fairthorne, R. A. (1954). The theory of communication. *Aslib Proceedings 6,* 255–267. Reprinted In *Towards information retrieval.* London, Butterworths, 1961.

Foster, R. N. (1986). *Innovation: The attacker's advantage.* New York, Summit Books.

Freeman, C. (1982). *The economics of industrial innovation* (second ed.). London, Pinter.

Galbraith, J. K. (1969). *The new industrial state.* Harmondsworth, England, Penguin.

Hawke, R.J. (1989). *House of Representatives Parliamentary Debates (Hansard).* Commonwealth copyright. Canberra, Australian Government Publishing Service, 8 May.

Hilmer, F. (1985). *When the luck runs out: the future for Australians at work.* Sydney, Harper and Row.

Hirschhorn, L. (1988). Computers and jobs: services and the new mode of production. *In* R. M. Cyert and D. C. Mowery, eds., *The impact of technological on employment and economic growth.* Commissioned by the Panel on Technology and Employment of the Committee on Science, Engineering, and Public Policy of the National Academy of Sciences, National Academy of Engineering, and the Institute of Medicine. Cambridge, Massachusetts, Ballinger.

Hughes, T. P. (1989). *American genesis: a century of invention and technological enthusiasm 1870–1970.* New York, Viking.

Ichimura, T., R. Muramatsu, and K. Ishii, (1986). A method for analyzing information behaviour in needs assessment. In H. Hübner, Ed., *The art and science of innovation management: an international perspective.* Amsterdam, Elsevier, pp. 131–141.

Jones, B. (1987). Concluding address. *In* T. Barr, Ed., *An information society for Australia: the promise and the threat: proceedings of a conference.* Melbourne, Commission for the Future.

Jones, B. (1982). *Sleepers wake! Technology and the future of work.* Melbourne, Oxford University Press.

Jones, B. (1990). *Sleepers wake!* (second ed.) Melbourne, Oxford University Press.

Jussawalla, M., D. M. Lamberton, and N. D. Karunaratne, Eds., (1988). *The cost of thinking: information economies of ten Pacific countries.* Norwood, New Jersey, Ablex.

Kanter, R. M. (1984). *The change masters: corporate entrepreneurs at work.* London, Allen and Unwin.

Kelly, H., and A. Wyckoff, (1989). Distorted image: how government statistics misrepresent the economy. *Technology Review,* February/March, 52–60.

Kingston, W. (1977). *Innovation: the creative impulse in human progress—industry, art, science.* London, John Calder.

Lamberton, D. M., Ed., (1971). *Economics of information and knowledge.* Harmondsworth, England: Penguin Books.

Lamberton, D. M. (1983). Information economics and technological change. *In* S. Macdonald, D. Lamberton, and T. Mandeville, Eds., *The trouble with technology: explorations in the process of technological change.* London, Pinter, pp. 75–92.

Link, P. L. (1987). *Marketing of technology: an Australian perspective.* Melbourne, Nelson Wadsworth.

Macdonald, S. (1983). Technology beyond machines. *In* S. Macdonald, D. Lamberton, and T. Mandeville, Eds., *The trouble with technology: explorations in the process of technological change.* London, Pinter, pp. 26–36.

Machlup, F. (1962). *The production and distribution of knowledge in the United States.* Princeton, Princeton University Press.

Machlup, F. (1980). *Knowledge: its creation, distribution, and economic significance: vol. 1, Knowledge and knowledge production; economics of information and human capital.* Princeton, Princeton University Press.

Madison, J. (1910). Letter to W. T. Barry, August 4, 1822. In G. Hunt, Ed., *The Writings of James Madison comprising his public papers and his private correspondence, including numerous letters and documents now for the first time printed.* New York, Putnam's, v. 9 (1819–1836), 103.

Maguire, C., and R. Kench. (1984). The introduction and diffusion of technological innovation in industry: an information research perspective. *Progress in Communication Sciences 4,* 163–204.

Ministry of International Trade and Industry. (1980a). The vision of MITI policies in the 1980s. Tokyo.

Ministry of International Trade and Industry. (1980b). Vision of the small and medium enterprises and their policy directions in the 1980s: based on materials furnished by the Guidance Division. Tokyo.

Mintzberg, H. (1973). *The nature of managerial work.* New York, Harper and Row.

MIT Commission. (1989). *Made in America: regaining the productive edge.* Cambridge, Massachusetts, MIT Press.

Mooers, C. (1960). Mooers' Law or, Why some retrieval systems are used and others are not. *American Documentation 11,* 204.

Mowery, D., and N. Rosenberg, (1979). The influence of market demand upon innovation: a critical review of some recent empirical studies. *Research Policy 8,* 102–153.

Organisation for Economic Co-operation and Development. (1987a). *Innovation policy: France* (February). Paris.

Organisation for Economic Co-operation and Development. (1987b). *Innovation policy: Ireland* (March). Paris.

Oxford English Dictionary. (1989). Second edition, Vol. 7, Oxford, Clarendon, pp. 997–998.

Peters, T. J. (1987). *Thriving on chaos: handbook for a management revolution.* New York, Knopf.

Peters, T. J., and R. H. Waterman, (1982). *In search of excellence: lessons from America's best-run companies.* New York, Harper and Row.

Porat, M. U. (1977). *The information economy: definition and measurement, vol. 1.* Washington DC, U.S. Government Printing Office.

Porter, M. (1990). *The competitive advantage of nations.* London, Macmillan.

Porter, M. (1990a). The competitive advantage of nations. *Harvard Business Review, 68*(2), 73–89; 92–93.

Prestowitz, C. V. (1988). *Trading places—how we allowed Japan to take the lead.* New York, Basic Books.

Roberts, E. B. (1988). Managing invention and innovation, *Research Technology Management, 31,* 11–31.

Roberts, E. B., and A. L. Frohman, (1978). Strategies for improving research utilization, *Technology Review, 80,* 32–39.

Roberts, K. H. (1988). UNESCO's General Information Programme, 1977–1987: its characteristics, activities and accomplishments. *Information Development 4,* 208–238.

Rogers, E. M. (1983). *Diffusion of innovations* (third ed.). New York, Free Press.

Ronayne, J. (1984). *Science in government.* Melbourne, Edward Arnold.

Rosenbloom, R. S. (1978). Technological innovation in firms and industries: an assessment of the state of the art. In P. Kelly and M. Kranzberg, Eds., *Innovation: a critical review of current knowledge.* San Francisco, San Francisco Press, pp. 215–230.

Rosenbloom, R. S. (1983). Introduction. *Research on technological innovation, management and policy, vol. 1.* Greenwich, Connecticut, JAI Press, p.x.

Rothwell, R. (1983). "Information and successful innovation." London, British Library Research and Development Department. (BL R&DD report no. 5782).

Rothwell, R., and W. Zegveld, (1981). *Industrial innovation and public policy: preparing for the 1980s and the 1990s.* Westport, Connecticut, Greenwood Press.

Rothwell, R., and W. Zegweld, (1985). *Reindustrialisation and technology.* London, Longmans.

Schlefer, J. (1989). Making sense of the productivity debate: a reflection on the MIT Report. *Technology Review,* August/September, 28–40.

Schramm, W., Ed., (1954). *Process and effects of mass communication.* Urbana, University of Illinois Press.

Schramm, W., Ed., (1971). *Process and effects of mass communication* (rev. ed.). Urbana, University of Illinois Press.

Schumpeter, J. A. (1939). *Business cycles: a theoretical, historical and statistical analysis of the capitalist process, volumes 1 & 2.* New York, McGraw Hill.

Schumpeter, J. A. (1943). *Capitalism, socialism and democracy.* London, Unwin Hyman.

Shannon, C. E. (1949). *The mathematical theory of communication.* Urbana, University of Illinois Press.

Sweeney, G. (1989). Introduction: information and corporate growth. *In* E. Punset and G. Sweeney, Eds., *Information resources and corporate growth.* London, Pinter, pp.1–15.

Tyler, M. (1981). Telecommunications and productivity: the need and the opportunity. In M. Moss, Ed., *Telecommunications and productivity.* Worcester, Massachusetts, Addison Wesley, pp. 1–51.

von Hayek, F. (1937). Economics and knowledge. *Economica 4,* 33–54.

Waterman, R. H. (1987). *The renewal factor: how the best get and keep the competitive edge.* Toronto, Bantam Books.

Zuboff, S. (1988). *In the age of the smart machine: the future of work and power.* New York, Basic Books.

2

The Process of Innovation

We now know that there is little difference between entrepreneurship whatever the sphere. The entrepreneur in education and the entrepreneur in health care—both have been fertile fields—do very much the same things, use very much the same tools, and encounter very much the same problems as the entrepreneur in a business or a labor union.

—P. Drucker, *Innovation and Entrepreneurship,* p. 28.

We cannot yet develop a theory of innovation. But we already know enough to say when, where, and how one looks systematically for innovation opportunities, and how one judges the chances for their success or the risks of their failure. We know enough to develop, though only in outline form, the practice of innovation.

—P. Drucker, *Innovation and Entrepreneurship,* p. 34.

There is now a body of findings, principles, and hypotheses by which we can attempt to explain, predict, and we hope influence the process of innovation in industry, commerce and services.

—M. A. Sirbu, "The innovation process in telecommunication," in *Telecommunications and Productivity,* p. 185.

Major innovations and the need for them are beyond the foresight of *masses* of people.

—E. M. Tauber, "How market resesearch discourages major innovation," in *Readings in the Management of Innovation,* p. 435.

Chapter Synopsis

Innovation is examined as a system. Inputs (such as new technologies) are processed into outputs (such as new products) and feedback is derived from interactions with the market, culture, and general environment in which the innovations operate. The bias in the literature toward technological innovation is acknowledged and the reasons for this are explored. Technology push and market pull are discussed as inputs to innovation along with other aspects of supply and demand in the process. Discussion is pursued of the role of other variables in innovation, such as size of organization and the relationships between productivity and innovative capability in organizations, industries, and countries. The idea of product life cycle is explored in relation to the inequalities of opportunity for innovation and so are the effects of expectations of economic gain.

In discussing the "processing" or management of innovation in organizations, strategies are examined in the light of the innovation signals suggested by Drucker (1985). Examination of outputs of the innovation system leads to discussion of some of the key organizational factors that have been identified and of attempts to systematize them. The role of feedback in the system is discussed in the light of findings of a variety of communications researchers and economists, which suggest some of the practices by which the signals of innovation potential are transferred among organizations.

The chapter concludes that innovation is a matter of organization, which demands the use of information and communication strategies capable of covering and assimilating new data from many different sources and systems.

2.1 The Idea of a System

Innovation is the application in any organization of new ideas, whether they are embodied in products, processes, services, or in the systems of management and marketing through which the organization operates. The process by which innovations spread operates in many different strata in society. They may be passed from one person to another, one organization to another, or from country to country. In business, industry, education, and government and in social institutions generally, innovation may be studied from several perspectives. There is the level of the organization—the firm, the school, the department, the professional society; the level of the industry or interest group, whether aerospace, librarianship, or social work; and the level of the region, country, or any other geographical entity, down to village and up to global level.

Long-established understanding lets us know that innovation moves (or is diffused) in sometimes mysterious ways. The source of the technology that built and put in place the statues on Easter Island may remain forever open to speculation. On much more common ground, so may the channels of diffusion of children's playground games and jokes. Similarly, the origins and the rate of spread of the neologisms or new slang phrases that sweep the world may be permitted no more than the attentions of the occasional sociologist or linguist and the occasional feature newspaper article. But for the reasons adduced in Chapter 1, it would be foolish to have such a laissez-faire attitude toward the promotion and management of innovation that has important economic and social implications.

As a general phenomenon, innovation can be understood in very broad terms. Rogers (1983), for example, defines it as "an idea, practice or object that is perceived as new by an individual or another unit of adoption" (p. xviii). The "unit of adoption" chosen for particular attention in this book is the organization, which again can be defined in very general terms, as it is by Rogers and Agarwala-Rogers (1976), as "a stable system of individuals who work together to achieve common goals through a hierarchy of ranks and a division of labor" (p. 26). At the same time, even in focusing on organizations as this book does, the innovation process in them cannot be studied without considering the actions of individuals and their interactions with each other and with the organization. Innovativeness within the individual is usually referred to as creativity and is often left to the psychologists and biographers to explain in terms of individual experience. But creative ideas in organizations have to come from people, and their creativity is therefore an important organizational variable in the innovation process. As Amabile points out in work on a model of creativity and innovation in organizations, "there is a two-way influence between the individual and the organization. What happens in the organization is significantly influenced by individual creators, but individual creators are significantly influenced by what happens in the organization" (Amabile, 1988, p. 151). In other words, innovation is a system in which people as individuals and in organizational groups are elements. In order to examine individual and group interactions in organizations as they innovate or fail to innovate in the products, processes, or services produced by their organizations, it seems useful to adopt an approach that acknowledges that we are trying to understand not a static phenomenon but a system.

A system is a set of interrelated parts that operate in combination to produce outcomes and in which the operation of each part affects the operation of all other parts. Morton (1971) phrases the definition more succinctly: "A system is an integrated assembly of specialized parts acting together for a common purpose" (p. 12). In extending the explanation he relates the system both to its environment and to the other systems of which it forms part. He writes,

> The pattern always is one of a group of entities, each having a specialized, essential function. But each is dependent for its system effectiveness upon its couplings to the system's other parts and the external world. Each entity of the

Figure 2.1
General idea of a feedback system.

> system receives information or energy from its neighbours and from the system's environment; each entity processes this information or energy in its specialized way and sends its outputs to the rest of the system and to the external world. We must think of every system as part of some larger system—as part of its environment—for only in its interactions with its environment are the system's inputs and outputs defined (p. 12).

The most economical model of a system consists of the classic diagram (Figure 2.1) in which *input* precedes *processing,* after which comes *output,* which is connected back to *input* with a dotted line marked *feedback.* The feedback line is intended to indicate that the system's output into the environment affects future inputs.

A system is regarded as more or less "open" or "closed," according to the extent to which it exchanges information with or interacts with its environment in this process.

Figure 2.2 indicates how the innovation process can be viewed as a particular case of the general system of Figure 2.1 Inputs are the sources which may trigger innovation. Processing refers to the strategies and practices which, whether planned to do so or not, affect the management of innovation within the organization. Outputs are the new products, processes, services, methods of organization or behavior that result from innovation inputs and processing. Feedback is considered from two points of view. One considers communication of information throughout the system and in exchange with the environment. The other relates more generally to the diffusion of innovation. The environment of innovation is explored, not only as an important aspect of the discussion of strategies (part of processing, as discussed in Section 2.3 of this chapter) but also in considering the external and internal conditions which seem to make organizations more or less successful in implementing innovation.

Those interested in the process of innovation have much knowledge at their disposal on the elements of innovation. The elements, or "entities" in Morton's terminology, are numerous but identifiable. It is rather in how "each entity receives information or energy from its neighbours and from the system's environment" and in the nature of the "interactions [of the

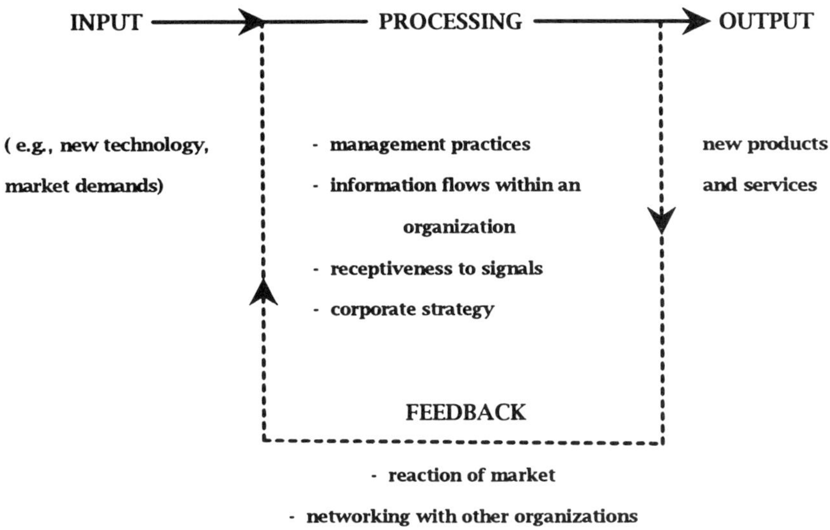

Figure 2.2
System with feedback as applied to innovation.

whole system] with its environment" (p. 12) that complexity and controversy lie.

The broad systems approach of Figures 2.1 and 2.2 will be used throughout this chapter as a framework in which to examine in more depth some key elements of the innovation process. The models of innovation set out in Chapter 1.3 (e.g., Figures 1.5, 1.6, and 1.7) are elaborations of the basic systems model in that they show explicitly various selections from the many entities and interactions that operate.

In order to uncover and unravel the entities and interactions that particularly affect the part played by information services in and for organizations, it is necessary to look at the knowledge and experience that has been accumulated about the innovation process in firms in industry and business and in public service institutions in education and government. Research on innovation has been carried out in diverse disciplines in many places and under many different assumptions. In the context of innovation, the meaning of research can be usefully extended to include all sorts of controlled observation or organized inquiry, with results that are publicly available. In this way, our study can include the realities of innovation practice as recorded in a multitude of sources. These include reflections on experience of research managers such as Morton (1971) of Bell Telephone Laboratories and Pake (1986) of the Xerox Corporation, of management consultants and entrepreneurs (Drucker, 1985), and of captains of industry such as Sloan (1963) in his memoir of General Motors. There is also interesting evidence in histories of research organizations (such as, Bernstein 1984), in biography and the history of invention (such as, Hughes, 1989), and in general social history (such as, Beniger, 1986)

As was stated in Chapter 1, this large and amorphous body of knowledge related to innovation has not been integrated into one coherent model. On the other hand, similar features and patterns have arisen at comparable stages in the innovation process in quite different environments, and their predictive value may be exploited. In particular, the similarities among innovators have been established. As Drucker (1985) writes, "We now know that there is little difference between entrepreneurship whatever the sphere. The entrepreneur in education and the entrepreneur in health care—both have been fertile fields—do very much the same things, use very much the same tools, and encounter very much the same problems as the entrepreneur in a business or a labor union" (p. 28). Drucker here uses the terms *entrepreneur* and *entrepreneurship* for the concepts of *innovator* and *innovation,* as expounded in this book.

One great danger looms over attempts to study innovation as a system, that is to study its elements and their interaction with each other and with the environment. This is the tendency to assign to technology a dominant, even a deterministic role. Technology, which is in essence an identifiable, specifiable way of doing anything, has always been an important element in innovation, as in all human systems. The glamor and the efficacy of scientific discovery and technological invention have been features of world history at least since the late eighteenth century. The achievements and the marketing of organized "big science" during and since World War II have already been referred to in Chapter 1. (See Chapter 1, page 8, this volume) Technology is becoming more not less important in both private and public enterprise. Horwitch and Sakakibara (1986), have remarked "Only in this decade have we witnessed the surprisingly rapid emergence and easy acceptance of technology as a major strategic variable throughout the globe for both corporations and national governments" (p. 83). No wonder then that technology has come to assume a central place in discussions of innovation in both research and policy circles. Our aim is not to deny its importance but to try to put technology and technological information into perspective within the whole innovation system.

Essentially, the technology bias is inescapable. Technological innovation has been studied much more intensively than that flowing from any other source. For one thing, its importance in capitalist economies is accepted by all, whether their interest is theoretical or practical. (See Chapter 1, section 2.1.) For another, the process of technological innovation often leaves trails or at least traces from which trails may be reconstructed. By contrast, the diffusion of social innovations in organizations or communities tends to leave less evidence of where, when, and how the new ideas arrived and how decisions were reached and implemented regarding their adoption. Data on technological innovation are therefore more plentiful, more instructive, and probably more exciting than those documenting more subtle but just as significant changes in opinion, attitude or behavior. Using the systems model adopted in this chapter may at least help us to appreciate that technological and social elements interact in the innovation process, and many historical examples of innovations demonstrate this interdependency.

In the remainder of this chapter the innovation system is approached in terms of the generalized system diagram shown in Figure 2.1. For the reader's convenience, the elements or entities in the diagram are repeated here. Inputs are the sources which may trigger innovation. Processing refers to the strategies and practices which, whether planned to do so or not, affect the management of innovation within the organization. Outputs are the new products, processes, services, methods of organization or behavior that result from innovation inputs and processing. Feedback is considered from two points of view. One considers communication of information throughout the system and in exchange with the environment. The other relates more generally to the diffusion of innovation. The environment of innovation is explored, not only as an important aspect of the discussion of strategies under processing but also in considering the external and internal conditions which seem to make organizations more or less successful in implementing innovation.

2.2 Inputs or Sources for Innovation

2.2.1 Demand and Supply

Invention is obviously an input to innovation, and while the most dazzling inventions may be technological, their chances of being applied as innovations seem to depend on factors other than technical brilliance. McCormick's invention of time payment by installments so that farmers could afford his harvester is hardly to be compared with the Wright brothers invention of their flying machine. But how far would the aircraft industry have advanced without the complicated web of payment by means other than cash in hand, which is now involved in the purchasing and indeed in commissioning the development of new planes? But need the invention or the new idea precede recognition of its utility? Which needs to come first, the problem or the solution?

These arguments are closely related to those about whether the stimulus for innovation should be "technology push" or "market pull." Can the inputs for successful innovation be new ideas or does the need for the new products, processes, or services have to be first or at least simultaneously recognized in the marketplace? These arguments about technology push versus market pull permeated much of the early literature, especially in the so-called tracer studies. Most notable of these were Project Hindsight, TRACES (Technology in Retrospect And Critical Events in Science), and Project SAPPHO. Project Hindsight was initiated by the United States Department of Defense to examine the role played by research in the development of weapon systems. (Isenson, 1969). The emphasis of TRACES was on chains of concepts and discoveries leading up to six innovations (Illinois Institute of Technology, Research Institute, 1968). Project SAPPHO, conducted by the Science Policy Research Unit at the University of Sussex, England, used a paired case study approach in which each pair consisted of one attempt at innovation that was successful and another that was relatively unsuccessful or a failure (University of Sussex, Science Policy Research Unit, 1972). All three studies found methodological difficulties in tracing the origins of innovation, and doubts were later cast by Mowery and Rosenberg (1979) that the findings of all three were any but artifacts of the methods used. However inconclusive the results of empirical investigation, arguments about the relationship between science and technology and about the relationship between the existence of knowledge and its useful application were also featured in much subsequent macroeconomic debate regarding the extent to which governments should fund disinterested or "curiosity-driven" research in science, technology, or any other field.

In the 1960s and 1970s the argument seemed to be settled in favor of market pull. Thus the so-called linear model, by which innovation proceeded from discovery or research through development to application, was discredited. This has already been discussed in Chapter 1 (pages 8–9, this volume). At a meeting of the American Association for the Advancement of Science in San Francisco in 1974, Derek De Solla Price described the claim that research leads to useful outcomes as one "fit only for grant applications" (Maguire, 1974, p. 6). The cry for market-driven innovation took over. But it was not long dominant. Much of the evidence gathered in investigation of innovation did not fit, because, as March (1981) noted, in organizations "changes often seem to be driven less by problems than by solutions" (p. 568). Some of the historical evidence was also at odds with the theory that successful innovation could be sourced to the needs of the market. For example, many of Elmer Sperry's several hundred patents became successful civil and military innovations in the late nineteenth and early twentieth century. A recent historian (Hughes, 1989) has described Sperry as "a solution looking for feedback problems," which he found and solved in "a remarkable range of applications" (p. 68). Another dimension has been added to the study of innovation as a system by the development of marketing as a practical skill and as an academic discipline. Marketing is above all an information exchange process, and its practice and study have yielded many insights into the innovation process. Thus, despite the difficulties of innovating with new knowledge which Drucker (1985) regards as "the riskiest and least successful source of innovation" (p. 130), he has also noted that science often pushes the entrepreneurial imagination and also that "anything genuinely new creates markets that nobody before even imagined" (p. 190).

Another question is whether innovation is more likely in conditions of strong demand for the organization's products or services. Again the evidence is mixed. Schmookler (1966) found that innovation was stimulated largely by demand growth, yet Abernathy (1978) said, "The present data on innovation fail to confirm the idea that major technological innovation lags behind demand growth" (p. 63). Drawing on his study of the automobile industry in the United States, he reports that "some of the most important innovations to the industry were made under weak demand conditions and made apparently to stimulate demand." And he adds, "There is no indication that major advances were delayed by slow market growth" (p. 63). In relation to macroeconomic conditions, sometimes studied in the setting of the Kondratiev long waves discussed in Chapter 1 (pp. 5–6), empirical evidence seems evenly divided on whether innovation is more likely to be stimulated in good or bad economic times. Van Duijn (1983), for example, argued that innovation is a result and not a cause of economic conditions and his empirical findings support the "prosperity-pull" argument. Kleinknecht (1983), on the other hand, argued that because innovation is inherently risky, it will occur more during a time of depression when everything is risky, and he also produces empirical evidence to support his "depression-trigger" argument.

What Abernathy (1978) found to be much more compelling than prevailing demand conditions was the structure of the industry. He wrote, "In the automobile industry the most important explanatory factor in innovative activity seems to be the competitive strategies of the major firms" and "when a few firms control most of the market their competitive strategies are of overriding importance in defining the course of technological progress" (p. 63).

The operation of supply and demand in innovation is not confined to industrial and commercial applications. The history of warfare and its tools provides many examples where technology push and demand pull stimulated rapid and expensive innovation. The rise of air power is a case in point. The airplane was invented with little thought of military application. As World War I got underway, both sides realized that airplanes made useful tools for reconnaissance. This prompted a demand for fighter planes to shoot down the enemy's scouts. More powerful engines were developed to allow the scouts to escape from the fighters. The new engines allowed airplanes to carry a "useful" payload, such as bombs, which opened the way for a whole new pattern of warfare: aerial bombardment, which demanded a new organization, the Air Force. And so the crazy spiral has gone on, with new technologies leading to new weapons, which prompt the demand for counterweapons (and new organizational systems to handle them), which in turn spur newer weapons that can get round the counterweapons, and so on.

An interesting example of how a new market can exert its pull through government intervention is a commercial innovation that has had major economic effects since its introduction in the eighteenth century—the wide use of banknotes as a new form of money (as distinct from coins of precious metal). Galbraith (1975) entertainingly describes how the market needs of the American frontier were accomodated to the orthodox monetary doctrines of the east coast by a de facto loosening of government regulation in the newer states. The tool was already invented but had not been widely used until the market impelled it.

Galbraith (1975) explains it as follows:

> For the new parts of the country as they were opened up, there was the right to create banks at will and therewith the notes and deposits that resulted from their loans. While there were state regulations specifiying the cash to be held in reserve, these were enforced with a light and gracious hand. In consequence, as civilization, or some approximation came to an Indiana or Michigan crossroads in the 1830s, so did a bank. Its notes, when issued to a farmer to buy land, livestock, or other simple equipment, put him into business. If he and others prospered and paid off their loans, the bank survived. If he and others did not so prosper and pay, the bank failed, and someone—perhaps a local creditor, perhaps an eastern supplier—was left holding the worthless notes. But some borrowers from this bank were now in business. Somewhere, someone holding the notes had made an involuntary contribution to the winning of the West (p. 94).

2.2.2 Structure, Size, and Life Cycle

Some structural factors may obstruct an organization from entering the innovation system. In terms of Figure 2.1, they may be negative inputs.

The structural factor most frequently discussed in this context is the size of the firm in industry and business. Again the evidence is mixed. Sirbu

(1981) says, "Studies show that radically new products occur disproportionately in small firms" (p. 189). Sweeney (1989) refers to "the relatively small minority of larger firms which are progressive and innovative" (p. 14). Drucker (1985) on the other hand, affirms otherwise. He writes, "That large businesses do not and cannot innovate is not even a half-truth" (pp. 147–148). Some aspects of these arguments regarding size of operation and frequency of innovation inputs have been recycled in discussion of geographic competitive advantage. Thus an Australian review cites as one of the changed perspectives in the innovation literature between 1984 and 1988 the realization that "small countries are not 'little' big countries" (Centre for Technology and Social Change, 1988, p. 11). The implication that small countries, like small firms, have different roles in the system of innovation can be detected in some of the discussion of product life cycle in relation to innovation.

Drucker (1985) goes on to argue that it is not size that is an impediment to innovation in a firm but the existing operation itself, especially the existing successful operation. The product life cycle has already been mentioned in Chapter 1 (pages 10–11). At the beginning of the life cycle of a technology, major innovations change the functions of the product in application or the basic way it is made. Such innovations give way to incremental change as the means of improvement in the later stages of development, until standardization of production processes improves productivity but makes the organizations or parts of organizations that use them rigid and resistant to change. The product life cycle concept is readily extended to any new idea or practice adopted by an organization. Once brought into the organization, the novelty is adapted in a series of minor ways that may add up to very large improvement in the overall operation. Inevitably, once the innovation has been successfully incorporated into operations, there is resistance to the introduction of ideas for competing novelties. Abernathy (1978) reminds us that "stated generally, to achieve gains in productivity, there must be attendant losses in innovative capability; or, conversely, the conditions needed for rapid innovative change are much different from those that support high levels of production efficiency" (p. 4).

The more mature the technology, and of course the more it is used, the more efficiently the product can be made. Economists refer to the "learning curve" during which an absolute decrease in cost is achieved with cumulative volume of production. The mature technology also represents investment in plant, training, and so on. No wonder that when a radically new technology comes along, the "attacker" from outside, that is, the emerging firm with the new technology but with little stake in the old, is in a much better position to adopt the innovation. Thus Foster (1986) subtitles his book on innovation *The Attacker's Advantage*.

The bases for decisions on inputs of new technology are clearly different in organizations where continuing improvements are still being made in existing products and processes, where the technology may be mature but not to the point of diminishing returns. Pake (1986), writing as head of research for the Xerox Corporation, points out neatly that in this case, "the new technology is pursuing a moving, not a stationary target, and its performance goals often have to be tightened as the new development proceeds" (p. 20).

Application of this product life cycle idea to innovation allows appreciation of the unevenness in opportunity for innovation and also explains why the companies that appear to have all the necessary technological expertise do not necessarily take advantage of apparent opportunities for innovation. It has been remarked, for example, by Abernathy (1978) and others, that despite accumulations of capital and engineering skills in the United States at the beginning of this century, the major transportation companies in the railroad industry did not become the innovators in the fledgling automobile industry, and neither did the gaslight companies prove capable of assimilating the opportunities offered by discovery and development in the distribution of electric light.

It may be useful to adopt the idea of the innovation life cycle when taking into consideration all the factors that will bear on an organization's openness to inputs of new ideas and to the strategies and policies adopted in reaching decisions about implementation. These matters are further discussed in section 2.3 of this chapter. Bottom-line considerations in business and industrial enterprise have also provided inputs to innovation.

2.2.3 Economic Expectations

Another key input in determining whether an organization innovates is its economic expectations. Von Hippel (1988) proposes that "analysis of the temporary profits ('economic rents') expected by potential innovators can by itself allow us to predict the functional source of innovation usefully often." In reviewing his own extensive empirical studies, he reports that "in all cases studied, it did appear that innovating firms could reasonably anticipate higher profits than noninnovating firms" (p. 5). Throughout his work, Von Hippel (1988) is careful to compare like to like among innovations, organizations, and industries, and he is sensitive to differences. He has provided evidence from the several industries that he studied that "the functional source of innovation differs strongly across the several types of product and process innovation explored" (p. 28).

Central to Von Hippel's thesis is the idea of *functional relationships*. Organizations and individuals can be categorized in terms of their functional relationships to innovation. These are the relationships through which they derive benefit from an innovation. The background to the common assumption that innovation is technological innovation has already been discussed. Such innovation is usually embodied in products, and this leads easily to the further assumption that the innovations arise with the manufacturers of these products. Von Hippel (1988) recognizes that functional relationships are not confined to manufacturers or even to users and suppliers of their products and processes. Indeed he assures us that "any functional class is a potential source of innovation under appropriate conditions" (p. 4). Among the functional classses Von Hippel lists suppliers, customers, competitors, and so on. One aim of this book is to explore the conditions under which information service providers may constitute a functional class for innovation.

In our overall attempt to gain better understanding of the process of innovation, the notion of functional relationships is important because it directs attention to formerly unnoticed aspects of the reality of the process. In arguing that "attempts to direct or enhance innovation must be based on an accurate understanding of the sources of innovation" (Von Hippel, 1988, pp. 9–10), Von Hippel points to the United States government's concern that semiconductor process equipment firms in the United States are losing their market edge. Since Von Hippel's studies show that innovations in most process equipment come from users, he argues that the semiconductor manufacturers may be falling behind because the United States user community is falling behind, rather than the other way around. Official concern and a good deal of economic commentary on the computer industry may therefore have been misdirected.

The complexity that has emerged in discussion of inputs to the system makes very unlikely the achievement of innovation by any kind of technological, economic, or government policy fix. At the same time, a good deal has been achieved in the sorting out of more and less effective variables in the initiation of innovation, and it is possible to examine the extent to which the process can be managed within the organization and within society generally.

2.3 Processing or Managing Innovation

2.3.1 Picking up the Signals

Much of the work on the management of innovation as a process concentrates on technological innovation and is often focused on management of research and development (R & D) facilities. The article by Brown and Karagozoglu (1989), which suggests a systems model of technological innovation, deserves to mark the beginning of a new trend of more coherent studies. As Brown and Karagozoglu (1989) point out, "The fragmented and contradictory findings of past research call for departures from an atomistic focus towards more comprehensive investigations" (p. 15).

Any comprehensive investigation has to take into consideration all types of innovation, as well as what Schon (1971) termed "the dynamically conservative plenum into which information moves" (p. 90). Drucker's book, *Innovation and entrepreneurship* (1985), is notable, not only for his wide historical perspective but also because he has drawn on his own theoretical knowledge and practical involvement in management to offer broadly based and confident prescriptions for the effective management of innovation. Readers are referred to the book to enjoy the full flavor of the "war stories," in other words, the anecdotes of successful and unsuccessful innovations, drawn from many centuries and many countries. In setting the scene, Drucker describes innovation as both a cause of and a response to change. He characterizes the innovator as searching for change, responding to it, and exploiting it as an opportunity. He argues that "change provides the opportunity for the new and different" and that "*Systematic innovation therefore consists in the purposeful and organized search for changes, and in the systematic analysis of the opportunities such changes might offer for economic or social innovation*" (Italics Drucker's) (Drucker, 1985, p. 31).

The "organized search for changes" that Drucker recommends is primarily a search for information. In particular, the innovator or the innovating organization needs information about the social, economic, and technological environment into which an innovation might go, as well as information about the innovation itself. More precisely, Drucker discusses seven signals of change, each of which can alert a potential entrepreneur or an organization to an opportunity for innovation. These opportunities are to be found in

1. the unexpected;
2. the incongruity;
3. changes in industry or market structure;
4. process need;
5. changes in demographics;
6. changes in public perception; and
7. new knowledge, both scientific and nonscientific (Drucker, 1985, pp. 35–129).

Drucker describes the first four as lying within the enterprise while the other three involve changes outside the enterprise or industry. But he also stresses that the borders of these factors are blurred and overlap. He writes:

"They can be likened to seven windows, each on a different side of the building. Each window shows some features that can also be seen from the window on either side of it. But the view from the center of each is distinct and different" (Drucker, 1985, pp. 35–36).

The seven windows are discussed in this section in some detail because of the management implications of having these vantage points staffed and assimilated into the overall reporting processes of the organization.

1. The Unexpected

One source of "the unexpected" may be the appearance of customers from a category other than that at which a company's product has been aimed. For example, all the early electronic computers were developed for scientific use, for crunching through large complex calculations, such as those that arise in astronomy and ballistics. When business became interested in buying computers for mundane purposes, such as payroll, Univac company, which made the most advanced computer at that time, was surprised but not interested. IBM, although equally surprised, seized the opportunity. In doing so IBM not only adapted its machines to meet the new market, it also introduced important management innovations, one of which was "bundling," which is the inclusion in the one price package not only of hardware and software but also of related services, such as training and programming.

Often detection of unexpected customers depends on the quality of the sales data available in the company's internal management information system. Because unexpected customers may hide behind a surprising peak in sales to a particular distributor, it is vital for the prime supplier to get out in the field to find out the reality behind the data on blips in sales. Who exactly are the users and what exactly are they looking for? The relevance of this idea to the management of innovation in all organizations, whether offering products or services, commercial or otherwise, is obvious. The importance of point of sales data has long been recognized, and in commercial enterprise product bar codes and scanners have made its collection much more copious and accurate. The importance of sales data also helps to explain both the widespread adoption of lap-top computers for the sales force in many organizations and the confident forecasts that pen computers will also be widely used at point of order.

2. The Incongruity

In any environment, alertness to the unexpected in consumer or client behavior may often also uncover Drucker's second innovation signal, the incongruity.

An important type of incongruity is that between what the industry thinks it is supplying and what the customers think they are buying. This Drucker (1985) describes as a signal that an industry is ripe for change. The shipping industry is often cited as an example. For many years shipping companies perceived themselves as supplying ships to carry a customer's goods. But what the user of shipping really wanted was smooth and cheap delivery of goods from his factory to his customer. Ever faster ships were introduced with ever greater carrying capacity and fuel efficiency and thus lower cost to the shipping companies but not to the shippers. Their goods simply piled ever faster on the waterfront at each end.

"Cheaper" ships hardly benefitted the users, because the cost of the sea voyage was, even in the 1950s, outweighed by the cost of packing, loading, unloading, and unpacking. The innovation of the container in the 1960s, which decoupled the packing and loading process from the voyage, saved the shipping industry. In the 1980s several shrewd transport companies (such as the Australian company Thomas Nationwide Transport) were able to expand worldwide by offering a further innovation: complete door-to-door service, with the shippers not having to concern themselves directly with how the goods traveled or with clearing them through customs.

Examples can also be found in the field of reference books. The incongruity of sending people who cannot spell to consult dictionaries was perceived by the publisher who produced *The Misspeller's Dictionary* (Norback and Norback, 1974). In this dictionary words are arranged in alphabetic order of common mis-spellings with references to correct versions. Managers gain the information needed to spot the opportunity for this kind of innovation from careful study of the market and assumptions about that market. There may be a whole new market out there that is not being served. For example, many of the end-users of mainframe computers in the 1970s did not really need or use the full power provided; a small, cheap, desktop machine was all they needed to do simple calculations and data processing. But this fact was hidden from suppliers because the people they sold to were the computer departments of large organizations, who (partly to maintain their own prestige) tended to specify the biggest and smartest machines their budget would allow.

The information needed to spot such incongruities, at least in anecdotal form, is usually available but is accessible only to people already connected with the industry, whether as suppliers or customers. Some of the opportunities to innovate that both these groups have arise because they have access to such information ahead of others in the industry, such as equipment manufacturers. Reference has already been made to the empirical evidence of the conditions for nonmanufacturer innovation in many industries, and it has been skillfully collected and analyzed in Von Hippel (1988).

3. Changes in Industry or Market Structure

These may arise from social change. The market for the popular newspaper, Lord Northcliffe's innovation in the late nineteenth century, was created by structural change in an industry, namely the education industry. Schooling in Britain changed in the nineteenth century from being the preserve of a few, mostly the rich, to a service to the masses, with the introduction of government-funded schools, which charged no fees. This innovation in turn forced the existing private schools to re-examine their operations and to innovate their own teaching practices.

Such external change, especially by governments, has often led to major industry restructuring, which, in turn, allows new operators to enter. Industry restructuring can also arise from technological change. A classic example is the introduction of the transistor to the electronics industry in the 1950s. Barely any of what were then the major electronics firms survived as major players; a whole new crop of companies grew up on the basis of rapid and focused R & D in the new technology. One of the classic studies of organizational innovation, Burns and Stalker (1961) had already demonstrated that only companies capable of adopting new forms of "organic" rather than "mechanistic" structures, including less authoritarian leadership styles, had survived the earlier challenge of transition from electrical to electronic engineering.

If technological change is likely to presage these structural changes in industries and markets, there is obviously a need for organizations to monitor closely the R & D scene in which they are involved. This is sometimes alleged to be most effectively achieved by the organization's own involvement in R & D. This was one of the findings of an extensive review of an Australian government scheme designed to foster investment in R & D (Price Waterhouse, 1985). Cohen and Levinthal (1989) also argue for recognition of the role of R & D in enhancing the firm's ability to assimilate and exploit existing information. Research in India suggests too that firms that have imported technology are more likely both to have their own R & D programs and to spend more on them than firms that do not import technology (Katrak, 1989). The advantage to companies of pursuing their own R & D is also strongly associated with the importance of sharing of information in industry, which is discussed in section 2.5 on feedback, this chapter. On the other hand, the difficulties of having the results of an organization's own R & D implemented as innovations within the organization are well known. In order to combat this and the wider problem of lack of communication among technical, marketing, and top management personnel, some corporations, such as Matsushita, have set up systems of internal quasi-markets that govern the interface between R & D and operating units (Bartlett and Ghoshal, 1989, pp. 123–124). There is also the closely related phenomenon that is often referred to as "not invented here"—the phenomenon by which attempts to import innovations in manufacturing, service, or management practices are resisted because they did not originate within the organization, or within the particular local branch of the organization. Allen (1977) has described the general phenomenon and Bartlett and Ghoshal (1989, p. 119) have pointed to the difficulties that it can cause in a multinational corporation seeking to leverage its global resources by transferring innovations from one country to another.

4. Changes in Demographics

Some information on changes in demographics is available for all countries, though the accessibility, scope, reliability, and up to dateness of such statistics may differ from place to place. Demographic data concern the numbers and distribution of populations in various categories such as age, ethnicity, income, and educational levels. National census-taking is more or less regular and the results processed more or less promptly and in more or less detail. More discussion of the sources of demographic data is entered in Chapter 4. It is sufficient to notice here that to obtain such data does not require inside knowledge of a particular industry. The public availability of up-to-date and reliable demographic statistics is in fact one of the features of an advanced industrial society. Demographic data can be used to predict, often years in advance, opportunities for innovative services.

One such example is the change in age structure of the population of Western countries as the post-World War II baby boom works its way through the age ranges. Initially this offered opportunities for child-care services. Then, with the need to build more primary schools to meet the boom, came the opportunity for innovators to redesign the layout and teaching methods of schools (open plan, etc.). Later still came the opportunities offered by the new teenage market (pop records, fancy dress, etc.). And so on up the process, to the opportunities in the 1990s for innovative forms of aged care, as many of the baby-boomers are unable to look after their aging parents, whom innovative medical technology has kept from dying sooner.

These opportunities can be predicted, even as to timing, years in advance based on publicly available information, such as the census data just mentioned. In managing the innovation process, organizations need to allocate resources to give proper attention to the collection and interpretation of such data. Also necessary in managing any enterprise is a willingness to realize that the future may look different from the present. An example of an innovator making use of demographic change in a different way is the successful United Kingdom computer software firm staffed entirely by highly qualified young mothers working from home (Shirley, 1989).

5. Changes in Public Perception

Information is much harder to come by on changes in public perception, but they too give rise to opportunities for innovation. Here the facts may not change, but the way people perceive them does. For example, related to the factual, demographic changes in the population structure of Western countries—but very distinct from them—is the tendency for the baby-boomers now in their forties to perceive themselves as still youthful. A generation ago, persons in their forties or fifties perceived themselves as past the stage of great physical activity. But this is not true today. We now have a boom in fitness-related activities, both in terms of commercial workout facilities and for producers of novel fitness systems, such as home gym machines, which enable the user to exercise out of public sight. Similarly, an innovator may use skillful marketing to move the image of a product away from a perception that it is old-fashioned, unexciting, or unappealing. An example is the success in Australia of "calamari rings," which sell much better than "sliced squid" would ever do.

Great skill is needed to read such changes in perception, since they are often hidden in contradictory information. Popular magazines and lifestyle supplements in newspapers may give a clue, but often do not because their editors have not picked up the change either. Market research in this case will be useful only if the entrepreneur already has a feel for the right questions to ask. And timing is critical in seizing such opportunities, as they may be fleeting.

6. Process Need

Process need opportunities inside an industry arise from weak links in the value chain[1] of that industry, particularly in the production and distribution processes. For example, in the nineteenth century there existed fast printing presses and large urban populations sufficiently literate to consider buying a newspaper, but until the technical innovation of mechanical typesetting, little could be done to fill this need.

Where there is a bottleneck in the process, and especially where this bottleneck is only a small but essential link in the chain, there is an opportunity for an innovator to corner a market. Often it is even possible for users to specify exactly what is required of the innovation. For example, during the First World War, the Germans were cut off from natural nitrate rock, but they needed the nitrates for explosives and fertilizers. Nitrogen is abundant in air. The problem was clearly one of chemical engineering: to chemically transform Nitrogen from its passive state in air to a chemically reac-

[1]The value chain is a concept made known mainly through the work of Michael Porter (1985) which is further discussed in the next section of this chapter.

tive form. The solution was found by a concerted effort by the top chemists in the country. They invented the Haber process for making ammonia (NH_3), and it is still in use today.

The information needed to bring in such an innovation is, first, knowledge of the industry in order to specify what is needed, and second, the specialized technical knowledge and skill from which to find a solution. In some industries, for example, scientific instruments, this information is more readily available to the users of equipment than to the producers. If the users can also capture the "economic rent" of improvements to the process, then they become a significant source of innovation, as documented by Von Hippel (1988).

7. *New Knowledge*

Some of the difficulties of using new knowledge as an input to the system of innovation have already been discussed in section 2.2. The simplest case for management seems to be that in which the problem to be solved is agreed and recognized. The Haber process mentioned previously, for example, built on new scentific knowledge: in this case, detailed measurements of the thermodynamic properties of ammonia. But this knowledge was gathered for a specific purpose and to build on the existing knowledge of thermodynamics. Such cases are the essence of technical development, the *D* component of the R & D divisions of organizations.

Unsolicited solutions coming from the *R* component of R & D, whether the research was originally conceived as pure or applied, are much more difficult to turn into successful innovation. Many of the most dramatically transforming inventions of history have their origin in pure research. Penicillin and the transistor are examples already referred to in this book. But in both those cases, getting them into commercial application required a good deal more than the initial scientific discovery. It took time, money, and a perception that the extra effort was going to be worthwhile. Or, to use Von Hippel's hypothesis (1988), "innovating firms will be found among those whose analyses lead them to expect a rent they consider attractive" (p. 44).

Monitoring the organization's operations and also the wider environment is obviously part of management's task in maintaining a lookout for the signals of opportunities for innovation described by Drucker (1985). There is also relevant knowledge about the strategies that can be employed within organizations to bring innovations to the marketplace and about the factors which seem to enhance and to jeopardize their chances of commercial success.

2.3.2 Designing the Strategies

For any organization to work effectively, its members have to share at least a broad consensus on what the organization is trying to achieve. To articulate this purpose is one of the main functions of corporate planning. Its other main purpose is to outline the means through which the organization can most efficiently achieve its objectives; that is, how the resources of the organization are to be deployed.

Theoretically, these considerations together determine the organization's need and potential for innovation. However, an organization's actual capacity to innovate also depends strongly on the informal, personal, status system that provides the internal motivation for each individual. As Burns and Stalker (1961) point out in their classic study of innovation, "individuals seek to realize other purposes than those they recognize as the organization's" (p. 91). There is no one strategy for human resources management adopted by all successful innovative organizations. There is evidence however that they are characterized by personnel policies that do not seek to impose rigid hierarchical modes of communication and which reward and therefore positively reinforce innovative behavior (i.e., positive feedback in terms of Figure 2.1).

In an interesting discussion of what they call "implementation inputs," Brown and Karagozoglu (1989) claim, "The successful implementation of innovative ideas in organizations depends on four crucial factors: the organizational structure, the quality of information flow, the relevant manpower flows, and the specification of key roles for innovative action." They also point out that "the appropriate structure has been found to depend on the complexity of the innovation project and the particular stage of the innovation process" (p. 12). There seems, however, less clear evidence to support their further claim that "the generation of ideas for radical innovation projects seems to be facilitated by organic structures. Implementation activities, however, seem best handled in mechanistic structures" (p. 12).

The key personal roles specified by Brown and Karagozoglu (1989) are (1) gatekeeping, (2) idea generating, (3) project championing, (4)project management, and (5) sponsorship by senior management. The role of technological gatekeeper was identified and described by Allen (1977), and they and some of their relatives who are notable for their boundary-spanning activities within and outside the organization are mentioned also in Chapter 3 (p. 94) and further discussed in Chapters 4 and 5. The project or process champion has also proved important at least in the creation of awareness of potential innovation and in the organization's decision on whether to take it to trial. Like gatekeepers, innovation champions seem to occur naturally, although their effectiveness naturally increases with their seasoning in the politics of the organization. Idea generating is also a natural outcome of communication among intelligent people, but the ultimate usefulness of the ideas will be increased depending on the breadth of the base on which they are formulated. Hence the popularity with management in industry of new product teams in which research, manufacturing, and marketing aspects of the organization are represented. The need for project management is obvious, and the nearer it can be to the inventor or primary group of innovators, the more effective it is likely to be.

Having people, ready, willing, and able to carry out these roles is essential to enable an organization to pick up inputs (on the left of Figure 2.1) and process them through to the outputs of innovation—new products and services (on the right of Figure 2.1). We would suggest that marketing is also a vital factor in the implementation of innovations; this topic is taken up in the next section.

Because of its central importance for all managers, there is a vast literature embracing titles like strategic planning, corporate planning, and strategic management. Naturally the literature tends to focus on the strategic management of commercial businesses, but in the political and economic climate of the 1990s other organizations such as government departments, universities, hospitals—in fact all public service institutions—are increasingly being asked to develop and implement businesslike plans for the management of resources.

Brown and Karagozoglu (1989) define the overall corporate strategy as the "large-scale plans dealing with the opportuntities and threats faced by the organization" (p. 11). Among these large-scale plans in commercial enterprises will be those related to the pursuit of economic gain. Porter (1985) distinguishes three major, but very distinct, routes that a firm can travel, in order to maximize its long-term profitability. These are cost leadership, differentiation, and focus on a selected market.

Cost leadership refers to the firm's outputs of products or services being offered at the lowest cost. Differentiation refers to the strategy by which a firm offers, right across the market, a characteristic or characteristics that distinguish it from its competitors. Some examples of such characteristics are better after-sales service, easier purchasing channels, or higher quality in some other sense. Within a focused, or "niche" market, a firm can do well by differentiation, or by being the lowest cost producer, or simply through having got there first with a product or service for which it can satisfy the well-defined market and from which it may derive monopoly benefits, at least for a time.

A company has to make a conscious choice which of these basic strategies to pursue, bearing in mind its own present culture, resources, and competitive advantages, and also the structure of the industry. (The implications for the company's information requirements depending on which of the strategies it pursues are taken up in Chapter 3.) This basic choice then largely determines such other strategic considerations as export strategy, acquisition strategy, technology strategy, and information strategy. The innovation literature stresses the importance of technology *policy,* which suggests a broader context than *strategy,* but no clear-cut distinction is preserved. Whatever the nice distinctions to be made between policy as setting the overall objectives and strategy as laying out the ways in which the objectives are to be achieved, in the literature the terms seem to be used interchangeably.

An organization's technology policy or strategy essentially maps out the path through which it progresses from inputs to innovation (left side of Figure 2.1) to outputs of innovation (right side of Figure 2.1)—or indeed whether it takes such a path at all. Maidique and Patch (1982) point to the very strong links that have to exist between technology policy and overall corporate strategy. They argue the suitability of a technology policy for a particular organization depends on whether the overall strategy is early-to-market, second-to-market, late-to-market (that is, cost minimization), or market-segmentation (focusing on niches). Translation is easily made into the terms suggested by Porter (1985).

The typical concerns of a technology policy are listed by Brown and Karagozoglu as: "(a) the extent of technological risk taking to be assumed; (b) the nature of the technology programs to be pursued; (c) obsolescence-related considerations; (d) the extent of involvement with external sources in developing technology (e.g., subcontracts and joint ventures) as opposed to internal development; and (e) the competitive posture of the company with respect to new product development" (Brown and Karagozoglu, 1989, p. 11).

Rothwell and Zegveld (1985, Chapter 2) summarize the extensive literature on factors that distinguish successful attempts to innovate from unsuccessful ones. Among the key corporate factors listed is

> having a long-term corporate strategy in which innovation plays a key role. Firms need a strategy in order to obtain synergies between R & D projects, manufacturing projects and marketing projects (p. 75).

Likewise, Dodgson (1989) concluded:

> While it is impossible unequivocally to assert that there is a strong positive correlation between the existence of a technology strategy and corporate success . . . there is a considerable amount of evidence showing that significant advantages are attained by firms with appropriate technology strategies . . . such strategies have long-term horizons, link technology well with other facets of corporate development, build upon existing skills and compe-

> tences, are often international in focus, and can be stimulated and implemented best by managers prepared to learn from past successes and failures (p. 220).

In the business literature, inevitably dominated by concern for technological innovation, a systems view of the whole operation can be seen emerging. For example, in the Australian review of the innovation literature from 1984 to 1988, the Centre for Technology and Social Change (1988) noted that "Technological innovation is increasingly seen not as a technical or an investment problem but rather one of managing organisations that transform knowledge" (p. 35). Such management requires that a firm can obtain the knowledge that it needs to transform, either from within or from outside itself. The "make or buy" decision about where to obtain knowledge is an important one; some of the circumstances on which the answer depends are discussed in Chapter 4.

The authorities quoted in this section emphasize the importance of technology strategy as part of corporate strategy. Whether one chooses to dub it technology strategy or policy, it cannot be neglected. This is because, as Porter (1985) points out, technological change can do all the following:

1. raise or lower entry or mobility barriers (can a change be easily initiated?);
2. alter the capital requirements for competing in a business (e.g., by raising the ante for R & D);
3. change the cost of switching suppliers (e.g., retraining);
4. change the relative power of buyers and sellers (e.g., by making available alternative products);
5. change fixed costs (e.g., supertankers);
6. introduce new products which offer alternatives to the customer.

Many of these consequences can readily be seen to apply to organizations in education and government and to public service institutions generally. For example, the Australian Taxation Office (ATO) in the late 1980s consciously decided that the most effective way in which they could minimize the amount of unpaid tax was to concentrate their attention on big taxpayers (such as large companies) and on individuals who had particular potential (because of the nature of their work) for making dubious claims. To match this corporate strategy, the ATO had a corresponding technology strategy: they brought in a massive new computer system with the capacity to match banking records to individual's returns and to pick out anomalous or "high risk" returns for detailed analysis from the millions submitted. In this way, low-level labor could be used to enter the data supplied by taxpayers (with very little first-pass checking by tax officers), leaving their skilled accountants to concentrate on the cases thrown up by the big computer (Australian Tax Office, Tax chaos 1992). The new system throws much more of the work of preparing and substantiating tax returns on the individual taxpayer—a change that the tax office can enforce because of its monopoly position. But the office also offers incentives to the taxpayer through quicker refunds, especially if the taxpayer makes use of the new technology offered to lodge his or her return electronically (i.e., without ATO staff needing to key it into the ATO computer, thus saving on their costs). The introduction of these procedures has required major restaffing and retraining, extending over the decade over which the new system has been brought on-line.

The Open University in Britain is an example of an educational innovation that took advantage of new technology (television) to reach a whole new market for distance education. The Open University not only offered educational alternatives not previously available to thousands of people in Britain, it also developed new print, video, and audio products as curricular materials, and these have found global markets.

The "product life cycle" was discussed in Chapter 1 (pages 10–12) and in relation to inputs to the innovation in this chapter (page 45). It may also be a helpful notion in technology strategy formation.

In analyzing strategy, Langrish (1989) has compared the management of innovation to the card game of draw poker. In draw poker players attempt to improve their competitive position by obtaining new cards to replace some of their old ones, just as firms seek to improve their competitive position by replacing old technologies with new ones. In each case, there is a set of rules determining which hand is better than another hand, the possibility of improving one's own hand, the possibility of competitors improving their hands, and a price to be paid for either withdrawing from competition or for remaining in competition. Moreover, in both cases, it is easier to improve a poor hand than an already good one (diminishing returns on efforts at product improvement), and in both cases choices have to be made between different types of improvement (do you break up a pair to try for a flush, do you improve the motor in your existing model of motor car, or go for an entirely new model?).

Somewhat less colorfully, Freeman (1982, 1988) and others have pointed out that very different technology strategies are appropriate for firms at different stages of the product cycle. Freeman (1982) describes these as offensive, defensive, and imitative. All have implications for information needs. For example, even the imitative firm needs good scientific and technological information in order to be informed about changes in production techniques and about what products to imitate!

There are many ways in which a firm can acquire new technology. In the 1950s and 1960s, two of the main sources by which firms acquired new technology were through their own R & D laboratories (themselves a major social innovation of the late nineteenth century) and through licensing. Trends in the United States (Friar and Horwitch, 1985) and in Australia (Centre for Technology and Social Change, 1990) suggest that there has been a swing towards more cooperative modes, such as joint venturing and cooperative R & D between firms. Perhaps most innovative of all are undertakings involving not only firms in an industry but also labor unions (Kazis, 1989). Obviously in such coalitions the need for an effective technology strategy in each of the organizations concerned becomes at once more pressing and more complex.

Information service strategies for the capture of relevant new technological information are discussed in Chapter 3, where the notion of an information technology strategy is also explored. The discussion of strategies in the context of the systems model has so far opened for us the possibility that the contradictions in some of the empirical work on innovation in business and industry may have arisen because the life cycles of products, processes or technology, and of innovation itself have been poorly understood. This possibility is pursued in the next section of this chapter on the outputs of the innovation system.

2.4 Innovation Outputs

In the model of Figure 2.2, the outputs of the innovation system are new products, processes, services, and changes in management methods and attitudes. Whether these outputs are successfully implemented is ultimately decided in the marketplace.

The concept of marketing is often limited in popular thinking to the promotion and distribution of products and services. Marketing in fact begins with the design of the product or service and continues with its pricing as well as promotion and distribution.

It is also recognized however that market research techniques are unlikely to yield reliable data on the future market for radically new consumer goods. As Tauber points out: "Major innovations that challenge established thinking and habits tend to create dissonance when the consumer is first exposed. The resulting decision dilemma can discourage expressed enthusiasm for the product." Tauber also points out that "products fill needs, but consumer ability to understand or willingness to acknowledge all but the simplest needs is limited" (Tauber, 1982, p. 435).

There are several good stories of new consumer products that bear this out. Among them are the 3M Company's dilemma at what uses could be found for sticky tape and later for the adhesive which has proved so useful on Post-it™ labels, although the first reactions to an adhesive which sticks only until it is gently pulled off were not promising (Fry, 1987).

Innovations in marketing methods also tend to be overlooked in the concentration on technological innovation. Notable examples include the following:

1. home selling by housewives (e.g., Tupperware™ parties)
2. franchising (e.g., McDonald's restaurants, where the central organization provides basically only ideas and tools)
3. payment by installments, which allowed McCormick in the mid-nineteenth century (unlike his rivals) to sell his reapers to the many farmers who did not have enough cash or bank security to buy one straight out
4. direct mail advertising

Outputs of the innovation system are most readily recognized in the consumer goods market. While they are not so readily identified and slower to take effect, the market's operations also affect innovative outputs in major service industries, such as education. There is also a market in new methods of industrial organization. One of these is the Japanese innovation of "Just-in-time" manufacturing, whereby inventories of components are kept to a minimum. This innovation was certainly associated with greater flexibility made possible by automated control of manufacturing technology in large scale plants in heavy industry. The idea has, however, spread to consumer goods makers and retailers (Feder, 1991). In all environments, "Just-in-time" depends also on the innovations in information processing technology embodied in products and services as varied as bar-coded labels and fibre optics. The outputs of innovations in information processing technology are further discussed in Chapter 3.

Marketing is an exchange process, and therefore information flows in both directions with every transaction. Less obvious perhaps is the importance for innovation of an exchange process of active communication between the different parts of a firm concerned with R & D, production, and marketing. Rothwell's interactive model of innovation (Figure 1.7) emphasized such internal links, the strength of which in Japanese firms is one well-known reason for their success in "second wave" innovation. Freeman (1988) has argued that the strength of such links arose from the practice of reverse engineering (or creative copying), which necessarily brought production engineers into the "development" process. The outputs of innovation are therefore strongly associated with the communication and feedback processes within and outside the organization. This may be regarded as another sign of the close association of innovation with information processes. It also makes separate treatment of feedback or communication in the innovation system somewhat artificial, but there are aspects of information flow that can be conveniently treated under the separate heading because of their relationship to the system as a whole.

2.5 Feedback in the Innovation System

Feedback is information derived from the operation of a system, which may be used to modify inputs to the future operations of that system. In most machine systems the process is automatic. Systems managed by human decisions react selectively to feedback. Signals about the operation of the innovation system may, for example, be ignored or simply unnoticed.

The marketplace is the obvious source of feedback in innovation. (See Figures 1.6, 1.7, and 2.1.) It represents the reaction in the environment outside the organization not only to changes in products, process, and services but to new ideas. Marketing is the attempt to manage feedback as a communication process, and the need for management resources to be devoted to the identification of and reaction to market signals with appropriate strategies has already been stressed in this chapter.

There are also other less obvious sources from and channels through which feedback enters the innovation system. One is identified by Von Hippel (1988) as "information know-how trading" (p. 6). He defines this phenomenon discovered in his field research as "essentially a pattern of informal cooperative R & D" which involves "routine and informal trading of proprietary information between engineers working for different firms" (p. 6). He proposes that know-how trading between rivals is a general and significant mechanism that innovators can use to share (or avoid sharing) innovation-related costs and profits with rivals.

Rogers and Larsen (1984, Chapter 5, "Networks") documented a similar phenomenon among high-technology specialists working in Silicon Valley. Part of this know-how exchange is undoubtedly important in maintaining professional reputations in the scientists' and engineers' peer groups, not to mention in maintaining visibility as good prospects for offers of better jobs. But such exchange seems largely to be at least deliberately overlooked if not actively sanctioned by management in most firms. As Von Hippel (1988) points out there are rules, albeit informal and unwritten, and he notes that trade is only carried out with those who can reciprocate in kind. He also noted an instance where firms in active rivalry for a particularly large government contract appeared to have suspended know-how trading for the duration of the bidding period. But for most of the time, in many of the environments in which he had researched, informal know-how trading seems to have acted as a more cost-effective form of cross-licensing of technology than could have been formally set up.

There is also evidence that know-how, which Von Hippel (1988) defines as "the accumulated practical skill or expertise that allows one to do something smoothly and efficiently" (p. 6), is much more effectively imparted on a person to person basis. At least one elegant empirical investigation suggests that building one of the early lasers from published sources may have been impossible to anyone who had not actually seen it done (Collins, 1974). The importance of knowledge exchange within the firm has also been recognized (see pp. 61–62) in the context of the success of Japanese firms in maintaining strong communication links among the parts of an organization. As Brown and Karagozoglu (1989) remind us, "Information flows depend on people and hence the manpower flow from one organizational unit to another becomes a vital factor in the [technological innovation] process. By transferring people, specific kinds of knowledge are also implicitly moved from one organizational unit to another, thus potentially aiding the innovation process" (p. 12).

Such links are often created on an ad hoc basis, by organizations seeking to innovate, in product, process, or new project development teams brought together, usually on a temporary or part-time basis. These interdepartmental links are believed to arise naturally in small firms founded specially to develop and commercialize some new scientific discovery. According to the Social Policy Research Unit (SPRU) database of innovations in the United Kingdom, such new technology-based firms (NTBFs) account for about a quarter of the technical innovations in that country. This proportion has increased rapidly over the last decade (Centre for Technology and Social Change, 1988).

Such experience, by no means confined to the United Kingdom, has prompted governments to try and create infrastructures favorable to NTBFs (such as, technology parks, tax breaks, and advisory and information services targeted at small firms). It has also prompted many large firms to promote "intrapreneurship"—the fostering of small units within the company—but separate from the existing divisional structure—to achieve major innovation. Experience shows that there are many traps in managing these units, which Brown and Karagozoglu (1989) describe as "venture units . . . staffed with temporary appointments from R & D and marketing" (p. 12). Conflict may arise in the clash in cultures between the innovation-oriented and productivity-oriented staff brought together in them. The development of the IBM personal computer by a venture unit, an independent business unit in the company's parlance, is an example of a notable success of the method and has been acknowledged as "Perhaps the best example of an IBM 'business within a business'" (Rodgers, 1986, p. 209). The development of both NTBFs and of venture units are innovations in themselves—

innovations in organization meant to improve the effectiveness and especially the speed of radical innovation. In industry, links to other companies are increasing in importance as a means of promoting innovation. Collaboration with other firms in the same industry for "pre-competitive R & D" is increasing as the scale of investment required increases in some industries (Fusfeld and Haklisch 1985; Organisation for Economic Co-operation and Development, 1988; Centre for Technology and Social Change, 1990b). Such collaboration is actively fostered by some governments, for example in the ESPRIT program in the European Community, Alvey in the United Kingdom, and in the many research associations sponsored by the Ministry for Trade and Industry (MITI) in Japan. The collaboration may well be international. The main result of such collaborations is often the creation and sharing of useful knowledge.

Sometimes collaboration with firms in a different sector is a fruitful source of innovation. This is particularly true between producers of new "tools" (intermediate goods) and the users of such tools (Von Hippel, 1988). For example, a steelmaker may work with a shipbuilder to develop a new steel having special properties needed for a new design of vessel, such as stiffness and lightness required for a submarine hull. Such collaboration would usually make only incremental innovation in the tool, but this may allow a steep improvement in the end device (e.g., a whole new class of ships). Organizational changes of the types just described form an important part of technology strategy.

These ideas take us into the broader topic of communication in the innovation system, which is pursued in our examination of the environment of innovation in section 2.6.

2.6 The Environment of Innovation

The study of communication in Silicon Valley (Rogers and Larsen, 1984) represents just one aspect of the "diffusion of innovations" which has been a major focus of the work of Everett Rogers (1962, 1971, 1983). His research has embraced innovation of every kind in agriculture, education, medicine as well as business and industry, and in many countries and cultures. His models of the diffusion process and his work generally has found wide acceptance and incorporation in other theories. He has identified the five attributes of innovations that affect rate of adoption in the environments in which application is under consideration: (1) the relative advantage, (2) compatibility, (3) complexity, (4) trial-ability, and (5) observability, that the innovations are perceived to possess. And in studying the different rates at which innovations are implemented, he has categorized adopters as innova-

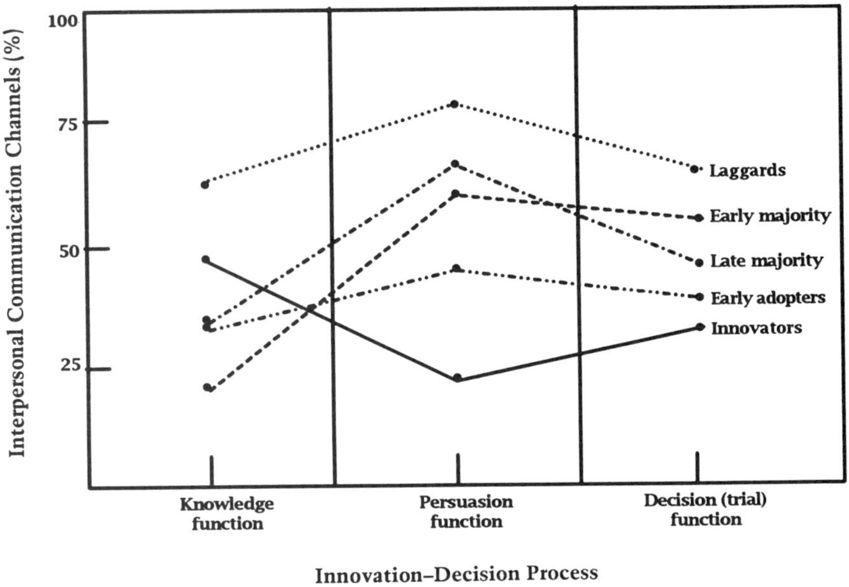

Figure 2.3
The importance of interpersonal channels for later adopters (Rogers, 1983, p. 202) derived from Beal and Rogers (1960). (Reprinted with the permission of The Free Press, a Division of Macmillan, Inc. from "Diffusion of Innovations," Third Edition by Everett M. Rogers. Copyright © 1962, 1971, 1983 by The Free Press.)

tors, early adopters, early majority, late majority, and laggards. The pace at which adoption is made depends on the time it takes adopters to work through the knowledge function, persuasion function, and decision (trial) function in the innovation-decision process (Rogers, 1983). A model derived by Rogers from a study of adopters of 2,4-D weed spray in Iowa is reproduced here as Figure 2.3. It illustrates the finding that interpersonal channels are relatively less important for earlier adopters than for later adopters. Anyone interested in the process of innovation will find Rogers (1983) the most comprehensively helpful work available. In Figure 2.4 his model of independent variables related to organizational innovativeness is reproduced (Rogers, 1983). This model is especially helpful to students and to managers of innovation in organizations; there is now widespread acknowledgement of the importance of the organizational setting and therefore of the dynamics of the firm, government department, school, library, hospital, or wherever the innovation is to be implemented.

We accept the soundness of the views expressed by March (1981) in that organizations are continually changing naturally and adapting to their environments, not optimally but sufficiently for their survival. At the same

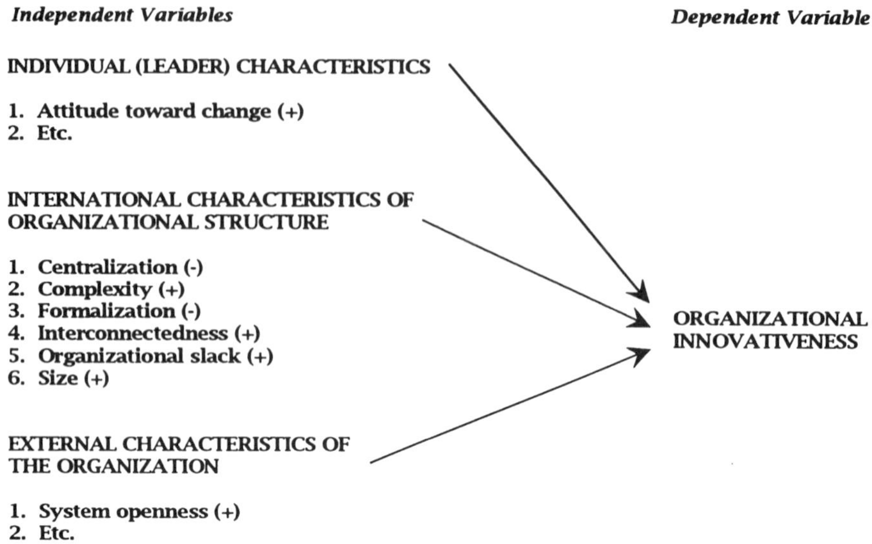

Figure 2.4
Independent variables related to organizational innovativeness. (Source: Rogers, 1983, p. 360.) (Reprinted with the permission of The Free Press, a Division of Macmillan, Inc. from "Diffusion of Innovations," Third Edition by Everett M. Rogers. Copyright © 1962, 1971, 1983 by The Free Press.)

time, it has become clear that innovation is at least partly a matter of organization. To keep an organization ready to adapt rapidly and sensibly to its environment, in other words, to innovate, is a major challenge and task for management. It involves, first of all, a recognition of the circumstances in which innovation is needed, and second, the establishment of formal structures and encouragement of informal cultures within the organization that are conducive to innovation. Rothwell and Zegveld (1985) divide the successes and failure in industrial innovation according to performance on seven factors. These are (1) external or market related communications ; (2) internal communications; (3) project planning and control; (4) technical efficiency before commercial launch; (5) top management's will to innovate; (6) good after-sales service and user education; and (7) committed key individuals, instanced by product champion, business innovator, and technical innovators or inhouse entrepreneurs. Innovation remains an untidy, human process, a system marked by iteration rather than linearity, by risk rather than certainty, in which recognition of different needs and conditions at different stages in the process is required. But the innovation process is a system in which all factors interrelate, as this chapter has sought to show using a rudimentary model, and as Brown and Karagozoglu (1989) have demonstrated in a model that goes much closer to the complexity of the process.

Again, like Sweeney (1987) we contend that for an organization to become conducive to innovation, it has to become a "learning system." Kingston (1977) devotes a whole chapter to innovation as learning, in which he emphasizes the distinction made in the nineteenth century by John Henry Newman between "real" knowledge (which we have made part of ourselves) and "notional" knowledge (which is there somewhere but to which we do not attach any special importance).

In innovation, decisions about which information is of special importance —which is to be known and which can just be known to exist—are crucial to the success of the system. In other words, it is not so much information flow as the communication of appropriate information that is vital.

In Chapter 3 we will argue that to be able to innovate with less risk and to manage the innovation system with less uncertainty, every organization needs an information strategy. The Centre for Technology and Social Change (1988) concluded from its study of the literature's accumulated knowledge on innovation that management needs to systematize what may have been in the past experience based on informal systems of learning. These requirements increase as private and public enterprise becomes more knowledge-intensive, as is happening in almost all industries and in public service institutions today.

This requires more thoughtful management and increased expenditure, particularly on some of the information strategies discussed in Chapter 3 as the means for converting information sources into information resources and services.

References

Abernathy, W. J. (1978). *The productivity dilemma: roadblock to innovation in the automobile industry.* Baltimore, Johns Hopkins University Press.

Allen, T. J. (1977). *Managing the flow of technology: technology transfer and the dissemination of technological information within the R & D organization.* Cambridge, Massachusetts, MIT Press, pp. 161–180.

Amabile, T. M. (1988). A model of creativity and innovation in organizations. *Research in Organizational Behavior, 10,* pp. 123–167.

Bartlett, C. A., and S. Ghoshal, (1989). *Managing across borders: the transnational solution.* Boston, Harvard Business School Press.

Beniger, James R. (1986). *The control revolution: technological and economic origins of the information society.* Cambridge, Massachusetts, Harvard University Press

Bernstein, Jeremy (1984). *Three degrees above zero: Bell Laboratories in the information age.* New York, Scribner's.

Brown, W. B., and N. Karagozoglu, (1989). A systems model of technological innovation, *IEEE Transactions on Engineering Management 36,* 11–16.

Burns, T., and G. M. Stalker, (1961). *The management of innovation.* London, Tavistock.

Centre for Technology and Social Change. (1988). *Innovation for the 1990s: new challenges for technology policy and strategy,* a report for the Department of Industry Technology and Commerce. Canberra, Australian Government Publishing Service.

Centre for Technology and Social Change. (1990). *Strategic alliances in the internationalisation of Australian industry [for the] Department of Industry Technology and Commerce.* Canberra, Australian Government Publishing Service.

Cohen, W. M., and D. A. Levinthal, (1989). Innovation and learning: the two faces of R & D *Economic Journal 99,* 569–596.

Collins, H. M. (1974). The TEA set: tacit knowledge and scientific networks. *Science Studies 4,* 165–186.

Dodgson, M. (1989). Conclusions: Realising technological opportunities. In M. Dodgson, Ed., *Technology strategy and the firm.* London, Longmans, pp. 219–230.

Drucker, P. F. (1985). *Innovation and entrepreneurship: practice and principles.* London, Butterworth-Heinemann, Ltd.

Feder, B. J. (1991). "Moving the Pampers faster cuts everyone's costs: consumer-goods makers and retailers find that 'just-in-time' works for them too." *New York Times* (July 14) p. F5.

Foster, R. (1986). *Innovation: the attackers advantage.* New York, Summit Books.

Freeman, C. (1982). *The economics of innovation* (second ed.). London, Pinter.

Freeman, C. (1988). Japan: a new national system of innovation? *In* Dosi *et al.,* Eds., *Technical change and economic theory.* London, Pinter, pp. 330–348.

Friar, J., and M. Horwitch, (1985). The emergence of technology strategy: a new dimension of strategic management. *Technology in Society 7,* 143–178.

Fry, Art (1987). The Post-it note: an intrapreneurial success *Advanced Management journal 52,* 4–9.

Fusfeld, H. I., and C. S. Haklisch, (1985). Co-operative R & D for competitors *Harvard Business Review 63,* 60–76.

Galbraith, J. K. (1975). *Money: whence it came and where it went.* Harmondsworth, England, Penguin.

Horwitch, M., and K. Sakakibara, (1986). The changing strategy-technology relationship in technology-based industries: a comparison of the United States and Japan. *Research in Technological Innovation, Management and Policy 3,* 83–135.

Hughes, T. P. (1989). *American genesis: a century of invention and technological enthusiasm, 1870–1970.* New York, Viking.

Illinois Institute of Technology, Research Institute. (1968). *Technology in restrospect and critical events in science (TRACES).* Chicago.

Isenson, R. S. (1969). Project Hindsight: an empirical study of the sources of ideas utilized in operational weapon systems. *In* W. H. Gruber and D. G. Marquis, Eds. *Factors in the transfer of technology.* Cambridge, Massachusetts, M.I.T. Press, pp. 155–176.

Katrak, H. (1989). Imported technologies and R & D in a newly industrialising country: the experience of Indian enterprises *Journal of Development Economics 31*(1), 123–139.

Kazis, R. (1989). Rags to riches? one industry's strategy for improving productivity *Technology Review* August/September, 42–53.

Kingston, W. (1977). *Innovation: the creative impulse in human progress.* London, Calder.

Kleinknecht, A. (1983). Observations on the Schumpeterian swarming of innovations. *In* C. Freeman, Ed., *Long waves in the world economy.* London, Butterworths, pp. 48–62.

Langrish, J. (1989). The draw poker theory of innovation management: illustrations from the automotive industry. *In* S. B. Lundstedt and T. H. Moss, Eds., *Managing innovation and change*. Vienna, IIASA.

Maguire, C. (1974). Reorganizing information resources for decision-making: [report of] an AAAS/ASIS symposium. *Lasie, 4*(5), 3–7.

March, J. G. (1981). Footnotes to organizational change *Administrative Science Quarterly 26*(4), 563–577.

Maidique, M. A., and P. Patch, (1982). Corporate strategy and technology policy. *In* M. L. Tushman and W.L. Moore, Eds., *Readings in the management of innovation*. Boston, Pitman, pp. 273–285.

Morton, J. A. (1971). *Organizing for innovation: a systems approach to technical management*. New York, McGraw-Hill.

Mowery, D., and N. Rosenberg (1979). The influence of market demand upon innovation: a critical review of some recent empirical studies. *Research Policy 8*, 102–153.

Norback, P., and C. Norback, Eds., (1974) *The misspeller's dictionary*. New York, Quadrangle/The New York Times Book Co.

Organisation for Economic Co-operation and Development (1988). *Technological co-operation agreements between firms, and the formulation of national technology policies*. Paris. (Document no. DSTI/SPR/88.11).

Pake, G. E. (1986). From research to innovation at Xerox: a manager's principles and some examples. *Research on Technological Innovation, Management and Policy, 3,* 1–32.

Porter, M. E. (1985). *Competitive advantage: creating and sustaining superior performance*. New York, Free Press.

Price Waterhouse. (1985). *The promotion of indigenous I R & D in Australia and the effectiveness of the Industrial Research and Development Incentives Scheme*. Canberra, Department of Industry Technology and Commerce.

Rodgers, F. G. (1986). *The IBM way: insights into the world's most successful marketing organization* (with Robert L. Shook). New York, Harper and Row.

Rogers, E. M. (1962). *Diffusion of innovations*. New York, Free Press.

Rogers, E. M. (1971). *Communication of innovations: a cross-cultural approach* (second ed., with F. Shoemaker). New York, Free Press.

Rogers, E. M. (1983). *Diffusion of innovations* (third edition). New York, Free Press.

Rogers, E. M., and R. Agarwala-Rogers (1976). *Communications in organizations*. New York, Free Press.

Rogers, E. M., and J. K. Larsen, (1984). *Silicon Valley fever: growth of high-technology culture*. New York, Basic Books.

Rothwell, R., and W. Zegveld, (1985). *Reindustrialization and Technology*. London, Longman.

Schmookler, J. (1966). *Invention and economic growth*. Cambridge, Harvard University Press.

Schon, Donald A. (1971). *Beyond the stable state*. New York, Random House.

Shirley, S. (1989). Corporate strategy and entrepreneurial vision, *Long Range Planning 22,* 107–110.

Sirbu, M. A. (1981). The innovation process in telecommunication. In Mitchell L. Moss, Ed., *Telecommunications and productivity*. Based on the International Conference sponsored by the Center for Science and Technology Policy, Graduate School of Public Administration, New York University, January 29–30, 1980. Reading, Massachusetts, Addison Wesley, pp. 184–198.

Sloan, Alfred P. (1963). *My years with General Motors*. New York, Macfadden-Bartell Corp.

Sweeney, G. (1987). The entrepreneurial firm as a learning system in the information society. *The Information Society 5,* 91–99.

Sweeney, G. (1989). Introduction: information and corporate growth. In E. Punset and G. Sweeney, Eds., *Information resources and corporate growth*. London, Pinter, pp. 1–15.

Tauber, E. M. (1982). How market research discourages major innovation. *In* M. L. Tushman and W. L. Moore, Eds., *Readings in the management of innovation*. Boston, Pitman, pp. 431–435.

Tax chaos. (1992, July 28–31). *The Bulletin*.

University of Sussex, Science Policy Research Unit. (1972). *Success and failure in industrial innovation: report on Project SAPPHO*. London, Centre for the Study of Industrial Innovation.

Van Duijn, J. (1983). Fluctuations in innovation over time. *In* C. Freeman, Ed., *Long waves in the world economy*. London, Butterworths, pp. 19–30.

Von Hippel, E. (1988). *The sources of innovation*. New York, Oxford University Press.

3

Information Services: Fundamental Issues

Information reflects the synergistic combination of medium and message.

—K. Levitan, *Information Resources as "goods" in the Life Cycle of Information Production*, p. 46. Copyright © by John Wiley & Sons, Inc. 1982. Reprinted by permission of John Wiley & Sons, Inc.

It is the creative use of information which allows people to work smarter.

—B. L. White, *The Technology Assessment Process*, p.131. Copyright © 1988 by Blake L. White. An imprint of Greenwood Publishing Group, Inc., Westport, CT. Reprinted with permission.

Information without an informant, without a person who tells something —is information in an only metaphoric sense.

—F. Machlup, *The Study of Information*, p. 657. Copyright © 1983. Reprinted by permission of John Wiley & Sons, Inc.

The key element in services is the interposition of human expertise between client and system.

—R. S. Taylor, *Value-Added Processes in Information Systems*, p. 180.

Like the Sorcerer's Apprentice, we are awash in information. And all the sorcerer has left us is a broom.

—N. Postman, *Technopoly: The Surrender of Culture to Technology*, p. 69.

Chapter Synopsis

The importance of innovation and information has been examined in Chapter 1 and the innovation process has been probed in Chapter 2. This chapter seeks to achieve understanding of the nature and function of information services. This understanding is meant to provide a firm base on which to think through opportunities and problems of information services in any environment. The approach is to seek first understanding of concepts closely related to information services, namely, information systems and information technology, and then to pursue distinctions among information sources, information resources, and information services. Distribution of information is clearly a function of any information service and so the nature of information markets is examined, along with the relationship of information services to the invisible assets of any organization. Organizations may themselves be regarded as information systems and the place of information services within them calls for examination. This is important not only in building a theoretical base but in dispelling illusions that any information service, inside or outside a particular organization, can attain a monopolistic position.

The influence of information technology on the provision of information services and on modern society generally is both pervasive and profound. Digitization of symbols and signals at once underlies all applications of information technology and at the same time constantly enlarges the possibilities for new applications. This chapter examines the effects of digitization of text and telecommunications on developments in the roles of information specialists, management strategies in organizations, and the design and distribution of information products and services.

The last section of the chapter suggests criteria and measures for the value of information services, and it also pursues ways in which value may be demonstrated within the organization and in broader environments than the bureaucratic structure and political jurisdiction in which any particular information service is embedded.

3.1 Definitions and Distinctions

3.1.1 Information Systems and Information Technology

The definition of *information systems* put forward in Chapter 1 was "the means of capturing, storing and channelling information." This definition was deliberately made general and inclusive. At such a level of generality the whole universe or even the whole of life may be regarded as a vast interlocking information system. Arrival at a definition more helpful in understanding information services requires attention to some of the factors that distinguish different types of information systems. Pursuit of such distinctions is made more challenging by what Machlup (1983) has called "semantic quirks in studies of information" (p. 641).

The purpose of working through the most important of these quirks is to arrive at deeper understanding of the nature and functions of information services. This understanding is at once more theoretical (abstracting what is essential in the mission and functions of all information services) and more practical (allowing more soundly based decisions on what is appropriate for particular information services).

In removing unhelpful connotations perhaps the first dismissal from the concept of information systems ought to be those systems that are truly mechanistic. Buckley (1983) points out the distinction between "simple systems with constant internal states and systems with varying internal states" (p. 602). In the former he explains "the outputs are a function only of the inputs, and given a particular input at any time, the output must always be the same." In the latter, on the other hand, "the outputs are a function of both the inputs and the internal state at a particular time, and thus, the same input may result in different outputs at different times or vice versa." Buckley concludes that "simple systems, including S[timulus]/R[esponse] systems, do not 'process information,' but only react to signals." In this sense publications like bus timetables or price lists, and computerized systems like automated teller machines are also mechanistic "simple systems."

Machlup (1983) goes further and insists that "real" information systems are human systems. He writes:

> The similarity of the working of homeostatic feedbacks in physiological and in man-made systems makes the use of the term information in both living and nonliving systems acceptable *as long as one does not forget that the term is used as a metaphor* [Machlup's italics]. Real information can come only from an informant. Information without an informant—without a person who tells something—is information in an only metaphoric sense (p. 657).

The informant does not have to be physically present in the system. He or she may no longer be alive so long as the message has been recorded in some surrogate form in the information system. Similarly, in computerized information systems the no longer present human informant may have contributed the design of the algorithm according to which data on the system's ongoing operations are gathered, processed, and delivered in answer to inquiries. The extent to which the data in an information system can be shaped by the inquirer varies according to the interface provided by the system designers and the inquirer's skill in manipulating that interface.

Interfaces that give much more power to the inquirer are being introduced in the digital environment in so-called knowledge-based systems. In such systems "knowledge specific to the problem domain is kept separate from the procedures which manipulate it" (Ford, 1991, p. 10). Manipulation procedures can then be packaged in software as tools by which inquirers can not only search the data in the system but exploit and interact with those data much more fully and freely. Increasing numbers of these tools for building knowledge-based systems are becoming available for personal computers. This software is not expensive and can be used by people without conventional programming skills to build quite complex information systems.

Computers and telecommunications are not essential to the concept of an information system. Some organizations in industrialized countries and many in less developed countries operate with information systems that place little or no reliance on the manipulation and transfer of machine-readable data. In a generalized definition very similar to that adopted in this book, Levitan (1982) reminds us that "an information system generally refers to the interrelated processes of gathering, organizing, storing, retrieving and disseminating information items." She immediately proceeds to this warning: "People often, and mistakenly, equate an information system with a computer. The two are not synonymous. A computer is merely a machine. It becomes an information system when activated by a user through programs which carry out the functions cited above" (p. 49).

Undoubtedly the developments in knowledge-based systems, based partly on their ability to operate on heuristics as well as algorithms, have begun to transform the interactions that the user can have with computerized information systems. But the user remains essential to the information system concept. We may conclude then that information systems will continue to include both human informants and humans wanting to be informed. At the same time information technology will continue to extend the range and depth with which human knowledge can be stored and made available to inquirers through information systems. Hence the need for recognition that information systems and information technology are closely related concepts.

Information technology has resulted from computer technology and telecommunications technology, and more recent developments represent the marriage of the two. But the range and scope of information technology and its pervasive influence on human activities demand a less mundane definition. In a gloss that nicely suggests both technological bases and social significance, Zuboff (1988) explains:

> *Information technology* is a label that reflects the convergence of several streams of technical developments, including microelectronics, computer science, telecommunications, software engineering, and system analysis. It is a technology that dramatically increases the ability to record, store, analyze, and transmit information in ways that permit flexibility, accuracy, immediacy, geographic independence, volume, and complexity. Information technology has a unique capability to restructure operations that depend upon information for the purposes of transaction, record keeping, analysis, control, or communication (p. 415)[1].

[1]Selected excerpt from approximately 7 pages from *In the Age of the Smart Machine: the Future of Work and Power* by Shoshana Zuboff. Copyright © 1988 by Basic Books, Inc. Reprinted by permission of Basic Books, a division of Harper Collins Publishers, Inc.

The transforming capability of information technology can be demonstrated in all aspects of information handling. The continuing changes in information specialities, in management generally, and in information products and services are pursued in section 3.2. But the transformations are in no way confined to information systems and information services. Information technology is not only pervasive in the modern workplace, whether factory, office, or professional suite: Its effects impinge on virtually all aspects of social life. The possibilities that information technology offers for innovation not only in itself but in all products, services, and ways of organizing human activity seem limitless. Just two examples are offered here. One is the inclusion of microprocessors in household appliances. Another is the use of digital communications to network security systems ranging from the protection of property to the validation of signatures.

The perspectives from which information technology and information systems are viewed can lead to some difficulties in reconciling our understanding of the terms. From the top down, in the macroview, information technology is embedded in the information systems that are the large building blocks of the infrastructure of a society. In this view, for example, the education system or the social services system are information systems. At the microlevel, however, in the management of any particular organization, whatever its mission, we may do better to work within a definition that, while general, associates information systems more closely with the management of organizations. In her work on information services strategy and infrastructure in large organizations, Marianne Broadbent (1988) defines information systems as "formal sets of organized activities that add value to messages being processed and use information technology in doing so" (p. 6). The first part of this definition is derived from Taylor (1986, p. 202), and, with Broadbent's addition fits very well in the modern context. It allows the distinctions that need to be made between information systems and information services in organizations. As was noted previously, computers are not essential to the concept of information systems, although they are in use in organizations, large and small, in public, private, and not-for-profit sectors in industrialized countries and in many such environments in developing countries. In its general sense, information technology may be regarded as any specifiable way of creating, storing, manipulating, and disseminating information, including the technology of pencil and paper. Thus Broadbent's definition of information systems may serve in all environments.

In search of a definition of information services this chapter proceeds in an attempt to dispel some other semantic quirks that surround distinctions among information sources, resources, and services. Chapter 5 is devoted to more technical aspects of information technology and something of the history of its impact on the provision of information services.

3.1.2 Information Sources, Resources, and Services

Information sources attract two connotations. One is that of the stores or locations in which information is kept. So a source of information may be an object, a place, an organization, or a particular person, whether, for example, an encyclopedia, a database, a warehouse, a library, a telephone number, or an expert. Sources may be personal or impersonal, public or private, passive or interactive, stored locally or remotely, to which immediate or delayed access may be available, and access may be easy or difficult to arrange. In its second connotation, information sources are virtually indistinguishable from information *channels* because the latter may be written, such as a book or words in some other printed or processed format, or verbal sounds, such as as a telephone or data line. In discussion of information phenomena, the term *channel* is not reserved for the communication channel in the telecommunications sense. In fact, in the telecommunications environment, identity of source and channel is likely to be less obvious. In access to a telecommunications network, for example, the ultimate address of the information (that is, on which computer and even in which files it resides) is usually unknown and irrelevant to the information seeker, as is the particular path or channel through which data are requested and delivered. The presence of telecommunications therefore may exacerbate the difficulty of distinguishing or even recognizing the source of information.

This feature of digital information systems is often referred to as *transparency*. Users, unaware of the processes by which and the locations at which their instructions are carried out, are able to see through them. The difficulties that may result from this transparency in digital information systems in preserving the integrity of information, and even in preserving the concept of authorship, are discussed in section 3.2.2.

Confusion between information sources and information channels may be regarded merely as a semantic replay of old arguments about form versus content or about McLuhan's more recent, pungent adage that the medium is the message (McLuhan, 1962). Levitan (1982) refers to other work in which the expressions *conduit* and *content* are used. Thus information resources are defined as having "two basic components: conduit, the physical facilities used for gathering, storing, processing and distributing information; and content, the information sources and elements" (p. 45).

The fusion of conduit and content aspects in the concept of information is well expressed in Levitan's pithy statement, quoted at the opening of this chapter, that "Information reflects the synergistic combination of medium and message" (Levitan, 1982, p. 48). But is there a distinction to be made between information sources and information resources?

Sources become *information resources* when their relevance for the user

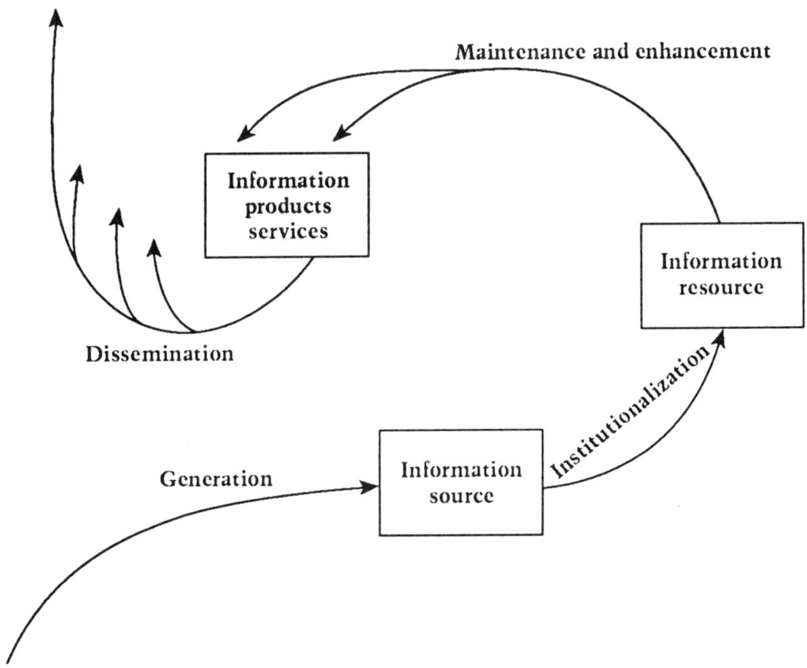

Figure 3.1
Life cycle of information production: simple version (source: Levitan, 1982, p. 47). K. Levitan, *Information Resources as "goods" in the Life Cycle of Information Production*. Copyright © John Wiley & Sons, Inc. 1982. Reprinted by permission of John Wiley & Sons, Inc.

has been recognized or optimized in some way and a suitable conduit has been engineered. Levitan (1982) understands information resources as information sources that have been institutionalized in some way and can thus be reused. The idea of organization for reuse is essentially what lies between the information source and the information resource. The source is in a sense the raw material: the resource is the product, at least partially processed. No one who has been subjected to a showing of a friend's unedited holiday photographic slides or videotapes needs to be reminded that information sources need to be organized for use.

In explication of the total system through which information moves, Levitan introduces the concept of the "Life cycle of information production." The two figures in which she gives first a simple and then a detailed version of her concept are reproduced as Figures 3.1 and 3.2. Figure 3.2 gives a good impression of how the partially processed contents of the information resource are further enhanced in a repackaging or reproduction process for dissemination as information products or services.

Levitan (1982) also points out that "once created, information sources, resources, and products/services can be and are combined in limitless ways"

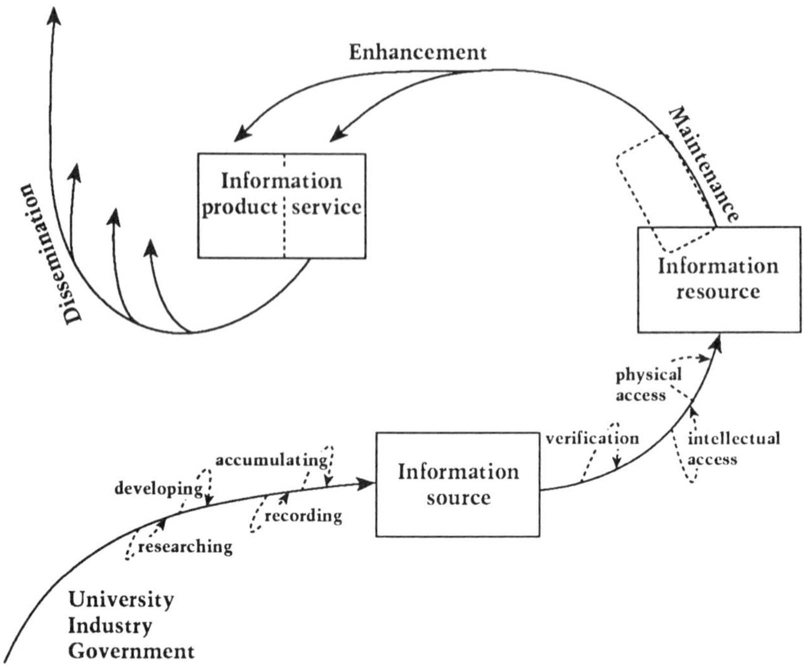

Figure 3.2
Life cycle of information production in detail (source: Levitan, 1982, p. 48). K. Levitan, *Information Resources as "goods" in the Life Cycle of Information Production*. Copyright © John Wiley & Sons, Inc. 1982. Reprinted by permission of John Wiley & Sons, Inc.

and that such convergence is especially apparent in our electronic age, so that "a concrete entity—be it a document, library, computerized management information system, insurance company, bank, university, etc.—can be an information source, resource, product, or service. In order to determine its function, hence its economics, it must be placed in its proper life cycle" (p. 49).

As a simple example, a book on global warming in a bookshop is a source of information. The same book on library shelves and with entries describing it in the library catalog may become a resource. From another perspective, the book in the library may remain a source of information that becomes a resource only when it is recommended by a lecturer. It may indeed then become a scarce resource, the management of which demands its confinement within the library building and retraction of borrowing time to a couple of hours per person. In the digital environment where copying and reproduction facilities are widely available, it is highly likely that books and other documents in high demand will be the basis of new products and services. At least those parts of the book on global warming that the lecturer judges of particular relevance to his students are likely to be repackaged and redistributed by the library or another agency inside or outside the university if suitable copyright arrangements can be made. On a wired campus the relevant parts of the book may, along with other documents in high demand, be accessible to students as an online service through a network.

Thus the roles played by the same information entities differ according to where they lie in any particular cycle of the generation, institutionalization, maintenance, enhancement, and distribution of information products and services. Without this realization of the contingent nature of entities in the process, attempts at analysis of information phenomena must remain superficial. Even placed in their proper life cycle, it is apparent that information products and services present challenges to economic theory based on the production and exchange of commodities. The need for understanding markets in terms of the peculiar properties of information as well as in terms of commodity exchange is discussed in section 3.1.3. Before proceeding to that discussion, the distinction between information resources and information services needs to be resolved.

Levitan (1982) offers a definition for information resources that so emphasizes proactive functions that it seems to leave little territory for information services. She writes:

> An information resource is an integrating mechanism. It stands at the midpoint in the life cycle of information production and brings together, on a continuous basis, information sources with information users. The users may be end users *or* repackagers. To carry out its function, an information resource must coordinate agents and activities which
> (1) develop mechanisms of access to information sources,
> (2) provide continuous access to the resource,
> (3) manage and maintain the resource,
> (4) repackage and distribute its products and services (p. 49).

These functions are carried out, not only by any reasonably functioning library, but also by any reasonably efficient accounts or finance department within an organization. Our discussion is focused on organizational settings, but these functions could also be seen to describe the work of professional consultants, attorneys, physicians, and so on, even though the information sources that they turn into resources for their clients may be largely their own personal stock of knowledge.

Levitan's categorization of functions is important in abstracting the essence of what has to be added to information sources to make them available for use. It can also serve as a useful reminder that the ability to act as an information resource is not limited to those organizations or parts of organizations that are designated as information services. The definition of an *information service* offered earlier in this text was a specialized organization or department of an organization whose major function is to capture, store and transmit information to people, departments or organizations outside the information service (see Chapter 1, p. 22). All departments and all members of an organization perform some information functions, even if such functions consist only of regular reports on usage of raw materials or signing a time book. Thus the emphasis of the definition has to be on the provision of information as a major function of the information service department and its staff. In this context, the term *major* connotes both the proportion of available time spent in the repackaging of information for use outside the service and the degree to which such repackaging is differentiated according to the particular needs of clients.

An organization or department of an organization that is designated as an information service is often focused on the provision of access to some defined subset of available information or to a defined subset of the population of information users.

Yet the media of mass communication, even those that seek global coverage of audience and of program material, also have elements that would satisfy the general definition as information resources. Their claims to be information services remain limited because by nature they have to aim their messages at large groups rather than attempt to provide the variety of both content and conduit appropriate to the diversity of human information needs and cognitive styles. The apparently effortless worldwide sweep and coverage, especially of television, masks the enormous selectivity of the mass media. In attenuating drastically the amount of data received, the editors cut down choice of topics, points of view, and depth of coverage of issues. In Tasmania, Australia's island state, as part of the curriculum in government schools, students enjoy access to the Australian Associated Press (AAP) wire service. In assignments they trace how many and how much of the stories carried by the wire service ever get into television, newspapers, and radio reports and how they are presented. The results show that students gain appreciation both of the need for the media to cut in order to achieve coverage and of the effects of such cuts on the comprehensiveness of news generally and on the accuracy of particular stories.

The difference between information resources and information services emerges as one of degree rather than of kind. Those information resources in which provision of information services is the primary function will be distinguished mainly by the quality of their interfaces with their users, in terms of variety, appropriateness and interactivity offered. The less the services are tailored to the variety of human needs presented, the more the entity stays at the level of an information system rather than approaching information resource or information service level. From this statement we may also deduce that the existence of an information system or systems is necessary but not sufficient to an information service. The quality of the relationship of an information system to its users will be determined by the quality of the interface with them, and the more targeted, informative, and responsive that interface is, the more likely is it to constitute an information service.

If a distinction has to be made between information resources and information services, it may best be by the addition of a stronger marketing emphasis to the four functions of an information resource listed in Levitan's definition (1982) quoted previously. In addition to providing mechanisms for continuous access to the information resource, managing and maintaining it, and distributing products and services, a stronger marketing emphasis would involve paying more attention to the discovery and definition of user needs in order for the products and services to be appropriately designed and modified. Emphasis would also fall on the place from which the information service is available or the network in which it is distributed, with the aim of maximizing its accessibility to users. Care would also be exercised to ensure that the price (monetary and nonmonetary) was attractive to users, while costs of supply remained rewarding to private enterprise or affordable to public enterprise. A marketing emphasis would also provide appropriate promotion for the information service in both publicity and public relations that would give the information service an identifiable image in the marketplace and create and maintain awareness of the particular products and services.

In the provision of library and information services there has been for at least twenty years a strong interest in the study of user needs. While much of this inquiry has not been particularly well focused and has often been criticized on methodological grounds, it marks part of the change in attitude of librarians from focusing on collections to focusing on users and marketing services to them. There is a healthy professional literature on the theory, methods, and outcomes of user studies in the information field, dating back to Brittain (1970) and a number of techniques have been developed for the study of information needs.

One such is the community analysis technique, developed in the public library sector in the United States, for studying the library and information needs of whole communities. Using this approach the library gathers as much data as possible regarding the characteristics of its community. Examples of data include such elements as population ethnicity, socioeconomic characteristics, commercial activities, transportation and shopping patterns, and educational and social services. Using the results of a community analysis a library can develop appropriate collections and services. For example, Kirwin (1979), in a community analysis for the Pitkin

County Library in Aspen, Colorado, an affluent community with a seasonal population, found that the affluent were not a service priority but the seasonal workers were. A highly fluid population indicated the need for an outreach program in the ski areas for the larger winter population. In another example, the public library in Washington County, Virginia, identified one-third of their service group as in the 0–19 age group and thus determined that one-third of the collection should be provided for this service group. (Carter, 1979)

The strategies for changing information services from collection-centered to client-centered organizations will be discussed in some depth in Chapter 6. Techniques of community profiling and of user studies generally have much in common with those of market research. The characteristics of markets that information products and services have to enter are examined in the following section as are the mechanisms by which information may be accumulated as invisible assets in organizations and in society.

3.1.3 Information Markets and Invisible Assets

3.1.3.1 Efficiencies and Deficiencies

Ten years ago, Parker (1981) prophesied that information technologies would be the focus of attention for the 1980s but that the main benefits would come in the 1990s. "In that decade," he wrote, "the focus will shift to the myriad of *information goods* and *services* [italics Parker's] that require and will utilize the new infrastructure." Parker further explained that "the focus will need to be on obtaining productivity gains in the information sector of our economies and the development of new information goods and services" (p. 77).

There is no question that new information goods and services have proliferated and development of new information technologies continues. Even as one technology becomes commonplace, such as the facsimile transmission of documents, new systems come into being that tend to complement the capacities of the older technology. For example, telecommunications interfaces are created by the insertion of a fax board in a personal computer. This repackaging makes possible more than the transmission and reception of facsimile messages by personal computers. In systems such as that used by the Australian Securities Commission since 1990, images of the annual reports, which by law all Australian companies are obliged to file, are stored on optical disk in a compressed FAX format. Lawyers and others who search the database on-line on the Commission's mainframe computer can have the selected documents faxed to their personal computers. The system is all automated. Requests generate cues from the mainframe to the optical disk and the turnaround time is about half an hour. Imaging technology allows the economical input of reports in a wide variety of sizes, paper surface and impression qualities, typefaces, and even handwritings. The power of facsimile technology is combined with that of automated document retrieval to provide search and delivery.

At the same time, new systems for digital encoding, storage, and dissemination of image data exert pressure for the creation of digital networks, especially integrated services digital networks (ISDN), capable of carrying large amounts of data at high speeds and with high levels of accuracy. Indeed it becomes difficult to allocate goods and services to particular enabling technologies, because the goods and services rely increasingly on combinations of technologies—optical character recognition, facsimile transmission, imaging systems, local area networks, fiber optics, and so on. The consequences of technological convergence generally are probed further in section 3.2; section 3.2.4 pays particular attention to the design, development, and distribution of information products and services. Technical characteristics of telecommunications networks are discussed in Chapter 5.

One approach to measuring the overall productivity of information goods and services is to look for evidence of the use made of them. The results of empirical investigation suggest that information services are seriously under-used, despite the huge sums spent on them in public, private, and not-for-profit sectors. There are two aspects of this under-use: first, the information service is used by only a fraction of the people to whom it is accessible and to whom it has *prima facie* relevance; second, those who use the information service make use of only a small fraction of its capacity. This result emerges whether the studies are focused on the information service or on some abstract concept such as the relationship of use of information services to productivity. For example, after a study in which Hayes and Erickson (1982) applied an econometric model, the Cobb-Douglas productivity model, to data for two years from fifty United States industries, they reported that "the results show that there is a demonstrated relationship between increased added value (and therefore profitability) and investment in information resources. Beyond that, the evidence suggests that manufacturing industry is using far less than the optimal amount of information services" (p. 313).

Machlup (1979a) described the market mechanism as "the largest and most effective information system in existence" (p. 113) and some of the rationale for such a claim has already been discussed in Chapter 1, section 5. Why then is information apparently not efficiently distributed through information markets? One cause has been identified by Lamberton (1984) who explained that "problems of how to measure the productivity of information combine with the absence of user charges to ensure overproduction of data" (p. 13).

At the other end of the marketing chain, blame for inequities in distribution of information, or for under-consumption if you like, has been placed on the managers of information services. For example, Tucci (1988) has claimed that, especially in not-for-profit organizations, many library and information professionals espouse an organization-centered rather than a customer-centered perspective. According to Tucci, "They see their collection of books and resources as inherently desirable; the responsibility for nonproductive use of these resources is placed on the customers who are viewed as either ignorant and unmotivated or arrogant and too proud to admit their lack of knowledge about information" (p. 61). Earlier research in British university libraries by Oldman and Wills (1977) provides evidence of the prevalence of the same phenomenon, which they described in marketing parlance as "product orientation" (p. 158). Oldman (1977) also probed the problem of nonuse of information and came up with factors that inhibit information use under three headings: organizational, attitudinal and cognitive. Lamberton (1989) has also made the point that there are "usually significant information differentials in terms of possession of information, access to information and capability of using information" (p. 19).

Methods of defining individual and group information needs and some of the ways in which information services can bring about improvements in the distribution of information, for example, through more sophisticated market segmentation strategies, are addressed in Chapter 6.

Less tractable aspects of deficiencies in information markets may be attributed to their innate complexity, which is derived from the nature of information and of the systems in which it is gathered, stored, and distributed. As Levitan (1982) has pointed out, "In the life cycle model information production occurs during each phase. Each phase can be viewed as an information market, producing not one but three different types of information 'goods': information sources, information resources, and information products/services" (p. 50). (See Figures 3.1 and 3.2.)

Fundamental to the complexity of information markets is the fact that marketing phenomena are at work in all human communication. These include all exchanges of meaning ranging from apparently simple matters of fact to complex theories and the promotion of political causes. For example, in an article that provides powerful evidence of the pervasiveness of marketing elements in human communication, Peter and Olson (1983) neatly turn upside down the old arguments about whether marketing is a science to argue that science is marketing. They illuminate the complex process by which scientific theories are "priced" and they conclude that because much of science is concerned with the exchange of ideas, and because exchange processes are the core of the marketing discipline, that a marketing perspective can lead to a better distribution of scientific ideas and better understanding of science. Peter and Olson's theory could also be applied in assessing the cost, and therefore the likelihood, of adoption of particular innovations in different environments.

On the other hand, seeking to understand the infrastructure of information markets requires, as Levitan argues (1982), specification of all relevant conditions and actions connected to both market-supplied and institution-supplied information. This is because information production involves not only the traditional economic market but also the institutional infrastructure of the economy. *Market-supplied information* refers to the usual feedback on demand and supply obtainable from the purveying of any commodity or service. It answers the questions on who buys the product or uses the services, in what quantities, when and from which suppliers. This is the information from which some of Drucker's signals for innovation, already discussed in section 2.3.1 of Chapter 2, can be picked up. *Institution-supplied information,* on the other hand, is that produced, transferred, and exchanged because of the infrastructure of the economy. It is derived from the laws, regulations, customs, and agreements established in both public and private sectors, as well as being inherent in the cultural norms of the environment in which the information is produced. It could be thought of as the context, a third element to be added to content and conduit. A foreigner, for example, may have relatively little difficulty in finding out the circulation of a particular newspaper and where the copies are sold. None of this information however necessarily reveals the conditions, legal and political, under which the newspaper is produced, let alone the unwritten as well as written agreements between labor and management, or between proprietors and contributors or distributors, to which the newspaper may be subject. Any of these factors could have substantial bearing on the paper's circulation.

It is hardly to be wondered therefore that information markets do not function as straightforwardly as commodity markets. As was pointed out in Chapter 1, information has some peculiar characteristics as a commodity. (1) It is not diminished with use—indeed often augmented; (2) its value is often hard to estimate in advance of use; (3) its cost is usually independent of scale of use (except as some licensing/royalty agreements try to regulate); (4) the greater part of the cost of information is often the cost incurred by the recipient.

The complexity of information markets is also increased by the number of products and services likely to be offered in them. As Burk and Horton (1988) explain: "Unlike most consumer goods, however, the finished information goods 'consumed' by users represent a very broad spectrum of customized products because each user assigns a different marketplace utility to the same information product or service, based on the user's unique consumption context. In contrast, the uses of non-information goods and services are much more generic and standardized and therefore their marketplace utility and price are far easier to ascertain" (p. 18).

Judgments of the cost and value of information are complicated by the externalities that information goods and services exhibit. As Levitan (1982) points out, "An externality refers to a positive or negative economic effect that extends beyond the control of the traditional marketplace" (p. 50). Ownership, public good and technical externalities are among those which apply to information goods and services, and they are derived again from the innate characteristics of information. For example, how is ownership to be apportioned when a resource may well be augmented rather than depleted with use? Information resources are often not owned the way one owns an item purchased in the marketplace and "reflect not simple ownership but complex systems of property rights" (Levitan, 1982, p. 51). Responsibility for the creation, maintenance, and accessibility of information is often spread over many "owners" or stakeholders. Therefore, there are "ownership externalities," which are the positive or negative effects of our inability to enforce ownership. Levitan (1982) suggests that "Information is not 'owned' in the sense that manufactured, tangible items can be owned. Rather, information reflects the rights of all those involved in the life cycle of production. Computers now provide the means of keeping a record of such rights, but we are lacking the proper incentives" (p. 51).

3.1.3.2 Ownership Issues

Issue can be taken with the assertion that computers can identify or apportion rights to all those involved in the life cycle of information. To illustrate this argument it is not necessary to seek out epistemological complexities in the accumulation of knowledge. Ample illustration is available in the apparently straightforward case of the attempts of a stakeholder to claim copyright in a large on-line bibliographical database.

In 1982 the On-line Computer Library Center (OCLC) claimed copyright in its bibliographical database, constructed from Library of Congress Machine Readable Cataloging (MARC) and other cataloging records contributed by OCLC member libraries, many of which deal with OCLC through membership of regional library networks in the United States. None of the other stakeholders were about to yield to OCLC ownership of the records or the right to determine their use. Copyright and the use of OCLC-derived records appeared on many meeting agendas including those of the American Library Association and the OCLC Users Council. For individual libraries, ownership meant their right to use and reuse the records that they had created. Special meetings were arranged to discuss the issues (e.g., "The ownership of bibliographic data—OCLC's experience," 1985). The right to free access to data in all forms if the data came from publicly supported bodies, including libraries, was strongly articulated (Intner and Schement, 1987).

At the end of 1987 the OCLC trustees adopted new guidelines for the use and transfer of OCLC-derived records, in the hope of putting an end to the dissension begun five years earlier. The new guidelines state unambiguously that each member and nonmember library may use records without restriction and may transfer records of its own holdings, without restrictions, to other libraries (Mason, 1988). The answer to who owns the databases may be no one: on the other hand, in view of the lively debate that OCLC's claim to exclusivity provoked, a better answer is probably everyone. The broad issues concerning rights to intellectual property in electronic form have been the subject of report by the Office of Technology Assessment of the United States Congress (Office of Technology Assessment, 1986). This report has been the source of helpful guidance in matters of electronic information ownership, for example, to the Library of Congress Network Advisory Committee (1989) in its exploration of the issues of particular relevance to library networks. It would be a mistake however to believe either that legal concepts of intellectual or industrial property are proving adequate to the electronic challenge. The uneasy fiction of having to regard computer programs as literary works is just one example of what must surely be a temporary response to profound change (Library of Congress Network Advisory Committee, 1989, pp. 18–21). Another reaction has been the increased use of contracts and licences to cover access to and use of information. These arrangements are made outside the provisions of existing intellectual property law.

3.1.3.3 Public Good and Private Enterprise

Public good externalities also derive from the characteristics peculiar to information, which Levitan (1982) describes succinctly as "nonexclusivity, nondepletion, and nonrivalry in consumption and use" (p. 51). Moreover, the exclusion of individuals from use of information may be both difficult and antithetical to the purpose for which the information resource has been created. The polite fiction of the "need to know" as a principle for the provision of access to information by members of organizations or of the general public has lost credibility. In democratic societies the "right to know" of the individual has been widely recognized in legislation and in administrative practice in the past twenty years. The United States Freedom of Information Act was enacted in 1966 and is the legal basis for public access to the records of federal government agencies. Katz and

Plocher (1989) describe the legislation as having "served effectively as an instrument and a symbol of open information policies in our democratic society" (p. 132). Similar legislation has been passed in several other countries, including Australia. Technological trade secrets are increasingly traded to gain other information benefits (as mentioned in Chapter 2, p. 62); but for other kinds of information, the problems of creating awareness in individuals and organizations of their need to know are receiving much more attention than those of rationing information.

The provision of information resources often demands high setup costs and high continuing fixed costs especially for those resources needed to support national decision-making. In fields vital to national well-being, these resources often can only be afforded by government through their own executive departments and agencies. In fact, only government has the legislative power to command disclosure of some of the information vital to the well-being of society. Examples spring to mind in education, health, and the environment. Who other than a government could afford, for example, to maintain an information resource for the registration and control of pharmaceutical drugs such as the U.S. Food and Drug Administration? Regardless of the degree to which large-scale information gathering and analysis functions can be contracted out to private or not-for-profit enterprise, costs are such that it is reasonable to set up only one such resource of this magnitude. This leads to needs for regulation of this "natural monopoly" and often involves government participation in the marketplace. Technical externalities derive from the economies of scale available from increased use, which decreases average unit costs. In the past decade there have been in all Western industrialized countries efforts to ensure that the user pays for this public or government information. There have also been dire warnings that democratic societies may pay dearly in the long term if such charges lessen the knowledge, understanding, and interest of people at large about the bases on which public policy is made and the ways in which it is put into practice.

In instances where an already vibrant information industry exists, such as in the United States, the potential for conflict between government and private sectors over the provision of information services has been realized. The System Development Corporation (SDC) in 1977 lost its chance to acquire a government-produced database at nominal cost when the United States Court of Appeals upheld the National Library of Medicine's argument that the MEDLARS (Medical Literature and Retrieval System) tapes were not "records" under the Freedom of Information Act (Appeals Court denies SDC MEDLARS tapes, 1977). By 1980, however, the National Library of Medicine was not able to deny commercial database vendors access to the on-line version of MEDLARS (MEDLINE to become available on Lockheed, 1980). At the outset and for many years thereafter, only a publicly funded enterprise could have borne the costs of creation and distribution of this database, which covers the world's medical literature published in journals. But rapid changes in the cost to productivity ratios of the various information technologies bring rapid changes in market relationships. Technological developments, including enhanced telecommunications, increasingly offer faultless, fast, and cheap migration of digital text and images. In this dynamic environment, information products and services that initially only a public sector organization could have afforded to supply, and for which government subsidy has seeded a market, now attract entrepreneurs who see opportunities for innovation that will tap new markets.

The conflicting interests of advocates of the public interest and entrepreneurs are well represented by Patricia Glass Schumann, president of the American Library Association (ALA) in 1991–1992 and Paul Zurkowski, founder and former president of the Information Industry Association (IIA) in the United States. Zurkowski believes in a "Republic of Information" in which global flow of information is regulated by the marketplace, without government controls. "The wonderful thing about information," he asserts, "is that no one ever made a fortune by sequestering it. But you have to get paid for it. How do you generate wealth if you give it away on the streets?" (cited in Sherwood, 1990, p. 41). Patricia Schumann, on the other hand, argues that the marketplace is far too uncertain and inequitable a mechanism for distribution of such a vital necessity as information. One of her particular targets has been information policies of the United States government that favor privatization of government information, which in Schumann's view make "the Jeffersonian ideal of an informed citizenry a more distant possibility for many Americans" (Schumann, 1992, p. 189). Arguments regarding the rights and responsibilities of the government and private sectors in the production and especially the distribution of information goods and services are now at least ten years old. (See, for example, National Commission on Libraries and Information Science, 1982.) More recently, conflicts of interest within the private sector have arisen. One such conflict has been generated by the desire of the United States Regional Bell Operating Companies (the Baby Bells) to enter the electronic information industry. Their entry is opposed by groups presently in the marketplace, such as the MCI Communications Corporation, Mead Data Central, and the American Newspaper Publishers Association, who believe that the entry of the Bell companies would generate unfair competition.

In another dispute that entails the rights to distribution of information by the private sector, Dialog has taken legal action against the American Chemical Society (ACS), a professional society but one that has received government subsidy in the past for its publication program. In mid-1990, Dialog filed an antitrust suit against the ACS charging that the ACS has damaged Dialog by limiting its access to information in the Chemical Abstracts and Chemical Registry databases. Essentially, the problem is that the

ACS will allow other vendors to retail its bibliographical files but not carry the accompanying abstracts online. ACS has filed countersuit accusing Dialog of fraudulent and deceptive accounting procedures, which robbed the ACS of millions of dollars in royalty payments in the years when its databases were distributed by Dialog. Years of dissension with Dialog influenced the ACS decision to become a database vendor and distribute its own products online. Fears are widespread that whatever the outcome, chemical information users will suffer since the courts are unlikely to provide incentives to cooperation (Quint, 1990; O'Leary, 1991).

There are also economies of scope in information markets, because it is often more cost effective to produce two or more products or services together than to produce them separately. This applies especially to the employment of information technologies and the exploitation of digital information. It is unlikely, however, that most entrepreneurs will want to take over the entire burden of the collection, organization, and supply of information on all topics or for an unlimited market. There will, however, continue to be ample ground for dispute between public and private sectors and within both. That this is so remains more attributable to the nature of information than to the recalcitrance of particular individuals or vested interests.

Levitan has contributed a very useful analysis of the characteristics of information that so complicate consideration of it as a marketable commodity. She writes:

> The economics of information resources defy a basic assumption about traditional economic goods: that of independence of producer and consumer, of production and consumption. Information resources exist as a result of interdependence of production and consumption. Information markets are not comprised of mutually exclusive components. Rather the entire production cycle reflects a network of interrelated subsystems which permit and facilitate multiple, nontraditional roles for consumers and producers, as well as for government and private industry (Levitan, 1982, p. 52).

3.1.3.4 Invisible Assets

Lamberton (1989) identified another basic economic characteristic of information and information channels that has emerged from information-sector measurement and mapping. This is that "the stock of information and the organizations created to handle information have the characteristics of capital" (p. 19). The idea of information as capital and therefore part of an organization's assets also underpins the advocacy by Burk and Horton (1988) of information life cycle management and information resource management. They describe these functions as referring "to the application of traditional management processes, particularly resource management principles, to the stewardship of an organization's information resources and assets" and as "the process whereby organizations optimize the spending of their information resource dollars to achieve their strategic objectives" (p. 10).

Yet recognition of information as an invisible asset within the organization may be difficult to create and sustain. Martin *et al.* (1991), for example, concluded from a study of 249 companies in the United Kingdom that marketing of the information management concept "must start from the assumption that whatever is claimed to the contrary, management is basically ignorant of the wider ramifications of information, whether this entails the range of formats available, its implications for the bottom line or its strategic significance" (p. 218).

It seems then that many organizations in industry and commerce have not yet accepted what Itami (1989) calls his "basic and very simple thesis [that] all invisible assets are based on one kind of information flow or another" (p. 37). He argues that invisible assets are "the only source of long-term competitive edge for the firm" (p. 40). It is also interesting that the "four key reasons" with which he sustains his argument are in essence just those which were revealed as the major complicating factors in the operation of information markets. According to Itami (1989), long-term competitive edge derives from information-based invisible assets because (1) most of them cannot readily be bought in the marketplace, for instance, brand names or advanced technological production skills; (2) they require on-going, conscious and time-consuming efforts—competitors do not have easy access to them and imitation takes time and building their own takes even longer; (3) they allow you simultaneous multiple use, because they are information-based; and (4) the value and the amount of the invisible assets will increase over time as they are used (pp. 40–41).

Itami's advice on how to build invisible assets will be revisited and referred to the management of information services in Chapter 6. Although his references are to firms in commerce and industry, and often to Japanese firms, what he has written about invisible assets is true of all organizations. As he has pointed out:

> The firm is an organisation made up of people who exchange information, communicate with each other and either store this information or tell someone else about something which they think is important. The effectiveness of this process is highly dependent on the corporate culture. In the framework of information flows one can define corporate culture as the distinctive characteristics of the patterns of information processing shared by the members of an organization (Itami, 1989, p. 39).

How then are information services within organizations to be linked with and differentiated from the information processing that is a major function of the organization and of all its parts?

3.1.4 Organizations as Information Systems

Arrow (1979) has remarked that "specialization in information gathering is one instance, in my view the most important instance, of the economic benefits of organization," and that "of all forms of division of labor, the division of information gathering is perhaps the most fundamental" (p. 310). The division of responsibilities for collection, analysis, and communication of information is at the core of all organizations. Organizations are of course ubiquitous. As Beam (1983) reminds us, "Whenever a continuing and reasonably stable pattern emerges from the joint effects of the separately decided behaviors of two or more parties, the relation they form is called an organization" (p. 615).

Information processing—that is, the creation, collection, storage, treatment, and distribution of information—forms a major part of the activity of every organization. It is commonplace to describe an organization as an information system. It may also be helpful to recognize that one source of variety among organizations is the degree to which information processing is formalized within them. Beam goes on to point out that:

> As social systems, organizations span the analytic gamut from purely controlled (formal) organizations to purely uncontrolled (informal) organizations, with a continuum of mixtures (semiformal organizations) in between. Formal organizations, such as governments or business enterprises, possess a controlled [sic] subsystem that acts on behalf of the whole system and has the capacity to communicate with, induce motivations of, and instruct its subsystem role- occupants to behave in the way it (the control system) desires (Beam, 1983, p. 616).

Many managers may smile wryly at the degree of abstraction in this definition and find the bloodless obedient "subsystem role-occupants" hard to reconcile with the people who answer to them in the organizational hierarchy. Many would argue that organizations, including formal organizations with strong overall management subsystems as defined by Beam in the quotation cited above, tend to house competing information systems that are sometimes secretive with each other, often duplicative, and nearly always insufficiently coordinated. The essential role of management is to shape the management information system so that it is capable of exploiting the organization's other information systems, including those that gather news from the environment, in order that reasonable decisions about the organization's future can be made.

According to Stinchcombe (1990) "The core of structure of organizations" is "information processing, and the core information to be processed is the earliest information that indicates what sort of world (i.e., future) the decisions are being made for" (p. 2). He goes on to explain that:

> The crucial thing for an organization from this point of view is to be where the news breaks, whenever it breaks. Information is "news" for the organization

> when it is a first appearance of some sign of how the future is going to be, in a respect crucial to the organization. The argument then is that news about one sort of contingency facing an organization (e.g., fluctuations in the quality of raw materials) is likely to be found in a different place than news about another sort of contingency (e.g., the risks of a hostile takeover) (p. 3).

For Stinchcombe (1990) this orientation to news explains why top managers prefer their information "live," from conversations, telephone calls, inspections, problems brought in by subordinates, and so on. Furthermore, because different organizations operate with different major constraints, hence uncertainties, and hence different sources of news, they need to grow different types of structures of information collection and processing. And these structures will also need to differ in different parts of the same organization (Stinchcombe, 1990).

Stinchcombe (1990) also warns that "to administer news about one sort of uncertainty with a structure built to handle another kind" is "the central administrative mistake" (p. 23). The implication is clearly that a different information management system is needed for every different sort of uncertainty. In a sense, each section of an organization, with its own methods of data collection, analysis, and distribution, needs to act as an information resource for all other sections. Consider the role of the finance department. It looks to internal sources from which it gathers data on income and expenditure and costs generally, and to external sources for other factors affecting and likely to affect the organization's financial condition. Not only is its official mission different from that of the marketing or production or personnel departments, so are its unwritten rules and tacit understandings. Even before trying to accommodate the different methods again by which an R & D department is likely to produce its "news," we can see why the effectiveness of different parts of organizations as information resources for each other is apparently low, whether such divisions are based on function, geographic location, or product or service speciality.

Problems of creating effective management information systems have not been solved in computerized organizations, where they have often been dignified with the capitalized initialism MIS. The citation record of Russell Ackoff's article "Management Misinformation Systems" (Ackoff, 1967) is enough to suggest that it continues to strike a chord. The computer power is usually greater and the modeling techniques more sophisticated in the construction of decision support systems (DSS), but they also seem to give little satisfaction among executives for whom executive information systems (EIS) are now being developed. Advances in techniques for the design of such systems are described in Chapter 5, but accusations continue that they report the wrong things in far too high volume while missing the right things all too frequently. The problems are not trivial. Consider for example the spate of complaints about company accounts and how poor a guide they are, not only to future investment but to the present true state of the financial health of the company.

It seems then, that none of the recognized areas of organizational uncertainty are yet covered by *trustworthy* information systems. As Stinchcombe (1990) explains, "A trustworthy system of information, in short, is one that does not routinely deceive its users about the uncertainty of the conclusions reached on the basis of that information but at the same time does not burden them with information about stable features of the environment" (p. 14).

The topic of communication in organizations is one that has received an immense amount of attention from sociologists and psychologists as well as organization theorists. Organizations are human systems, and many factors intervene to complicate the automation of any but the least subtle of their communications. For one thing, informal structures based on individual and personal preferences and antipathies coexist with the formal structures in all organizations. The flow of information through these informal structures at once facilitates and complicates the task of formal systems for the collection, processing, and distribution of information within organizations.

A good deal has also been discovered in empirical investigations of organizations about other roles important in information processing and in particular in the importation and distribution of information from outside the organization. As already mentioned in Chapter 2 (pp. 55–56), the occupants of these roles are variously termed gatekeepers, boundary riders, and boundary spanners. They are naturally occurring phenomena, roles of which are often mimicked by departments and individuals within organizations and by outside agents and agencies that have formally designated information service functions. In particular, information services within organizations see part of their role as including not only the collection, repackaging, and distribution of information but the responsibility to draw attention to the relevant external "news" in order to make new syntheses of internal news. The extent to which information services themselves make news may be argued to depend on the degree of information analysis that their mission involves. The extent to which an information service is capable of recognizing the relevance to the organization of data that arises externally to it depends on knowledge of the organization—of its formal structure, mission, uncertainties, its communication systems, and of informal as well as formal roles of individuals in information processing.

The nature of information services may thus be claimed to include the concept of information resources with not only the addition of a marketing emphasis (as discussed in section 3.1.2) but also addition of particular knowledge of the organizations that they serve and of the information systems operating within those organizations. This point of view and the techniques of mapping the information resources in organizations are set out in detail in Burk and Horton (1988).

Another attribute that organizations need is memory. The extent to which formally designated information services play this role differs with the nature and purpose of the organization, its longevity, and the significance of its history. In maintaining the short-term memory of an organization, obviously all operating departments have a role to play. The organization's formal requirements for that memory are embodied in its records management and archives appraisal procedures. The former may include not only file-handling procedures but also rules and conventions regarding, for example, the minuting of telephone and other verbal communications. Appraisal procedures are applied to decide which of the organization's records are to be retained for which lengths of time. That these procedures need to be rational and even ruthless with paper-based records is witnessed by the fact that Australia's largest corporation, the Broken Hill Proprietary Company Limited, each year disposes of about six tons of the paper-based records generated by its operations.

Responsibilities for the long-term memory of organizations relate to the archival significance of past operations. In large corporations and in government settings, records appraisal guidelines are often drafted. Universities and research libraries often set up collecting archives to ensure that records of significant organizations are preserved to support future scholarship when the organizations see no further need for them or when the organizations themselves cease to exist. However, the extent to which the organization's information systems need to serve the past and the future as well as the present is not the least of the complications that makes challenging the design of both management strategies and information services.

Added challenges posed by the digitization of information to information managers attempting to satisfy an organization's memory needs are discussed in section 3.2.2. They are only a part of the opportunities and problems brought about not so much by information technology *per se*, but by the reduction of the building block of information to a common operational unit, the binary digit.

3.2 The Digital Environment

3.2.1 Convergence and Diversity

The ability to express symbols and signals in digital codes that can be used to encode, store, and transmit all types of recorded information is changing the way the world works. The convergence of digital data is brought about by portability from one system to another and by the flexibility with which the same data can be used for different purposes. Thus data created or modified in a word processing system can migrate to an electronic mail system or to a desktop publishing system and may be carried over any one of a variety of networks and in any of a number of interrelated code systems. No wonder that both repackaging and repurposing have been adopted in the language of the multimedia systems which have been made possible by the integration in the digital environment of codes for media as different as sound, moving and still pictures, and text. The possibilities opened by such convergence in the raw materials, the building blocks, at the same time as such diversity in applications were imagined only by the visionaries until a decade or so ago. The World Brain imagined by H. G. Wells and Vannevar Bush's Memex are probably the outstanding examples (Wells, 1938; Bush, 1945).

When confronted with threat of change, the human tendency is to look for guidance to analagous historical events. Thus the effects on Western civilization of the introduction of printing from movable type are often used as a framework for attempts to study the contemporary effects of the digitization of the symbols in which records are encoded and of the signals by which they are moved. The representation and telecommunication in digital codes of text, sound, and still and moving pictures offer to bring about changes in all aspects of human life, which will be as or more profound and more widespread than those that resulted from the invention of printing from movable type in Europe in the second half of the fifteenth century. The effects of the adoption of printing were profound and have continued not only to intrigue scholars, such as Eisenstein (1983), but to attract large numbers of lay people to exhibitions and television presentations on the subject. Examples are the International Printing Machinery and Allied Trades Exhibition entitled "Printing and the Mind of Man" presented in London in 1963 and the subsequent book on its contents (Carter and Muir, 1967), as well as the television series "Civilization," presented by Sir Kenneth Clark, which emphasized the effects of printing on the development of Western culture. The book on the television series continues to sell well (Clark, 1969).

From its earliest applications, printing has expanded and extended the memory of mankind, and, as in all technologies, printing as a process has a life cycle in which its capabilities and efficiency have been continually enhanced. Technical barriers have been turned into opportunities with progressive improvements in contributing technologies, such as type-founding and ink-making as well as mechanical typesetting and indeed in every aspect of the process. Flexibility and portability of printed media have been much enhanced since the development of photography in the nineteenth century as well as by twentieth century copying technology, especially since the invention and exploitation of xerography. Application of digital capabilities to the printing process has again transformed not only speed of production but spread of access to printed data. Thus to this point, in most organizations, derisive use of the phrase "paperless office" is justified.

Printing also encountered and could be argued to have caused political as well as social problems. Neither temporal nor spiritual rulers were happy to relinquish to printer-publishers control of the provision of information to the people at large. The Church was especially opposed to printing of the Christian scriptures in the vernacular languages. Some of this opposition may be attributed to concern for the integrity of the text of the documents, though no priestly caste ever readily suffers loss of its exclusive rights of access to and interpretation of texts. Some analogy may be seen here to the early negative reactions of mainframe computer professionals to the introduction of microcomputers, which put computing power into the hands of everyday, unordained users. Traces of these attitudes may also be detected in the concerns of archivists and librarians about loss in the digital environment of successive versions of documents and of alterations made (whether in draft treaties or manuscript poems) to the collective memory of society. This idea is pursued in section 3.2.2.

Copyright is another concept that had to be expanded after the introduction of printing from movable type. Even then it took two hundred years to bring into general acceptance in Western Europe the notion that the creative contributions of authors should be protected at the same time as new information is made available for the good of society at large. On the other hand, the idea was quick to arise among monarchs and other heads of state that granting and registering monopoly rights to printers was a great way to raise revenue and to control the flow of information. Sociopolitical problems derive from the digitization of information and are just as pervasive and maybe less tractable than those wrought by printing. Difficulties in establishing ownership of intellectual property in digital form have already been mentioned in section 3.1.3.2. Another example lies in the social and political ramifications of transborder flows of digital information, which bring problems for despots and patriots alike that were unthought of in all the years when travelers and postal bags could be searched by customs officials at borders of countries anxious to exclude particular printed documents for whatever reason.

Acceptance of the new medium of printing and its innovative products was neither immediate nor universal. Fifteenth century people of quality, such as the Duke of Urbino, would have been ashamed to have had printed books in their libraries, if a contemporary seller of manuscripts is to be believed (Vespasiano, 1963). Those who are pioneering electronic publication with no paper equivalent may see an analogy here as they tend to be scorned either as visionaries or feared as radicals, the outcome of whose efforts will be to disrupt the orderly accumulation and distribution of knowledge and maybe even power. The way to respectability for electronic journals is being forged by initiatives like the publication of the *Online Journal of Current Clinical Trials*. This is a joint venture of the American Association for the Advancement of Science (AAAS) and the Online Computer Library Center (OCLC), in which AAAS developed the editorial content and focus and OCLC developed its programming and technology. Billed as "the world's first peer-reviewed medical journal distributed by computer" (Schieber, 1992, p. 33), publication began on the network on July 1, 1992. Its progress and acceptance will be watched with interest as important indicators of whether electronic publishing can be managed to preserve the level of quality control achieved in the printed literature of science and scholarship.

Analogy with the history of printing in Western society may be pursued a little further. Just as the early printed books took the manuscript books as their model so have printed books and other documents formed the models for all the early schemes for computer manipulation of text. This is predictable in view of McLuhan's observations more than twenty years ago that new technologies are "driven" from the rearview mirror provided by established technologies and that the old media provide the content of the new media (McLuhan, 1964). In fact, the models adopted for document production in the digital environment have been driven by views through three different rearview mirrors: office documentation, publishing, and do-it-yourself printing. In all three there has been recognition of the importance of standards, but their separate development of standards for the solution of essentially similar problems. There are now, however, some signs of convergence among the sponsors of these three different formal approaches to the creation of printed documents. These approaches are represented by the acronyms that describe the major concerns of each, that is, ODA (office document architecture), SGML (the standard generalized markup language) and DTP (desktop publishing).

ODA has been developed by the computer and data processing companies involved in the word processing (WP) and office information systems business. Their quest is for a method to interchange documents regardless of which word processing system may have been employed in their preparation. Publishers need SGML to allow their typesetters to talk to each other in different firms and even in the same organization. SGML also facilitates repackaging of data. For example, the same codes can drive typesetting machines and be input into online retrieval systems. SGML offered early hope to authors of a single satisfactory format for all publishers. Attempts were made in the early days to require authors to prepare manuscripts with the codes to control whatever typesetter their publisher used. But authors were in fact relieved not by SGML but by the developments in WP in the ODA sector, which increasingly have made the data on disks prepared in one system readily transferable to ASCII text or to the format of another WP system. There has been widespread cooperation among manufacturers such as in the ODA consortium in which IBM, DEC, Bull, UNISYS, and ICL are working to develop features that will further facilitate easy interchange.

Useful translation facilities or file-exchange programs are now standard features of almost all personal computers in the MSDOS and Apple Macintosh families. The barrier between MSDOS and Macintosh machines has been breaking down for at least three years and the joint development project on which the two companies entered in 1991 will soon remove all barriers to interoperation. This is not to suggest that the spirit of rivalry is dead. Microsoft and ACE have formed a consortium and are developing systems that may be incompatible with those developed by Apple and IBM, though the tide seems to be turning strongly in favor of interchangeability.

Another convergence taking place is that between WP and DTP. In their 'pure' forms, DTP transcends WP as it makes possible not just the encoding of text but of complete documents preserving all the details of page layout, font style, formatting, diagrams, graphic images, and so on. This is achieved with software that used to be generally rated easier to use than the systems common in the other two environments. Increasingly, however, WP software packages have added DTP features and in both sectors "windowing" with pull-down menus has made for increased ease of use. DTP software is usually not self-contained and needs other programs (for example, graphics and WP) to feed information to it, while WP can accept information from other software.

It is obvious that many of the problems of structuring and interrelating electronic text and the codes that control its disposition in printed format are common to the three environments. Thus ODA, SGML, and DTP can be regarded as rivals, among which the writers of Project Quartet (1990) regarded DTP as the front-runner. They wrote: "Perhaps the real importance of DTP is to be found in its power to manipulate the computer object, rather than to imitate the printing press" (p. 68). It may be argued that WP systems are so versatile and the digital text so susceptible to new forms of indexing and reformatting that WP has or is acquiring equal power to manipulate the computer object. These and other matters for dispute regarding technological developments are pursued in Chapter 5. There can, however, be no dispute that truly innovative applications of the nonlinear possibilities of electronic publishing, that is, of the electronic preparation and delivery of documents, have hardly begun. In fact the final analogy to be drawn is to suggest that like printing before 1500, the applications of digital systems for the creation and communication of information are in their cradle period, and the systems, services, and products of today should be regarded as electronic incunabula. Much remains to be discovered and developed in the underlying technologies for storage, transmission, and display and in the software tools needed to allow the creative manipulation of electronic information. Much also remains to be learned at the technical level, or at least has yet to be embodied in usable digital tools, before we can claim even the ability to deal in a uniform manner with data in multiple modes and to assimilate new modes easily. This discussion proceeds with sections on the effects of the digital environment on information specialities and specialists, on attitudes and strategies of management in organizations of all types, and on information products and services.

3.2.2 Effects on Information Specialities and Specialists

Convergence in the digital environment allows easy combination of media and brings down the walls between information management applications at all levels, within and between organizations. The electronic data interchange (EDI) application by which tax preparers in the United States may transfer clients' income tax returns to the Internal Revenue Service is one example. Digitization also de-emphasizes distinctions between managing the carriers of information and managing information as a resource. The environments in which digital information is stored need no longer determine either the physical, administrative, or intellectual arrangements for access to the information content. Thus boundaries that were once well marked between information specialities begin to blur, and the spread of responsibilities for information management among different agencies changes.

There is, for example, interesting debate in relation to public and corporate records on the changing roles of archivists, records managers, and systems analysts. These arguments also involve changing responsibilities, in relation to electronic records, of archival repositories and the agencies that created the records. Whatever their mission, organizations create and keep records for three purposes: to do business; to support the conduct of their business; and to document the organization's activities. Thus staff are paid, goods are ordered, and so on, in the doing of business, and supporting documents are kept and accumulated in files, while documentary evidence is built up in policy decisions recorded in minutes of meetings and, in general, as proof that internal rules and external laws and regulations have been obeyed in the conduct of the organization's business.

Records managers traditionally have kept track of the movement of records in files and have administered rules about file-classification, file-handling, and file-access. As Thibodeau (1991) points out, "What distinguishes records from other forms of recorded information is that they have a specific connection to the conduct of affairs" (p. 1). The role of archivist overlaps with that of records manager as the archivist has responsibilities for identifying and preserving those records that have permanent value. Therefore, as Thibodeau (1991) remarks, "The recognition of archival value is a recognition that, at a given stage or state, records have evidential or informational value apart from their instrumental use in the operating environment" (p. 2).

Electronic records bring in a third player with the systems analyst, or whatever job title is attached to the specialist who designs the systems in which electronic records are made and manipulated. Decisions made in the choices of software, hardware, and telecommunications very much affect the records manager's ability to locate, retrieve, and cumulate data from wanted files and the archivist's ability to appraise the records of lasting value and to see that they are retained. Archivists are themselves divided on how to cope with electronic records. Thibodeau (1991) argues that "to preserve the historical truth of the records requires that they be removed from the operating environment and transferred to an archival environment." An archival environment he goes on to define as "one in which the records are protected from changes which would diminish or destroy their historical character" (p. 3). Bearman (1991), on the other hand, argues strongly that, providing the archives have intellectual control, it does not matter where the records or the users are. He remarks that only one public archival repository in the United States (the North Carolina State Archives) provides online public access to its catalogs for patrons. From this apparent lack of orientation towards public access, Bearman draws the conclusion that among archivists, "Unfortunately custodial habits have devalued intellectual control." His paper closes with the broadside that "the archival repository is as a strategy for the electronic age what the walled city became with the invention of gunpowder, an indefensible bastion and a liability" (p. 24).

Many archivists recognize with Hedstrom (1991) that "Electronic records provide archivists with much more powerful tools to perform many traditional archival functions, while simultaneously offering a long list of possibilities for new services and functions." As she further explains, "Much of the value that archivists have added to paper records, by arranging, describing and indexing them, is now added by the original creators of the records when they design the search and retrieval capabilities of automated systems" (p. 26). Clearly debate will continue on how much of the archivist's traditional role in the provision of a range of finding aids for records has been and should be taken over by the systems analyst/designer.

Digital information is so much more readily sampled, compacted, searched, or as current jargon puts it, *repackaged* and *repurposed,* that the line between the short-term and longer-term use of records begins to blur. The time period over which searches are conducted in the digital environment may be determined by a few keystrokes, in contrast to the time and effort required to search over longer time periods in archival repositories of records on paper that are usually stored in sites remote from those in which the results of the search are required. The concept of a separate physical repository for archives seems irrelevant in this environment, but the problems of archival treatment of electronic records do not end with the ability to "read the files." The need to preserve the context in which the contents of files were created remains a challenge.

Many skirmishes on the borders of librarianship and archives administration take place over the degree of similarity between archival records and library materials. Some of these territorial disputes have been about rights of ownership, but more have been about the treatment of manuscripts and personal papers in research libraries. Much more often they have been related to methods by which intellectual access should be provided to the contents of the manuscripts and personal papers and other archival materials commonly held in library collections. Archivists' disquiet usually focuses on the librarians' approach to materials item by item. Archivists argue that this ignores the materials in their groups and the process and context of their creation, which are in fact the very qualities essential to understanding archives and their value and integrity as documents. In the digital environment the scenes of these conflicts have moved into the arena of integration of archival information systems with bibliographical systems. The cause of this relocation of debate is largely the existence of extensive online bibliographical networks.

Some of the difficulties encountered by archivists when they compromise traditional attitudes to try to take advantage of electronic library networks have been demonstrated by Michelson (1987). Her investigation of eighty-six of the ninety archives repositories contributing records to the archives and manuscripts collection (AMC) file on the research libraries network (RLIN) confirmed the unsuitability for archives of standards of bibliographical description prepared for library materials, such as Library of Congress subject headings. But she also discovered the effects of total lack of standardization of terminology among record groups with similarities. Michelson (1987) concluded: "Adopting library standards used with bibliographic utilities creates problems in providing access to archival holdings. But automating through this route also offers advantages. In addition to mainstreaming primary source materials into the library research community and enhancing access to archival holdings, this process can provide an effective way to gain needed education in information systems, challenge archivists to begin transforming internal practices, and encourage the development of a body of users expert in archival automation" (pp. 200–201).

McCrank (1986) puts forth bolder ideas:

> Old cornerstones of archival theory and practice, original order, provenance, and respect des fonds, need to be reconsidered in automated environments. These principles evolved in manual environments where physical arrangement had to preserve original order to save context and thereby assist evaluation and interpretation. Such concerns apply as well to machine-readable records; they cannot be discounted entirely, but may be modified. Studies comparing access by provenance and by content indexing suggest that the latter cannot replace the former, because each method of retrieval operates differently. Searchers familiar with organizational structures are already familiar with the data structure of an archives, and can search more efficiently by that means than can a searcher unfamiliar with the organization. The latter seem to need indexing alternatives. The two methods together seem to produce the best results in archives; the same might be true in libraries if online catalogs allowed searching by provenance (p. 74).

Just which items in libraries would benefit from access by provenance, that is, by the organizational settings, in the broadest sense, which gave rise to their creation, is not a question to be pursued here. This discussion however indicates that the tasks of information storage and retrieval (ISAR) are similar in various specialist cultures; the digitization of information has made these similarities more evident. Handling digital information has also simultaneously created necessity and opportunity for formulation of sounder more broadly based theory on which to pin ISAR practice and the principles of systems design. The strengthening of the theoretical literature is witnessed in work such as Vickery and Vickery (1987) and in contributions to the *Annual Review of Information Science and Technology* in the past decade. At the same time critics such as Diener (1992) remind us that there is much further to go in grasping the opportunities presented by digital information. Diener (1992) writes that, "grasping the idea of managing the information content rather than the information carrier is relatively difficult to operationalize. Information has to exist somewhere to be manageable, so it is easy to revert to the same old ways of managing the carrier, the thing in which it exists" (p. 26).

Cook (1991) lists among the questions that archivists must answer,

"Do they appraise information or records?" (p. 53). But archivists are by no means the only specialists to have opted to manage the carriers rather than the information. In corporations, as in government agencies, the chief information officer, or information manager position proves very often to refer to the management of computers, telecommunications, records, books, and other physical carriers of information. The idea of managing the information itself as a resource usually gets no further than maintenance of the software that manages the information. The specialists in the information carriers (and museum and art gallery curators could be added to this list of archivists, librarians, and records managers) and the data processing specialists are struggling to come to terms with the challenge of managing information content.

The picture comes to mind of a digital mudslide in which information specialists struggle to hold a footing as the ground grows ever softer in the migrations and combinations of data once thought to have been safely compacted behind stout retaining walls. Admirably clear statements of aims may be made, such as that by Hedstrom (1991) that "archival records need to be protected from changes in their content and character that would diminish their ability to reflect the information available to an organization at the time it was acted on" (p. 28). Means of achieving these and other information management aims in the digital environment are, however, not yet in place.

In the older information specialities of librarianship, archives administration, and records management, there is also some difficulty in identifying which parts of the traditional knowledge and skills bases remain pertinent. Again in all three environments the characteristics of digital information increase flexibility of access, which in turn decreases the need for searching expertise. There is a transfer of power to the user that may be perceived as a challenge to the authority of the professional. This is similar to the transfer of power to the user in the data processing environment with the advent of microcomputers, which has already been commented upon in section 3.2.1. Chapter 5 also discusses end-user computing.

Some of the professional knowledge and expertise of traditional information specialists is or ought to be embodied within the digital information systems in increasingly sophisticated interfaces. The digital environment is bringing about convergence of data and systems and of storage and access mechanisms. Yet in order to contribute their expertise and understanding to the creation of better interfaces and thus help supply the information needs of wider constituencies in different media, information specialists have to accept, somewhat paradoxically, broader as well as deeper roles. In fact, information specialists who are not flexible and willing to learn and change may be caught up in an electronic pincer movement, of which the transfer of power to the information service user forms one flank and the greater importance of access over storage forms the other.

The position of information services within organizations is far from stable. One obvious sign of this is the number of special libraries in corporate settings and in government agencies that have been closed down in the last ten years in North America, Europe, and Australia. The marginalization of these library and information services owes a great deal to the attractiveness to the modern private and public enterprise of "just-in-time," (which has already been mentioned in Chapter 2, p. 61) rather than "just in case" methods. Just in time concepts were first adopted in manufacturing and in retail selling to allow the cutting of inventories; the whole concept is made possible by better management of information about production schedules and market demands. It therefore seems only fitting that it should also be applied to the management of information services, because dealing with documents in electronic or digital form can (at least in principle) save on time, space, and labor. There is reason also for some caution. The United States automobile industry has discovered that strikes of short duration in the plants of parts suppliers can be disproportionately disruptive in the large companies if they hold no inventories. Information providers may also be properly wary of operating without local inventory as the supply of digital information can be subject to interruptions that may be technical, industrial, or political in origin.

The progressive convergence of information systems and services based on digital data makes ever more difficult discernment of the joins, seams, or stages in the continuum between information systems, information resources, and information services and between the specialists who seek to provide services based on digital information. Many information specialists have been reluctant to concede that digital information is bringing down the walls between their specialities, but there is general recognition and concern at the tendency of digital information systems to obliterate traces of their own creation and growth.

Archivists have been quick to point to the dangers inherent to the quality of records unless their context is preserved. Related difficulties at the document level are those of keeping track of different editions of a text and those of having for reference various versions of a document, whether an international treaty being developed in the local area network environment of a government department or in the editing of a much less exalted text by individual authors. The ease with which WPs make copies of text may be transformed from boon to fatal proclivity, especially in the hands of nonspecialist users. This is part of the challenge that digital data offer to the managers of information at all levels in their custodial roles and is a consequence of the fluidity and interchangeability of digital data. In an admirably broad view of this combination of problem and opportunity, Neill (1987) points out:

> The history of intellectual access to the store of knowledge is a history of the tension between the fluid uniqueness of the individual inquirer and the essential stability and concreteness of the store of knowledge itself. One of the most important problems facing the next generation of librarians will be the relative "fluidity" of information stored electronically. The potential for losing first editions of any publication with the ability we have in a computer store to erase, correct, or change without leaving a paper trail threatens the credibility of publishers and authors when the corrections cannot be checked against the originals. There is, of course, the promise . . . that the fluidity of the computer will be a more appropriate store of knowledge for the searching process of the unique and fluid inquirer (p. 208).

Meadows (1991), introducing a collection of essays that examine the roles of different information specialists, also remarks on "the current state of flux in the information world." He notes that "change, especially that due to computerization, is blurring the dividing lines between author and publisher, publisher and librarian, and so on" (p. viii). In one of the essays in this collection, Feather (1991) provides evidence of this blurring of roles in relation to publishing. He points out that "the development of the computer has impinged on the publishing industry at almost every point" and that this impact has to some extent changed the balance of editorial and entrepreneurial power, with authors who can readily become their own publishers using DTP facilities. Feather argues that: "short runs of worthwhile publications of limited, but genuine, interest have become economic possibilities for the first time since the general abandonment of hand-printing for commercial purposes in the middle of the nineteenth century." As he points out, "This is a cultural, as well as a commercial, revolution" (p. 72).

When publishers have sought to exploit the new product innovation possibilities of digital data, such as database publishing, they have had to learn a whole new range of skills. Those skills are beginning to overlap with those of librarians and other information service providers. Appreciation of the similarity of the skills needed by information specialists in handling digital information is leading to what Feather dubs "recognition that the distinctions between the various sectors of the information industry are becoming blurred almost to the point of oblivion" (Feather, 1991, p. 75).

Thus in Feather's view, technology has allowed a far greater diversity of publishing than has ever been possible before, and at the same time the flow of knowledge and information, even through commercial channels, is subject to far fewer economic restraints than was the case before cheap and efficient information technology was widely available. In the blurring of the boundaries between "published" and "unpublished" information the concept of private publishing has disappeared. Feather concludes that:

> The new technologies of information handling have revolutionized the publishing industry as they have all other aspects of the world of knowledge. Publishing is a key element in the process of storing and disseminating knowledge and enlarging the boundaries of human understanding. Indeed, the barriers between publishing and other areas of the information world, always somewhat artificial, are now visibly collapsing. Libraries "publish" information, just as publishers store information in databases and provide access to it (p. 75).

In his essay on "Librarians and knowledge" in the same collection, Line (1991) argues that "There is no escaping a changed role for libraries; either they drift into it, they are forced into it, or they plan for it as a deliberate policy, with much more emphasis on fast and efficient access, organized not as a supplement to the main service but as an integral part of it" (p. 87). Obviously, if libraries are to change librarians must change them. The same strictures could be applied to other information specialist organizations. The need for change is impelling in all information service environments. Digitization has created the means and at least some of the need for change. Some of the consequences are obvious on the big screen, not only in the computer and telecommunications industries but in industrial restructuring throughout the economy. One example is in the financial sector. Interchangeability of roles and blurring of boundaries between organizations are obvious in the developments in which financial services, such as credit unions, large retailers, stockbrokers, and other organizations, take on functions that have traditionally been associated only with banks. The next subsection of this chapter examines the effects of the digital environment on attitudes and strategies employed within organizations.

3.2.3 Effects on Management Strategies in Organizations

The ability to reduce text, sound, and pictures to digital codes means simply that "the same data can be processed by many devices and media" (Miles, 1988, p. 7). This deceptively simple facility has already brought about and will continue to produce profound change in the way in which human affairs are managed.

In the early days of computerization much faith and money were invested in the power of computers to manipulate digital data to build formalized information systems in organizations—systems that would provide information on a regular basis and in a predefined manner. The shortcomings of these systems—whether called MIS, DSS, or EIS—have been discussed on page 93, and it is not the formalized systems that have brought about most significant changes in the management of organizations. The impact of digitally based information in organizations has been both more subtle and more pervasive. Exclusiveness of access to information in the office was significantly weakened by the adoption of copying machines and virtually destroyed by digital systems. Digital information has proved not so much flexible as fluid, and its flow cannot be controlled by any group at any level within an organization or indeed among organizations. In fact, digital data and the telecommunications facilities that carry them (some of which are digital themselves) have provided the international currency for globalization of industry and commerce. Digital data flowing (even flooding) into new and unplanned channels have obviously brought new management challenges. Some of these challenges present as purely technical and somewhat superficial problems but when probed soon reveal depths of involvement with the organization's internal organs and the life-support systems by which it is attached to the outside world. Data security is one example.

The wider issues of rights of access to information and the rights to individual privacy have given rise to a spate of legislation in the United States, Canada, Australia, New Zealand, and other countries. The possible social consequences are such that an international expert on these laws has warned against "a surrender to the nagging doubt that technology is inherently elitist and autocratic and that democracy, with all its inefficiencies, cannot survive into the next century" (Kirby, 1987, p. 158). In contrast to the world view, however, at the management level within particular organizations, general guidance on the security requirements of digital systems can readily be given straightforward expression. For example, this is the advice given by Project Quartet:

> The security policy of the system provides the rules by which documents will be managed, protected, and distributed within the domain of clients and servers. The system recognises the following general security requirements:
>
> - authentication of clients and the server
> - integrity of documents, error reports and requests
> - non-repudiation of client actions
> - confidentiality of documents and requests
> - access control (Project Quarter, 1990, p. 39).

Yet anyone who has used office automation knows how difficult control over access can be to maintain. Apart from ubiquitous human error, usually blamed on the system, there are many cases when a copy of a document comes off a remote printer, apparently unbidden, though probably as likely through chance combination of symbols input at a keyboard as through sabotage or espionage. Or again, often through chance combination of symbols and circumstances, documents to which the viewer has no official access appear on his or her screen in answer to a "find file" or similar command. The ease with which some of the most secure systems have been broken into by hackers has caused embarrassment in defense and even royal circles, since 1984 when hackers broke into electronic mail files belonging to the Duke of Edinburgh, husband of Queen Elizabeth II. Yet few managers are prepared to give up the benefits of computer networking in order to increase data security. The quality and pricing of telecommunications facilities available will have a decisive influence on information policies in organizations and absolute data security will be demanded in very few environments.

It is difficult to separate this discussion on the effects of digital data on organizations from the effects of information technology (IT) generally—in fact it is difficult to separate the concepts from the management point of view and they are at least part of the same phenomenon. Information technology is fundamentally the creation, combination, storage, manipulation, retrieval, and dissemination of symbols according to instructions that are encoded in other sets of symbols. In less abstract terms it is the application of computing and telecommunications to the handling of digital data. Many authors have struggled with the apparently contradictory evidence on what IT does to organizations. Burton (1988) lists what he calls the "significant differences" over central topics as follows:

(a) IT will centralise/decentralise authority within the organization;
(b) IT will allow operational staff greater access to "management information," or it will strengthen control over the flow of information;
(c) IT will magnify/reduce the role of middle management as summarisers and filters of information up and down the hierarchical pyramid;
(d) IT will increase/limit opportunities for employee participation and involvement;
(e) IT will change/freeze existing organisational structures;
(f) IT will limit/increase job satisfaction;
(g) IT consumes capital/puts capital to work (p. 60).

Explanation of the existence of these dilemmas may be found in what Zuboff (1988) calls "the two faces of intelligent technology." She explains that

> information technology, even when it is applied to automatically reproduce a finite activity, is not mute. It not only imposes information (in the form of programmed instructions) but also produces information. It both accomplishes tasks and translates them into information. The action of a machine is entirely invested in its object, the product. Information technology, on the other hand, introduces an additional dimension of reflexivity: it makes its contribution to the product, but it also reflects back on its activities and on the system of activities to which it is related. Information technology not only produces action but also

produces a voice that symbolically renders events, objects and processes so that they become visible, knowable and shareable in a new way (p. 9)[2].

Zuboff pursues this insight in probing the dual effect of IT on organizations:

> Viewed from this interior perspective, information technology is characterized by a fundamental duality that has not yet been fully appreciated. On the one hand, the technology can be applied to automating operations according to a logic that hardly differs from that of the nineteenth-century machine system—replace the human body with a technology that enables the same processes to be performed with more continuity and control. On the other, the same technology simultaneously generates information about the underlying productive and administrative processes through which an organization accomplishes its work. It provides a deeper level of transparency to activities that had been either partially or completely opaque. In this way information technology supersedes the traditional logic of automation. The word that I have coined to describe this unique capacity is informate. Activities, events, objects are translated into and made visible when a technology *informates* as well as *automates* (pp. 9–10)[2].

The fact that the "information about the underlying productive and administrative processes through which an organization accomplishes its work" revealed by IT is in digital form intensifies its impact on three areas of management, namely:

1. Policy/strategy formulation and integration,
2. Organizational structure,
3. Distribution of power within and between organizations and between them and their customers/clients.

These areas are, of course, themselves interwoven, and it is important to remember with Miles (1988) that "IT is only one of the elements in flux in the current restructuring of political and economic life. Different countries and regions are as capable as ever of having radically different responses to apparently similar changes" (p. 10). And so of course are different organizations. There is also the insight gathered from Stinchcombe (1990) that different organizations need to grow different types of structures for information collection and processing. These points are an antidote to any impression that digital data just roll in appropriately to organizations and have predictable and similar effects. Information technology nevertheless exerts some powerful general influences on organzations in the three areas identified, which are now discussed in some detail.

[2]Selected excerpt from approximately 7 pages from *In the Age of the Smart Machine: the Future of Work and Power* by Shoshana Zuboff. Copyright © 1988 by Basic Books, Inc. Reprinted by permission of Basic Books, a division of Harper Collins Publishers, Inc.

1. Policy/Strategy Formulation and Integration

While discussion of means of bridging what have been called the information archipelagoes in organizations is reserved for Chapter 5, the impact of information technology and digital data on how an organization decides what to do (policy making) and how to do it (strategy) deserves mention. Controversy continues on the extent to which policy and strategy making in organizations is and ought to be implicit or explicit, on whether it is a formal, analytical process or a set of behavioral outcomes derived from the way in which power is exercised, or indeed as a pattern of action emerging from past decisions (Hax and Majluf, 1984).

But, in the presssure of burgeoning technology of all kinds, corporate attention has been much engaged in recent years with the necessity for organizations to adopt a technology strategy. Dodgson (1989) defines technology strategy as

> an understanding within a corporation—manifest among senior management but diffused throughout the organization—of the importance and potential of technology for its competitive position, how in the future that potential is to be realized, and how this complements the other aspects of strategy, such as finance, marketing and personnel (p. 1).

In many corporations it has proved to be a short step from a technology strategy to the adoption of an information strategy, for which the term information systems strategy seems to be used interchangeably. Broadbent (1988) offers for "information strategy" the definition, "patterns which can be detected in a series of actions aimed at strengthening the performance of information resources, information technology and personnel in order for the organization to succeed in its industry" (p. 5).

What seems to be of most concern to managers is the integration of technology and information strategies with business strategy. In a 1990 survey of major IBM mainframe users in all industries and in government agencies in Australia and New Zealand, the most critical skill for all organizations in the opinions of information systems (IS) managers was "aligning business and IS strategies" (Broadbent *et al.*, 1992, p. 33). The authors claim that these Australasian results are similar to findings in the United Kingdom, Ireland, and the United States, and among the several pieces of advice they offer for the achievement of better strategy alignment is:

> Developing organizational arrangements for information services which match the organizational infrastructure of the firm. If a firm is divisionalized with decision-making responsibility heavily devolved, the IS/T arrangements should mirror this, while taking cognizance of the firm's technological architecture (p. 36).

Like so much of the advice offered in the management literature this emphasizes the importance of integration of information policy and strategy with organizational structure and technology strategy. The idea of integration is also paramount in the concept of information resources management, which has also been popular in the literature for some years. According to Burton (1988)

> This combination of the strategic significance of information in an organisational context and the importance of good management of technology has created an interest in the wider concept of information resources management (IRM), an holistic approach to the management of both the technology (and all that pertains to it) and the information resources and assets of an organisation which are manipulated by the technology . . . IRM therefore goes beyond both the data processing manager's concern for technology and the information officer's concern for information resource provision and dissemination in order to create a new service to the organisation, a service geared to supporting an organisation's strategic objectives (p. 65).

The authors point out that these approaches to the management of organizations have become possible because of the ability to store, process, and communicate quickly and cheaply vast amounts of data stored in digital codes. Eason (1988) nominates microelectronics as the phenomenon that has provided "a way of integrating what have previously been separate ways of handling information; data processing on large mainframe computers, text on typewriters, photocopiers and printing machines, and communications via the telephone, radio and television" (p. 1). Whatever the phrase used to describe the catalyst for this integration of data, and the authors prefer to use "the digital environment," it is the integration of data that has made policy and strategy integration within and between organizations at once more feasible and more necessary.

2. Organizational Structure

Arguments about the effects of the digital environment on organizational structures usually center on whether greater centralization or decentralization is likely to result. Such arguments often have more to do with the distribution of power between the central and branch offices than with structures as such. Allen (1986) however has suggested that a computerized information system may in the management of engineering projects accomplish a goal that was formerly achieved through organizational structure. He forecast that the information system, through improved access to the literature, might obviate the need for colleague contact and thereby accomplish the goal for which the functional form of organization has been traditionally used. The crux of his argument was:

> At present, most projects are coordinated, as they have been for years, by means of periodic review meetings and written status reports or memoranda. There is absolutely no reason why such devices cannot be put "on line". The software for conferencing and "many-to- many" reporting exists and is rapidly being improved. As such electronic means for project coordination advance, the problems

> associated with coordinating project work across a matrix organization structure should be diminished considerably. In other words, information technology will be accomplishing the major goal for which project organization was developed. Information technology, in this way can be viewed as a substitute for the project form of organizational structure (p. 216).

Subsequent studies of the effects of online information systems, and especially of electronic mail in organizations, tend to confirm that the use of such facilities changes the pattern and nature of formal communications, such as regularly scheduled meetings, and that the opportunities they offer for natural development of contacts throughout the organization have led insecure managements to try to curtail and control their use (for example, Zuboff, 1988; Sproull and Kiesler, 1991). As Zuboff (1988) points out: "the structure of access to information expresses the organization's underlying conception of authority"(p. 392). Because organizational structures are built for the very purpose of structuring access to information, it is not surprising that digital information systems have brought structural changes. We should note, however, with Sproull and Kiesler (1991), that computer-based communication technology may move managers either to tighten controls over employees generally or to expand their access to information and their personal autonomy.

Buckland (1989) brings excellent logic and a wealth of historical evidence to support his contention that "delegation of decision making is inversely related to the effectiveness of information handling" (p. 329). Yet the whole process by which digital information has tended to become a corporate (or organizationwide) rather than a departmental asset has not necessarily reduced the power available at the periphery, either in branch offices or among clients or customers of the organizations affected. The effects on the distribution of power and on the organizational structures through which it is distributed seem to be much more complex.

3. Power Distribution

Zuboff (1988) has drawn sharp distinction between imperative control of management in the automating strategy and the consensual cooperative attitudes required in informating organizations. Under an informating strategy, the importance of the skill base has to be recognized—indeed she demonstrates from her case studies that analytical skills are essential for effective work with electronic text. The necessity for workers to gain knowledge and therefore power is vital. Towards the end of her book Zuboff (1988) writes, "To put it simply learning is the new form of labor" (p. 395). Earlier she presents detailed justification for her argument that "the cognitive demands of intellective skill suggest that computerization should be accompanied by a serious educational effort, if the informating capacity of the technology is to be exploited" (p. 217). Yet in one of the plants in which she carried out her study, the company had spent $200 million on new technology but did not have a budget item for training.

Zuboff also argues strongly that effective exploitation of the electronic text is not possible without comprehensive and continuing innovation. And that "if the technology cannot shoulder the entire burden of strategic change, it nevertheless can set into motion a series of dynamics that present an important challenge to imperative control and the industrial division of labour" (p. 308).

In an address given in 1980 Diebold prophesied that:

> Information technology is bringing about a change to a direct electronic dialog in which intermediary functions are integrated in ways which offer tremendous opportunity for innovative marketing. A corporation's information policy will bear directly on how aggressively the corporation can pursue these opportunities (Diebold, 1985, p. 61).

What seems critical is that access to the information on which these opportunities can be recognized and the intellective power to recognize them should be widespread in organizations, or as a member of one of Zuboff's more successful informating organizations is quoted as saying "'People can think no matter where they are in the hierarchy'" (p. 213).

The transfer of power to the user, such as in the change of emphasis from mainframe to microcomputing, has already been mentioned in this chapter (p. 104) and the history of this change is traced in Chapter 5. One well-established movement of power in organizations is that from specialists in to users of digital information systems, whether the shift is between departments in the same organization or between organizations and their customers. The information systems managers in Australia and New Zealand surveyed in the study by Broadbent *et al.* (1992) saw as an important necessity the need to promote their services within their companies and government agencies. Other evidence of the transfer of power to the users comes from a Delphi study of Australian industry (Hunt and Dampney, 1990), which gave strong support to the forecast that by the mid-1990s computer applications development would be a largely user-driven responsibility.

A more subtle power can be bestowed on both the managers and users of information services on account of the transparency of digital systems, "the additional dimension of reflexivity" to which Zuboff (1988, p. 9) has pointed. The "reflexivity" of these systems both reveals client behavior to information service managers and reveals to clients the behavior of the information service in response to their demands. How much easier it is in these circumstances for clients to form a constituency with power to exert pressure on the information service, whether the supplier is a library, an information brokerage firm, or an online database provider.

Broadbent (1991) claims that most large organizations now have what could be called a "federation of information services . . . that is, a range of information services for people working at different levels, developed from key information sources and using different types of information systems" (p. 7). Different approaches are taken in these different business units, but as Broadbent goes on to point out, "The bottom line is whatever approach is taken, it must support and stimulate the advantage gained from information resources and information technology." Some of the opportunities for meeting this challenge based on the information products and services possible in the digital environment are now discussed.

3.2.4 Effects on Information Products and Services

Opportunities for information to be packaged, marketed, and traded as a commodity began with the first message and writing systems thousands of years ago, but they have been dramatically expanded by the advent of digital information systems, which began about fifty years ago. At first the digital codes were strongly associated with particular machines, and nothing could be done with programs or data outside particular hardware configurations. Independence was established through stages that included in the early online systems access to dedicated terminals, such as the Beehive terminals that were for several years required for access to OCLC, and the special terminals needed to access LEXIS and other Mead Data Central databases, when these services were first made available.

This independence or portability of digital systems was achieved through the interplay of creative ideas pursued as competitive innovations in companies in the computer industry and in the packing down or universalizing of these good ideas in standards. One breakthrough was the introduction (in 1954) of the "high level" computer programming language FORTRAN, which enabled scientists and engineers to write programs that would run on almost any computer. The compiler programs (each written for a particular type of computer) converted the "universal" statements the scientists and engineers could understand to the machine code specific to each machine. An important portion of the infrastructure for the creation of digitally based information goods and services has been provided by organizations such as the American National Standards Institute (ANSI) as a national standards authority and the International Standards Organization (ISO) as an international body. Other parts of the infrastructure continue to be assembled in less formal settings and in many commercial ventures in which solutions, sometimes referred to as gateways or handshakes, are devised for linking particular systems. The national and international standards organizations will however remain important in the conception and achievement of large ideas, such as those related to the interconnection of systems. More discussion of the importance and the techniques of standardization in the digital environment is entered in Chapter 5.

As soon as digital codes could be used to drive typesetting machines, digital files of the contents of the printed media began to accumulate. The development of DTP and WP in the microcomputer environment now ensures that there are in industrialized countries very few contemporary documents that do not exist in a digital version. Facilities for the retrospective conversion of text to digital formats have become widespread with the use of digital cameras, scanners, and optical character recognition (OCR) systems. Optical technology has progressed so that, not only can pictures, on videodisc for example, be indexed with digital codes, but digital pictures can also readily be taken. Parallel developments have created digitized sound, animation, and full motion video. Commercial initiatives have led to the development of many innovative products such as the multimedia productions, which include combinations of print, videodisc, digital sound, and hypertext interface. On a broader level the availability of digital data from many sources and in many forms can lead to the creation of a whole new genre of products and services.

Geographic information systems (GIS) represent one such example. Bjerklie (1989) describes GIS as yielding "dynamic ways to visualize, compare, and analyze spatial relationships among large amounts of diverse data" (p. 57). Collected from data sources as various as satellites, street directories, and census excerpts, GIS have various applications in land use studies, traffic control, and site selection for businesses and public utilities. Bjerklie (1989) reports that Pizza Hut used GIS in many United States cities for the optimal placing of their pizza-to-go outlets. As he explains:

> Having geographic information in digital form gives researchers and policymakers a powerful handle on it. Computerizing maps provides the means to meet a great range of highly specific needs, since users can selectively extract required information from a massive database (p. 58).

Digital systems have also given entrepreneurs much better insight into which parts and combinations of the data available can be made into products and services that are the users' required information. Reference has already been made to Zuboff (1989) and her description of information technology as providing "a deep level of transparency to activities that had been either partially or completely opaque"—a capacity for which she coins the verb "informate" (p. 9). She also points out that this informating capacity can be ignored or suppressed. It may indeed be argued that it was for a long time ignored in many of the integrated library management systems that proliferated as bibliographic data became highly standardized and the software for its control highly adaptable for use on many different hardware platforms.

At the same time some feedback on user behavior has been obtained from operating information systems and from deliberate *ex post facto* inquiry into transaction logs. (See, for example, Bates *et al.*, 1993). At the commercial level, competition makes it imperative that the record of use reveal at least the macrodata on which sources are being used and by what clients and at what times. Most of these data are of course proprietary to the companies supplying the products and services, obtained through market research firms specializing in the information industry, such as the Link Company in the United States and Monitor in Europe.

At the microlevel the digital systems have made possible much more accurate targeting of sales prospects in every field, based often on buying behavior recorded in transactions already entered by the individual, for example in incurring credit card debits. Although it is a capacity still to be fully exploited in the commercial and especially in the publicly funded sector of information products and services, there is no doubt that designers of information products and managers of information services have better methods than they have ever had for recording and studying user behavior and deducing from it user preferences. There is also increasing, widespread disquiet as to how evidence of past consumer behavior may be put to use. Concerns have surfaced in a number of environments about the rights of the individual to information held by credit bureaus and the rights of access to past borrowing records in libraries. Awareness among United States librarians of the Library Awareness Program of the Federal Bureau of Investigation led to a campaign spearheaded by the American Library Association in which Congressional inquiries revealed that the bureau had not only sought records of individual borrowers but had also made records of those librarians whom it considered less than cooperative in supplying information (Foerstel, 1991). This incident is another reminder of the increased need for protection of privacy, by both legislation and the ethical standards of information professionals.

The range and sophistication of information products and services available have created a transformation in the expectations of users. Part of this transformation stems from the fact that the digital environment has created a climate in which clients are emboldened to demand the properties that they have always wanted in information services but previously knew it was futile to request. One example is the lukewarm response of biomedical researchers in Project Quartet when they were offered unlimited access to

ADONIS, the service that makes available from CD-ROM (compact disk read-only memory) high-quality copies of articles from selected medical journals. "Their objections were not to the system itself but to the fact that more material was not currently available, that is, they objected to the limited journal coverage" (Project Quartet, 1990, p. 48). These users also made it clear that coverage included not only breadth, in number of journal titles, subjects, and so on, but also depth in terms of the number of years covered by the database.

For years librarians could only smile wanly at undergraduate students naive enough to ask whether the online catalog included the journal articles as well as the books in the library. Now with the mix and match properties of computerized systems well established, libraries have responded by mounting databases of serial indexes or providing users with transparent access to remote catalogs, indexes, and abstracting services. The Melvyl system of the University of California may serve as an example. Originally applied to the union catalog of the libraries on the nine campuses of the University of California, Melvyl was from the outset designed with the idea that other databases would be provided over the system. Thus University of California users have access through it to Medline, Current Contents, Inspec, and many other databases, and all users (many of whom come in via the Internet) may use Melvyl as a gateway to other systems. Except in the most progressive library systems, however, and in corporate environments where the cost can readily be charged out to clients, online access to external databases has remained largely the prerogative of the privileged. It is hardly surprising therefore that the information product that has received most enthusiastic welcome from users is the CD-ROM on which more technical detail is given in Chapter 5. CD-ROM has been likened to what happened with text processing a few years ago when widespread access to WP and DTP software gave individuals power over the tools of production. According to Project Quartet (1990), "CD-ROM just alters the balance of power in significant ways, largely in favour of the user" (p. 71).

CD-ROM not only offers democratization of access but also allows creation of much better interfaces than can be afforded with the line speed available for access to remote online services. Part of the wider access derives from the readiness with which CD-ROM products can be mounted on local area networks. Increasingly, they are also transforming access to isolated people over wide area and telephone networks. Such access can be made available from information services of no great sophistication or wealth. The experience of the small university college in a country area of Australia, which provided dial-up access to CD-ROM for its external students (Van Dyk, 1992), has many replications elsewhere in the world.

In the publishing sphere, CD-ROM has proved a boon especially for government agencies obliged to make available large sets of data at frequent intervals. It has been reported that the United States federal government published more than 500 CD-ROMs in 1991, with the largest group containing census data (Gey, 1992). However daunting this volume of data may be to any information service hoping to confine CD-ROM access to a single PC, it may also prove the answer to the dilemma of governments cutting costs by cutting back on the distribution of information, especially statistical information.

There is no doubt that CD-ROM products will gain a considerable market share in the multimedia environment. Because of the much greater bandwidth demanded for digital transmission of sound and pictures than for text, online access to multimedia services is unlikely to be available in any mass market. Experience and experiment continue to uncover ways in which to economize on the amount of data that has to be transmitted to decision makers. For example, Project Quartet (1990) found that the user in control of the progressive enhancement of an image will in general halt the reception of data at an early stage, usually very soon after he or she begins to comprehend the picture contents. In fact, "initial studies have indicated that around 6% of the total information in an image is sufficient to make identification possible, at which stage either the image may be rejected or the resolution selectively enhanced" (Project Quartet, 1990, p. 135).

Implementation of these and other bandwidth-saving ideas will enhance the attractiveness of CD-ROM as well as online products and, at least in organizations in which there are local area networks and a reasonable demand for a particular multimedia product, the CD-ROM format is likely to prevail. It must immediately be acknowledged, however, that such predictions are hazardous if not foolhardy in situations where innovative advances in technology are continuous and where they are occasionally brought together with creative innovations in public policy, as in the National Research and Education Network (NREN) on which there is more discussion in Chapter 5.

Forecasting the range and scope of information products and services likely to be available in the future is therefore difficult. Forecasting that there will be more of them in ever more attractive packages is easy. The buy or make decisions that now confront information service managers can only proliferate, as changes in cost to productivity ratios of the various information technologies constantly alter the basis of "make or buy" and "which to buy" decisions by consumers in information markets.

The convergence of DTP and WP already discussed (see p. 99) has enhanced options for the creation of information products. Developments of the past two to three years have made possible the production of high quality printed output from microcomputers and laser printers. Before this the only way to produce such quality output from computer-generated text was to use elaborate embedded formatting codes with which to drive a typesetter, such as the Unix-based text processing systems or on very expensive purpose-built equipment, such as that used in the newspaper printing industry.

Now virtually any organization, and many private individuals, have the power to produce printed output of a quality that enhances public image and that carries connotations of permanency and worth. With some attention to the different design requirements of the screen environment, highly acceptable electronic publishing can also be achieved in the microcomputer environment. While academics remain skeptical of the rewards of electronic publishing, the ability to produce high quality printing is a threat to the competitive advantage of academic publishers. The smaller investment of the occasional publisher whether academic department or community organization makes it easier than for the professional publisher to provide frequent updates and in general to supply information that is generally more timely and more accurate. The ability to provide short runs frequently—so-called publishing on demand—is also attractive because it fits in so well with the just-in-time philosophy espoused by manufacturing, construction, retail, and transportation industries, which has already been mentioned (see p. 105).

The extent to which repackaging and repurposing of digital information is to be done in-house, by commercial enterprises in the information industry or by public agencies, is a matter of continuing controversy. Conditions will vary by case, place, and time, and no certain prescriptions are possible, although some guidance on the factors to be considered is offered in Chapter 6. No discussion of information products and services would be complete, however, without mention of the latest, least-planned, worldwide, and minimally predictable digital information product, namely the Internet and its contents.

The Internet, which came to birth early in 1991, probably has at least some tens of thousands of users, provides connections with probably over one million computers in universities, colleges, schools, and other organizations in at least twenty-eight countries and has been described as a chaos rather than a universe of data. The size of this universe has recently been estimated at more than three million files, representing 165 gigabytes of data available from 1044 sites from which files can be downloaded, which are commonly known as file transfer protocol (FTP) sites. Source code and system code account for 43% of the files and 49% of the storage; text files account for 10%, archives created by newsgroups for about 12%, and personal computer programs, data files, computer images, computer games, and executable program files for approximately 14% of the files (Dillon *et al.*, 1993). One of the hot topics on Internet bulletin boards is the future of the Internet itself. Questions of how much of its contents can remain free and for how much longer clearly concern not only its present users but have national, international, and even global implications. The Internet and its undoubtedly more technologically sophisticated successors may be accessible to a privileged, comparative few, or they may become instruments so widely available that they tend to obliterate considerations of distance and difference and even the notion of the nation-state. Because the bottom line will be based on economic arguments, it is fitting that the promise of the Internet should be followed by discussion of the value of information services.

3.3 The Value of Information Services

3.3.1 Judgment of Value

Estimates of value differ according to the time, place, and personality of the person (or culture of the group) making the estimate as well as to intrinsic properties of the phenomenon being judged. This applies whether what is being judged is a commodity, service, course of action, person, or philosophy. Obviously, judgments differ, even in the relatively simple area of judgment of the exchange value of a commodity. Opportunity costs (for example, if I buy this carpet will I have to forego my vacation in Europe?) and political issues (for example, will this one look good enough to keep up with the Joneses with their Persian carpets?) and a host of nonmonetary aspects of price (for example, how much trouble will it be to keep this carpet in good condition? will it make the rest of my furnishings look shabby?)—all these considerations apply.

Popular pejorative use of the term "value judgment" suggests that there are superior judgments that are independent of bias, presumably because they are made independently of any established set of values: in other words, that purely objective judgments are possible and are to be preferred. We would suggest that, on the contrary, judgments can be objective only over a relatively limited set of clearly defined phenomena and in circumstances in which no judgment outside the confines of an algorithm is required. Even in these cases, if any aspect of human behavior is to be embedded in the algorithm, its natural variety will have to be attenuated into a set of manageable assumptions. In most cases the variables considered and their interactions cannot be subjected to valid and precise measurement in advance. Therefore, almost all judgments of value must be based on the subjective deliberations of a person or group, whether immediately or remotely in time. In organizations, such judgments are influenced by the culture of the organization; at the same time, they help to create and maintain that culture. In fact, Itami (1989) defines corporate culture as "the distinctive characteristics of the patterns of information processing shared by the members of an organization" (p. 26).

The degree to which judgments may be considered "objective" is bound up with measurement and units of measurement. The utility of measurement, and of the reduction of commodity values to measurements in units of currency, is not to be questioned. On the other hand, the validity of measurement is not immutable. For example, the value of currencies, and wages, and other features in the countries using them is recognized as more accurately measured by units of comparison drawn from the price of an identical basket of goods and services in other countries than by prevailing exchange rates. *The Economist* annually publishes the Big Mac Index, which is regarded as a more accurate and stable measurement of the comparative value of currencies than the exchange rates ("Big MacCurrencies," 1992).

Variables pertaining to information cannot be as neatly packaged as a hamburger. In discussing information markets in section 3.1.3, we came to terms with the heterogeneity of both supply and demand for information. Taylor (1986), discussing the concept of value in general, employs the term "use value," which he describes as "basic to exchange value, because use value establishes the conditions for the exchange of one thing for something else" (p. 12). But the use value of information usually is subject to wide variation among users and is difficult to calculate in advance. When he extends the notion of value to information, Taylor (1986) also calls up the phrase "apparent value of information," which he sources to King Research, Inc. (King *et al.*, 1982). This phrase is used to connote "not only a formal dollar price a client is willing to exchange, but also the time and effort a client is willing to invest in order to receive what is perceived as benefits from the information process" (p. 15). Among the features of information that complicate judgments of its exchange value is the difficulty a prospective purchaser may have in getting enough detail from a supplier who has, of course, to guard against revealing enough of the information to make it unnecessary for the prospect to purchase the rest.

A corollary is seen in that the difficulty of posing a question is proportional to one's lack of knowledge of the topic. So, if one asks a question to which one already knows the answer the artificiality of the question is usually obvious. It is, for example, seldom difficult to identify "Dorothy Dixers," a term sometimes applied to questions asked by arrangement, often in parliaments or other political settings, to give the respondent a chance to demonstrate his or her carefully rehearsed knowledge and perspicacity. Other examples of the genre are to be found in some of the questions asked of students in reference courses in library schools and of contestants in quiz shows—questions of such particularity that they could not possibly have been posed unless the answer was known to the questioner.

The problem of giving away only enough proprietary or commercial information to engage the buyer's interest in the exchange is played out on many stages and with great uncertainties, for example, by those attempting to license rights to patents or to negotiate license arrangements for technology based on secrecy agreements. These difficulties are often overlooked, especially by the providers of information services in the public and not-for-profit sectors. Their preoccupation is likely to be with the superabundance of available information from which they want to channel to their customers all that it relevant to them and, as far as possible, only that which is relevant to them.

In section 3.1.3 (see pp. 83–84) Lamberton (1984) attributed overproduction of information to insufficient regulation by the market mechanism. More profound and disturbing causes are postulated by Postman (1992) who is the latest in a thin but long line of critics of the optimism with which Western culture has embraced succeeding information technologies from writing onwards. Postman (1992) describes the present condition of the United States as *Technopoly* and asserts that "one way of defining a Technopoly is to say that its information immune system is inoperable" (p. 63). He goes on to claim that "the First Amendment to the United States Constitution stands as a monument to the ideological biases of print" and that the founding fathers did not write "a single line . . . that does not take for granted that when information is made available to citizens they are capable of managing it" (pp. 66–67).

But Postman (1992) argues that, with the invention of the telegraph, technological change disrupted the understanding on which the nation was based. As he puts it, "The telegraph removed space as an inevitable constraint on the movement of information, and, for the first time, transportation and communication were disengaged from each other." Strictly speaking, carrier pigeons, beacons, semaphores, the penny post, newpapers, and even wampum belts and message sticks removed the space constraint on movement of information long before the invention of telegraphy. Postman also claims that "telegraphy created the idea of context-free information" and "made information into a commodity, a 'thing' that could be bought and sold irrespective of its uses or meaning" (pp. 67–68).

Whether telegraphy made information into a commodity or simply made it into a phenomenon that could be traded more widely, as well as whether the success of telegraphy is largely owed to growth of demand for the daily newspaper or vice versa, remain debatable points. To suggest, however, that information became with telegraphy a commodity that could be exchanged regardless of its use or content seems an overstatement not in accordance with historical or contemporary fact. On the other hand, no one would want to argue or forego the elegance of Postman's rhetoric on today's superabundance of information:

> From millions of sources all over the globe through every possible channel and medium—light waves, airwaves, ticker tapes, computer banks, telephone wires, television cables, satellites, printing presses—information pours in. Behind it, in every imaginable form of storage—on paper, on video and audio tape, on discs, film, and silicon chips—is an ever greater volume of information waiting to be retrieved. Like the Sorcerer's Apprentice, we are awash in information. And all the sorcerer has left us is a broom. Information has become a form of garbage, not only incapable of answering the most fundamental human questions but barely useful in providing coherent direction to the solution of even mundane problems. To say it still another way: The milieu in which Technopoly flourishes is one in which the tie between information and human purpose has been severed, i.e., information appears indiscriminately, directed at no one in particular, in enormous volume and at high speeds, and disconnected from theory, meaning, or purpose (pp. 69–70).

Postman follows up his attack on the belief that information per se has any value with the claim that fast access to information otherwise unavailable has nothing to offer our most serious problems, which are not technical and do not arise from inadequate information. Neither nuclear catastrophe, death by starvation, nor family breakdown will occur on account of inadequate information.

Postman makes his point that the value of calculation, speed, and voluminous information has been overemphasized, but, argued another way, perhaps there has not been a nuclear confrontation because of the information available about the types and numbers of weapons available to warring parties and the likely consequences of their use. Information about problems of less-privileged groups certainly cannot be said to remove self-interest, but maybe victims of famine and civil strife get more relief and more engagement of attention to their problems than they would without such widespread distribution of information about their plight.

Whatever the limitations of Postman's argument he has effectively made the point that information per se (for which data may be a better term) is not necessarily at all useful. It is doubtful that many writers on the value of information would disagree. In fact Taylor (1986), though his rhetoric is milder than Postman's, has seen just as clearly problems of control of both quantity and quality inherent in the use of information technology. He writes:

> Today's computer networks and office terminals, though still very complicated because of lack of standardization, make vast stores of data available to those who have the money, patience, and time to use them. These newer technologies are,

> however, based on old information processes. As a consequence they will not only carry all the problems of the earlier processes, but will magnify those problems, such as overload or poor data quality (p. 57).

Not only in the work of Taylor (1986) but in many others (for example, Simon, 1971 and Feldman and March, 1981), a continuing theme is that the function of information services and information specialists is increasingly to keep information out of environments where it is irrevelant. This approach to the reduction of information overload is dubbed "noise reduction" by Taylor (1986, p. 57). As he explains:

> The explosive growth of potentially relevant information in research, managerial, educational, social and policy contexts is altering the information environment in rather basic ways. This does not mean that we have too much information; it means rather that the systems that filter, transmit, and distribute information do not operate well. The inadequateness is due in part to a failure to understand the contexts from which the need for information arises and to the perceptions we hold concerning the information systems themselves (p. 24).

The importance of context in giving meaning to information has been firmly established. Taylor (1986) recognizes that "a message has value only in context" (p. 16). Dervin (1980) has charted the progress of communications research as "conceptions of information are moving from observer constructions to user constructions" (p. 91). Taylor's research and scholarship from a background in librarianship and information science have brought him to a comparable understanding. He has stated his belief that "Value is not inherent in nor is it carried by a message" and that "'usefulness' means that a person or group of persons have chosen a particular message for one of several reasons"(Taylor, 1986, pp. 14, 16). Any judgment of information value cannot proceed independently of use value, which in turn has to be based on acknowledgement of the primacy of the judgment of the information user.

This chapter has already discussed the continuum on which information sources are transformed into information resources, which are in turn transformed into information services by the addition of arrangements for regular and reliable access, and of marketing strategies by which the resources are customized and contextualized for use in a particular environment. Many authors have suggested that in seeking to evaluate information services distinction should be made between (1) value of the information content of messages, that is, value of the meaning and (2) value of the information resources (services, technologies, and systems) that store, process, analyze, package, and deliver messages (Braunstein, 1979; Machlup, 1979b; and Taylor, 1986). Adoption of this approach carries the danger of a return to the unproductive content/conduit debate of the past. In this chapter we have gained deeper understanding of the synergy of form and content in information delivery and of the importance of the context in which the information system operates. We may therefore expect that the value of content will often prove difficult to separate from the added value provided by the information service. With this in mind, we may find it interesting to probe some of the criteria and perspectives from which the value of information products and services has been judged in practice.

3.3.2 Perspectives and Criteria

In keeping with the book's theme, the focus in this discussion of perspectives and criteria for the value of information services is on organizations rather than individuals and on formal information systems. This does not mean that either the rich diversity of human differences nor the important role of informal communication of information within and without organizations is to be discounted. Both are crucial factors that shape the environments in which information services are fashioned and delivered. Therefore in this book we emphasize the importance of user-imposed judgments of the value of information and the information service operators' understanding of the contexts in which their services are to be used.

Perspectives on the value of information services and information itself may be *technology-driven, content-driven* and *user-driven*. Table 3.1 shows some of the approaches to the value of information and indicates how they fit into this categorization. The terminologies used are those of the authors indicated. The bases of all these approaches are discussed in the following text.

Postman's excoriation of the technology-driven approach has been presented above and his warnings of the consequences of uncritical "garbage in–gospel out" attitudes to computers are timely (Postman, 1992). Technological opportunity has been important in extending the range and utility of information products and services. An outstanding example is the range of

Table 3.1
Perspectives on the Value of Information Services

Technology-driven	Content-driven	User-driven
Information technology approach (Black and Marchand, 1982)	Library science approach (Black and Marchand, 1982)	Value added (Taylor, 1986)
Information resource management (Black and Marchand, 1982)	Organization theory (Black and Marchand, 1982)	Marketing (Maguire and Willard, 1990)

products and services developed by the Institute for Scientific Information, which are based on Eugene Garfield's early perception of the opportunity that the text-handling abilities of computers offered for automated citation indexing (Garfield, 1979). The spectacular failures have come when the capacities of the technology have been mistaken for the properties required by customers. When information service managers are inexperienced in the purchase of computer hardware and software but dazzled by the system's capacities, bad judgments of both exchange value and use value have led and will continue to lead to useless purchases. In commercial consumer products, the discipline of the market seems to work with a delay proportional to the utility of the product. Postman (1992) has a good story about how short-lived the telephone lie detector was in the market. Inappropriate products and services offered on a noncommercial basis are not used, and in the longer term clients may not even accept delivery of them, whatever the technology involved. But it would be absurd to suggest that technology was not a factor in the judgment of value. The image of advanced technology attracts prestige, and its novelty attracts customers. Its presence may be politically warranted if it is adopted by the competition, by more upscale institutions that the information service wants to emulate, or simply if it is widely adopted. One example here is the rash of purchases of tattle-tape electronic book control systems in the entrances of university and public libraries from the late 1960s. Relatively expensive equipment was purchased by relatively poor institutions in large quantities, initially from one supplier (the 3M Company). Bingham (1976) was probably the first to point out that there has been very little questioning, either at time of purchase or in subsequent operations, of the value of these systems from the point of view of preventing theft. On the other hand, their adoption has been so widespread that not to install a system would these days seem irresponsible on the part of library management.

Content-driven perspectives on value presume an ability to assess the quality of the collections of information based on objective criteria. But this viewpoint is hard to sustain when subjected to examination in any real life situation. The contents of university libraries, for example, do not represent the librarians' judgment of the best that has been thought and said. As Postman (1992) points out, the curriculum already represents the institution's judgments on the value of subjects and aspects of subjects which it has chosen to teach. An example of collection-driven evaluation is the system known as Conspectus, which was developed by the Research Libraries Group in the early 1980s and sponsored by the Association of Research Libraries (Gwinn and Mosher, 1983). As an innovation in library management, Conspectus can be said to have achieved wide and rapid diffusion. It has been applied in many other countries including Canada, France, Germany, the United Kingdom, and Australia, and considerable resources have been spent on its adaptation and implementation, for example, on on-line databases containing the results, and verification studies of some of those results. There has been some criticism of the shortcomings of Conspectus as a method and some suggestions in the United States that, while Conspectus has been useful in indicating where collection strengths lie and in directing scholars to them, it has not achieved its primary goal, which was a coordinated national collection development policy for libraries. Lucas (1990), for example, has pointed out that "the Conspectus has now been completed by research libraries across the United States. Using a six-point scale, participants have rated their collections in seven thousand subject categories. Despite its wide adoption, however, the Conspectus has yet to be used to construct a national collection development policy" (p. 199). To date, however, criticism of the Conspectus approach to collection evaluation and development seems to have been confined to skepticism about the validity and reliability of measurements and their political usefulness in defending library budgets in hard economic times. Fundamental issues do not seem to have been confronted. Questions could, for example, be raised about the relationship of comprehensiveness of the collection to the likelihood of availability of items when they are required. There is also the question of the embarrassing redundancy of collections revealed in many library use studies, notably the Pittsburgh study (Kent *et al.*, 1979).

Black and Marchand (1982) describe the technology-driven and content-driven perspectives in different and somewhat broader terms. They characterize the dominant approaches to assessing the value of information as the *information technology approach* and the *information/library science approach*. They point out that "while the universe for the former is that of automated technology, for the latter it is the library system" in which "value criteria are premised primarily upon the specific functions of the acquisition, storage, and retrieval of information" (Black and Marchand, 1982, p. 196). They classify both of these approaches as belonging to "the functional interpretation of information management," wherein "the two aspects of transfer and content are minimally related to each other and can be separated without excessive distortion" (p. 196). This is both repetition and extension of the idea that content and conduit can be studied separately in the analysis of information services.

As a contrast, Black and Marchand (1982) also discuss "the process interpretation" wherein "transfer and content have to be linked for a fuller understanding of the value of information" (pp. 196–197). Approaches that they place within the process interpretation are those of information resources management, organization theory, and the economics of information. These approaches differ in nature and objectives. Information resources management is "fundamentally a resource accounting procedure to control the costs associated with the information explosion" (Black and Marchand, 1982, p. 205). The organization theory approach "sees its objective to be the organization's ability to transmit, in an accurate form, the key pieces of information needed to make faster and better decisions" (p. 209). The economic theory of information, on the other hand, is "primarily a statistical or probability theory of the amount of information needed to reduce uncertainty in decision making" (p. 211). (This is a narrower usage of the phrase economics of information than that adopted in Chapter 1 of this book.) All these process approaches have in common emphasis on quality rather than quantity of information and on the costs of information, including the consumption costs, rather than, as in the functional approaches, on its benefits.

Separating the mechanisms for the transfer of information from the substance and the substantive use of the information itself is hazardous. To admit this is not to suggest complete abandonment of the functional approaches to the value of information services. But one does need to recognize that a focus on the supply of information storage and delivery systems makes it difficult to adopt a user-driven perspective on value.

To obtain a user-driven perspective, Taylor (1986) recommends a value-added approach to information services. This is based on the recognition that "a message . . . is given value by a 'user' who sees its potential 'usefulness' because he or she is in a particular environment and can relate the message to the problems and tasks of that environment" (p. 15). Taylor relates this value-added perspective to information systems and services, as he explains: "Since messages carry potential for value, value added processes are defined as those activities of information systems which provide mechanisms that (a) can signal this potential, and/or (b) can relate the potential to a specific problem in a specific environment" (pp. 16–17). Taylor (1986) also sets out clearly the criteria by which an information system ought to be judged:

> The merit of an information system is determined by its success (a) in signaling the potential for value of messages; (b) in combining, interpreting, and reexpressing information content in addressing or clarifying particular problems; and/or (c) through system flexibility, in allowing users to develop routines adapted to their individual needs and styles (p. 203).

Taylor (1986) also postulated the criteria on which information users measure value, which are shown in the first column of Table 3.2. In the second column he lists the values added by value-adding activities, and the third column includes examples of specific enhancements through which these values may be implemented. His full table of user criteria and added values is reproduced as Table 3.2.

The Taylor model offers a sound base on which more precise and

Table 3.2
User Criteria and Values Added

User criteria of choice	Interface (value added)	System (Value-added processes: examples)
Ease of use	Browsing	Alphabetizing
	Formatting	Highlighting important terms
	Interfacing I (mediation)	
	Interfacing II (orientation)	
	Ordering	
	Physical accessibility	
Noise reduction	Access I (item identification)	Indexing
	Access II (subject description)	Vocabulary control
	Access III (subject summary)	Filtering
	Linkage	
	Precision	
	Selectivity	
Quality	Accuracy	Quality control
	Comprehensiveness	Editing
	Currency	Updating
	Reliability	Analyzing and comparing data
	Validity	
Adaptability	Closeness to problem	Provision of data manipulation capabilities
	Flexibility	Ranking output for relevance
	Simplicity	
	Stimulatory	
Time-saving	Response speed	Reduction of processing time
Cost-saving	Cost-saving	Lower connect-time price

Source: Taylor, 1986, p. 50.

detailed criteria and measures for information services could very well rest, and against which any existing information service could be weighed. The value-added approach can also be enriched by the adoption of a *marketing perspective*. As Maguire and Willard point out:

> The marketing perspective provides a helpful framework in which to consider the management of library performance because it focusses attention on the clients, and on the exchange relationships with them as the purposes for which the library exists. The demands of collection building and maintenance and the complexities of the library's technical services operation conspire to make library staff much more likely to be orientated to products and processes than to client service (Maguire and Willard, 1990, p. 271).

Similar warnings of the difficulty that libraries have in adopting a marketing approach are frequent in the literature reviewed by Tucci (1988). In such an approach, quality is determined by what the customer wants rather than by what the service can most conveniently supply. The marketing perspective requires cultivating channels through which clients can communicate their expectations and reactions. Such an approach involves strengthening the weak links often experienced, especially in publicly supported information services, between customer preference and satisfaction and input of resources. Use studies have repeatedly found that many potential customers are unaware of the existence of the information services and that most of those who use them are ill-informed about the range of different services offered. Therefore the marketing approach also involves the use of publicity and promotion of information services.

The value-added approach, as adumbrated by Taylor (1986), may be judged to include the marketing approach, or to have thoroughly assimilated it. His wisdom on the value of information is summed up as follows (Taylor, 1986):

> The value of information cannot be measured in precise terms prior to its use. Value is not inherent in, nor is it carried by, an information message. A message has value only in context. It is given value by its users. Consequently a message has potential for value. This means that the better we understand the environment in which the output of a system will be used, the better we will be able to estimate the potential value of those outputs, and to design systems accordingly (p. 203).

Taylor (1986) goes on to suggest that "*a posteriori*, the value of information might be measured by its apparent value—the sum of dollars expended by the user, plus time and energy dollars [sic] costs, and the opportunity costs lost in not doing something else" (p. 203). Some such *a posteriori* measures have been tried in the demonstrations of value discussed below.

3.3.3 Demonstrations of Value

At the macrolevel, the mathematical demonstration of under-use of information in United States industry by Hayes and Erickson (1982) has already been cited. Their findings have been supported by Braunstein (1985) who came to the same conclusion after analysis of United States industrial data using different econometric models.

At the microlevel, Koenig (1990) describes several attempts to extrapolate and quantify the value of information services, ranging from the Exxon Research Center library in the mid-1970s through an evaluative study of NASA's information services in the late 1970s, to the suite of studies carried out by King Research, Inc. The King studies have done the most to develop methodologies that take into consideration the user's time and costs. These studies go back to 1979 (King and Roderer, 1979), in consultancies in many environments in the United States, in public service and private enterprise, in manufacturing plants, publishing enterprises, and educational and library systems, including public libraries in the United Kingdom.

The King methods have analyzed the value of information services to the organization from several angles. One is by measuring the value of the time (represented by salary and overhead) that the users are willing to expend on the information services. This value is expressed as a proportion of the amount spent in providing the information services. Another method is to calculate the additional cost that would be incurred if there were no in-house information service and the documents made available through it had to be obtained elsewhere. The King studies have also established that professionals in organizations spend a relatively fixed proportion of their time on information seeking and reading. On this basis they have calculated in several environments the amount of reading that would have to be foregone if more time had to be spent on information seeking. In all three methods it is interesting that surprisingly stable ratios have been recorded in a variety of environments. They are of the order of 20:1 for value of the users' time spent in using in relation to the amount spent in providing the information services and 8:1 for the cost of obtaining required documents from alternative sources versus the costs of an information service which would provide them. The third category of studies indicates that the costs of reading time that would have to be foregone without the information services would be very high. In their study of the energy database of the United States Department of Energy, King *et al.* (1982) reported that had the energy database not existed there would have been a loss of 300,000 searches and almost 2.5 million readings (a value equivalent to $3 billion). The methods used by King Research are similar to the "contingent valuation" methods used to evaluate environmental amenities, which like information services clearly have positive value but an ill-defined market (Pearce *et al.*, 1991).

Koenig (1990) has reviewed the work on R & D productivity from the management literature and his own work on the pharmaceutical industry, all of which indicate the superiority of research teams that are more open to information from external sources and which make more use of information services overall. At the same time it must be admitted that studies of the value of information are most easily applied to academics and to research-based knowledge workers. Matarazzo *et al.* (1990) in a survey of 167 corporations found that even though senior managers expressed very high regard for their corporate library and information centers, there was litttle consensus about how those services should be evaluated or about how the library or information center added value to the organization.

According to a recent survey of a diverse mix of large Japanese corporations, firms there place a tremendous value on information and do not feel the need to justify information management expenditures (Prusak and Matarazzo, 1992). The authors remark that "many issues that absorb Western information systems researchers, such as how to determine the value of an information management system or how to justify the investment and measure the payback of an information center, become far less important in an environment that considers information management an essential cost of doing business" (p. 6). Such attitudes are not confined to Japan. The technical services manager of a multinational food company reported to an Australian survey that his company spent $5 million per year on its extensive information service worldwide and that the cost of foregoing it would be great, because "over a couple of decades, we would not be in the market place" (Maquire *et al.*, 1987, p. 56).

Management's intuitive appreciation of the longer term value of information services has not served to protect those services when their salience to the core business of their organizations cannot be demonstrated. This is obvious from recent widespread curtailment of library services in government agencies and business corporations already mentioned on page 105. Broadbent (1992) quotes Eason (1988) to point out that "the inclusion of multiple stakeholder perspectives is essential in any process which seeks to go beyond . . . technical system performance" (p. 3). Broadbent (1992) goes on to argue that the perspective of senior managers has often been missing in both the literature and practice of information and library services. As Buckland (1983) did in his identification of the "double feedback loop in library service," Broadbent (1992) recognizes that "links between management and users are essential in ensuring an information management perspective on the performance of the I[nformation] S[ervices] U[nit]" (p. 4) and that those links will not exist unless they are forged by the information service managers.

Broadbent (1992) reports on an interesting attempt to build on the King techniques, and usefully codified in Griffiths and King (1991), by combining cost-benefit analysis with a technique called priority and performance evaluation (PAPE). As she describes it

> PAPE seeks quantitative and qualitative input from managers, users and ILU [Information and Library Unit] staff about the areas in which the ILU should be directing its major efforts, together with an assessment of the current performance of the ILU in those areas. . . . It may indicate differing perceptions which require resolution, in order for the ILU to focus its efforts in areas where the organisational stakeholders perceive that they gain maximum benefit. The output from this approach facilitates the development of a series of well-grounded Critical Success Factors (CSFs) for the ILU as viewed by the major organisational stakeholders (p. 4).

The technique was applied in evaluation of a national information resource center and the library and information service of an Australian state government agency. A list of result areas was developed, and users of the information service and senior management were asked to rank the priority that should be afforded each of them in the organization and then to give performance ratings for the information service in each of these areas.

Differences between priority and performance judgments are of interest and so are the priorities offered overall and by different groups. Overall, timeliness, currency, and accuracy of information services and products were considered most important. As Broadbent (1992) points out, "For any organisation, the results have primarily a diagnostic value: areas of strength and weakness are identified and can be ranked in priority order for management consideration and action" (p. 7). Depending on the match between priorities and performance, result areas can be labeled "waste," "OK," "success," and "killer."

In attempting a cost-benefit analysis of the current awareness services offered by the two agencies, Broadbent (1992) acknowledged the difficulties inherent in applications of this approach to information services. These are (1) lack of agreement about nature and measurement of costs within the parent organization; (2) the different time frame over which costs and benefits usually accrue; (3) the control of the user rather than the information service over the use of materials; (4) the fact that user's willingness to purchase does not necessarily mean awareness of the full benefit of the purchase to be derived from the service; and (5) lack of a control group that can be deprived of the information service and then compared with those who had access to it. Within these limitations, Broadbent evaluated the current awareness services in terms of the following criteria:

1. Cost savings and cost avoidance in users' time
2. Cost of alternative products and services
3. Impact and usefulness of the information to the organization

Two alternate scenarios were proposed. In one, the current awareness services were not provided: in the other, outsourcing was postulated for preparation of current awareness services and document delivery. Removal incurred cost increases of around twenty-four times the cost of providing the information service in the organization, a figure not very different from the recurring approximately twenty times reported by the King studies. In dollar terms there was not much difference between the costs of outsourcing and in-house provision, once the notional allocation of the serials budget is included in costing the in-house facility. Broadbent (1992) concludes that the values added in-house by greater speed of delivery, greater knowledge of the organization and its members, and greater confidentiality, cannot be represented in dollar terms. This is a great pity since those qualities are clearly crucial to the quality of the information service provided.

Again, while few of these figures and none of the anecdotal evidence about value may satisfy cost accountants, Broadbent (1992) reports that the reaction of management in both organizations to these evaluation techniques was very positive. She is also an advocate of the process of evaluation. She writes:

> In our experience of evaluation of different types of services and systems, the interaction which takes place as part of the process is at least as important as the product or report at the end of that process. Ongoing evaluation, aimed at improvement in service, and changes to policies and resource allocation, is central to good management in any enterprise (p. 14).

Judgments of value are inseparable from the attitudes and beliefs of the people who make them. Thus the better the attitudes and beliefs of the stakeholders have been assimilated, the more the information service is likely to serve their needs. At the working level, the purpose of the information service has to be consonant with that of the organization. At the broader level, this discussion of value may also serve to point out the necessity of inquiring into what value an organization or a society wishes to derive from its information services. Thus the guidelines set out for evaluation of information services in Chapter 6 will be premised on the particular purpose or purposes of the service as well as the general purpose of assisting the organization in effective innovation. In that framework, there is much assistance to be gained from the research into and development of performance indicators for information services pursued in the last twenty years and in particular in the transfer of perspectives of value to the viewpoints of both the user and the management.

This chapter has sought to clarify the nature of information services both by associating them with and separating them from information systems, information sources, and information technology. Separation of information services from information resources has proved neither possible nor necessary in our analysis. Underlying all this discussion is the understanding that information is a trinity consisting of content, conduit and context. Although this notion is abstract, it is also useful in avoiding the practical dangers that lie in the temptations to regard outpourings of data, regardless of the sophistication of the technology involved in their production, as information if it is, to use Postman's phrase, context-free. Extension of this idea to information services indicates that any criterion of their value that is not strongly related to use and users, even though the links may be indirect, should be rejected. Thus armed, we can proceed in Chapter 4 to the consideration of information sources that can contribute to successful innovation.

References

Ackoff, R. L. (1967). Management misinformation systems. *Management science, 14*(4), BB147–BB156.

Allen, Thomas J. (1986). Organizational structure, information technology, and R&D productivity. *IEEE transactions on engineering management 33*(4), 212–217.

Appeals Court denies SDC MEDLARS tapes. (1977). *Government Publications Review 4,* p. 142.

Arrow, K. J. (1979). The economics of information. *In* M. L. Dertouzos, and J. Moses, Eds., *The computer age: a twenty-year view.* Cambridge, Massachusetts, M.I.T. Press, pp. 306–317.

Bates, Marcia J., Deborah N. Wilde, and Susan Siegfried, (1993). An analysis of search terminology used by humanities scholars: the Getty Online Search Project report no. 1. *Library Quarterly 63*(1), 1–39.

Beam, R. D. (1983). Towards a system-based unified social science. *In* F. Machlup and U. Mansfield, Eds., The study of information: interdisciplinary messages, New York, Wiley, pp. 607–618.

Bearman, David (1991). An indefensible bastion: archives as a repository in the electronic age. *In* David Bearman, Ed., *Archival management of electronic records.* Archives and Museum Informatics technical report, (13), 14–24.

"Big MacCurrencies" (1992). *The Economist 323*(7755) (April 18), 81.

Bingham, Richard (1976). *The adoption of innovation by local government.* Lexington, Massachusetts, Lexington.

Bjerklie, David (1989). The electronic transformation of maps. *Technology Review* April, 54–63.

Black, Sena Hoosenally, and Donald A. Marchand, (1982). Assessing the value of information in organizations: a challenge for the 1980s. *Information Society Journal 1*(3), 191–222.

Braunstein, Y. M. (1979). Costs and benefits of library information: the user point of view. *Library Trends 28,* 79–87.

Braunstein, Y. M. (1985). Information as a factor of production: substitutability and productivity. *The Information Society 3*(3), 261–273.

Brittain, J. M. (1970). *Information and its users: a review with special reference to the social sciences.* New York, Wiley.

Broadbent, M. (1988). Information services strategy and infra-structure in large organizations: research proposal. Melbourne, 1988, unpublished manuscript.

Broadbent, M. (1992). Demonstrating information service value: linking priorities, benefits and performance. Paper presented at the Australian Library and Information Association Biennial Conference, Albury, September.

Broadbent, M., P. Lloyd, A. Hansell, and C.N.G. Dampney, (1992). Roles, responsibilities and requirements for managing information systems in the 1990s. *International Journal of Information Management 12,* 21–38.

Buckland, Michael K. (1983). *Library services in theory and context.* New York, Pergamon.

Buckland, Michael K. (1989). Information handling, organizational structure, and power. *Journal of the American Society for Information Science 40*(5), 329–333.

Buckley, W. (1983). Signals, meaning, and control in social systems. *In* F. Machlup and U. Mansfield, Eds., *The study of information: interdisciplinary messages.* New York, Wiley, pp. 601–606.

Burk, D. F., and F. W. Horton, (1988). *InfoMap: a complete guide to discovering corporate information resources.* Englewood Cliffs, New Jersey, Prentice Hall.

Burton, Paul F. (1988). Information technology and organisational structure. *Aslib Proceedings 40*(3), 57–68.

Bush, V. (1945). As we may think. *Atlantic Monthly 176*(1), 101–108.

Carter, John, and P. H. Muir, (1967). *Printing and the mind of man: a descriptive catalogue illustrating the impact of print on the evolution of western civilization during five centuries.* London, Cassell.

Carter, Martha (1979). *Community analysis in respect to library service.* Washington County Library. January. (ERIC ED 17547).

Clark, Kenneth (1969). *Civilization: a personal view.* London, British Broadcasting Corporation.

Cook, Terry (1991). Appraisal in the information age: a Canadian commentary. *In* David Bearman, Ed., *Archival management of electronic records.* Archives and Museum Informatics technical report, no .13, 50–56.

Dervin, Brenda (1980). Communication gaps and inequities: moving towards a reconceptualization. *Progress in Communication Sciences 2,* 73–112.

Diener, Richard A. V. (1992). A tale of two paradigms, or whatever happened to IRM? *BASIS 18*(2), 26–27.

Diebold, J. (1985). *Managing information: the challenge and the opportunity.* New York, Amacom American Management Association.

Dillon, Martin, Erik Jul, Mark Burge, and Carol Hickey, (1993). *Assessing information on the Internet: toward providing library services for computer-mediated communication: results of an OCLC research project.* Dublin, Ohio, On-line Computer Library Center (OCLC).

Dodgson, Mark (1989). *In* Mark Dodgson, Ed., *Technology strategy and the firm.* London, Longmans.

Eason, Ken (1988). *Information technology and organisational change.* London, Taylor & Francis, pp. 1–10.

Eisenstein, Elizabeth (1983). *The printing revolution in early modern Europe.* Cambridge, England, Cambridge University Press.

Feather, John (1991). Publishers and knowledge. *In* A. J. Meadows, Ed., *Knowledge and communication: essays on the information chain.* London, Library Association Publishing, pp. 59–76.

Feldman, M. S. and J. G. March, (1981). Information in organizations as signal and symbol. *Administrative Science Quarterly 26,* 171–186.

Foerstel, Herbert N. (1991). *Surveillance in the stacks: the FBI's library awareness program.* Westport, Conn., Greenwood.

Ford, Nigel (1991). *Expert systems and artificial intelligence: an information manager's guide.* London, Library Association Publishing.

Garfield, Eugene (1979). *Citation indexing: its theory and application in science, technology and humanities.* New York, Wiley.

Gey, Fredric C. (1992). Networked resource sharing of CD-ROM information banks. *ASIS 1992 Mid-Year Meeting: Networks, telecommunications and the networked information revolution.* Silver Spring, Maryland, ASIS, pp. 114–123.

Griffiths, Jose-Marie, and Donald King, (1991). *The evaluation of information centres and services.* London, North Atlantic Treaty Organisation, Advisory Group for Aerospace Research Development (AGARD).

Gwinn, Nancy E., and Paul H. Mosher, (1983). Coordinating collection development: the RLG Conspectus. *College and Research Libraries 44,* 128–140.

Hax, Arnoldo, and Nicholas S. Majluf, (1984). Strategic management: an integrative perspective. Englewood Cliffs, New Jersey, Prentice-Hall.

Hayes, R. M., and T. Erickson, (1982). Added value as a function of purchases of information services. *The Information Society 1*(4), 307–338

Hedstrom, Margaret (1991). Archives: to be or not to be: a commentary. *In* David Bearman, Ed., *Archival management of electronic records.* Archives and Museum Informatics Technical report, no. 13, 25–30.

Hunt, R. and C. N. G. Dampney, (1990). *Future management of information systems: a Delphi study of Australian industry.* North Ryde, New South Wales, Macquarie University.

Intner, Sheila S., and Jorge R. Schement, (1987). The ethic of free service. *Library Journal 112*(6), 50–52.

Itami, H. (1989). Mobilising invisible assets: the key for successful corporate strategy. *In* E. Punset, and G. Sweeney, Eds., *Information resources and corporate growth*. London, Pinter, pp. 36–46.

Katz, Steven L., and David Plocher, (1989). Federal information policy development: a citizen's perspective. *In* Charles R. McClure, Peter Hernon, and Harold C. Relyea, Eds., *United States Government information policies: views and perspectives*. Norwood, New Jersey, Ablex, pp. 115–138.

Kent, Allen *et al.*, (1979). *Use of library materials: the University of Pittsburgh study*. New York, Dekker.

King, Donald W. and Nancy K. Roderer, (1979). Information transfer cost/benefit analysis. In *Information and industry*. Proceedings of the North Atlantic Treaty Organization, Advisory Group for Aerospace Research and Development (AGARD) Technical Information Panel's Specialists' meeting, 1978. Neuilly-sur-Seine, AGARD. (AGARD CP-246).

King, Donald W., Jose-Marie Griffiths, Nancy K. Roderer, and Robert Weiderkehr, (1982). *Value of the energy data base*. Work performed under Contract No. A105–800R11232. Rockville, Maryland, King Research, Inc. Submitted to Technical Information Center, U.S. Department of Energy, Oak Ridge, Tennessee.

Kirby, Michael (1987). New technology and international privacy issues. *In* Trevor Barr, Ed., *Challenges and change: Australia's information society* Melbourne, Oxford University Press, pp. 146–158.

Kirwin, Florence (1979). *Community analysis of the Pitkin County Library*. Aspen Colorado. February. (ERIC ED 176776).

Koenig, M.E.D. (1990). Information services and downstream productivity. *Annual Review of Information Science and Technology 25,* 55–86.

Lamberton, D. M. (1984). The economics of information and organization. *Annual Review of Information Science and Technology 19,* 3–30.

Lamberton, D. M. (1989). The regional information economy: its measurement and significance. *In* E. Punset, and G. Sweeney, Eds., *Information resources and corporate growth*. London, Pinter, pp. 16–25.

Levitan, Karen B. (1982). Information resources as "goods" in the life cycle of information production. *Journal of the American Society for Information Science 33*(1), 44–54.

Library of Congress Network Advisory Committee. (1989). Intellectual property issues in the library network context: proceedings of the meeting, March 23–25 1988. Washington, Library of Congress. (Network planning paper no. 17).

Line, Maurice B. (1991). Libraries and knowledge. *In* A. J. Meadows, Ed., *Knowledge and communication: essays on the information chain*. London, Library Association Publishing, pp. 77–89.

Lucas, Thomas A. (1990). Verifying the Conspectus: problems and progress. *College & Research Libraries News 51*(3), 199–201.

Machlup, F. (1979a). An economist's reflections on an Institute for the Advanced Study of Information Science. *Journal of the American Society for Information Science 30*(2), 111–113.

Machlup, F. (1979b). Uses, value, and benefits of information. *Knowledge: Creation, Diffusion, Utilization 1,* 62–81.

Machlup, F. (1983). Semantic quirks in studies of information. *In* F. Machlup and U. Mansfield, Eds., *The study of information: interdisciplinary messages*. New York, Wiley, pp. 641–671.

Machlup, F., and Mansfield, U., Eds. (1983). *The study of information: interdisciplinary messages*. New York, Wiley.

Maguire, C., A. D. Weir, and L. Wood, (1987). Scientific and technological information: its use and supply in Australia. Canberra, Department of Science, Scientific Development Division.
Maguire, C., and P. Willard, (1990). Performance measures for libraries: statistical, organizational and cosmetic. *Australian Academic and Research Libraries, 21*(4), 262–273.
Martin, W. J., C. A. Davies, and A. J. Titterington, (1991). Marketing the concept of information management to top executives. *Journal of Information Science 17,* 209–220.
Mason, Marilyn Gell (1988). Copyright in context: the OCLC database. *Library Journal 113*(12), 31–34.
Matarazzo, J. M., L. Prusak and M. R. Gauthier, (1990). *Valuing corporate libraries: a survey of senior managers.* Washington, D.C., Special Libraries Association in cooperation with Temple, Barker & Sloane, Inc.
McCrank, L. J. (1986). The impact of automation: integrating archival and bibliographic systems, *Journal of Library Administration* 7(2/3), 61–98.
McLuhan, Marshall (1962). *The Gutenberg galaxy: the making of typographic man.* Toronto, University of Toronto Press.
McLuhan, Marshall (1964). *Understanding media: the extensions of man.* London, Routledge & Kegan Paul.
MEDLINE to become available on Lockheed. (1980). *On-line Review 4,* pp. 411–412.
Meadows, A. J., (1991). Introduction. In A. J. Meadows, Ed., *Knowledge and communication: essays on the information chain.* London, Library Association Publishing.
Michelson, Avra (1987). Description and reference in the age of automation. *American Archivist 50,* 192–208.
Miles, Ian (1989). Information needs for the information economy. *International Journal of Information Management 9,* 275–288).
National Commission on Libraries and Information Science. (1982). *Public sector/private sector interaction in providing information services: report to the NCLIS from the Public Sector/Private Sector Task Force.* Chairman: Robert M. Hayes. Washington, D.C., Government Printing Office.
Neill, S. D. (1987). The dilemma of the subjective in information organization and retrieval. *Journal of Documentation 43*(3) 193–211.
Office of Technology Assessment, (1986). *Intellectual property rights in an age of electronics and information.* Washington, D.C., Office of Technology Assessment of the United States Congress.
Oldman, C. (1977) Marketing library and information services. *European Journal of Marketing 11*(6), 460–474.
Oldman, C., and G. Wills, (1977). *The beneficial library.* Bradford, MCB Publications.
O'Leary, Mick (1991). DIALOG and the American Chemical Society play a high stakes game. *Online 15*(1), 15–20.
The ownership of bibliographic data—OCLC's experience: a symposium. (1985). *Journal of Academic Librarianship 11*(4), 196–205.
Parker, E. (1981). Information services and economic growth *The Information Society 1*(1), 71–78.
Pearce, D., A. Markandaya, and E. Barbier, (1991). *Blueprint for a green economy.* London, Earthscan.
Peter, J. Paul, and Jerry C. Olson, (1983). Is science marketing? *Journal of Marketing 47,* 111–125.
Postman, Neil (1992). *Technopoly: the surrender of culture to technology.* New York, Knopf, pp. 63–119.
Project Quartet. (1990). Bill Tuck, Cliff McKnight, Marie Hayet and David Archer, Aus. London, British Library Research and Development Department. (Library and information research report no. 76)

Prusak, Laurence, and James Matarazzo, (1992). *Information management and Japanese success.* New York, Special Libraries Association.

Quint, Barbara (1990). Conflicting trends. *Wilson Library Bulletin 65*(4), 96–102.

Schieber, Phil (1992). Online Journal of Current Clinical Trials begins electronic publication. *OCLC Newsletter 198,* 33–34.

Schumann, Patricia Glass (1992). Cynicism, euphemisms, and seductive hyperbole about privatization. *American Libraries 23*(1), 189.

Sherwood, Diane (1990). Welcome to the Republic of Information. *Information Today* 7(5), 40–41.

Simon, H. A. (1971). Designing organization for an information-rich world. In M. Greenberger, Ed., *Computers, communications, and the public interest.* Baltimore, Maryland, Johns Hopkins Press, pp. 38–52.

Sproull, Lee, and Sara Kiesler (1991). *Connections: new ways of working in the networked organization.* Cambridge, Massachusetts, MIT Press.

Stinchcombe, A. L. (1990). *Information and organizations.* Berkeley, University of California Press.

Taylor, Robert S. (1986). *Value-added processes in information systems.* Norwood, New Jersey, Ablex.

Thibodeau, Kenneth (1991). To be or not to be: archives for electronic records. *In* David Bearman, Ed., *Archival management of electronic records.* Archives and Museum Informatics Technical report, no. 13, 1–13.

Tucci, V. K. (1988). Information marketing for libraries. *Annual Review of Information Science and Technology (ARIST) 23,* 59–82.

Van Dyk, M. T. (1992). ROMOTE: an off-campus dial-up service for CD-ROM databases. *Lasie 22*(6), 148–155.

Vespasiano, da Bisticci (1963). *Renaissance princes, popes and prelates: the Vespasiano memoirs: lives of illustrious men of the XVth century.* Translated by W. George and E. Waters. New York, Harper and Row.

Vickery, Brian, and Alina Vickery (1987). *Information science in theory and practice.* London, Butterworth.

Wells, H. G. (1938). *World brain.* Garden City, New York, Doubleday.

White, Blake L. (1988). *The technology assessment process: a strategic framework for managing technical information.* New York, Quorum Books.

Zuboff, Shoshana (1988). *In the age of the smart machine: the future of work and power.* New York, Basic Books.

4

Information Sources for Innovation

It is striking, though, how often innovators are those firms that are simply looking in the right places, unencumbered by or unconcerned with conventional wisdom.

—M. Porter, *The Competitive Advantage of Nations,* p. 48. Reprinted with the permission of The Macmillan Press Ltd. and The Free Press, a division of Macmillan, Inc. from *The Competitive Advantage of Nations* by Michael E. Porter. Copyright © 1990 by Michael E. Porter.

Proactive search for technical and market inputs, as well as receptivity to information sensed from external sources, are critical aspects of technology-based innovation.

—E. B. Roberts (1988, *Managing Invention and Innovation,* p. 13)

By drawing information from a wide cross-section of sources—banks, academia, the mass media, industry and labor—Japan's system of industrial policy making averts the danger of making major errors in judgment owing to bottlenecks in information flow.

—D. I. Okimoto, *Between MITI and the Market: Japanese Industrial Policy for High Technology,* p. 34.

Viewed as a system of information collection and dissemination, Japan's system of industrial policies may have been among the most important factors in Japan's high rate of industrial growth.

—R. Komiya, "Planning in Japan", in *Economic Planning, East and West,* p. 221. Copyright © 1975 Harper Collins.

Chapter Synopsis

The sources of information relevant to innovation are explored in this chapter. For this exploration, sources are categorized as far as possible according to whether they reside inside or outside the organization. Examples are offered of some of the notable and diverse attempts that have been made by governments, often in coalition with industry, to spread innovation benefits by transferring technology and diffusing new products, processes, and services. We have chosen to refer to these as information resource systems.

This chapter identifies agents and agencies through which information services are delivered in organizations and discusses their roles in general and in relation to particular services in different countries. These agents and agencies, which may be regarded as both sources and channels of information, are classified first according to their location within or outside the organization, and second by the functions they serve. Descriptions are recorded of some of the experiences accumulated by the agencies in diffusing innovations. From these stories, some of the innovations that the agencies have themselves adopted in the transfer of information also emerge incidentally and allow them to offer services with added value.

4.1 Introduction

The quotations at the opening of this chapter suggest that looking in the right places for information is important in successful innovation, whether the search may be so much a part of the organizational culture as to appear serendipitous or so energetic as to be a marked feature of organizational and even national strategy. As has been pointed out in Chapter 2, innovation is a complex process in which many elements interact. In technology transfer, for example, there are many other elements involved besides an awareness of technological opportunity. After a technology is identified, some mechanism must be used to acquire it, such as internal R & D effort, a joint venture, a license, an assignment, or a manufacturing, supply, distribution, or franchising agreement. A clear distinction is therefore preserved throughout the chapter between the sources from which individuals or organizations learn of the existence of ideas, attitudes, products, processes, and services previously unknown to them and the reaching of decisions on whether and how to go about acquisition of a particular technology whether it is to be applied to a product, process, or service. Thus the patent system and patent alert databases will be mentioned as sources of information about new technologies and about the people and firms with expertise in particular technologies. Much less attention is given to those aspects of information management concerned with negotiation of the licenses, secrecy agreements, and so on, through which patented technology may be bought, sold, protected, and exploited. While this book makes no attempt to give advice on such matters, the discussion of information sources and information flow offers some implications for preferred policies in the formulation of corporate strategies regarding joint ventures, takeovers, and so on, through which organizations may also acquire technology.

Throughout the chapter, the emphasis tends to be on group behavior and, whether explicitly or not, on probabilities of behavior. Just as no one person can represent the total mind of an organization, neither can generalizations about organizations, or the average behavior of members of a social class, or of a trade or profession, represent every individual behavior. In all empirical research there is the temptation to collect data true to a particular place at a particular time and then to attempt to apply findings universally. There is also the danger, in attempting to make sense of such research, that empirical evidence will be accumulated however disparate the sample characteristics and the environments in which the projects have been carried out. Care is taken in this chapter to give enough of the background of the quoted studies to allow readers to make their own judgments regarding the generalizations proposed. The diversity within as among organizations is part of the rationale for this book's argument that flexibility and proliferation of options for accessibility mark the most effective information systems and services.

4.2

Categorizing Sources of Information

In Chapter 3 we noted that the concept of information sources entails two connotations: the stores in which information resides, such as an object, person, or place; and the channels through which it is distributed. As discussed in Chapter 3 (pp. 76–77), differentiation between source and channel, or message and medium, is hard to maintain. Thus, in this chapter the information sources and channels are differentiated only when it is necessary to remind ourselves, for example, that members of the organization often act as channels for information from sources outside the organization. In general, our position is that of Levitan, already quoted in Chapter 3, namely that "information reflects the synergistic combination of medium and message" (Levitan, 1982, p. 48).

Discussion of the sources of information for innovation in organizations could be structured in many ways, and from many perspectives. This book attempts a global view in which all providers and consumers of information services are included, rather than a partial view in which the perspective is limited to any particular specialist group, whether chief executives, financial managers, librarians, information system managers, professional practitioners, researchers, or records managers. There are several ways of structuring a review of sources that fit in with this global approach. One is according to whether the sources are internal or external to the organization; another is according to whether they are formal or informal. A sectoral approach could be adopted, according to which industrial, governmental, educational, or public service activities were covered. A cross-sectoral approach could seek to look at sources by category of innovation. Another possibility is to structure the review according to the stage of the process of adoption of innovation involved.

In the internal and external approach, sources of information are divided between those that are available within the organization and those from outside. The extremes of this approach may be seen in some organizations where the accounting section is responsible almost entirely for collection, analysis, and diffusion of internal information, and the library is responsible almost entirely for external information. One criticism of this approach is that the dichotomy is hard to sustain because individuals within the organization, such as managerial boundary riders and technological gatekeepers, are constantly bringing information from outside sources, and thus such information can then be assumed to be internal.

Using the formal and informal approach, information sources are organized according to whether they yield formal data, such as in print format, or informal, interactive, usually oral communication. In fact, except for formal lectures, formal could be taken as coextensive with impersonal and informal with personal sources. But the same argument could hold true with the division between internal and external in determining the fast boundaries between formal and informal. Formal and informal sources of information are essentially interdependent, and in communication systems such as electronic mail, the messages may surely be either formal or informal.

Categorization of sources by the sectoral approach could be based on the Parker (1976) and Porat classification (1977), in which economic activities are divided among extraction (mining and agriculture), manufacturing (including construction), tangible services (such as transport and retailing), and information services (including banking, insurance, and education). In the cross-sectoral approach a review of sources could be adopted by division of innovations across all sectors into new products and processes, new services, and management changes. And in the innovation adoption process, information sources could be reviewed by looking at sources under the five headings of awareness, interest, evaluation, trial, and adoption.

Neither the sectoral nor the cross-sectoral approaches are adopted in this review. Both these call for perspectives that focus on phenomena related more to differences in organizational context than to the similarities in organizational dynamics that facilitate the study of conditions for innovation as a universal phenomenon.

The question arises as to the relationship of information sources viewed from the three perspectives preferred here, which are the internal–

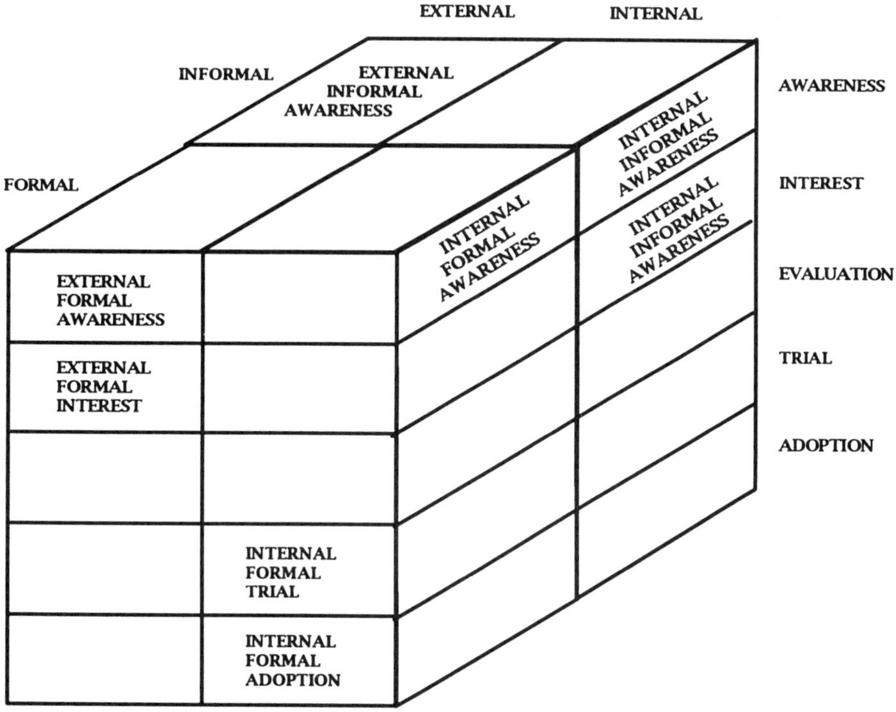

Figure 4.1
Information sources matrix (20 cells; samples completed).

external, the formal–informal, and the five stages of the innovation adoption process. This relationship can be illustrated by the examples provided in Figure 4.1.

Each approach that has been mentioned provides only one cut across the possibilities of information sources. In the chart in Figure 4.1 each cell represents an example of an information source. For example, one cell represents a formal, external source, used in the interest phase. If a sectoral approach was to be adopted, as suggested in Figure 4.2, the source can then be further defined as to whether it is, for example, a new service in the sector of information services, such as banking. A specific example of this might be a written report (formal) generated by a governmental agency (external) for the purpose of informing management who want information (interest) relating to the use of home information systems (new service) used in the banking industry.

While this structure helps isolate many different segments of informa-

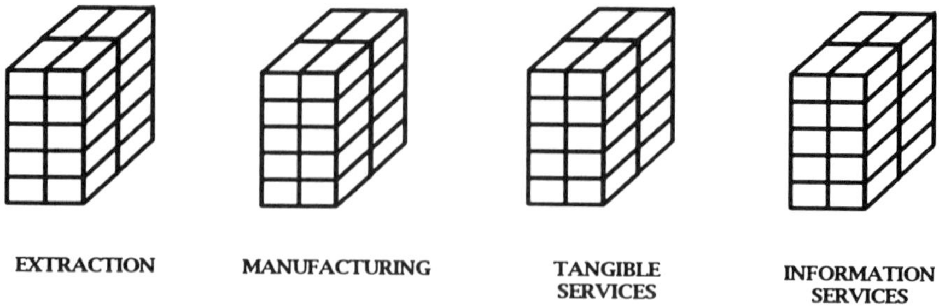

Figure 4.2
Information sources matrix divided by sectoral approach.

tion sources, our purpose is to provide some categorization that can provide an easy basis for discussion. Thus, from our viewpoint the categorization of sources according to whether they are internal or external appears the most appropriate. This approach has been used in the literature and the concept is most applicable as the first cut for the broadest spectrum of organizations. And the underlying point is that, as necessary, the other means of categorization may be subsumed under this discussion.

4.3 Categories of Information Sources

A number of researchers have outlined possible categories of internal and external information. Kono (1988) provides a list of important information necessary to decide on a product concept and to generate ideas for successful new products. Kono was presenting contrasting results between the companies he classified as high performance and low performance. His quantitative results have little meaning outside the context of his survey, although it is interesting to remark that a lesser proportion of the low performance companies made use of all but two or three of the sources listed. Kono's list is reproduced as Table 4.1 without the percentage results. The items listed are many and varied. They are also helpful in framing our discussion of the sources from which information for innovation may be obtained.

A study conducted by Keller of the Industrial Technology Institute of Ann Arbor, Michigan, provides a measurement of information activity of a population of manufacturers who responded to a questionnaire (Keller, 1986). Her study indicates that technical and product information is critical to this group. Respondents also relied heavily on information from

Table 4.1
Sources of Important Information Necessary to Generate Successful New Product Ideas and to Decide on Product Concept

Survey of growth areas by own company
Published forecasts on growth areas
Long-term forecasts on industry structure
Long-term forecasts on technology
Special market research to find needs
Survey of the actual usage of related products
Survey of deficiency of present products
Information on materials and new materials
Information on substitutes
Claims, customer cards
Reports and suggestions of salesmen
Information from sales channels and trading companies
Interviews with consumers
Information from monitors
Information from trade periodicals
Information from suppliers
Newspapers, periodicals, government publications
Successful products of foreign companies and other companies
New product development trends among competitors
Observation of related products in exhibitions or in the stores
Information on patents
Articles in academic periodicals
Scientific information in trade publications, newspapers, periodicals, and government publications
Papers of academic meetings and conferences
Opinions of experts on technology
Opinions of experts on the use of products
Trends in competitors' research
Trends in the economy and politics overseas
Economic trends in the domestic area
Trends in government policies
Trends in important resources
Strength and weakness of research capabilities of own company
Strength and weakness of marketing capabilities of own company
Strength and weakness of production capabilities of own company
Information from testing of new product

Source: Adapted from Kono, 1988, pp. 139–140.

journals and on information provided by colleagues. Keller provides lists of information types used by this group, including names of people, telephone numbers, intelligence reports, technological forecasts, product evaluations, bibliographic references, and conference details. Also included in her study is a list of communication mechanisms used by this group, such as person-to-person contacts, the grapevine, memos, newsletters, staff meetings, and electronic mail systems.

From his study of United States and Japanese researchers in high technology firms, Cutler (1989) provides a list of the principal technology transfer mechanisms, and they are definitely information laden. These include meetings, seminars, and intensive conferences; professional society meetings; journal publications and newsletters; international conferences; advisory boards, councils and committees; study missions, site visits and trade shows; patent and licensing agreements; consulting arrangements; joint university and industry research projects; and visiting scientists and resident researchers (Cutler, 1989).

Link and Tassey (1987) list internal and external sources of technology-related intelligence to support R & D. Their list includes the following external sources: formal and informal interactions among peers; information obtained at meetings, seminars, and conferences; information gathered during study missions; customers, especially important if R & D is market-driven rather than technology-driven; technical equipment suppliers; consulting firms; universities; publications and information database systems; and governmental agencies and laboratories. Internal sources include internal peer groups, such as the planning and marketing personnel; new employees who previously worked for competitors; and reverse engineering of competitors' products (Link and Tassey, 1987).

From the literature generally and from the studies just discussed, important sources of information for innovation emerge as:

1. Internal Sources
    a. Peers (formal and informal interactions) including those in other departments of the organization, for example planning and marketing personnel for R & D staff (includes information from customers and suppliers formalized internally through groups such as marketing).
    b. New employees
    c. Internally generated data and reports
2. External Sources
    a. Peers (formal and informal interactions)
    b. Meetings, seminars, conferences, study missions
    c. Publications
    d. Electronic information services

Collaborative efforts among groups such as universities, governmental agencies, laboratories, consulting firms, and other such agencies are discussed later in this chapter.

4.4 Internal Sources

4.4.1 Internal Peers

In any organization internal peers can include co-workers or colleagues in the same unit or individuals within other units, such as marketing and planning groups. An important ingredient for innovation is information flow among peers—peers are also probably the most common source for information. Peers may be located within or outside the organization in which one works. Members of the same occupational group in one's own and other organizations and members of the same organization at the same hierarchical level may be regarded as peers. Along with many other observers, Mailloux (1989) has noticed that engineers, after first using their own knowledge base, tend to turn to peers and co-workers as sources of information, rather than to the literature. Similarly, Krikelas (1983) describes various studies, such as that by Prentice (1980), which indicate that the most common source of information is a co-worker.

Information flow among peers can be informal, such as when individuals meet to discuss a solution to a problem or in casual conversation of nonspecific topics of mutual interest. There are often also formal groupings arranged for specific organizational purposes, such as new product teams, in which people from different departments of an organization and from different disciplines are brought together in the hope that they will not only achieve specified project goals but also develop peer relationships in doing so. Some of the barriers and gateways to communication in organizations have been discussed in Chapter 3 (section 3.1.4) and other aspects of communications among different groups in organizations are raised in section 4.6 of this chapter.

4.4.2 New Employees

New employees, whether they have previously worked for competitors or for other units of the same organization, have been recognized as important sources of innovative ideas. Rogers (1982) noted that it was not only shortage of skilled personnel that accounted for the high rate of job mobility among semiconductor professionals in the Silicon Valley. A second important reason was "the desire to obtain technical information from a competing company" (p. 116). Rogers concluded that "'Head hunting' in the Silicon Valley can be a Machiavellian game of byzantine strategies and counterstrategies, with the exchange of technical information as one of its purposes" (p. 117).

The movement of personnel has long since been identified as an important vehicle for the importation of new information and new ideas into industrial firms. Internal transfers have also been viewed as beneficial in bringing new ideas to bear in the different sections of an organization. The utility of information embodied in people who can interact, explain, demonstrate, and argue hardly needs further discussion. But the importance of such invisible assets is a point to which we will return in Chapter 6, offering guidance for the design of effective information systems and services to promote innovation.

4.4.3 Internally Generated Data and Reports

Discussion of the data and reports generated internally as sources of information for organizations needs to be prefixed by acknowledgement of the turbulence brought about in information management in organizations mainly through the changes in information technology. Ten years ago, faculty of the Harvard Business School wrote of "the information archipelago" in organizations (McKenney and McFarlan, 1982; McFarlan and McKenney 1983; McFarlan *et al.*, 1983). The three islands that made up the archipelago were in fact islands of information technology: office automation, telecommunications, and data processing. The authors regarded these as information services, in the sense that they are tools that members of the organization can use to manage information. The articles urged integrated management and set out the principles by which companies should operate to resolve the two main conflicts likely to arise. The first was identified as that between innovation and control, and the second as that "between the IS [information services] department and users in developing skills for dealing with the new technology and in setting priorities" (McFarlan *et al.*, 1983, p. 91).

One resolution of the latter argument suggested by the authors depended on the extent to which the sharing of data was necessary among different divisions or departments of the corporation. The more such interdependence exists, the more the corporate database approach has merit. They defined the corporate database in loose terms as "a collection of files at a central location for reference by multiple users" (McFarlan *et al.*, 1983, p. 96). The information archipelago articles also make the point, which much subsequent history has reinforced, of the impossibility of telling where the application of an information technology may lead.

One of the stories told to illustrate this point was as follows:

> A large grocery chain acquired a system of point-of-sales terminals. The retail division bought these terminals (with the support of the IS manager) to help store managers control inventory. Once installed, however, the systems evolved quickly into links to central headquarters, which used the data to modify forecasting, measure advertising effectiveness, and manage warehouse stock levels for the whole chain. This linkage is seen by all involved as providing significant value added.
>
> This unplanned linkage was very expensive because the communication protocols in the terminals were incompatible with those in the computers at headquarters. No planning for compatibility had been undertaken, since the retail division had not intended to use the computers in this way when it had bought its terminals. Further, even if the organization had considered such use, management probably would have seen the costs of the resulting system as prohibitive (McFarlan *et al.*, 1983, p. 92).

McFarlan *et al.* (1983) remark that this and other cited examples "illustrate that it is often impossible to foresee and plan for the full range of consequences before introducing IS technology and that excessive control and a focus on quick results in the early stages can inhibit learning about a system" (p. 92). There is also in the examples cited evidence of the digital information undertow, which, as has been discussed in Chapter 3 (Section 3.2) tends to escape if not to subvert attempts at management and control as well as prediction of its direction.

The information archipelago articles proposed a much more centralized solution than has proved possible, again at least partly through underestimation of the capacity of digital information systems to subvert centralized authority. McKenney and McFarlan, (1982) saw the future thus:

> In summary, at present a number of organization patterns are possible as companies move toward adopting and combining all information services. This heterogeneity is transitional, and most businesses will eventually merge management of these islands under one organization, certainly for policymaking, planning, and control—and in many settings for line control and execution. The timing of these moves in any organization depends on such factors as corporate structure and leadership style, the speed at which a company usually adopts new technologies, flexibility in staff assignments (for example, to remove deadwood), and current development priorities (p. 113).

In fact, the last decade has seen the rise and fall of both the information center and the CIO (chief information officer). Carlyle (1989) reports the results of a survey in which "What CIOs say they are really victims of . . . are unsympathetic corporate cultures, uncertain job expectations and the stigmas attached to IS because it is an immature discipline" (p. 12). One of the other causes of the lessening of centralized IS power in organizations is identified as outsourcing, of which Carlyle remarks: "This off-loading trend started in the federal government and is now spreading to state and local governments, as well as into the commercial sector" (p. 13). And he adds to the list of causes of breakdown of centralized control end-user control of IS dollars and computer-aided software engineering (CASE) tools. All this has added up to "a shift in the locus of responsibility for IS within companies to independent business units and line organizations" (Carlyle, 1989, p. 15).

White and Christy (1987) reported that "the principal current concern of corporate information centers is the support and management of end-user computing," (p. 451) but "They are noticeably deficient when it comes to establishing overall goals and objectives, measuring performance, setting up adequate control and security mechanisms (including audit trails), educating end-users in control and security techniques, providing advanced training and support, and coordinating end-user application development efforts" (p. 457). If this assessment is just, the corporate information center, as tried in the 1980s, cannot be rated either as a useful source of information or infrastructure for the production of internal information.

On the other hand, the difficulties in establishing any section of an organization as a reliable information source for others are notorious. Gupta and Wilemon (1988) point to the problems in communication between R & D and marketing personnel. After a study of eighty companies, they remarked that:

> Unfortunately, communication between R & D and marketing managers is impeded because R & D would like clear, unambiguous and precise answers to what new product characteristics potential customers will demand and at what price, while marketing, on the other hand, would like R & D to freeze their new product as soon as possible to facilitate market exploration, testing and business planning. Both groups seek to gain certainty from the other while retaining the option of being uncertain themselves (p. 41).

The conflict in aims between marketing and technical staff came out in another study of communication. A former marketing manager in the Australian food industry complained to Maguire and Lovelace that:

> The problem with technical people is that they often want to improve the product, without recognizing the fact that consumers may prefer the "worse" product. For example, the technical people managed to make a chicken noodle soup without MSG (monosodium glutamate) but the public didn't like it. The technical people actually slipped the change in without telling marketing (Maguire and Lovelace, 1988, p. 41).

Gladstein and Caldwell (1985) argue strongly that the importance of management of the boundaries between groups in organizations has been overlooked in favor of concentration on decision making within groups.

		Direction of Information and Resource Flow	
		In	Out
Who Initiates the Transaction	Group	SCOUT	AMBASSADOR
	External Agents	SENTRY	GUARD

Figure 4.3
Boundary roles in groups (source: Gladstein and Caldwell, 1985, p. 162).

Their particular reference is to the effectiveness of new product teams, for which the boundary roles that they suggest are shown in Figure 4.3.

In these roles, "The scout brings information or resources needed by the group in across the boundary" while "The ambassador role involves carrying information, resources, or other outputs that the group chooses to transmit to others" (p. 162). Another role, that of the sentry, protects the group from intrusive information. "The sentry polices the boundary by controlling the information and resources that external agents want to send into the group, acting as a filter deciding who can give input, how much of that input will be admitted, and when the flow of input must stop. The sentry protects the group by allowing it to work with minimal distraction." The guard, on the other hand, "monitors the information and resources that others request from the group and determines what the group will release in response to these demands" (p. 163).

The roles are of course, even in a small group, not necessarily played by any one person, nor is any one member of the group likely to be limited to only one role. On the larger stage it may be argued that the organization as a whole also needs to have these roles played in relation to the environment in which it operates. (One of the authors who worked there at the time recalls that a factor in the failure of the ground-breaking library automation at Florida Atlantic University in the mid 1960s was the number of visitors who came to see what was going on. The lack of an organizational sentry was felt especially in the winter months. The publicity about the library automation project generated by the university's public affairs office in national and international news sources was only too effective.) Examination of the external sources of information for innovation suggests that the scout, ambassador, sentry, and guard roles are indeed played, although their tracing may prove difficult in the labyrinth of connections through which an organization exchanges information with its environment.

Before entering into discussion of sources external to the organization, we should note that almost all organizations have another artery of information: one dealing with accounts. Subsidiary parts (divisions) report annually, monthly, or even daily on their income and expenditure, always with the stated aim that central management can get a picture of the financial health of the organization. But this is a formal channel, and almost always operates strongly only in one direction, carrying information to the center. In some organizations, financial controls of this type dominate managers' thinking, acting as an incentive for divisions to concentrate on making the short-term figures look good. This charge was, for example, made about ITT in the 1970s (Sampson, 1973). This of course acts as a great disincentive to innovation in anything other than accounting practices.

Likewise, formal divisional contributions to the organization's annual report do little in themselves to foster communication between separate divisions such as R & D and marketing. Neither do corporate plans, however glossy, unless they come after or immediately before wide consultation and are thus offering a formal expression of what is already, or soon will be, the informal culture of the organization.

4.5 External Sources

One of the effects of the information management revolution in organizations in the last twenty years has been to lessen the control that managers can exercise over contact that members of an organization can have with external sources. In public bureaucracies, especially up to and beyond World War II, regulation was often in force that all correspondence had to be addressed to the chief officer and that all outgoing correspondence went out under his (and it was, of course, his not her) name. As organizations grew, the chief officer's signature was increasingly a rubber stamp with initials added by duly authorized members of the organization empowered to sign for him. The first heavy salvo to breach this control was the telephone, whereon employees soon transacted business and could not be monitored, nor could the letters they drafted to external sources. Now access to facsimile machines, end-user computing, and local and wide area networking open the way for exchange of information with external sources so easily and informally in ways that leave so little trace that this alone makes shaky our attempt to draw a firm line between internal and external sources of information. It also, of course, makes it much harder to keep organizational secrets.

4.5.1 Peers and the Importance of Informal Sources

There are many groups external to an organization in which peers of individuals within the organization are likely to reside. These can include, as indicated previously, individuals and groups in other firms who have similar education, interests, and positions. Contacts with peers are often made and sustained through professional society membership, conference attendance, and similar activities in which opportunities for professional, business, and social contacts are intermingled. Leadership in peer groups is established on reputations built through publications, speeches, and professional activities, such as membership of ad hoc and standing committees.

The phenomenon of the *invisible college* was first noticed in a study of communication patterns among scientists. In an invisible college the scientific community communicates through a personal network of colleagues and contacts prior to the dissemination of information through publications or meeting presentations. Crane (1972) defines an invisible college as a "network of productive scientists linking separate groups of collaborators within a research area" (p. 54). Over the years the term has sometimes been extended to refer loosely to the personal networks that all members of information-based occupations have and through which we exchange ideas, whether in a meeting of academic minds or in some of the "information trading" already discussed in Chapter 2 (p. 62). The role of the *gatekeeper* in the transmission of technical information within R & D laboratories, which was first noticed by Allen (1977), has also been mentioned in Chapter 2 (p. 55). This role can operate both in scanning the environment external to the organization and in scanning the rest of the organization for information relevant to the work or project group. Thus the gatekeeper adopts a role close to that of the scout in the Gladstein and Caldwell (1985) table set out in Figure 4.3, though it has been argued that gatekeepers have natural affinity for this role and possess personality traits that motivate them to participate in many groups and in more information-gathering activities than their peers.

The gathering of information through peers is a method for acquiring information that is preferred by many individuals as their primary source. The reasons are obvious in terms of immediacy, interaction, shared frames of reference, and so on. And the empirical literature confirms the preference. In a discussion of information seeking behaviors, Krikelas (1983) notes that when individuals turn to external sources for information they tend to seek person-to-person contact. Manufacturers in the survey by Keller (1986) alleged that their most common need for information was for names of individuals who could assist in solving a problem. In a review of the literature dealing with engineering information systems, Mailloux (1989) notes that engineers tend first to use their own knowledge base consisting of experience, personal files, vendor data, and the like. If this is inadequate, they then tend to turn to co-workers and peers, rather than to the literature. Cutler (1989) in a study of the high-technology transfer practices among Japanese and United States researchers in the fields of robotics, biotechnology, and ceramic materials, already referred to on page 148, points to the fact that their preferred method of information gathering is through person-to-person contacts. He states that "the most preferred and also the most effective technology transfer mechanisms are people-intensive rather than paper-intensive," and that "this effort amounts to approximately two-thirds of the effort." His conclusion is that high-technology transfer is primarily a "contact sport" (Cutler, 1989, p. 21). This conclusion could have been drawn much earlier, at least for the United States semiconductor and solar engineering industries, from Everett Rogers' 1982 study of information transfer among Silicon Valley firms (Rogers, 1982).

There are, however, problems associated with too much dependence on peers as sources of information. In a group of Australian social workers in a hospital agency, relationships were strong with professional peers in other hospitals but weak with the medical experts outranking them in the hospital hierarchy. Information on which to base counseling of parents of children with birth defects tended to be derived from peers with whom the social workers could communicate easily rather than from medical specialists in their own hospital, even when the specialists were known to be particularly knowledgable of the medical condition involved (Maguire *et al.*, 1976).

In business and industry peer contact may not give adequate coverage of information. At a meeting on United States competitiveness at the Congressional Research Service of the Library of Congress discussion highlighted the need for United States business and industry to access foreign research and technology. The problem noted was that the United States does not use available information. One of the main issues raised was that it is less common for individuals to have peer contacts in other countries whom they could contact for information. It was noted, for example, that engineers in the United States do not read much and use the gatekeeper concept more, making use of both external and internal peers in doing so. This report suggests that while this approach may have been fine in the past it will not serve today with the rise of an international literature and global competition (Change the Way You Think about Using Information, 1988).

The acquisition of adequate information typically requires multiple sources. Brown and Karagozoglu (1989) indicate the importance of flow of external and internal data in technological innovation. However, information flow, through the literature, in patents, and other formal, impersonal sources, by itself is not adequate in achieving major innovation. The need for person-to-person communication in passing on the know-how associated with most technology transfer has long been identified in the literature. The importance of tacit knowledge was brought out in a study of the building of one of the early laser systems by Collins (1974). Intensive study of work in automated environments by Zuboff (1988) has confirmed the importance of tacit knowledge in all types of work.

Emphasis on informality in communications reinforces the familiar wisdom about the importance of informal networks in information transfer. Perhaps we should remind ourselves that informal sources of information have also long been recognized by marketing specialists as important in takeup of product innovations by consumers. Engel *et al.* (1981) wrote: "Word-of-mouth, or personal, communications play a critical role in the adoption of new products . . . Traditionally, it has been postulated that as an individual moves through early stages and toward adoption, the individual increasingly turns to other individuals for confirming information" (pp. 479–480). An Australian study asked 69 technical managers in industry which of their sources of scientific and technological information they would be most reluctant to give up. Personal contacts were nominated by 19 (28%) of managers but 14 (20%) of the managers insisted that both formal and informal sources of information were vital to them and that they would answer the question only on this basis. As the technical manager in a new biotechnology company put it: "All [sources] are important—insufficient informal leads to missed formal information" (Maguire *et al.* 1987, p. 53).

As in other countries, peer groups are important sources of information for Japanese business and industry and their effectiveness may be enhanced by other features of Japanese corporate society. As Itami (1988) has pointed out, the Japanese corporate system is quite amenable to the accumulation of technological information. The social organization of the Japanese corporate system fosters this through long-term employment and this, in turn, fosters the development of strong personal information networks, both inter- and intra-firm based.

The Japanese have also organized opportunities to help small firms compensate for their lack of internal sources of information, especially R & D information, by forming networks for gathering information related to innovation. The formation of such networks in Japan, through industry associations and R & D associations, is actively encouraged by the Ministry for Trade and Industry (MITI) as a key element of industry policy. Through interaction developed through personal acquaintance or leadership of another agency, such as the government, information is exchanged on products, processes, marketing, and management. Through network development, reciprocal visits to factories can be arranged and seminars organized. As appropriate, technological resource sharing can occur, resulting in mutual utilization of an innovation or perhaps joint development and production (Furukawa *et al.*, 1990).

It should probably be stressed that the role of MITI in Japan is not so much as a source of information directly applicable by companies but of assistance and encouragement in the formation of effective information networks. These linked informal and formal networks include quasi-governmental organizations, not-for-profit industry promotion agencies, industry associations, and research associations. All of these have the function of extensively sharing information and building consensus about future policy directions. As Okimoto (1989) remarks: "It is this network of ad hoc informal ties, not just MITI's formal organization or the structural characteristics of Japanese industry, that gives industrial policy and government-business interactions the resilience and adaptability for which Japan is renowned" (p. 152).

4.5.2 Meetings, Seminars, Conferences, Study Missions

Another rich source of informal information and personal interaction is attendance at meetings, seminars, and conferences, and through engagement in site visits and study missions. Using a sample of 55 Japanese and 51 United States researchers in industry, government, and university R & D organizations in the fields of robotics, biotechnology, and ceramic materials, Cutler (1989) notes that in Japan and the United States the mechanisms most preferred for effecting high technology transfer were meetings, seminars, and talks. Cutler also reported that 93% of the Japanese in university settings and 80% in industrial settings indicated attendance at least twice a month at technical meetings outside their organization; the corresponding percentages for the United States were 43% and 17%. In Japan, 59% indicated that they had attended at least one international conference in the past two years; the corresponding percentage for the United States was 28%. Comparable figures gathered in an Australian study for regular attendance at overseas conferences were 16% for technical managers in industry and 13% for government and university researchers. (Maguire *et al.* 1987). From her survey of United States manufacturers Keller (1986) determined that a good percentage of respondents attended two to three conferences a year. Only a small percentage (1.9%) never attended a conference. Those who attended conferences noted that the "opportunity to learn about new ideas/technologies" was the major benefit (p. 126).

Cutler also reports from his survey that study missions and site visits were highly rated by the Japanese as mechanisms for effecting high technology transfer (Cutler, 1989). Irvine and Martin (1984) referred to a Japanese technological consulting firm who annually sent a 50-person team to the Hanover Trade Fair. The consultants explained:

> You can sometimes find demonstrations of important prototypes which have not yet been commercialized. There we find out state-of-the-art technological "seeds." The sales people at the fairs are often only too willing to tell us in detail what they are doing. Every single booth is visited, discussions are held, and all the technical literature collected. Afterwards it is all carefully digested, analyzed and stored (p. 131).

The enthusiasm with which Japanese business people have gathered and used scientific and technological information has not always accorded with ideas in the United States and other countries about fair trade in information. Several Japanese companies have been sued in the United States for alleged infringements of patents of American companies. Cases include

1. Corning Glass v. Sumitomo Electric over the making of fiber optic cables (1987),
2. Honeywell v. Minolta over an automatic focussing, technology (1988)
3. IBM and Fujitsu over software controlling mainframe computers (dispute dating to 1982, settled in 1987).

Individual researchers have also been known to complain after Japanese visitors have been in their laboratories. An Australian rheologist is reported as having described collaborative research with the Japanese as "like sharing a chicken with a wolf." He had been upset by an incident when a Japanese visitor to his laboratory had taken photos without permission of new instruments being developed there (Japan: how to make collaboration work, 1988, p. 25). This publication goes on to comment that "Japanese eyes, including those of their researchers (most of whom are in, or closely associated with, industry) are always firmly on the potential downstream product, unlike the more academic Australian scientists." Innovation in other words may or may not be in the eye of the beholder.

4.5.3 Publications

The emphasis placed on informal sources in this chapter so far should not be allowed to obscure the importance of formal sources. The need for both has already been mentioned. Indeed the point to be taken is the interdependency of formal and informal sources. Formal sources of information may be referred to collectively as publications. An increasing, but still small proportion of publications now consist not only of words and pictures on paper, but of records of words, pictures, and sound on digital media. Some few publications appear only in digital form. In general the availability of publications in electronic form has meant swifter and more flexible access to newer information for those who can afford it. The features of digital information sources and the products and services based on them have already been discussed in Chapter 3. Discussion of electronic information services is also pursued in Section 4.5.4. Discussion of sources in print form is pursued here, but it should immediately be noted that a rapidly increasing proportion of these publications are also made available in electronic form for *full-text* searching.

Published sources of information related to innovation are many and include technical reports, textbooks, conference proceedings, product documentation, patents, standards, directories, and so on. Journals, however, remain the most used and the most prized of formal sources, not only among scientific researchers but among specialists of all kinds. The term "journals" is used here to include not only the scientific and professional journals but also the trade magazines. In science-based industry distinctions between scientific journals and trade literature become increasingly blurred, and some of the most significant of the journals are produced by organizations in the "trade." Obvious examples are *AT & T Bell Laboratories Technical Journal* and the *IBM Journal of Research and Development.*

Most journals are published in the United States and other Western countries, where professors perform both research and teaching. It has been noted that Japanese journal publications do not necessarily contain reports of new work, in contrast to United States publications where editorial policies emphasize the requirement for new or original work (Cutler, 1989). This different emphasis may partly explain the greater likelihood that members of Japanese organizations will go to conferences and meetings to gain new information.

Among the United States manufacturers Keller (1986) studied, the most cited information source important to job performance was journal literature (67.6%), followed by colleagues (40.8%), and conferences (40.4%). But it was also pointed out by the respondents that maintaining currency with the published literature was difficult. Anxiety about keeping up with the flood of current published information is often expressed by respondents in information-use studies. Sometimes this takes the form of hostility towards the most prolific source. For example, an Australian computer scientist in a university complained that "there are more [journal] articles than anyone can read and at a cost no one can afford" (Maguire *et al.*, 1987, p. 26). In the same study as many of the technical managers (20, or 52%) reported reading scientific journals as reported communicating with colleagues when asked how they kept up-to-date with technical information. An impressive 78% (54 managers) reported reading trade magazines for the same purpose (Maguire *et al.*, 1987 pp. 30–31, 38).

Obviously, indexing and abstracting services that lessen the anxiety of users about keeping up with the literature will be commercially successful. We may note in passing the high value added to the contents pages of journals by their regular listing in the different disciplines that make up the *Current Contents* series published by the Institute for Scientific Information. The characteristics of successful literature-alerting services are discussed in Chapter 6. It should be remarked here though that coverage of the trade literature in printed indexing and abstracting services has been poor and that this deficiency has recently begun to be addressed in the electronic database services.

Newspapers and news magazines form a subset of the journal literature, the contents of which are of particular interest to politicians and to government employees at all managerial levels. For many decades, considerable value has been added to newspapers by the cuttings services. Extracts on topics, often preselected according to clients' requests, are cut from newspapers and labeled with their source and date. Such a service may be provided by the library service within an agency or a corporation or may be purchased externally from a commercial service. The clippings files in newspaper and newsmagazine libraries have traditionally formed the single most important source of information. In research libraries, and in local history collections in much smaller public and academic libraries, as in information units in other organizations, the newspaper clippings have often been the most important component in the vertical files of current and historic material filed under the name of the topics that make the pictures and stories relevant in the particular environment of a library or other information service. There is also a genre of journal publication dedicated to summarizing and disseminating the literature from diverse sources on a topic or a cluster of topics. One such is *Information Hotline* (vol. 1, no. 1, 1969+) which, as its longevity indicates, has proved very useful in bringing together information about the myriad aspects of information policy, information technology, and information services. More recently, newsletters about media content have proliferated on the electronic database services. *Newsearch,* for example, is a daily index of news stories, information articles, and book reviews from nearly 2000 of the most important newspapers, magazines, and periodicals, as well as the complete text of *PR Newswire.* The contents of the newswires are well represented in databases such as *Newswire ASAP. Newsnet* was among the earliest services to see the niche for electronic newsletter publishing. It began by publishing more than one hundred newsletters in 1982 and also introduced *Newsflash* as an electronic news clipping service, run on the database (Conniff, 1982). Ten years later *Newsnet*'s coverage has extended to several hundred newsletters online as well as offering gateways to other services.

In environments where knowledge of the content of the mass media can be critical to electoral or corporate success, media analysis units have been set up where the electronic as well as print media are constantly monitored and the content recorded for later analysis and discussion. The House of Commons in Ottawa, Canada, offered from a broadband communications system installed in 1984 video services that included an electronic news clipping service (Hogers, 1984). Subsequently, almost all legislatures have installed similar services.

4.5.3.1 Patents

Database services have also enabled increased access to the patent literature and this literature has special interest for technology transfer and innovation. Discussion of database services is pursued in the next section, but opinions have differed so on the use and usefulness of the patent literature that it seems more sensible to discuss the patent databases here in the Publications section. Content may be augmented in the database version but far more important is the greater accessibility and the manipulation of data which the electronic format makes possible. Databases such as the series including the CLAIMS family of patent databases cover virtually every aspect of United States patents and patenting activity. They provide, for example, access to citations, abstracts, continuations, reassignments, reexaminations, extensions, and expirations. In April 1993, Dialog Information Services announced that United States PATENTS FULL TEXT had been made available online. This file contains the complete text of more than 1.4 million patents issued by the United States Patent and Trademark Office since 1974. The availability of this file transforms access to the text of the patent literature of the world, since, of course, many of the patents issued in the United States originate in other countries.

Positive views about the usefulness of patents as a source of information about innovation and many other topics have been expressed by

Ashton and Sen (1988). Their article indicates that business planners have typically used marketing information to help set future direction. While allowing that this information is essential, the authors suggest that another component is also needed—information dealing with technological developments. Such information is needed so that companies can anticipate changes and make the appropriate decisions for future developments. According to the authors, patents can provide information on a competitor's strengths and weaknesses, or they can focus on the strengths and weaknesses of an industry or a technology. Patents information can provide an analysis of possible ventures and acquisitions, management of a company's own patent portfolio, R & D management, and product and market surveillance. Ashton and Sen (1988) also see some problems with patents. Timeliness is an issue since there is an inevitable lag between the issuance of a patent and the patent document and thus public availability of the information. They also mention that not everything is patented and what is patented and available may not be readily comprehensible.

The patent literature has long been rated under-used as a source of technical information. The reasons are not far to seek. Patents are often written in a style designed to conceal rather than reveal information. The style and diction adopted in patents have been referred to as "patentese." An interesting discussion of the patent literature is found in an article by Dunford (1987). He alleges that some organizations make conscious efforts to discourage utilization and diffusion of a developed technology. This can be accomplished by various methods, such as patent consolidation whereby a company gains control over key patents through R & D efforts and buying up existing patents and by a patent "Blitzkrieg," when large numbers of patents are used to block the path of would-be competitors. This account has some echoes of findings by Rogers (1982) in Silicon Valley that "much technological information is not patented by private firms" (p. 118) and that "patents are not an effective means of preventing information exchange in the solar and the microprocessor industries" (p. 119). Patents are seldom listed among the sources from which firms acquire new technology. Yet stories abound of competitors who failed to find what was readily available to them in the patent literature. One example is the availability in the world patent literature of Ben Lexcen's design of the winged keel on Alan Bond's boat which eventually won the Americas Cup, briefly, for Australia in 1983. Chester (1984) reports: "Everyone is aware of the steps the Australian team took to keep the configuration of the keel secret, and the antics of other syndicates to discover the secret. Even before the final series of races started the secret was available to the public at Patent Offices in Europe and Australia" (p. 7). At the same time Chester (1984) also warns that "The role of patents in the innovative process should not be over-emphasisized. They play a minor role, but this role can be of significant importance if a commercially viable product results" (p. 2).

Many information users in commerce, industry, and government remain unconvinced, not only about the usefulness of the patent literature but about the patenting system. The costs of obtaining and defending patents have soared and doubts have been expressed about their utility to any but the largest corporations. There have also been complaints that in some countries, such as Japan where it takes five years to obtain a patent but where public disclosure of content is made after 18 months, local firms are given ample time to engineer around the pending patent. Again, on the positive side, others have remarked that, however out-of-date the patents taken out may be, the literature announcing and indexing them, especially when in electronic form, provides a useful source for identification of who has done what where and therefore of which people and which institutions are likely to be involved in further developments of similar technology. For example, the C.E.O. of an Australian medical electronics firm told one of the authors of this book that he has found this a useful method of identifying manufacturers for the microchips that it designs as it constantly seeks to upgrade the performance of its heart pacemakers and hearing device implants. State universities can also benefit from the royalty payments from well-managed patent programs. It has been reported that in 1991–1992 the University of California system made more than $28 million from patent royalties, a figure up by more than 40% from the previous year (UC innovators assemble to learn more about patenting, 1993).

Patents remain one of the important ways in which our society seeks to reward those who invent, invest, and innovate while at the same time to encourage the rapid spread of new knowledge for the benefit of all. Patent systems for the protection of industrial property, like copyright systems for the protection of intellectual property, no doubt worked better when economies were national rather than global, when the pace of technical change was not so frantic, and when new contributions were more easily identifiable among existing knowledge. More equitable ways of allowing exploitation of innovative technology and ideas worldwide are desirable. A factor in evolving better systems is the access to external sources of information now available to organizations of all sizes in all countries through the electronic information services discussed next.

4.5.4 Electronic Information Services

The concept of an information service can include a number of components, including methods for indexing and abstracting of materials, production of printed indexes and abstracts, document delivery, and associated reference and referral services. Existing information services provide a variety of these components. Some are only print-based and provide indexes and abstracts. Many of the print services that exist are also available electronically, and are known as databases. Some of the database services available for news clipping and newswire services have already been mentioned above. In addition, there are some information systems that are only available in electronic form. There is no doubt about the popularity of databases in providing access to information. Examples from the literature attest to this from various perspectives. For example, Matarazzo and Prusak (1990) note that managers of library managers (that is, the more senior managers to whom those who are in charge of libraries report) identify database searching as the key library service. The past few years have witnessed the rapid development and growth of the online and CD-ROM database service industry. Developments of the technology continue, some of which, such as videodisc and WORM discs, will be discussed in Chapter 5.

Large numbers of databases are already available on a wide spectrum of topics. For example, in 1990 it was estimated that there were 4465 distinctly named databases, produced by 1950 database producers (Cuadra Associates, 1990). There are a large number of commercial online database vendors, ranging from those who provide access to a large number of different databases, such as Bibliographic Retrieval Services Inc. (BRS) and DIALOG, to those who develop in-depth services for one market segment, such as Mike Bloomberg whose service covers all aspects of the money and stock markets (Stern and Zweig, 1991).

One of the effects of the comprehensive commercial services available to all on demand has been to dull the competitive edge of large corporations. In the early development of computer-based information services only the largest corporations, the British-based chemical conglomerate ICI Limited was an outstanding example, could afford to develop and provide access for their staff to digital information. Parts of these services were literature-based and parts based on the corporation's own proprietary information, such as its R & D. Thus the advances in hardware, software, and telecommunications and the entrepreneurs, like Roger Summit of DIALOG, who took advantage of the technology democratized access to information.

There are many advantages to the use of databases. Their use facilitates quick access to information and provides additional search capabilities unavailable in print-based sources. Electronic access to remote databases can also be cost-effective to an organization since charges occur only when the databases are being used. For example, an organization need not subscribe to print copies of an infrequently used indexing or abstracting service. Remote access also provides a wealth of information that the users would not have available otherwise. The databases available include indexes and abstracts of the literature, in which are bibliographic citations, with or without abstracts, to periodical and newspaper articles, to the report literature, and to the patent literature, as discussed previously. There are also catalogs of libraries and of taxonomic collections and collections of numeric data ranging from census data and stock market prices to technical properties of engineering materials. As the capacities of computer storage devices and telecommunications lines continually expand, increasing numbers of the literature-based databases are being made available in full text, and more value is constantly being added to these services through additions such as statistical analysis software with interfaces that make it relatively simple and graphically elegant for the users to apply to whatever subsets of the data in which they have particular interest.

There are two forms of access to available databases: (1) online and (2) CD-ROM (compact disk read-only memory). Online databases are accessed through a terminal or a personal computer that has a modem or which is part of a local area network. CD-ROM databases are copies of online databases (or other digital reference sources) that have been placed onto a laser disk. A CD-ROM database is accessed through a personal computer that is connected to a CD-ROM player. A user subscribes to a CD-ROM service that periodically provides updated discs. For online databases the basic requirements are a personal computer, a modem, communications software, and a phone line or connection to a local area network. To access commercial services, arrangements for a subscription with a database vendor are needed. Commercial vendors provide access to a variety of different on-line databases at a fee that can vary depending on which database is accessed. Telecommunication charges for linking the local site to the database vendor are also a component of the overall online cost. Costs accrue every time an on-line search is performed. In some systems, billing is made available through a phone company or public telecommunications utility so that the user does not need a subscription to every available database service. This facility is sometime referred to, as in the French Minitel system, as a kiosk service.

CD-ROM databases have the following requirements: a personal computer, a CD-ROM player with interface card, the CD-ROM disk. A subscription service is established with a vendor who provides periodic CD-ROM disk updates, such as on a quarterly basis. The cost of the service also varies according to whether network access is provided to the disk and the number of terminals connected to any such network. One advantage of CD-ROM databases is the fact that there are no "on-line connect" charges—usage is not cost-sensitive and so does not need to be controlled as with online databases. Advances in CD-ROM networking technology, especially the capacity to provide local access to many different disks, are also transforming the range and depth of information to which individuals may have access from their own workstations.

Developments in networking and networked information services in the United States have culminated in the setting up of the National Research and Education Network (NREN) under the High Performance Computing Act. Both research and policy aspects of the NREN are analyzed in McClure *et al.* (1991). There already exists a global network of networks of which an important part is the Internet—a loosely-organized international collaboration of autonomous, interconnected networks that supports host-to-host communication through voluntary adherence to open protocols and procedures defined by Internet Standards—which has spread from the United States, based on the NSFNet (the National Science Foundation network) and the earlier ARPANET (in the Department of Defense). Access to this network is supported now by educational and government institutions in about thirty countries, and its use is available cost-free to members of those contributing organizations. The consequences for public and private access to networked computing power and information services in the United States (and probably most of the world) will be very much affected by the decisions to be made by President Clinton and the United States Congress on the future financing and control of the NREN. At this stage, however, it is obvious that the Internet and the entire global network of networks, subsidized and commercial, is a very large source of information of potential use in innovation.

It is also already obvious that implementation of global networks will bring extra challenges as well as extra benefits in the diffusion of information. Researchers in fast-moving fields, such as computer science and parts of nuclear physics, already use the Internet as a journal-substitute. The flurry of work in 1989 on "cold fusion" was largely communicated through the Internet, and this left researchers having to sort out the quality of the reports without the assistance of the refereeing system used by traditional journals. There has long been acknowledgement that genuinely new ideas are much more difficult to have promulgated in the journal literature of science than those that are within existing paradigms and consonant with personal beliefs of editorial boards and referees. Peter and Olson (1983), already discussed in Chapter 3 (pp. 84–85), have argued that the more original the idea the higher the price of acceptance. The "free-for-all" of the Internet may even evolve into a more robust system, less dependent on the law of cumulative advantage, by which opportunities to publish as to obtain grants of various kinds and other distinctions of rank and reward have been shown to be skewed towards those who have had initial advantages in their educational choices. The Internet may serve therefore as another reminder of the changes wrought by diffusion of digital data (already discussed in Chapter 3, section 3.2), which are continually increasing the disciplinary, class, and geographical fronts over which the impacts of advanced communications and information technology are felt.

Some of the databases that are at the heart of electronic information systems are more specific to our concern for innovation than others. These include several large systems that have been established to control the indexing and abstracting of materials, and in addition to disseminate and transfer information on a wide array of topics. Typically, these large systems utilize a variety of means to accompish this, including, clearinghouses for the collection, processing, dissemination, and reproduction of information; on-line database and other bibliographic support services; paper announcements and reports; and consulting services. The purpose of such activities is to spin off developments to communities other than those in which or for which the initial research is pursued. A prime example of a single information system that assists in innovation, and which in effect was developed to assist in broad-based technology transfer, is that of the National Aeronautics and Space Administration (NASA). The NASA system is discussed in section 4.7 of this chapter.

4.6 Information Providers in Organizations

Chapters 1 and 2 demonstrated that information is an essential ingredient in the innovation process. In those chapters and in subsequent discussion in Chapter 3, the difficulty of separating content from channel, data from its communication has been raised. In this chapter the importance of informal sources (i.e., interactions with people) has been stressed. While it is immediately acknowledged that every member of an organization is to some extent an information provider, this section pays particular attention to those members and departments whose function it is solely or principally to provide information to other parts of the organization and in some cases to external clients. In our terminology the function of information providers is to find *already existing* information and provide it to others, adding to it varying levels of extra value depending on the circumstance. These providers typically include librarians and other information professionals, such as records managers and archivists; individuals involved in competitor intelligence; and marketing and public relations personnel. Acknowledgment must also immediately be made that today we are also witnessing the development of end-user information seeking, such as through the use of database systems marketed to and used by end-users. They too, like the professional information providers, will increasingly utilize technologies for access to external information, for organizing internal information, and for processing and delivering information. We must acknowledge then that, just as the discussion in Chapter 3, section 3.2.2 showed how indistinct the boundaries between information specialities are becoming, so too are the boundaries between the specialists and all members of increasingly information-intensive organizations.

4.6.1 Librarians and Information Professionals

It has been common for organizations, once they reach a critical point of information disarray, to set up a library and to hire a librarian to organize the collection and to provide information services. As a matter of note, there are more than 14,000 librarians and other information personnel who are members of the Special Libraries Association (United States and Canada). But what do information providers, such as librarians, understand of their role? How effective have they been in relating information to innovation issues? In an attempt to answer these questions, one of the authors of this book conducted an informal telephone survey of ten information providers, specifically special librarians at a number of engineering, aerospace, and high-technology related organizations.

The purpose of the survey was to determine whether the library knew or kept track of the impact of information services on the development of new products or new services; new techniques (of manufacture or production); new uses of existing products or services; new internal systems or operations; R & D efforts; the competitive edge, as in responses to requests for proposals (RFP), quick reponses to client needs, successful contracts; or other similar impacts.

When there were positive responses, the following questions were asked: on what units or components of the organization had the information service had a positive impact, for example, engineering, R & D, marketing; how had the library become familiar with the impact of the information service, and was there any formal system for such data collection; what sources or systems were used; and were there other units, for example, marketing or corporate, in the company that provided information services that might have assisted in any of the items listed in the previous questions.

Unfortunately, most libraries did not gather data on the impact of their information services either on in-house clients, or external customers. Those that did tended to have informal systems whereby a client happened to make a positive comment or sent a thank-you note about an information service. Several of these related not to innovation topics, but to winning patent infringement cases and other such benefits. One site gathered data on the time that on-line searching saved the requester in contrast to how long gathering the information manually, or by some other method, such as through personal contacts, would have taken. But this was for the purpose of justifying online searching costs rather than for tying the information provided to an innovation. Several examples were given whereby literature searching assisted in winning a contract or having a new patent awarded.

This limited and informal sampling of reality suggests that the alignment of special library goals with overall organizational strategy, and in particular with innovation strategies, may not yet be on the agenda. Support for this conclusion comes also from an Australian study of the value of information services in two public organizations reported by Broadbent (1992).

The value of the information professional and the corporate library was also probed in a recent study by the Special Libraries Association in the United States Matarazzo and Prusak (1990). The study was based on interviews with individuals who managed the managers (librarians) of 164 special libraries and information centers. Librarians were highly rated for the services they provided, in controlling expenditures and in adapting to change. Databases were cited as a key library service. But unfortunately, the study appeared to confirm the results of our telephone inquiries. Managers could not identify the library services that added the most value to the company (approximately two-thirds did not or could not respond to this question).

It has been noted in the literature that the librarian or information specialist has little stake in the results of research. The librarian provides the information or in some instances provides some value-added services, such as a state-of-the-art review of a particular topic. But the involvement stops here. While this approach may be satisfactory for existing technologies, individuals at Exxon Research and Engineering Company did not believe the same held true for previously unexplored technologies. "It is more difficult to assess both the technical and business obstacles and the potential for the development and commercialization of research in technological areas previously unexplored. . . . [An] information specialist is important as a means of achieving comprehensive information coverage and a high degree of confidence in the interpretation of the information. [What is needed is a new model which] . . . incorporates information as a major stimulus to enhance the definition, planning, goal-setting, and execution of a research program from the earliest stages through to commercialization" (Walton *et al.*, 1989, pp. 33–34). After a trial period of examining this approach, an information specialist was added as a full-time member of the corporate research unit. The information specialist "by applying information input and analysis important to the definition, planning and advancement of R & D programs . . . has become a source of expertise not available elsewhere in Exxon" (Walton *et al.*, 1989, p. 37).

4.6.2 Competitor Intelligence Personnel

In an attempt to ascertain whether there were other information providers who might be gathering data on the impact of their information services on innovation, another unit within organizations was considered as a possibility for review: the competitive intelligence unit.

Competitive intelligence is information with a strategic point of view, or in other words, information that is used to support the strategic planning of an organization and the corporate decision-making process. From the broad perspective it involves a determination of the strategies and goals of organizations with similar lines of business. In tactical terms it involves the gathering, analysis, and presentation of information dealing with such issues as acquisitions, new product development, new business ventures, new market entries, market shares, pricing, promotions, and customer viewpoints (Brody, 1989).

The functions of a competitor intelligence system are set out in Figure 4.4. Competitive information can be gathered from a variety of sources, including traditional library resources, such as directories, almanacs, printed indexes and abstracts, annual and other reports, and online databases; news clippings; news media transcripts; speeches; contract award listings; internal organization publications; contacts at international, federal, state, and local government agencies and professional and trade associations; product literature; information presented at conferences and trade shows; and information and documents generated by members of the organization who perform staff rather than line functions. It is an indication of the amount of interest in this area that a new company intelligence database has been announced by Information Access Company. This is a "convenience" database in that it extracts information from a number of their other databases to combine directory and bibliographic information on each entry (O'Leary, 1990).

Intelligence information gathered from these various sources needs to be organized into a database. As an example of the effort that some organizations invest in obtaining this information, Digital Equipment Corporation (DEC) has been reported to have 11 people who are collecting competitor information and placing it into a database system (Brody, 1989).

In preparation of this chapter, discussions were held with several individuals responsible for competitor intelligence to ascertain whether data

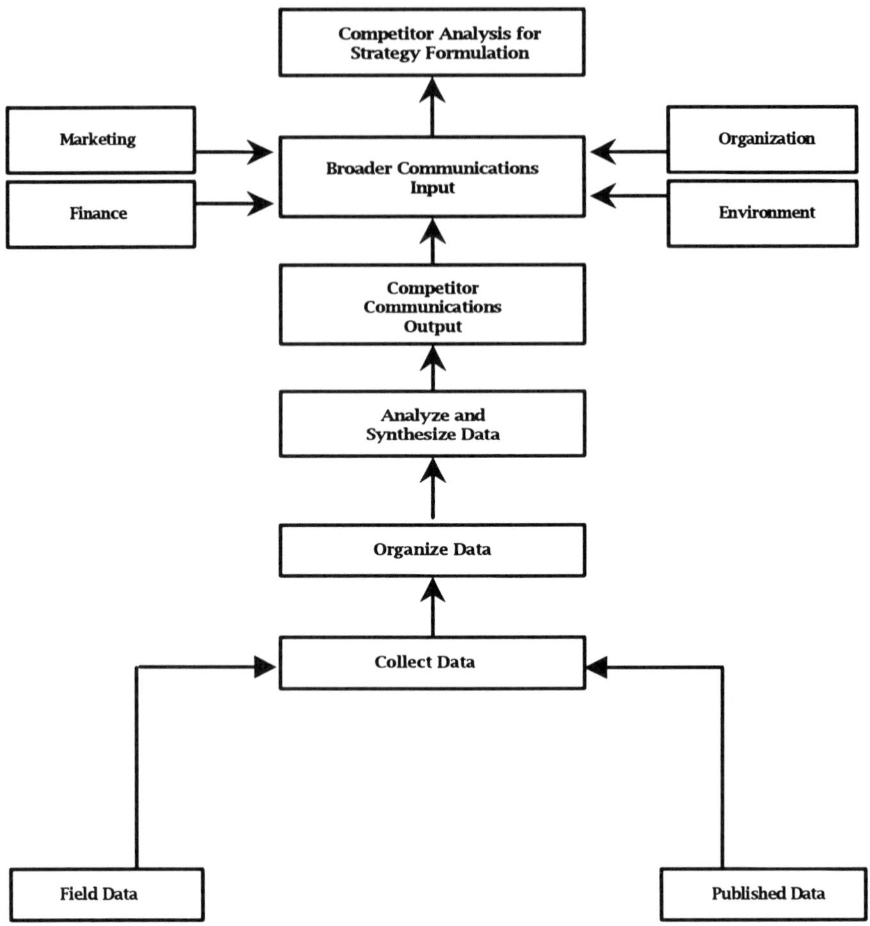

Figure 4.4
Functions of a competitor intelligence system (source: M. E. Porter, *Competitive Strategy;* adapted by C. Allgaier).

were collected on the benefit of the information provided. Actually, the same questions that were asked of the librarians in the informal survey were asked of these individuals. Some of the replies were similar to those from the librarians. Among competitor intelligence personnel it is also common to gather anecdotal comments to help justify or describe the benefit of the service. In some instances among them, too, an estimate of the dollars saved

Table 4.2
Sources of R & D Intelligence Used by Manufacturing Firms

Source	Mean response[a]
Marketing group	3.26
Manufacturing group	3.09
Technical equipment suppliers	2.69
Universities	2.62
Professional interaction with peers outside the firm	2.61
Customers	2.55
Informal interaction with peers outside the firm	2.44
Consulting firms	2.13
Reverse engineering of competitors' products	1.98
National Technical Information Service	1.89
Other government agencies (national laboratories)	1.80
New employees who previously worked for competitors	1.73

Source: Link and Tassey, 1987, p. 53. Reprinted with the permission of Lexington Books, an imprint of Macmillan Publishing Company from *Strategies for technology-based competition* by Albert N. Link and Gregory Tassey. Copyright © 1987.
[a]1 = never used; 4 = always used.

if the competitor intelligence information was not gathered or had to be gathered in another way had been used to assist in benefit analysis. But some more concrete efforts have been used since competitor intelligence gathering can be project-related. In competitor intelligence it is common to report on how much information support is provided to a product or project in terms of hours and expenses and to provide such data to project leaders for use in R & D costing and for eventual use in profit and loss statements.

An interesting study asked a group of R & D vice-presidents in manufacturing to evaluate, using a four-point Likert scale, sources of intelligence information. The results of this survey are displayed in Table 4.2. It is interesting to note in this study that internal groups dominate as the sources of information. The authors call attention to the fact that "while U.S. corporations have indeed begun to realize the importance of adopting a technology-based competitive strategy, they remain ignorant of the critical role of nonproprietary sources of technology in the success of a technology-based strategy" (Link and Tassey, 1987, pp. 53–54). It may also be wise to point out that the boundaries between internal and external information are by no means firm. In fact, the more senior the executive the more likely he or she is to get specialized information about external circumstances and events through internal filters.

4.6.3 Marketing Personnel

The importance of marketing information in the innovation process has already been pointed out in Chapter 2. Marketing information includes those data that are collected on an ongoing basis and organized into a system, typically computer-based, which facilitates analysis and evaluation of such data for decision-making purposes. Examples of data that can be a part of such a system include, external data, such as statistical and census data; advertising and trade information related to the specific industry; internal reports, such as financials; and actual marketing data, such as product lines, and customer and sales descriptions. In addition, marketing information also includes the data generated as part of specific marketing research projects.

While library and competitor intelligence and marketing personnel are involved in organizing, storing, retrieving, and transmitting information, marketing personnel are much more involved with processing and analyzing information for use in managerial decision making. Unlike the other information-based units we have discussed, marketing is an integral part of the corporate function. Top executives often become involved in the marketing process and have a vested interest in its success—top executives do not become involved in the library process. Marketing also involves a number of functions requiring the gathering and processing of information that are beyond the scope normally associated with library and competitive intelligence. These include such tasks as research design, sampling, questionnaire and interview development, and statistical analysis. Even though outsourcing of market research was commonplace before that of computer services, qualitative and quantitative research skills can be essential to marketing personnel in interpreting the significance and assessing the quality of market research done externally to the organization. One empirical study suggests that marketing personnel are highly dependent on personal, informal sources of information for new ideas, especially on the sales force and on brainstorming with colleagues. A few will depend a little on customers, personal contacts, and new recruits from other companies, and none on printed reports (Maguire and Lovelace, 1988, p. 329).

Reference has already been made in this chapter (see p. 152) to communication failures between marketing and other personnel. An analysis by Gupta and Wilemon (1988) of R & D managers from 80 companies outlined some of their problems in communicating with marketing personnel. According to this study, major reasons for R & D not using marketing information relate to the quality of the information. It was perceived by R & D to be incomplete, in that it did not always identify actual customer needs, it was too narrowly focused, and it was not provided when needed. On the other hand, a percentage of R & D managers indicated that they did not use information provided to them! Approaches for improvement include providing more quality information, and adopting a more cooperative and continuous effort in providing information (Gupta and Wilemon, 1988).

4.6.4 Other Providers of Information

There is other information that is generated within an organization, which may also be of interest to our concern with information for innovation. One that comes to mind is economic data covering such topics as inflation rates, personal incomes, interest rates, and unemployment figures. Corporate planning needs to integrate economic data because planning is based on a set of assumptions about the future. The ecomomist or a planning department generating economic data is concerned with trends and predictions for the economy in general and within an industrial or business setting in particular. Planning is interested, for example, in both the prospects for the sale of a product (say, beer) and the prospects for the sale of a specific brand (Adams, 1986).

Additional providers of information within an organization might also come from the planning department or some other unit that does technological forecasting. This may be a forecast on when a new process or product might be widely adopted, such as when a computer technology or a new operating system might have widespread industry utilization. Additionally, forecasting might focus on developments in an area, such as the supply of a particular raw material or component, within ten years.

No information will be of much use to an organization if it cannot be efficiently retrieved in time of need. This applies not only to "bundled" or "packaged" information (e.g., books, reports, videotapes, etc.) traditionally handled by libraries, but equally to the "loose" information embedded in correspondence, memoranda, policy development papers, and so on, which are traditionally handled by filing systems. Filed information cannot be retrieved easily unless it is logically and systematically organized, with a view to making its retrieval easy. Good practice in this regard (for example, systematically subdivided and fully named files free of acronyms) is all the more important in these days of frequent restructuring of organizations. While principles of good records management have been enunciated, for example by the Association of Records Managers and Administrators (ARMA, 1989), evidence is widespread of the careless handling of files in organizations and of the reluctance of management to spend serious money on upgrading of file handling systems. Frequent restructuring, which has been recommended as a strategy to promote innovation, results in rapid turnover of staff. This makes difficult the access to an organization's records traditionally available from personal sources if files could not be located, or perhaps more likely as a first resort in locating formal records. Such a source would be someone who knows what the background was, say to a policy decision twelve months ago, why other options were rejected, and where the papers are. In organizations where there is frequent change, however, the person who knew may no longer be working in that area or may quite possibly have left the organization completely. The person who has to follow up the original initiative must perforce have recourse to the written record, and in some organizations with which the present authors have dealt, this record is for practical purposes irretrievable because of poor records management practices, ranging from poor classification and naming of files to lack of quality control in filing.

Happily, useful guides have begun to appear on the general principles of electronic records management, including the retention and disposition scheduling for such records. One such is *Managing Electronic Records* (1990). There are also specialized works on the use of optical disk based systems, such as *The Use of Optical Disks for Public Records* (1990) and *Electronic Imaging RFP Guidelines* (1991).

4.7 Case Examples of Information Resource Systems for Innovation

Some government agencies have established mechanisms which attempt to spread innovation benefits by transferring technology and diffusing new products, processes, and services. We refer to these as *information resource systems*. The most ambitious of these systems is that provided by NASA. It is of particular interest because NASA has also fostered studies of the effectiveness of that system.

4.7.1 NASA

To assist in its mission of peaceful exploration and use of outer space, NASA "performs and contracts aerospace research, and provides 'spinoff' technology to aerospace firms and nonaerospace firms" (McCarthy, 1989, p. 241). "Spinoff" refers to the reapplication of a technology to another use, oftentimes considerably different from its original use. The technology is transfered by the following means: (1) through direct use whereby a NASA technology is used in the creation of a new product or process, the creation of a new company, or generation of a new application; (2) through creating or stimulating a market, such as when a NASA-developed technology has a much broader application than that originally intended; (3) through facilitating commercialization because a NASA-developed technology may have more credibility than other R & D-developed technologies and thus is used more quickly; (4) by providing problem-solving assistance; (5) through employee spinoff whereby an employee takes a technology and develops it for commercial use; (6) through spinoffs to other public agencies, such as where NASA provides a technology to another agency, for example, to an airport; (7) through professional activities, such as journal articles and conference papers (Chapman *et al.*, 1989).

To assist in performing this spinoff R & D technology transfer, the agency has created an extensive information system, known as the technology utilization (TU) program. Table 4.3 represents an overview of this program. In specific organizational terms, personnel are made available and centers have been established across the United States to assist in NASA's technology transfer process. These include the Field Center Technology Utilization officers who manage center participation in technology utilization activities; the industrial application centers (IACs) affiliated with universities and which provide users with information retrieval services and assistance to technical information; the industrial application center affiliates, which provide technology transfer information to state-sponsored business or local assistance centers: the computer software management and information center, which provides government-developed computer programs to other potential users; and application teams, which provide assistance in applying aerospace technology solutions to public sector problems (Spinoff, 1989). The IACs are central to our concern since they are oriented towards information dissemination, as opposed to the other components that focus on technical equipment and software distribution (McCarthy, 1989). As a specific example, the services of the NASA IAC (NIAC) at the University of Southern California include on-line database searching of NASA as well as other public and private databases, current awareness services, document reproduction, and delivery, and personal contacts with experts or NASA's application teams. Typical clients include industries and entrepreneurs who have technical information problems, need to find new applications, or gain competitive intelligence; businesses applying for government contracts or awards, such as the Small Business Innovation Research (SBIR) grants; and users desiring to search for patent information.

NASA has been most concerned with the success of its information transfer programs. In this context, the information utilization can fairly readily be translated into economic terms. There are numerous examples of such successes, a sampling of which is provided.

Table 4.3
Basic Attributes of the NASA Technology Utilization Program

Industrial Application Centers	Technical briefs and publications	STI information facility	Technology utilization officer (field center)	Application
Database searching	Technical support packages	Referral to Technology Utilization Program	Referral within Technical Utilization	Public sector projects in technology transfer
Referral	Spin-off magazine	Technical utilization documentation	Referral to application teams	Referral from Technical Utilization Centers
Consultation	Inventor/corporate information			
Information packaging		General NASA information	Develop technology transfer projects	Documentation projects
				Physical equipment transfer

Source: McCarthy, 1989, p. 248.

Aqua/Trends of Boca Raton Florida utilized the assistance of the Southern Technology Application Center at Florida Atlantic University to locate and furnish pertinent documents, advise on relevant seminars, and provide contacts with experts in the field. Using the information and contacts, Aqua/Trends was able to develop a micro-irrigation system to automatically tend indoor plants in locations such as hotels, restaurants, and building lobbies. These systems have been installed in over 100 locations throughout the United States (Spinoff, 1988).

The Electrosynthesis Company, Inc., of East Amherst, New York, utilized the services of NERAC, Inc., to conduct literature searches for their preparation of SBIR proposals. Using the information provided, the company has been successful in receiving R & D or limited production contracts to develop chemically modified carbon products (Spinoff, 1988).

Alcide Corporation developed a compound that was successful in sterilizing ultrasonic cleaning tanks by destroying bacteria, viruses, and fungi. At the same time, this compound was nontoxic to animals, plants, and humans and, thus, had potential for other applications. Alcide Corporation contacted NERAC to conduct literature searches to identify potential applications and businesses that might benefit from such a product. Using the results of these searches, Alcide developed and tested various applications for various markets. Several of these are now commercially available, including an air conditioning disinfectant for automobiles accepted by all three major United States automobile manufacturers, a disinfectant for contact lenses, and various oral care applications (Spinoff, 1988).

The NASA Industrial Application Center at the University of Southern California assisted Ceradyne, Inc., of Costa Mesa in conducting computerized literature searches. As a result of the information gathered, Ceradyne in conjunction with Unitek Corporation/3M developed Transcend™ ceramic orthodontic braces. With a production of over 300,000 pieces a month, the developers note that this product is the most successful orthodontic product introduction in history (Spinoff, 1989).

"Flashlight battery innovations typify aerospace technology transfers for consumer, home, and recreational applications" (Spinoff, 1989, p. 92). In this context, Rayovac Corporation of Madison, Wisconsin, developed Luma 2 Flashlight™, a high-powered corrosion-proof flashlight with a 10-year shelf life. Rayovac used various components from NASA's programs: a NASA-developed technology of the lithium power cell was employed in the final product, and literature searches were conducted for technical information dealing with flashlight batteries.

Various companies and entrepreneurs have developed new products based on information found in NASA's *Tech Briefs,* a publication that contains articles on "newly developed products and processes, advances in basic and applied research, improvements in shop and laboratory techniques, new sources of technical data and computer programs, and other innovations originating at NASA field centers or at the facilities of NASA contractors" (Spinoff, 1989, p. 132). More detailed information can be obtained by requesting a technical support package on particular innovations. For example, using technology located from *Tech Briefs* dealing with collapsible geodesic trusses used in the space program, Tensegrity Systems Corporation of Tivoli, New York, developed Tensegritoy™, a kit which allows students to understand scientific principles of structural stability. The kits are used by children as toys, as well as by architects, engineers, and technology instructors. This same technology has been used by the firm to develop lightweight display columns (Spinoff, 1989).

Another interesting innovation deals with the development of the Armor-Sight™ riflescope by the Bushnell Division of Bausch and Lomb. The NIAC at the University of Southern California performed database searches on graphite composites, and on bonding and porosity problems. Information from these literature reviews assisted the R & D engineers to develop this new product (Spinoff, 1989). A video has been prepared by Bushnell that describes this product. It is interesting to note that there is a discussion of how this product was developed through NASA spinoff technology. General Joe Engle, a consultant to Bushnell, describes how this product was developed using the transfer of knowledge from government projects to new uses in the private business sector, in this case from space technology to the sports hunter (Bausch and Lomb, 1989).

These various examples illustrate the usefulness of information systems in the transfer of knowledge and ultimately in the development of new, innovative products. NASA's publication, *Spinoff,* carries descriptions of examples of innovation. But in an attempt to gain a better understanding of the usefulness, or the benefits, of NASA technology spinoffs, an extensive study was undertaken recently to analyze the examples described in this publication between 1978 and 1986. Also included were any other examples identified in the *Spinoff* files but which were not described in the publication (Chapman *et al.*, 1989). It should be noted that these examples do not represent a random sampling of cases, but rather an identifiable group with contacts to individuals, companies, or products. Using a telephone interview process, 441 useful cases were identified. Through the interview process, data were gathered on the benefits of the technology transfer. These data were quantified according to the sales or savings in dollar terms or in percent of business, or by savings in personnel time, materials, maintenance, or R & D costs. These cost data were provided by representatives of

Table 4.4
Benefits Realized from NASA-Furnished Technology Case Applications from *Spinoff* Reports by Categories of End Use[a]

End-use description	Number of cases	Number of cases with sales or savings	Benefits realized (US$)[b] Sales	Savings	Total (US$)[b]
Communication/ data processing	51	32	171,007	51,964	222,971
Energy	30	13	203,500	15,613	219,113
Industrial (mfg. and process)	170	107	5,767,649	67,837	5,835,486
Medical	61	31	2,003,036	30,613	2,033,649
Consumer products	24	18	1,278,294	524	1,278,818
Public safety	27	16	347,888	555	348,443
Transportation	40	18	9,887,865	116,623	10,004,488
Environmental	16	11	16,962	21,788	38,750
Other	22	13	1,654,989	10,232	1,665,221
Total	441	259	$21,331,190	$315,749	21,646,939

Source: Chapman *et al.*, 1989, p. 54.
[a]Estimates were obtained from company officials or derived from company estimates of manpower or other types of savings. The 441 cases were reported in *Spinoff* magazine, 1978–1986; of these 368 had acknowledged sales or savings, but 109 cases could not be estimated as to extent.
[b]All dollar amounts in thousands.

the companies or calculated from company-provided estimates of personnel or other savings. Various benefit tables were prepared, including those by SIC (standard industrial code) and by specific technical application, such as insulation materials or medical instruments. Table 4.4 represents benefits data categorized into nine broad areas, representing the most comprehensive groupings possible.

Although Chapman's main finding relates to the benefit of the over $21 billion in sales or savings, other benefits, non-quantifiable in nature, were also identified as part of this study. These included: the provision of knowledge and technologies of a critical and valuable nature, such as a key R&D base; the opening of new areas of opportunity; assistance in creating an improved product or market share, or in meeting its competition; improved quality of work or life, promotion of safety, and help in meeting regulatory requirements; and the avoidance of misdirected R & D efforts (Chapman *et al.*, 1989).

NASA continues to present in *Spinoff 1992* what it terms "a representative selection of new products and processes adapted from technology originally developed for NASA mainline programs" (p. 49). The presentation is impressive, as befits a major public relations production of a major United States government agency. But one would have to be cynical indeed to fail to appreciate the startling variety of the applications listed in the five categories: consumer, home, and recreation; health and medicine; environment, industrial productivity and manufacturing technology; and computer technology. The stories told are interesting in themselves as well as in their variety, ranging from the design of boomerangs, sail boards, and orthopedic footwear to blood analyzers, rugged minicameras, and cans that will chill their contents by the relief of internal carbonization pressure when their tops pop. The NASA stories are also rich in insights into the sources of information for innovation. The publication *Tech Briefs,* which is designed to inform potential users of NASA technology available for transfer has already been mentioned in Table 4.6 and on pages [179–180]. In *Spinoff 1992,* the NASA writers report that while *Tech Briefs* "frequently inspires development of a spinoff product, more often [it] finds utility as a problem-solving tool for its government and industry readers" (p. 105). An illustration is the story of Air Products and Chemicals of Allentown, Pennsylvania, who needed to develop an apparatus to contain the high energy excimer laser beams used in their work on use of UV radiation. Commercially available beam blocks could not absorbe the UV light at the >500 watts output power generated by the lasers. The company read in *Tech Briefs* of related work on UV light absorption at the Jet Propulsion Laboratory (JPL), got a technical support package describing in detail the JPL invention, and went on to incorporate the NASA technology into its beam stops.

In many of the fifty-one stories of NASA technology transfer related in *Spinoff 1992,* the interaction of people in NASA laboratories and people in industry and government is essential to the process by which the existing technology is exploited to yield a successful product or process. One example is the Flogiston chair developed by Brian V. Park, a Scottish engineer resident in Texas, who read the NASA *Tech Brief* on neutral body posture, which was based on research in Skylab in the 1970s. When he inquired for more information, Park was invited to visit the Johnson Space Center by one of the engineers, who gave him personal help as well as documentation on neutral body posture and human factors in spacecraft design. The outcome of this interaction is a chair which is described as "a compromise between the Neutral Body Posture and Sasavana, a Yoga posture of relaxation" (Spinoff, 1992, p. 77).

NASA has also created national information resources that are unique in the history of government assistance to industry. One such is the NASA software bank, which has been very important in the agency's contribution to the Small Business Innovation Research (SBIR) program established by the United States Congress in 1982. There has never been a more concerted effort to have publicly funded technology adapted and extended for the wider benefit of society than that made by NASA through its publications, technology application centers in universities, and the stimulation of interactions between NASA scientists and engineers and engineers and entrepreneurs in industry. But there are several other systems that can act as important information resources for innovation.

4.7.2 Other Systems

Other large database systems can also be used to assist in the information transfer and innovation process. For example, various databases have been used, other than NASA, to assist in the application of defense technologies. A prime example is the Defense Technical Information Center (DTIC), which is a component of the United States Department of Defense (DoD) scientific and technical information program. DTIC provides "access to and transfer of scientific and technical information for DoD personnel, DoD contractors and potential contractors, and other U.S. Government agency personnel and their contractors" (DTIC, 1988). This is accomplished by DTIC's provision of a variety of services, including a variety of reference and document services relating to its own technical reports. Although classified materials are only available through specialized terminals with dedicated telephone lines, unclassified materials are released to the public through the National Technical Information Service (NTIS). In addition, DTIC manages IACs that provide in-depth reference service and access to subject matter experts. Products include generation of handbooks, state-of-the art reports, and evaluative engineering studies. Additional examples of databases that have been used for defense technology transfer include the Predicast databases, the American Institute of Aeronautics and Astronautics Aerospace database, and Commerce Business Daily. As with DTIC, through the use of these databases, users can review research and development efforts, locate new product and applied technology announcements, and monitor aerospace and defense contract activity.

The Center for Analysis and Dissemination of Demonstrated Energy Technologies (CADDET) is sponsored by thirteen countries, under the aegis of the International Energy Agency and the Organisation for Economic Cooperation and Development (OECD). It provides an international network of information to end-user sectors on demonstrations of energy-saving technologies. Specific activities include the collection, technical and economic analysis, and dissemination of information to the member countries, as well as identification and communication of policy implications, market choices, and the potential for commercialization. Distinguishing features of the information system are the value-added aspect and its international nature. Clues to the value-added aspects are in the key words "analysis" and "demonstrated" in its title. In the field of energy technology it is fairly easy to obtain reports (from the promoters) of systems as they are built, but it is much harder to obtain impartial analytical information about how they perform in practice. CADDET reports provide specific "practice" information, such as percentage of efficiency improvement, investment payback period, and existing user-base. Also noteworthy about CADDET is the level at which the published reports are pitched: although all about engineering, the reports are written so that accountants, politicians, and other decision-makers can understand them, while they give engineers a contact for further technical detail.

Among other notable examples of information resource systems are those created by the National Library of Medicine (NLM) and the Educational Resources Information Center (ERIC). The NLM provided in the Medical Literature Analysis and Retrieval System (MEDLARS), a very early entry in the development of computerized information retrieval systems and it also shaped the regional medical library network in the United States by its requirements and its statesmanship. It was also, with MEDLINE, the online version of the database, a pioneer in that field. The NLM also made contracts with foreign government organizations (for example, the National Library of Australia and the Australian Department of Health) to allow them to spin off its database and provide information retrieval services from it. The ERIC clearinghouses and the database were initiatives of the United States Department of Education, through which worldwide access has been facilitated, not only to reports of educational research sponsored by the department but to the educational literature as a whole. The sources listed in the ERIC database refer to a wide array of education topics, many of which, such as school improvement, are highly relevant to innovation.

The current debate about what roles should be played in the publication of government information by public and private sectors, to which reference has already been made in Chapter 3 (pp. 87–90), should not be allowed to obscure the enormous contribution made by the government agencies discussed in this section to the provision of information and to the technological and organizational innovations that were necessary to allow such provision.

4.8 Organizations to Promote Innovation

Various organizations, both public and private, are committed to the fostering of innovation and productivity. Some of these are specifically engaged in the information industry and have the provision of information as a major component of their function. Other organizations are concerned with the fostering of information transfer and innovation but are not specifically involved in information services. What follows is intended to be an illustrative assortment of these organizations. It is certainly not to be regarded as an attempt at a comprehensive listing.

4.8.1 Organizations for Innovation—Information Provider Organizations

The American Productivity and Quality Center is a not-for-profit research and educational institution that conducts action research projects, provides seminars, offers consulting services, and publishes materials on all aspects of productivity and quality of work life, including such publications as *The Productivity Letter, The Productivity Digest,* and the *MIPI: Multiple Input Productivity Indexes* (Thor, 1988). A focal point of the center is the library, which includes one of the largest collections of materials on productivity and work quality, including books, articles, statistical compilations, reports, corporate productivity guides, proceedings, presentations, and case studies. Information specialists provide information research and services.

The Information Retrieval and Management Service (IRMS) of the Graduate School of Library and Information Science of the University of Illinois provides various levels of information service. At the basic level, information from library and database search services is provided to clients. At more complex levels, the IRMS provides a current awareness service, analyzes and synthesizes information into reports (such as on manufacturing trends in Illinois), and consults with clients on their information services (*Information service expands under new name and director*, 1990).

The purpose of the Center for the Utilization of Federal Technology is to provide awareness to United States industry of governmental R & D and engineering efforts with particular emphasis on those efforts that might have potential or are at a significant stage of development. The center also operates the most active patent licensing program within the United States government and produces publications, such as *Government Inventions for Licensing Absract Newsletter* and *Directory of Federal Laboratory and Technology*

Resources, which announce available federal technologies and resources (National Technical Information Service, 1989).

4.8.2 Organizations for Innovation—Program Providers

In order to strengthen the industrial competitiveness of the State of California, a competitive technology program has been established. This program's goal is to accelerate market driven innovation through public–private technology-transfer projects (California Department of Commerce, Office of Competitive Technology, 1989). This program was inaugurated in direct response to foreign competitors whose governments support technology development. It draws upon cooperation among the private sector, national laboratories, private and public universities, the state and federal governments for the purpose of transfering basic or applied research and scientific discoveries into the design, development, and production of new or improved process, procedures, services, or products for the purpose of commercialization.

In other moves that could be regarded as program initiatives, it has been reported that United States and European companies are establishing research centers in Japan to monitor technology developments. These moves have been described as essential because of the globalization of industry in a Booz Allen and Hamilton 1988 study (*More companies doing R & D in Japan*, 1988).

4.9 Advisory Services

It is becoming more frequent for organizations to cooperate in R & D efforts and, in turn, to share information. There are many examples of such cooperative efforts, with a prime example being joint university and government agency and laboratory cooperation, such as that of the NASA Jet Propulsion Laboratory and the California Institute of Technology, the Information Science Institute and the University of Southern California. Doherty (1985) in his measurement of R & D productivity indicates that one measure concerns the external technical and scientific contractor and consultant. He lists a series of questions to ask regarding the quality, accessibility, continuity and stability, and the multidisciplinary mix. His assumption is that outside groups will be used as a normal matter of course.

In the United States, the National Science Foundation (NSF) has been instrumental in fostering university–industry cooperation on high-technology related innovations through the creation of centers, such as the Polymer Processing Center at the Massachusetts Institute of Technology. The overall goal of NSF funding is to have these centers become self-sufficient. To that end certain factors are essential: strong industry commitment to cooperation; extensive university support; high industry and university compatibility; and extensive industry personnel participation (Colton, 1987).

Another development in the United States is the inauguration of joint industry–government research consortia, such as the Microelectronics and Computer Technology Corporation (MCC) and the Semiconductor Manufacturing Technology (SEMATECH) Center, which assists United States companies in remaining competitive through development of generic technologies that member companies can adapt to specific markets. The chief executive of MCC states that the United States leads in the area of new technology creation. However, in the area of application and commercialization, the United States is not as successful. It is also noted that technology transfer in the United States is very linear, that is, there is no transfer until a project is completed or a specific milestone reached. For success, projects need collaborative efforts in developing the research agenda and in a continuous transfer process. A SEMATECH officer notes that a successful project is one in which 90% of the technology is transfered by the time of the final transfer. To that end, about half of the SEMATECH consortium's staff consist of individuals from member firms who serve a several year appointment. Continuous transfer is realized as these individuals use the technologies to refine and develop proprietary products (Corcoran, 1989).

Another example is the Commission of the European Community, which is concerned with technology transfer and has instituted a program entitled SPRINT (Strategic Program for Innovation and Technology Transfer). The objectives of this program are to foster cooperation between national organizations that already exist for the promotion of innovation; provide consultation on the development of national policies to aid communication in this area; and to provide greater availability of information on new research results and new technologies. The last objective is definitely information-laden. Specifically, the SPRINT information program is involved in a number of areas. The concern with the dissemination of European R & D results is achieved by the fostering of the Europeanization of conferences on technology and innovation—SPRINT can provide speakers to member states and can assist in conference translations. SPRINT is responsible for two information products: *EuroTechAlert,* an abstracting service providing access to the many technical reports generated throughout the community; and *ICONE,* a database that provides information and a comparative index to technical standards and regulations developed by member states. In addition, SPRINT has developed a telefax network for European technology transfer institutions, which in 1988 numbered about 100 members (Von Witzleben, 1988).

In some instances technical skills may not exist within a company and there is a need to go outside to hire a consultant or subcontractor. This is a common practice in the United States. Information is transfered in these cooperative ventures in both directions, and both organizations acquire additional technical information that they did not have before.

This chapter has categorized and explored the sources from which information useful in the innovation process is likely to be derived. As far as is possible, distinctions have been made between sources within and those external to the organization. As in all attempts to deal with information as a live issue, the content of messages has proved very difficult to separate from the channels and the context in which those messages are communicated. One of the criteria for the design of information services is therefore the need to plan around the communication patterns preferred by clients. Demonstration of this is to be found in large information resource systems as in small specialized information units within a particular organization. This chapter has also sought to indicate the range of initiatives that have been taken at government and industry level in order to create awareness of innovation opportunities and to lessen some of the risk.

Chapter 5 explores information technology from the point of view of its relevance to the process of innovation.

References

Adams, F. Gerard (1986). *The business forecasting revolution: nation—industry—firm*. New York, Oxford University Press.

Allen, T. J. (1977). *Managing the flow of technology: technology transfer and the dissemination of technological information within the R & D organization*. Cambridge, Massachusetts, MIT Press.

ARMA (1989). *ARMA: International Guideline for Records and Information Management*. Prairie Village, Kansas, ARMA International.

Ashton, W. Bradford, and Rajat K. Sen, (1988). Using patent information in technology business planning—I. *Research Technology Management 31*(6), 42–46.

Bausch and Lomb. (1989). Armor-sight riflescope. Bushnell, 2/2/89, videotape, 8:20 minutes.

Broadbent, Marianne (1992). Demonstrating information service value: linking priorities, benefits and performance. Paper presented at the Australian Library and Information Association Biennial Conference, Albury, September 1992.

Brody, Roberta (1989). Competitor intelligence and the corporate librarian. Proceedings of the Special Libraries Association Professional Development Program, Irvine, California, November 17, 1989.

Brown, Warren B., and Necmi Karagozoglu, (1989). A systems model of technological innovation. *IEEE Transactions on Engineering Management 36*(1), 11–16.

Burns, Tom, and G. M. Stalker, (1961). *The management of innovation*. London, Tavistock.

California Department of Commerce, Office of Competitive Technology. (1989). *Program solicitation fiscal year 1989–90*. Sacramento, California.

Carlyle, R. E. (1989). Careers in crisis. *Datamation* (August 15, 1989), 12–16.

Case, Thomas L., and John R. Pickett, (1989). R & D information systems. *Research Technology Management 32*(4), 29–33.

Change the way you think about using information (1988). *Research Technology Management 31*(4), 56–57.

Chapman, Richard L., Loretta C. Lohman, and Marilyn J. Chapman, (1989). *An exploration of benefits from NASA "Spinoff"*. Littleton, Colorado: Chapman Research Group, Inc., June 1989, NERAC Contract Number: 88–01.

Chester, D. (1984). Getting benefits from patents. *Lasie 15*(2), 2–11.

Collins, H. M. (1974). The TEA set: tacit knowledge and scientific networks. *Science Studies 4,* 165–186.

Colton, Robert M. (1987). University/industry cooperative research centers are proving themselves. *Research Management 30*(2), 34–37.

Conniff, Michael (1982). The arrival of Videotex/Newsnet: publishing goes online. *Computerworld 16*(11a), 66, 68–69.

Corcoran, Elizabeth (1989). Technology transfer: research consortiums look for ways to work with backers. *Scientific American, 260*(5), 98(2).

Crane, Diana (1972). *Invisible colleges: diffusion of knowledge in scientific communities*. Chicago, University of Chicago Press.

Cuadra Associates, *Directory of online databases*. (1990). Santa Monica, California.

Cutler, Robert S. (1989). A comparison of Japanese and U.S. high-technology transfer practices. *IEEE transactions on engineering management 36*(1), 17–24.

DTIC. (1988). *Defense Technical Information Center:* Alexandria VA; DTIC, March 1988.

Doherty, William J. (1985). *Measurement of productivity in an R & D environment*. Los Angeles, Applied Social Research Inc. August 1. Contract No: DAAG29–81-D-0100.

Dunsford, Richard, (1987). The suppression of technology as a strategy for controlling resource dependence. *Administrative Science Quarterly 32,* 515–525.

Electronic imaging RFP guidelines (1991). Silver Spring, Maryland, Association for Information and Image Management (TR27-1991).

Engel, James F., David T. Kollat, and Roger D. Blackwell, (1981). Diffusion of innovations. *In* Robert Rothberg, Ed., *Corporate strategy and product innovation* (Second edition). New York, Free Press, pp. 477–485.

Expert systems shrug off slow start for good growth according to Frost & Sullivan Report. (1990). *Information Today* (May), 43–44.

Furukawa, K., Y. Teramoto, and M. Kanda, (1990). Network organization for inter-firm R & D activities: experiences of Japanese small business. *International Journal of Technology Management 5*(1), 27–40.

Gladstein, Deborah, and David Caldwell, (1985). Boundary management in new product teams. *Academy of Management Proceedings: 45th annual meeting, San Diego,* pp. 161–165.

Gomelsky, V. (1993, 11 February). UC innovators assemble to learn more about patenting. *Daily Bruin,* 1 and 15.

Gupta, Ashok K., and David Wilemon, (1988). Why R & D resists using marketing information. *Research Technology Management 31*(6), 36–41.

Hogers, Hans P. (1984). Ottawa builds local net *Canadian Datasystems 16*(8), 32.

Information service expands under new name and director. (1990). *Graduate School of Library and Information Science of the University of Illinois Library School Association Newsletter.* Issue 6 (Spring), 1.

Irvine, John, and B. Martin, (1984). *Foresight in science: picking the winners.* London, Pinter.

Itami, Hiroyuki (1988). The Japanese corporate system and technology accumulation. *In* Kuniyoshi Urabe, John Child, and Tadao Kagono, Eds. *Innovation and management: international comparisons.* New York, Walter de Gruyter, pp. 27–46.

Japan: how to make collaboration work (1988). Canberra, Department of Industry, Technology and Commerce.

Keller, Karen A. K. (1986). Information use survey of manufacturers. *Proceedings of the American Society for Information Science 23,* 123–131.

Komiya, R. (1975). Planning in Japan. *In* M. Bornstein, Ed., *Economic planning, East and West.* New York, Ballinger, pp. 210–227.

Kono, Toyhiro (1988). Factors affecting the creativity of organizations—an approach from the analysis of new product development. *In* Kuniyoshi Urabe, John Child, and Tadao Kagono, Ed., *Innovation and management: international comparisons.* New York, Walter de Gruyter, pp. 105–144.

Krikelas, James (1983). Information seeking behavior: patterns and concepts. *Drexel Library Quarterly 19*(2), 5–20.

Levitan, Karen B. (1982). Information resources as "goods" in the life cycle of information production. *Journal of the American Society for Information Science 33*(1), 44–54.

Link, Albert N., and Gregory Tassey, (1987). *Strategies for technology-based competition: meeting the new global challenge.* Lexington, Massachusetts, Lexington Books.

Maguire, Carmel, and Robin Kench, (1984). The diffusion of technological innovation: an information research perspective. *Progress in Communication Sciences 4,* 163–204.

Maguire, Carmel and Eugenia Lovelace, (1988). Marketing in the Australian food industry. *Journal of Documentation 44,* 315–334.

Maguire, Carmel, Eugenia Lovelace, and Robin Kench, (1976). *The people you know: an investigation of information transfer among a group of Australian social workers in a hospital agency.* Sydney, School of Librarianship, University of New South Wales.

Maguire, Carmel, A. D. Weir, and L. Wood, (1987). Scientific and technological information: its use and supply in Australia. Canberra, Department of Science, Scientific Development Division.

Mailloux, Elizabeth N. (1989). Engineering information systems. *Annual review of information science and technology 24,* 239–266.

Managing electronic records. (1990). Washington, National Archives and Records Administration, Office of Records Management.

Matarazzo, James M., and Laurence Prusak, (1990). Valuing corporate libraries: a senior management survey. *Special Libraries 81*(2), 102–110.

McCarthy, Kevin G. (1989). Information transfer: NASA's information programs. *In* Charles R. McClure, and Peter Hernon, Eds., *U.S. Scientific and technical information (STI) policies: views and perspectives.* Norwood New Jersey, Ablex, pp. 241–267.

McClure, Charles R., Ann P. Bishop, Philip Doty, and Howard Rosenbaum, (1991). *The National Research and Education Network (NREN): research and policy perspectives.* Norwood, New Jersey, Ablex.

McFarlan, F. Warren, and James L. McKenney, (1983). The information archipelago—governing the new world. *Harvard Business Review 61*(4), 91–99.

McFarlan, F. Warren, James L. McKenney, and Philip Pyburn, (1983). The information archipelago—plotting a course. *Harvard Business Review 61*(1), 145–156.

McKenney, James L., and F. Warren McFarlan, (1982). The Information Archipelago—maps and bridges. *Harvard Business Review 60*(5), 109–119.

More companies doing R&D in Japan. (1988). [report of a Booz Allen and Hamilton study] *Research Technology Management 31*(1), 2–3.

National Technical Information Service. (1989). *NTIS products and services catalog*. Springfield, Virginia, U. S. Department of Commerce, pp. 12–14.

Okimoto, D. I. (1989). *Between MITI and the market: Japanese industrial policy for high technology*. Stanford, Stanford University Press.

O'Leary, Mick (1990). Company intelligence: a new convenience database. *Information Today* (April), 38–39.

Orsenigo, Luigi (1989). *The emergence of biotechnology: institutions and markets in industrial innovation*. New York, St. Martins.

Parker, E. B. (1976). Social implications of computer/telecom systems. *Telecommunications Policy 1,* 3–20.

Peter, J. Paul, and Jerry C. Olson (1983). Is science marketing? *Journal of Marketing 47,* 111–125.

Porat, M. U. (1977). *The information economy*. Washington, D. C., U. S. Government Printing Office.

Porter, Michael E. (1980). *Competitive strategy: techniques for analysing industries and competitors*. New York, Free Press.

Porter, Michael E. (1990). *The competitive advantage of nations*. London, Macmillan, p. 48.

Prentice, Ann (1980). Information seeking behaviors of selected professionals. *Public Library Quarterly 2,* 27–28, 58–60.

Roberts, Edward B. (1988). Managing invention and innovation *Research technology management, 31*(1), 11–31.

Rogers, Everett M. (1982). Information exchange and technological innovation. *In* Deverendra Sahal, Ed., *Transfer and utilization of technical knowledge*. Lexington Massachusetts, Lexington Books, pp. 105–123.

Rosenbloom, R. S. (1978). Technological innovation in firms and industries: an assessment of the state of the art. *In* P. Kelly and M. Kranzberg, Eds., *Innovation: a critical review of current knowledge*. San Francisco, San Francisco Press.

Sampson, Anthony (1973). *The sovereign state: the secret history of ITT.* London, Hodder and Stoughton.

Savage, Allan G. (1989). National Library of Medicine's MEDLARS: economic commodity or social good? *In* McClure, Charles R. and Hernon, Peter, Ed., *U.S. Scientific and Technical Information (STI) policies: views and perspectives*. Norwood New Jersey, Ablex, pp. 268–298.

Spinoff 1988. (1988). Washington, DC, NASA Office of Commercial Programs, Technology Utilization Division.

Spinoff 1989. (1989). Washington, DC, NASA Office of Commercial Programs, Technology Utilization Division.

Spinoff 1992. (1992). Washington, DC, NASA Office of Commercial Programs, Technology Transfer Division.

Stern, Richard L., and Jason Zweig, (1991). A new guy can do it better. *Forbes* (25 November), 122–127.

Thor, Carl (1988). Letter from President, American Productivity and Quality Center, to the authors, September 1.

The use of optical disks for public records: technical report for information and image management. (1990). Silver Spring, Maryland, Association for Information and Image Management. (TR25-1990).

Von Witzleben, Alexander. (1988). Information for innovation: the SPRINT Programme EURINFO-88. Brussels, European Community.

Walton, Kenneth W., John P. Dismukes, and Jon E. Browning, (1989). An information specialist joins the R&D team *Research Technology Management 32*(5), 32–37.

White, Clinton E., and David P. Christy, (1987). The information center concept: a normative model and a study of six installations. *MIS Quarterly* (December), 451–458.

Zuboff, Shoshana (1988). *In the age of the smart machine: the future of work and power*. New York, Basic Books.

5

Information Technologies and Their Use

The computer may enable the next big leap in the evolution of human intellect. Consider what the computer offers. It gives us direct, focused access to millions of publications from around the world. It allows us to, with almost unlimited capacity, store everything we know, and access it at will. It allows us to communicate with local, organization-wide, and global networks of colleagues with whom we might not otherwise communicate. It allows us to quickly sketch ideas in a variety of forms and freely manipulate those words, numbers, and images. With the advent of expert systems, the computer can even interact with us as a colleague would pushing us to be more creative and thoughtful. Computers are supplements of the mind.

—Mary E. Boone, *Leadership and the Computer*, p. 6.

The move away from mainframes toward smaller machines like personal computers, work stations and central information repositories known as servers has dramatically reduced profit margins for many computer companies and is in large measure responsible for the severe problems of IBM, the world mainframe leader.

—Andrew Pollack, "Mitsubishi Drops Mainframe Computers"
New York Times, January 12, 1993, p.C4.

Only in this decade have we witnessed the surprisingly rapid emergence and easy acceptance of technology as a major strategic variable throughout the globe for both corporations and national governments.

—M. Horwitch and K. Sakakibara, p. 83.

An inkling of possible revolutionary potential begins to appear with the emerging notion of hypertext.

—*Project Quartet,* p. 67.

Chapter Synopsis

Information for innovation may be, as Chapter 4 has demonstrated, derived from a multiplicity of internal and external sources and by many formal and informal methods. Tremendous amounts of information exist and continue to be generated at an accelerating rate, largely through the facilities of the information technologies used for creating, copying, and disseminating data. Fortunately, some of the technologies that have done most to create this flood or avalanche of information can also be used to control it. This chapter addresses the technologies available and the methods devised to accomplish information management in the broadest sense. Likely future trends are also discussed and so is the understanding of human behavior that must be incorporated in the design of information services.

The intention of this chapter is twofold. It is to inform readers of significant developments that have occurred in information technology and to alert them to likely developments that managers will need to maintain their awareness. This chapter is also inevitably, albeit incidentally, the account of a series of technological innovations that have had varying acceptance in the marketplace. The lessons that can be drawn from the experience of applying information technology in organizations are among the topics addressed in Chapter 6.

Inevitably, some of the data provided in this chapter on the capacities of hardware and software will quickly be superseded. The intention is not to give an up-to-the-minute state-of-the-art review, because none can remain so for long. At the same time the intention is not to deal with technical capabilities at such a level of generality that comparison of, for example, communication line speeds and capacities is not possible.

The chapter begins with discussion of specific technologies and associated hardware and software. It proceeds to a review of approaches and methods that have been used in the design and implementation of information technology-based systems. Some of the human factors that affect acceptance of computer-based information systems are explored along with the ways in which human needs and preferences can be determined.

5.1 Introduction

Technology has been defined as "systematic knowledge and action, usually of industrial processes but applicable to any recurrent activity" (McGraw-Hill, 1987, p. 145). In providing tools and techniques for action, technology at once adds to and draws from a knowledge base in which theory and practice interact and compact. At its most general, technology may be regarded as any definable specifiable way of doing anything.

Information technology is the creation, combination, storage, manipulation, retrieval, and dissemination of symbols according to instructions that are encoded in other sets of symbols. It is defined by the United Nations Educational, Scientific, and Cultural Organization (UNESCO) as "the scientific, technological and engineering disciplines and the management techniques used in handling and processing information; their applications; computers and their interaction with man and machine; and associated social, economic and cultural matters" (Stokes, 1985, pp. 114–115). In the context of our particular interest, information technologies may be employed in creating, communicating, processing, providing access to, and synthesizing information on innovation. In an organization, information technologies may be used, for example, to organize and make accessible internal information, to gather some of the appropriate external information, and to combine internal and external information to provide input for strategic decision making. The need for integration and conscious management of this information as a resource has been made obvious in work such as that by McFarlan and McKenney, which has already been mentioned in Chapter 3. These authors identified in organizations an "information archipelago" consisting of three separately developed "islands of information." These islands are data processing, office automation, and telecommunications. (McKenney and McFarlan, 1982; McFarlan and McKenney, 1983; McFarlan *et al.*, 1983). In this chapter we look more closely at some of the common geographic features of these islands, namely computer systems, including hardware, operating systems, and application software and languages; at local area networks (LANs) and fax (telefacsimile) technology and other features of office automation; and at the whole area of networking and communications. The growing blur enveloping attempts to separate and specify boundaries of digital technologies has been described in Chapter 3 (pp. 95–100). Any technology is likely to turn up on any one of the islands of the information archipelago within an organization, as well as in other contexts, such as CD-ROM databases in its library or EDI systems in its purchasing department.

This book makes reference to all of the information technologies but discussion revolves primarily around the computer, particularly the personal computer which, especially as a workstation in a networked environment, has become the center-piece of present-day information services.

5.2 Computer Hardware and Software

Computer hardware may be regarded as the equipment that implements the instructions embedded in the software. The term has been formally defined as "physical equipment used in data processing, as opposed to programs, procedures, rules, and associated documentation" (Rosenberg, 1984, p. 225). Throughout rapid and continuing diversification in hardware, there has been consistency at least in the tendency for each change to make the equipment smaller, more powerful, and less expensive per unit of work than the previous generation. These trends have increased immensely the number of people able to make use of the technology and the uses to which it can be put. Opportunities for application continually expand, including those that we are exploring for the application of information technology in the promotion of innovation in organizations.

Hardware has typically been classified in terms of the capacity of the computer, that is, according to whether the machine could be classed as mainframe, minicomputer, supercomputer, or micro- or personal computer. Mainframe equipment and philosophies dominated the market as the technical ability to make more and more powerful machines developed in the 1960s. Some challenge came to mainframe dominance with the development of the minicomputers in the 1970s, especially those available from Digital Equipment Company (DEC), such as the PDP and VAX series. Many academic libraries bought them with relish as stand-alone machines because they saw them as ways to extricate themselves from dependency on campus computing centers. The real challenge to the mainframe came, however, from developments in silicon chip technology. For a long time these effects were masked somewhat as the chips also made possible much faster and much less bulky mainframes. At the beginning of the 1980s, computer industry opinion tended to regard the microcomputer as a gimmick that would satisfy the hobby needs of professionals. A story related by Lawrence Magid, a computer analyst and writer, is that when trying to bring an Apple II into a university computing center he was told that the center didn't support video games (Magid, 1991). Mainframe experts often finished their dismissal of the microcomputer's prospects with the assurance that they had one at home!

Such attitudes were largely dissipated by the mid-1980s, by which time the inventors and entrepreneurs of personal computers had attained the status of heroes and their stories the stuff of legends. Steven Jobs and Steve Wozniak worked together in a garage to form the Apple Computer Company and sold their first computers through the mail. With their success they began in 1977 to work on the Apple II. Tandy/Radio Shack was already a major company when they released their first computer, the TRS-80 Model One in 1977. The Osborne became a popular portable in 1977. But it was not until 1981 that the IBM Corporation, the major force in the computing industry, introduced its first machine in the personal computer range, the IBM PC. The Macintosh, brought to the market by Apple in 1984, introduced the personal computer user to the icons and mouse of the first widely available graphic (or graphical) user interface (GUI). Again, it was several years later in 1987 that IBM introduced its new line of machines, the IBM PS/2, embodying the graphic sophistication begun by Macintosh. The early history of the PC, as told by Levy (1984), is most interesting in that it was the small entrepreneur and companies not in the computer field who were able to develop and bring innovations to the market, not the established computer firms. When IBM moved to develop a personal computer, the team working on the project was kept apart from, and thus protected from the rest of the company. This technique called intrapreneurship has already been discussed as an innovation strategy in Chapter 2 (p. 63). But as Magid (1991) notes, IBM did bring an aura of respectability to the fledgling PC industry.

The real competitive power of the personal computer has come through alliance with another area of technology, namely that of telecommunications and networking. The personal computer, operating in a LAN environment, can command speed and power that can not only satisfy technical requirements but that can also satisfy organizational requirements for the distribution of both power and responsibility.

In simple terms, the mainframe has a place when there is one major task to be accomplished, as for example in an airline reservation system. But the trend has been to opt for single larger systems rather than several smaller mainframe systems, and at the same time to continue to explore options, such as LANs (Ambrosio, 1992). The trend for the migration from mainframes seems to be established. Many new computer tasks, like product development, are being moved to workstations and personal computers linked in a network. On the other hand, existing "industrial strength computing chores," the phrase used by Lohr (1993, p. C1), will tend to stay on the mainframes, until the apparent cost savings from switching become overwhelming.

In certain market niches, support for minicomputer systems continues. There have been some recent noticeable successes in the minicomputer marketplace such as the IBM AS/400 (Verity, 1992), but the major hardware change has been the reduction in numbers of minicomputers in favor of PCs (Francis, 1989). This trend continues. Now, not only are PCs more powerful and less expensive than they were, but application software that originally required a minicomputer is now available for PCs on LAN-based systems. Furthermore with the increase in market size, software products for the LAN-based systems are superior to those written for the minicomputers. Minicomputers are not obsolete, however. Particularly for those organizations that already have one, the minicomputer can become a powerful server for a LAN—in other words, the minicomputer can serve to control communications and printing, to drive database functions, and to act as repository and switching device for network files. There are also developments to integrate other elements, specifically the Macintosh computer and the IBM PS/2 as desktop interfaces with the minicomputer. Projections indicate that the number of mainframe and minicomputers shipped through 1995 will remain flat. But the shipments of personal computers and workstations will continue its upward growth curve (Sherman, 1993).

Developments also continue at the highest end of the market, that is, in supercomputers, that category of machine that has the highest computation rate, highest memory, and highest cost in the marketplace at any given time. There are in fact two separate categories of supercomputers: the mini-supercomputer and the true supercomputer. The mini-supercomputer of which the price range falls within that of the mainframe, is a growing segment of the market. These are machines which, unlike the general-purpose mainframe, have special architecture for specific applications. (Electronic Industries Association, 1991, p. 50). The true supercomputer, on the other hand is geared towards scientific computations that require large amounts of memory, storage, and processing. There are, however, other applications for which such power is also required, notably sophisticated visual displays.

Another relatively new development has evolved round a computer built by connecting thousands of weak processors, using a parallel processor to make the various computer components work simultaneously on a problem. These have been dubbed "connection machines." Using this technology, the Thinking Machines Corporation has developed its latest machine with processing speed that could approach that of the supercomputer. One of the major applications of connection machines has been in the creation by the Thinking Machine Corporation, in collaboration with others, of a sophisticated management information system for a worldwide corporation, as is discussed later in this chapter (see p. 228).

Today's large computer installations allow choice of a variety of hardware levels in configurations that ought to be the most appropriate for the job. They could, for example, include personal computers that can operate on a LAN as well as provide connections to host systems, such as a mainframe and a superminicomputer; workstations that would have fast access to servers and more sophisticated host systems; remote access to a supercomputer; and connections to a multiprotocol network that would provide access to other global networks (University of Southern California, University Computing Services, 1991).

Software developments have been as dramatic as those in hardware. They have taken place in operating systems, programming languages, and application software. At first, hardware and software were provided together by the hardware manufacturer. But once technical developments allowed and business strategies recommended the unbundling of software and hardware, the impetus for software development moved from the hardware producer. (Discussion of software development is pursued in sections 5.2.4, 5.2.5, and 5.2.6.) Because the personal computer (PC) has become the dominant element in so many information systems and services, the next section is devoted to consideration of the technology that has allowed its remarkable rise.

5.2.1 The Rise of the Personal Computer

The development that has had the most widespread impact on the general public and therefore on the computer market has been the introduction of micro- or personal computers. Most of the discussion of technological changes undertaken in this chapter is related to them. Ample justification for this emphasis may be found in the facts that (1) the present focus of computerization and information systems development is at this level of hardware, particularly at the workstation level; (2) the market for this type of computer is great; and (3) companies, whether their specialty is hardware or software, are committed to innovation for this large base of computer users. In addition to these reasons there is also the fact that because of their wide availability and susceptibility to individual experiment, personal computers have been the catalyst for innovations not only in computer technology but also in products and services in many other fields, and in the organizational structures and procedures through which products and services are designed, made, and delivered.

Appearing from the end of the 1970s, personal computers were designed for a single user and brought computer processing power to a personal level. From modest beginnings, the CPU (central processing unit) power of these machines has developed to such a degree that in sophisticated systems it has come to rival that of the low-end mainframe systems. This trend in increasing the power of personal computers continues to be fueled by skilled marketing and the achievement of a high price to performance ratio. Increases in CPU speeds in PCs offer convincing evidence of the rate and scale of improvement in performance. CPUs are rated by the number of instructions they can handle in a given amount of time. It is easy to see why a CPU that can handle more instructions has the potential for being a faster, more powerful machine. One standard used to rate CPUs is the million instructions per second (MIPS). Many of the early PCs were based on a microchip that performed at a rate of under one MIPS. There is much more to making a computer fast than just the CPU chip, but trends in computer speed have been linked to the type of CPU used. Chip technology has progressed with each new generation faster than its predecessors. For example, the PCs with 80486 chips perform in the 10–12 MIPS range, which puts them in a class of performance equivalent in some ways to the much larger computers.

Another class of CPU chips has been built around a technology called reduced instruction set chip (RISC) and such chips now appear in PCs. Because of the high speeds of these RISC machines, which run, for example, at 20–25 MIPS, many have become popular with technical graphics users such as architects and designers who use the machines to run sophisticated graphics packages. In digital capacities, a picture is indeed worth many thousands of words in space taken, and therefore in the speed needed to fill a screen in the time required for real time operation.

Now that the hardware is becoming technically more advanced, PCs are beginning to support multiple concurrent users, in much the same way as mainframe computers. Borrowing some of the mainframe technology, PCs are beginning to be designed using multiprocessor architecture. It is especially attractive when multiple users are accessing the computer to do a variety of different applications. This facility may be especially attractive to individuals involved in different aspects of the innovation process, including data gathering and synthesizing, database creation, marketing and product development, and customer feedback analysis.

Some will argue that when twenty Intel 80486 chips are used in one computer, it no longer can be called a PC. But the main thrust of the technology is coming from the PC environment and multiprocessor machines can be expected to come much closer in price and in features to the PC than to the mainframe. One of the reasons that PCs are being made more powerful is that the cost of random access memory (RAM) has continued to decrease. The more RAM a computer has, the easier it is to process different applications simultaneously (a procedure called multitasking) and to handle more than one user (known as multiuser operation).

In addition to the rapid increase in computer speed, systems are offering the ability to store huge amounts of information. Disk capacities have grown in recent years. The first fixed disks that were available on the PCs could hold 10 megabytes of data (that is, about one million words of text). At the time, in the early 1980s, that capacity seemed considerable and the access time (that is, the time it took to find any location on the disk) seemed acceptable. Now it is possible to have a fixed disk that contains one gigabyte of data (that is, 1000 megabytes) and an access time that is one tenth of that attainable with the original disks. The interesting point of note is that both of these disks (the 10 megabyte and the 1 gigabyte) take up the same amount of physical space, roughly 5 × 8 × 3 in. The removable floppy disks, which originally held about 375 kilobytes (about 1/3 megabyte), are now available in smaller formats with higher capacities, such as 1.44 megabytes. Increases in movable disk capacities are expected to continue. For example, developments are occuring in removable disk storage that will make their capacities comparable to hard disk capacities. The floptical diskette is one example of the trend. This is a 3.5-in. diskette that can store 20 megabytes of data (Rosenblatt, 1991).

Disks (floppy as well as fixed) communicate with the CPU via a disk controller interface card. Early controllers could access two floppy disks and one hard disk. A development called the small computer system interface (SCSI—which rhymes with fuzzy) allows up to seven fixed disks to be controlled simultaneously by one controller. If 1-gigabyte disk drives were used, this would allow for a total disk memory capacity of 7 gigabytes.

There is, however, more to computer performance than fast CPUs and fast disks. Data move between all the devices within a computer on a "bus," which acts like a freeway for all the electronic instructions that are generated by the CPU. Just as freeways have the potential for traffic jams, computer buses have a similar potential, and the PC experienced just such a problem. The original PC bus had a width of one bit. Then appeared a bus that was two bits wide, an industry standard that stayed in existence for some time. Because the CPU and the RAM continued to increase in speed, more and more data were being sent down the bus, pushing it to its limits. As other components within the computer became faster, a new bus was needed to keep up with the other components of the system. Two different bus standards emerged, each giving similar boosts in performance to PC systems.

The micro channel architecture (MCA) bus was developed as a proprietary technology by IBM, which has since licensed it to a few other companies. The extended industry standard architecture (EISA) was developed by a consortium of companies, each resolved to make the architecture available to the industry as a whole. Both EISA and MCA attained faster performance by building a bus 4 bytes (that is, 32 bits) wide. And with performance standards increasing so quickly, further increases in bus width are expected. Mainframe computers have used wide bus design to deliver much of the performance they are known for, and it is a sign of the times that the same techniques are being applied to the PC market.

Continuing changes of the type described ensure continuance of the trend by which high performance PCs are used to do significant data processing jobs. Increased power does not necessarily imply increased bulk. PCs, as well as becoming more powerful, are also becoming smaller and are increasingly made to travel easily with the user wherever they are needed. And, as better screens have been made with liquid crystal display (LCD) technology, the size and weight have come down further. Rigid disk drives can be attached and portables can do without a drive by using a special cable to connect them to other PCs, thus enabling transfer of data without floppy disks. For example, in 1992 units were available with 40-megabyte fixed disks, an 80386 class CPU, and a full-featured keyboard. These machines weigh under six pounds and are small enough to fit within a standard briefcase. There are also computers with the same power as the original IBM PC, which weigh under 1 lb. and maintain a number of work-enhancement software packages loaded into permanent memory.

These portable computers open up new realms of applications for the PC. The largest use is by business people who need computing power wherever they go, whether it be for editing documents or manipulating numbers. Typically, the individual in management who owns a portable or laptop computer has a standard PC for use in the office. Another use is in the sales force—for recording orders and other customer needs and transmitting them to the company, whether by telecommunications link or wired upload into the company information system. The pocket or palmtop computer has established itself as a product: the market for the pen computer is just emerging from early technical problems with batteries and poor resolution in output. Typically, nomenclature is not yet standard and some companies are seeking to promote the term personal digital assistants (PDAs) as a separate entity from palmtops and pens (Louderback, 1993). Again typical of innovative computer products, standards tend to emerge after the first flush of marketing of the product on novelty value. The pen computer is following this path, with the announcement in April 1993 of the formation of an alliance of vendors to develop a standard for sharing pen-generated data across computer platforms ('Pen-computer standard', 1993). Portable computers contribute technology that is very helpful for just-in-time manufacture and warehousing, a trend already discussed in Chapter 2 (p. 61) and Chapter 3 (p. 105). Portables also generally allow more complete, more accurate, and swifter flow of information within an organization about its own operations. There is therefore no risk in predicting that the use of such products will become more and more commonplace in the conduct of everyday life.

5.2.2 Mass Storage Developments

Existing techniques for external mass storage have been improved and new ones invented. The original technology for external mass storage was magnetic tape, and over time ways to put more information on a smaller bit of tape were developed. Tapes now come in cartridge format, with the tape as narrow as 1/4 in. The quarter-inch cartridge (QIC) format has been an industry standard for some time. With a capacity of 525 megabytes and more, these cartridges measure about 3 × 5 in. It would take more than three of the large nine-track tapes of early digital storage to hold the same amount of data as one QIC cartridge. Development of larger capacity tapes in the QIC format has been confidently predicted (Thryft, 1990).

One of the latest formats introduced is the digital audiotape (DAT). These are the same tapes as are used to record music with high quality. DAT are in cartridges and can hold a little over 1 gigabyte of data. These cartridges hold as much information as more than eight of the old mainframe nine-track tapes would have held, and the DAT cartridge fits easily in a coat pocket. (Glass, 1990)

Other types of external storage device gaining in popularity in the PC market are loosely referred to as laser devices. All have the capacity to store huge amounts of data on removable media. The most familiar is the compact disk (CD), which is a 4-in. disk with the capacity to store 500 megabytes of digital information. Because of their immense capacity, many companies are encouraging CD use to reduce paper documentation. The Digital Equipment Company (DEC), for example, has done away with their product documentation paperwork, reducing storage requirements from a 4-ft-wide, ceiling-high bookshelf to the contents of two CDs. The use of CD format by United States government agencies, such as the Census Bureau, has already been mentioned in Chapter 3 (pp. 118–119). Obviously, CDs have potential application in all organizations that collect and need to retrieve from large stores of information.

The reason that so much data can be stored on one CD is because of the extremely close tolerances that laser technology allows. CDs operate much like the early phonograph record, with the thousands of "tracks" on the CD spreading out from the center in much the same way as the grooves of the vinyl albums. Because of the extremely high energy associated with the lasers in early CD machines, CDs were originally offered in a "read only" format. In 1990 NeXT, Inc., (the company that Steven Jobs left Apple to found) introduced the first PC class computer offering a writeable CD that could hold 256 megabytes of data. In 1993 competition from less expensive, but powerful, computer systems produced by other manufacturers forced NeXT to drop their hardware line to focus on software development (Weber, 1993b). Nonetheless, development of the writeable CD is not likely to cease. Although the write speed to the CD is slow compared to writing to other disks, the capability to store and transfer this amount of data opens still more opportunities.

When the information to be stored on CDs is sound or pictures, much more storage space is needed than for text. While one CD could hold about six copies of the Bible, it could hold about 35 min of high-fidelity music, or about 10 min of motion video. Still frame pictures may also be stored on CD, and this facility can be used in applications such as parts catalogs featuring full-color images of a company's complete line of products. Such catalogs could be distributed to regional sales offices and to major customers, and they would share the advantages of accessibility and space conservation, which have already been pointed out (p. 203) in the case of DEC, which has put its documentation on CD. A library in a competitor intelligence unit could use CDs to store competitors' product information. It is in fact impossible to put limits to the possibilities that CDs offer in regard to removable, fairly fast access data storage.

The CD-ROM publishing field is booming, and many academic and public libraries are subscribing to multiple services. Technical developments improve access to these products. Network access to CD-ROMs can be provided via a LAN, and concurrent access to more than one disk is made possible through the use of CD-ROM jukeboxes, also refered to as CD-ROM towers.

There are many other developments in optical disk storage techniques, including digital video interactive (DVI) and write once, read many [times] (WORM) disks. New products are continually brought to market embodying the technical advances. For example, the Sony Corporation has released a portable Data Discman™, a calculator-sized information retrieval system based on a 3.2-in. optical disk, capable of holding such titles as the Bible and the *Compton Concise Encyclopedia* ('Sony introduces hand-held system for data retrieval', 1991). Eaton (1989) provides a useful summary of the common optical products.

5.2.3 Output and Input Devices

Cathode ray tube (CRT) monitors have developed over the years as output devices for PCs from simple, character-based monochrome devices to high resolution units capable of displaying graphics in a range of 256 colors. A current standard used for graphic PC monitors, called the video graphics adapter (VGA) is capable of displaying a grid 600 pixels wide by 400 pixels high. A pixel is the smallest picture element addressable on a display screen. The VGA resolution (on a standard-sized monitor which is about 14 in. in diameter) produces smooth graphics for most applications. Screen resolution continues to be improved as, for instance in the high-performance graphic system, the extended graphics array (XGA), which handles resolutions on a grid of 1024 by 768 pixels.

There are also a high-end series of monitors, which are specifically designed for the ultra-high resolution necessary for drafting and design applications, such as might be appropriate, for example, in computer-based product design. Graphics of this quality require a significant portion of CPU power in order to provide the three-dimensional capabilities that these applications offer. So as not to take away from the main CPU of the computer, these sophisticated monitor adapters have separate dedicated processors that handle all the graphic instructions.

A noted computer analyst, Lawrence J. Magid (1991) has forecast that in the future CRT monitors will be replaced by flat active matrix panels that will display outstanding color images. Indeed, the flat panel display industry is growing and revenues in 1994 are expected to be over $4 billion (Lazzareschi, 1993). Homes and offices will have smart electronic wall panels, which can display computer data and video. In fact, there will be a trend towards a combined computer and TV display.

Computer printers have also evolved considerably. Three major technologies exist in the printer market, with the slowest and oldest being the impact type. The second type, which is still in wide use today is the dot-matrix printer. But the laser printer is the current state of the art. Using a technology very similar to that of copying machines, a laser printer produces quality output at a respectable speed. A side benefit of the laser printer is that it is almost silent in operation, which makes it attractive for quiet office environments. Standard resolution laser printers use a 300 dot-per-inch (DPI) matrix, which allows even curved lines to appear very smooth. Printing at a rate of between four and eight pages per minute, laser printers have emerged as the preferred technology for the business world. Mainframe computer centers have also switched over to laser printing technology and high speed printers are being used to print more than 50 pages per minute. Other developments in output technology include voice output, such as the Kurzweil Personal Reader, which can interpret a variety of text formats and convert them into speech, and color printers, which are becoming more affordable and have increasing high quality (O'Reilly, 1993).

A major aspect of any computer interaction revolves around the input of information, which is today primarily accomplished by the keyboard and the mouse. Alternatives include pen-based input, handwriting input, and voice recognition devices. A peripheral piece of hardware important to current PC input technology is the scanner, which is a device that processes a document, photograph, or other item of information on paper and transforms it into a digitized image, which can then be manipulated inside the computer. The software applications that can use these images vary: one uses the information as a graphic image; another called optical character recognition (OCR) converts the scanned image into text so that it can be used in a wordprocessing environment.

Although color scanners have begun to appear such as that unveiled by Macintosh at the beginning of 1993, the majority of scanners used with PCs are limited to imaging black and white. To achieve the subtle tone changes seen in a photograph, the scanner supports what are called gray scales. The most advanced scanners can handle 256 gray scales, making the PC image of the picture very detailed indeed (Antonoff, 1990). This detail is necessary for imaging systems to be useful to the graphics and art world.

Scanned images require a large amount of storage space. A standard 8.5 × 11 in. image, scanned at a normal resolution, takes about 1 megabyte of storage. It would be easy to run low on hard disk space if you worked with many images of this type. Data compression is one method used to reduce the space problem and the fundamentals of this technique are clearly explained in Lunin (1990). By running the data files through a processing algorithm, it is possible to obtain up to 94% savings of space, so the 1-megabyte file may only require about 66 kilobytes in its compressed form. The tradeoff with this technology is that running the compression/decompression algorithm takes time and it must be run each time a user wishes to access the image.

Applications of imaging technology range from the global to the local. Knowledge of the world's geology, geography, and resources has been augmented by the use of images derived from data transmitted by satellites in geostationary orbit. While the technology was developed for military applications, Landsat is probably the best known of these satellites. It was put into orbit in the 1970s by the United States and has since been joined by several others, including Seasat, from Europe as well as North America. These observations of the earth have formed the basis of a new discipline in geographic information systems (GIS) and much of the early development of data compression techniques was occasioned by the need to make sense of very large amounts of digital data from satellites.

Digitization allows images to be manipulated by software. Composite images can be formed, for example, to show the relation between crop types, soil types, and water availability in a particular geographical area. Effects can be created just like those an artist could achieve in retouching a picture. Areas of the image not in focus can be sharpened up and blemishes can be altered. Imaging systems can output these manipulated originals to very expensive typesetting machines (available at a per page price through professional typesetting houses). The images can also be output to laser printers. Image data can also be output to machines that can turn them into photographic slides.

5.2.4 Operating Systems

Advances on all fronts in hardware have of course been accompanied by advances in software. The operating system is the software that mediates between the applications programs and a level of instructions nearer to the machine's operations. A fuller definition indicates that it is "software that controls the execution of a computer program, and that may provide scheduling, debugging, input–output control, accounting, compilation, storage assignment, data management, and related services" (Rosenberg, 1984, p. 362). There are many types of operating systems available: Some are made to work on a variety of different types of hardware, and some are designed for only one specific type of machine.

Operating system software is written specifically for the type of function the computer is going to be used for. Generally, the more complex the function, the more complicated the operating system. In the early days of personal computing, all operating systems were single user. Apple, Amiga, Commodore, and IBM are all computer hardware manufacturers with machines that run different single-user operating systems. The most commonly used operating system in the world today runs on the IBM personal computer and the many work-alike brands, of which the total world population has been estimated at 100 million (Fallows, 1993). This is the Microsoft disk operating system (MS-DOS). Since the early 1980s, DOS has been improved and refined several times. Used heavily for business applications, DOS was pushed along to become the standard not because it is the best operating system, but rather because of the high popularity of the IBM PC and the vast amount of application software that has been written for it. And, since DOS is very low priced or even bundled in with computer purchases, it is popular with companies that have large numbers of PCs.

A second type of operating system described as multitasking is still only capable of having one user but more than one task can be operating at a time. The main task that requires the user's attention (for example, a word-processing program) remains on the computer monitor, while the other task is working away in the background. The background process could be a complex statistical analysis program that takes a long time to complete, and the user could spend the waiting time in writing a letter or memo. A multitasking successor to DOS is called operating system 2 (OS/2). This began as a joint effort of Microsoft and IBM but is now IBM's alone, as Microsoft has gone on to develop in its Windows environment an operating system with multitasking and other advanced capabilities. Multitasking operating systems must divide CPU resources between the different tasks. In addition, multitasking itself is a more sophisticated operating system than the single-user type, and can take more CPU resources just to run.

The third type of operating system is multiuser. By definition, multiuser systems are also multiprocessing, since each user that is working on the machine accounts for a separate process. Depending on the power of the CPU and the size of the computer, the number of users that can be working at once can go into the hundreds. The most obvious examples of multiuser systems are in the large mainframe environments. Systems like VMS from DEC and MVSA and VM from IBM are examples of operating systems with the potential for large numbers of users.

UNIX is a multiuser operating system that has gained high popularity. Developed originally at AT & T Bell Labs, UNIX was designed to be used by engineers and scientists. Because of its efficient design and built-in security features, plus its reasonable price, application software companies have considered UNIX an attractive development platform. Probably the most attractive feature of UNIX is that it is an open system and multiplatform. This means that the operating system will work on a range of hardware configurations from microcomputers to mainframes. A new competitor to UNIX on personal computers, workstations, and networks is the Windows NT operating system, a new operating system from Microsoft Corporation.

This open system approach has both advantages and disadvantages, but the benefits seem to outweigh the problems. Open systems promote competition among different developers and can lead to disputes and diverging trends. This is exactly what happened within the UNIX world. Two factions developed, with vendors lining up on either side of the fence. Led by IBM, Digital, Hewlett Packard, and other large companies, a group called Open Software Foundation (OSF) emerged to oppose standards that were being dictated by UNIX's original developer, AT & T. AT & T and Sun Microsystems formed an opposing group called Unix International (UI). Both groups have definite opinions on how the operating system should be developed for future releases. These differing opinions have caused some problems, but the overall effect of the competition should be a better operating system. Even those involved believe that the competition is good for UNIX (Tory, 1990).

Multiplatform open operating systems are very attractive because applications that are developed for one platform can be run on another with minimum conversion problems. A UNIX word-processing software package on a Sun workstation could also be used on a UNIX PC. The application is said to be "ported" (from the word portable, and ultimately from the Latin verb, *portare,* to carry) from one machine to another. On the other hand, proprietary systems (like those found on IBM mainframes) are designed to run on only one machine, therefore the software is not as easily shared among machines. From a user's point of view, much of this may not be important, but in the eyes of software developers and those in the computer industry watching marketing trends, the open systems approach is highly important.

One example of its importance is in the government open systems interconnection profile (GOSIP), which is further discussed on pages 255–256.

5.2.5 The User Interface

What is very important to the computer end-user community is the user interface. This interface is the communication link between the user and the machine. It is where the user meets the machine and it defines the way that users can go about their work. Changes in the computer interface are having major effects on operating systems, as well as the entire computer field.

The original computer interface was a cumbersome typewriterlike terminal that allowed the user to type the input, and then the CPU would respond by typing its response. Called a teletypewriter (TTY), these slow printing devices necessitated that the commands sent and received were brief and to the point. Operating system commands were also cryptic, nonstandardized, and therefore hurdles for beginners and infrequent users. The commands "ls" for list, "dir" for directory, and "listc" for list catalog are all commands used on different operating systems to get a listing of files.

The next development in computer interfaces appeared with the development of video display terminals (VDTs), cathode ray tubes, or computer monitors as they are more commonly called. These terminals allowed commands to be displayed much more quickly, and allowed the operating system to address the entire rectangular screen. Application software began to make use of this capability very quickly, but as far as the operating system went, the VDT just mimicked the line-for-line command and response scenario that originated with the TTYs.

Computer users who have a technical and scientific background usually get along fine with entering cryptic commands to communicate with the operating system, but such users are becoming the exception rather than the rule. As computers are applied in more and more fields, the typical user has no real interest (or need, for that matter) to get involved with complex operating system commands. Their need, rather, is to get the computer to perform the type of work that they need to do. Learning operating system commands has tended to be a necessary evil for users. In the mid- to late 1980s, however, everything began to change in the area of user interfaces and operating system commands.

The development that allowed this change was the ability for terminals to display graphic images in addition to the characters they traditionally projected. Graphics allow lines, curves, and designs to be displayed and, optionally, in a variety of colors. Graphics can also be used to display text with the added benefit that a character can be adjusted to appear in different sizes, with attributes like italic or bold, and using any of a variety of type styles. In contrast, the character-based nature of the original VDT allowed only one appearance for each character. When graphics first became available many application software programs made use of them right away. Operating system software, however, remained limited to a character-based command line approach until Apple released the first computer with a graphical user interface (GUI) when it shipped its first Macintosh computer in January 1984 (Cocula and Ryland, 1990). The idea behind the Macintosh (as well as behind GUIs in general) is that graphic symbols, menu bars, and windows are all manipulated with the help of a pointing device, a mouse, attached to the computer. This intuitive graphical representation may be more easily accepted by the user, especially one who is new to computing.

The convenience and ease of learning afforded by the GUI doesn't come without a price. Graphic-based software is much more difficult to program and takes more of the computer's resources than does a program using a character-based interface. Those experienced in keyboarding claim that it is usually considerably slower. After you have learned it, typing the word "dir" and hitting the enter key comes very naturally and quickly. Using the mouse to click on the appropriate boxes usually takes more time. For this reason, many of the GUIs also allow, as Macintosh did from the beginning, optional keyboard input as well as the mouse driven input (Hayes, 1990).

Microsoft Corporation began working on a GUI soon after the Macintosh was released. Originally called Windows, it was actually an application program that sat on top of the operating system (the DOS operating system) and insulated the user from the need to learn any DOS commands. A parallel development of a truly complete operating system based on the Windows look is the product called OS/2. As has already been mentioned in section 5.2.4, OS/2 is a multitasking (single-user) operating system. Both of these interfaces have made possible Macintosh-like interactions in the PC environment and added the ability to run an application program in a window, then reduce the window down to a small icon, while another windowed application is run.

Compared to DOS, UNIX is a very complicated operating system for a user to learn, and therefore a UNIX-based GUI was needed to remove some of the mystery of the system. The first GUI for UNIX was called Open Look and was provided with the Sun Microsystems' SunOS operating system. The OSF also developed their own GUI and patterned it very closely after the Microsoft Windows product. Called Motif, this windowing GUI has the backing of a large number of computer companies, and is believed to be the GUI that will emerge as a widely agreed upon and used standard in the years to come (Blackford, 1990).

Just as UNIX is benefiting from different companies being involved with refining the operating system, the GUIs for use with UNIX are being developed so as to communicate via a standard methodology. This will ultimately allow a user to have the same-looking user interface no matter which kind of computer or which kind of operating system is being used. Thus, in the jargon used to describe computer systems, they are open systems. So, in the UNIX world, even though Motif and Open Look are different, both adhere to a set of rules laid out by researchers at the Massachusetts Institute of Technology called the X-Window System. Now GUI software based on the X-Windows standard is available for the DOS-based computers. Adherence to a standard is important if two dissimilar machines are going to be connected together.

Standards are important in all communication—machine to machine, human to machine, and human to human. As protocols in the telecommunications environment or as shared conventions in applications programming, standardization helps to smooth physical and logical differences. The commercial scales appear to have tipped in favor of interconnectedness. Section 5.4, "Harnessing Information Technology for use," focuses on human factors in the management of technology, and there are strong indications that user demand will continue to fuel this trend. But it is also interesting to look at the shared effort and increasing productivity in programming made possible by advances in computer languages, and how increased sophistication in functionality is also occurring.

5.2.6 Computer Languages

In the early days of computing the only way to develop software applications was via a structured computer language. Although they have gone through many changes making them easier to use, for the most part computer languages still require formal training to master their usage. Most computer application software, however, is these days designed to be easily learned and used by many people. The use of application software accounts for the vast majority of user hours spent at computers today. A team of a dozen software programmers might create a wordprocessing application program that is purchased by thousands of users. Changes in computer languages will first be examined, and this will be followed by a discussion of the current trends in application software.

Computer languages have gone through major changes since the 1950s, and these changes can be characterized as different generations of languages, in which communication has moved from machine language to symbolic language to higher-level language. The third-generation languages (the higher-level languages), such as Fortran, Cobol, BASIC, Ada, and C, gave real power to the programmers and are most widely used today. With some exceptions, languages are independent of hardware and operating systems. So a programmer who learns the C language on a PC will be able to use the same knowledge to program in C on an IBM mainframe.

The basic features of all third-generation languages comply with certain logical constructs. Programs can test to see if certain mathematical conditions are true, and if they are, execute a series of commands. Programs can "loop," or do a number of things over and over until signaled to leave the loop. They can also read input from the keyboard, test it for certain qualifiers, and display it on the screen. Each of these actions, while basically simple in concept, require substantial numbers of program statements to implement.

The fourth generation of languages has emerged to accomplish two things. One is to reduce the number of repetitive tasks that are common to all programs, and the second is to make the syntax of the commands easier to use. Both of these goals reflect the trend towards more people with less experience entering the world of computer programming. And they also reflect the desire to reduce the amount of time needed to program an application. By specifying a command like "update" the compiler actually substitutes a whole series of third-generation codes that perform an addition to a certain file. Fourth-generation languages are becoming popular in the database programming world because of these time and resource saving features.

A radical change in sophistication is involved with the fifth generation of programming languages. The main thrust of this generation of languages is in the field of artificial intelligence (AI). Emphasizing topics referred to as knowledge systems, knowledge-based systems, or expert systems, the world of AI has developed slowly over the years. Originated in 1956 by a group at Dartmouth College, AI is a type of programming that attempts to have the computer solve problems or determine courses of action based on the type of information with which it is presented (Walker and Miller, 1990). The LISP language is the most popular example of an AI programming language today.

AI has had an impact on programming but a similar impact is seen in the area of application software. And, although much work has been done over the years with AI, the complex nature of its goal makes progress slow. In order for a machine to make decisions, a very exhaustive set of rules must be provided for the machine to follow. The rules make up what is referred to as the knowledge base and much time is required to specify all these rules. If a physics teacher takes twenty weeks to teach a class of students the introduction to physics, an expert would be required to provide very many specific rules and information for the same knowledge base to be embedded in expert systems software. This is one of the reasons that AI software is not widespread and also is very expensive to develop.

There are signs however that the market for expert systems is developing, as software becomes off the shelf, more affordable, less complex, and more under the control of the user. Until the late 1980s, the user usually had to hire, along with the software, a knowledge engineer from the vendors in order to install an application. The next big movement in the market is towards application shells that allow small and medium-size companies access to expert systems. Many systems now operate in manufacturing and in information industry applications, such as letters of credit, claims adjustment, and stock trading.

An interesting offspring from AI thinking is something called fuzzy logic. Developed in the mid-1960s at the University of California, Berkeley, fuzzy logic is a combination of innovative hardware and software ideas. The premise behind fuzzy logic is that in the real world, answers are not always as clear-cut as yes or no. "Fuzzy logic is an attempt to make machines reason more like humans—taking into account a number of factors that are not precise to make common-sense judgement. When fuzzy theory is applied to control systems in machines, a number of variables are represented in mathmematical terms that are analyzed simultaneously to make operational decisions" (Helm, 1992, p. D4). Standard digital circuitry distinguishes only two values (0 or 1), depending on its electronic state. Fuzzy chips have the ability to represent values between 0 and 1 based on the relative amount of electricity that flows through them (Savage, 1990).

Although it has only slowly been embraced by United States developers, the Japanese industry has been using fuzzy logic for some time now. Fuzzy logic is being used to adjust subway schedules to rush-hour peak load in Japan. The software adjusts train speeds, and assists in bringing trains to smooth stops within terminals. In another application, air conditioners can make temperature adjustments based on the number of people in a room. One major United States refrigerator manufacturer is using fuzzy logic to determine when it is time to defrost the freezer. Fuzzy logic is predicted to become a major area of development and to become a $2 billion industry within the next 10 years (Rogers and Hoshiai, 1990). It is already available in the wide area information servers (WAIS) protocols which, among other applications, may be used for searching the Internet and which are also mentioned in section 5.3.3.2.

5.2.7 Application Software

Application software consists of the programs that allow the user to get work done. The biggest change in this area has been prompted by the huge number of users that personal computers have brought into the field.

Increased competition among software companies has provided the user with a wide selection of software that addresses new needs as well as allowing choice among a series of offerings in the major application areas. Trends toward making application software easier to use have further added to benefits that end-users enjoy.

Although the bulk of application software still is character based, an increasing percentage is following the GUI formats discussed on pages 209–210. This adds to the ease of use of the software and allows more novice users to utilize it. Software developers have been financially motivated to listen to the demands of the users, and the users are unanimously asking for simpler and better software.

In Chapter 3 pages (pp. 98–99) we discussed the different bases from which text processing software has developed, depending on whether it was to be applied in the office with WP, the traditional publishing house with the standard generalized markup language (SGML), or in any of the many environments in which the linking of computers with high-quality printers has made on-demand or desktop publishing (DTP) possible.

Word processing is one of the most widespread application software types in use today. Developed as a successor to primitive text editors that were popular on mainframe computers, a word-processing program allows interactive editing of documents, enabling easy redrafting and merging of chunks of existing documents, without the need for extensive retyping. Most of the popular programs have features such as spell checkers, outlining, choice of fonts, line drawing, as well as page layout settings to produce any type of document desired. One feature that most of the popular packages offer is a way to see just how the document will look on the printed page. This is a handy feature when laying out complicated tables or columns of text.

Desktop publishing programs contain many of the features of word-processing software, but go even further in the ability to layout the format of a printed page. These packages are being used to control complex components of the printing process right from the PC. Desktop publishing does what used to be called typesetting, and has truly changed the printing business. Sophisticated packages like Ventura Publisher and PageMaker allow in-house departments to produce newspaper and other page layouts, to include graphic images that were digitized with scanners, and print the output to laser printers or high quality devices that produce camera-ready output. Although once much more difficult to use than a word processor, many of the features of desktop publishing software have been streamlined and are now incorporated in word-processing packages. While variety of type font and size is not to be confused with sound typographical design, in general, application of DTP techniques has improved the look of in-house documents and manuals in many organizations. A new development in DTP is the ability to exchange on various personal computer platforms final documents in published formats. It is noted that this may pave the way for electronic distribution of the wide array of materials, such as newsletters, which are now distributed in print form (Weber, 1993a).

Another major type of application comes under the heading of database software, which allows for the collection of, searching for, and manipulation of information about unique entities. The topic might be the characteristics of competitor products, the bibliographic and abstract information relating to relevant research publications and activities dealing with an area of R & D, or it could be addresses, phone numbers, and purchasing information on the customers of a current product. All and any topics on which files of information may be collected are susceptible to control by database-management software. An early arrival to the PC database-management software market was a product from Ashton-Tate called dBase. Still in use today, dBase also provided a fairly sophisticated third-generation programming language. Everyday users can use the software in its standard form but the programming features allow more advanced users to develop custom applications that are tailored specifically to an organization's needs.

A very popular trend in the database market, especially on computers that use UNIX, is the use of relational databases. Developed by researchers at IBM, the relational model of database design uses the theories of symbolic logic to define how data are organized. Database software that follows the relational model is especially useful when dealing with large applications and when storing large amounts of data. Relational database products can minimize problems that arise with redundant information and keeping data up-to-date. Relational database products have appeared on all levels of hardware systems. An example of a successful relational database system in the library environment is Carlyle Systems Voyager Series.

Client/server architecture (as used in the Voyager Series) is another feature that database software applications are providing. Although not actually limited to database applications, this technology is used to share the task loads when the database is on one computer and the user is sitting at another. This arrangement is called networking and will be discussed in a later section. The example is pursued a little further here as yet another technique for extending the range and power of a personal computer. If a user is sitting at a PC and communicating to a minicomputer in the next room (the mini is acting as a file server), rather than have the server do all the work, a client/server arrangement would allow the CPU in the PC to do all the work related to entering data on the screen, and only send information over to the server CPU when the information on the screen is correct. The main advantage of this technology is that more users can simultaneously use the database, and the database can be run on a less sophisticated computer that has less CPU power. This dramatically lessens the cost of implementing a database system.

Spreadsheet software, which manipulates tables of numbers and text, has been a workhorse for the financial markets for years now, and these days it is likely to be used not only in every report in an organization with quantitative data but in almost every student assignment as well. Most spreadsheets can also show the data graphically. Another feature commonly offered is the easy interchange of data between it and other application programs, such as a word-processing document. Some spreadsheet programs also allow three dimensional graphical representation of the data.

Presentation graphics represent another category of application software currently being used in the PC market. Packages such as Harvard Graphics, Micrographics Graph, and Corel Draw all offer advanced graphing and drawing features. The user can create simple textual graphs or complex line charts and then add textual information to complete the image. Standardized sets of symbols (called clip art) are either included with the software or can be purchased optionally to customize the appearance of the presentation. Output can be sent to laser printers for inclusion with documents or can be directed to slide-making devices to create presentation slides. Due to the high cost of these slide-making cameras, service agencies are available that will take the data (optionally sent in via modem) and image the slide for a reasonable fee. The main advantage of presentation graphics software is the ability to quickly do in-house what used to require graphic artists considerably longer to create and oftentimes had to be sent to an outside vendor.

As already mentioned, digital data are not limited to the storage and manipulation of text and numerical symbols nor to graphic images. They can also encode moving pictures and audio data. Many new databases carry an additional field type to handle these. Called binary large objects (BLOB), these fields are contained in the same record structure as the textual data. When a user accesses a certain record the lower part of the screen might display textual name and address information while a video still image is displayed in the upper part of the monitor. Databases of this type have new potential for categorizing individuals and are being used, for example, by law enforcement agencies for identification of suspects, not to mention in the amalgamation of student photographs with the rest of the student records in some colleges.

As well as, and in many cases associated with multimedia, are applications of the techniques of *hypertext* and *hypermedia,* which are predicted to have a major impact on approaches to computer interactions in the next few

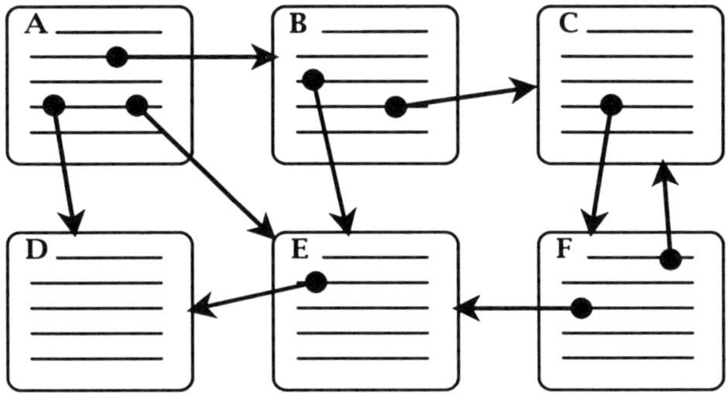

Figure 5.1
Simplified view of a small hypertext structure having six nodes and nine links (source: Nielsen, 1990).

years. Marchionini (1988) indicates that hypertext is to be regarded as the "electronic representation of text that takes advantage of the random access capabilities of computers to overcome the strictly sequential medium of print on paper" (p. 8). Burnett (1992) regards hypertext as the meta-organizing principle of the design; a metaphor for it could be a kind of invisible web underlying and supporting the information in the database perhaps. Hypermedia can be thought of as databases in any media using hypertext as the organizing principle. Essential to the idea of both hypertext and hypermedia is, as Nielsen (1990) points out, the notion that they are nonsequential. Figure 5.1 illustrates this concept and points out the hypertext structure as a network of nodes and links through which users navigate.

Assume that you start by reading the piece of text marked A. Instead of a single next place to go, the hypertext structure has three options for the reader: Go to B, D, or E. Assuming that you decide to go to B, you can then decide to go to C or to E, and from E you can go to D. Since it was also possible for you to go directly from A to D, this example shows that there may be several different paths that connect two elements in a hypertext structure (Nielsen, 1990).

Many interesting hypertext and hypermedia applications have already been created in library and information work. An early project involved the use of optical media and hypertext indexing of Chinese antiquities in the First Emperor of China Project (Chen *et al.*, 1988). A more recent application in the Micro Gallery at the National Gallery of Art in London combines digital reproductions of the gallery's pictures with indexes that provide information about artists, art, and even a printed guided tour to the pictures chosen to look at during gallery visits (Maguire, 1991).

Multimedia on the other hand is a more comprehensive term, encompassing the use of multiple media, maybe digital and analog codes, and the formats can include relational databases (in which data are represented as a set of tables, each one of which represents a relation), flat-file databases (in which all necessary descriptive information about data is stored in a location within the file itself), and hypermedia (the structure of which is indicated in Figure 5.1) (Burnett, 1992). Hypertext interfaces often work very well with multimedia applications. For example, Steve Mamber of the Department of Film and Television at the University of California, Los Angeles, has created a multimedia application in which images on a videodisc are indexed using hypermedia software on an MS-DOS processor (Maguire *et al.*, 1991).

Multimedia applications combine many hardware and software components. In addition to the PC with appropriate interface and display and enough storage, the typical components in multimedia include the following: (1) audio consisting of CD audio akin to the CD player found in the home, and waveform audio, which accepts and digitizes audio and stores the file on the computer for later playback; (2) musical instrument digital interface (MIDI) audio, which is a digital protocol for the transmission of musical data and which encodes every action performed on a MIDI musical instrument; (3) video, including a PC graphic adaptor and a video adaptor that can accept input from some TV sources and can operate as a videodisk and VCR controller, as well as allow for recording computer-generated images on videotape; (4) a video capture board, which allows for the digitization of single video frames; (5) a motion video board, which can capture and store multiple frames; and storage, including a hard disk and CD-ROM. (Miller, 1992; Hendall, 1992). Popular applications of multimedia are in *The New Grolier Multimedia Encyclopedia* (Grolier, 1992) and *Mammals: A Multimedia Encyclopedia* (National Geographic Society, 1990).

In addition to these examples there are hundreds of different kinds of applications software available. Developers are designing better interfaces and some standardization is being seen. Small but useful examples are, for example, on most DOS software, the F1 key (function key 1), which usually brings up a help window, and the escape key which usually is used to return to the previous screen. Software developers are hiring designers who have specific training in fields such as instructional technology, and who bring the psychological knowledge of how people learn best to the design process. The importance of these human factors is examined further in section 5.4.

The technological advances described so far have contributed to the major innovation in that most people spend at least part of their working lives using computers. The power of computers to effect changes in organizational systems, in attitudes and skills, and to influence profound social change has been very much extended and intensified by their ability to communicate with each other.

5.3 Networking and Telecommunications

Computers can now communicate with each other and with a range of peripheral devices, over distances small and vast, and with increasing speed and reliability. Technological advances in worldwide communications have ushered in a new era not only of computing power but of access to information services, at least in those parts of the world that have been able to develop extensive and reliable telephone networks. The transmission over the telephone network, not only of voice but more recently also of text and simple illustration through telefacsimile, laid the foundations for this age in which communication is taken for granted in developed countries. Predictions made earlier that rapid growth in computer networking would be the emphasis of the 1990s seem to be borne out in the developments of networks at local, regional, national, and global levels. These developments are now examined under the headings, local area networks, wide area networks and public networks.

5.3.1 Local Area Networks

Definitions of local area networks (LANs) are not precise regarding size in terms of area covered, number of devices connected, and connection speeds. The essential ideas are (1) that the LAN serves one working group of people, whether this is in a small organization or a department of a large one, and (2) that the hardware and software involved is accessible in terms of both cost and sophistication of knowledge needed for its installation and maintenance. The LAN is very much a product of the personal computer revolution. Its major application has been in the field of office automation (OA) which is another term difficult to subject to precise definition. Martin (1988), for example, defines it as a way of providing users with a better and more complete way to perform their work. Apart from the PC itself, the LAN has permitted the most significant advances in the field of OA. The LAN has gone a long way to bridging the distance between OA, telecommunications, and data processing, which, as mentioned already (see p. 197) have been regarded as islands in the information archipelago in organizations. The most popular PC LANs, such as Novell Netware and Banyan

Vines, offer similar features. The main distinction in function between LANs and other networks is that the high speed links they offer are mainly for the purpose of sharing resources, not running centralized applications.

By sharing resources and defining work groups that all have access to a common set of tools, the concept of interconnecting workers through technology is changing the way offices in commerce, industry, and government function, as well as other work groups such as academic departments in universities.

From a financial standpoint, sharing commonly used resources has a great cost savings potential. Sharing laser printers is a major reason that organizations set up LANs. With the cost of an 8-page-per-minute laser printer running at about $1700, it makes sense to use a LAN and share it among users. Telephone modems or other high-speed communication devices can also be put on the LAN and shared by a number of users. And, as the name *file server* implies, an optimum use of the LAN is to store data (files) on the server machine, which extends the amount of disk space and therefore the amount of data that each connected PC can access.

Networking in the UNIX environment is attractive in terms of the requirements of OA. UNIX offers the same functionality for file server operations as in a typical LAN environment but, in addition, UNIX has a sophisticated file addressing scheme built right into the operating system. Many UNIX versions support network file system (NFS), which is becoming a standard in the LAN arena. Versions of NFS are available for DOS PCs, so that an office worker can use a DOS system, and have the file server functionality running on the UNIX server.

In general, LANs are hard-wired. But it is interesting to note the development of WaveLAN, an NCR product that allows personal computers within a maximum radius of 100 ft to be connected without the use of cables. This could be an option for those facilities in which it is difficult to run wires, or in instances where PCs are moved quite frequently.

In addition to specific work enhancement software available on the network, office automation products available on the LAN include electronic mail (E-mail) as well as group schedulers. E-mail is described in more detail on pages 232–233.

The concept of the *workstation* has taken root and flourished in the LAN environment. For the majority of office applications a reasonably priced PC will suffice. But there is emerging another class of user who needs a computer that has more CPU power and greater flexibility than the low-end PC offers. To fit this requirement, the industry has introduced a new type of desktop computer, which has attracted the generic name workstation, a term already used several times in this chapter.

Getting a definition of what actually denotes a workstation can be difficult. Some say that since performance is linked to price, anything over $7500 is a workstation, but price is a very unstable characteristic at all points in the PC market. A more informative description is that a workstation is a computer that is networked to a file server and has an operating system capable of multi-tasking (Egol, 1990). Since much of the multi-tasking software makes use of multiple windows, most workstations are equipped with high-performance graphics monitors as well. What all description of workstations implies is that they possess greater power than PCs. These machines are being used for graphics applications such as computer aided design (CAD) and in many other applications and experiments. Many of the workstations offer much higher performance than minicomputers that would have cost ten times as much just a few years ago.

Image processing is very much part of the LAN environment of OA where it is seen as an aid to both the efficient storage and retrieval of documents and the reduction of the amount of hard copy (paper) generated during the day-to-day course of an organization's operations. Sometimes called the "paperless office," the concept is often scorned for its obvious lack of reality. But important applications of imaging technology have been made, which have averted the need to keep some very large paper files. Examples include the storage of income tax returns by the United States Internal Revenue Service and of credit card receipts by American Express. Imaging technology also has enormous potential in the areas of conservation, preservation, and journal processing in libraries (Lunin and Lynch, 1991).

The components necessary for image processing exist. Scanners can read in the images, and large hard disks or laser CDs can store them. High resolution monitors can display the images; LANs can move and share them, and high-speed laser printers can print them. The problem arises when all those components are to be connected into one system and be operationally efficient so that any user can access any document in rapid time. Investments have been made to create suitable systems. The 3M Company, for example, offers a high-end integrated system called the Docutron that delivers a system offering all the required functions (Vogt, 1989). To address the mass storage problem, an optical storage and retrieval (OSAR) system has been developed that uses a carousel type arrangement to access up to 204 optical disks (which use a similar technology to the CD), allowing as much as 530 gigabytes of data storage within the automated system.

The second hurdle to "the paperless office" is psychological. There is a human tendency still to believe that generating a photocopy of something keeps it frozen in time and always retrievable. Even though we know that a letter is stored away on the disk, it seems safer if we go ahead and produce something tangible. It will take time until users become more confident about the computer systems they use in their everyday work and forgo the need to generate hard copy. So far, indeed, computer systems have produced no artifact more useful in triggering action than a piece of paper. Again the image arises of an environment that is not paperless but in which there may one day be less paper.

5.3.2 Facsimile Transmission

One paper-based innovation of the past decade that has changed the world of OA and lent itself well to incorporation in PC-based systems is the telefacsimile or fax machine. To most users, fax, which can take, scan, and transmit in black and white any document over the telephone lines, is a fast postal service. Facsimile transmission was in fact a nineteenth century innovation. Invented by a Scottish engineer who patented it in 1843, the technology went through the usual curve of cumulative enhancement and the first commercial fax service opened in France in 1865. It ceased in 1870, with the outbreak of the Franco–Prussian War. Hunkin (1993) offers the following explanation of the failure of fax as a nineteenth century innovation: "The telegraph already provided a quick simple way of sending written messages, and the pace of business life was still slow enough for there to have been no real demand for sending drawings or pictures instantaneously" (p. 34).

The rapid dissemination of fax technology in the past decade may be explained in terms of the accessibility of the telephone networks for transmission, the simplicity of the human interface, and the promptness with which industry standards were established. Fax has proved especially useful for the transmission of line drawings, and it has been suggested that the speed and ease with which engineering drawings can be sent all over the world has allowed companies to undertake contracts that would previously have been impractical (Hunkin, 1993). Some extra impetus to fax development also resulted from its convenience in transmitting handwritten memoranda, especially in Japan, where early word-processing systems for kanji, the characters of the Japanese language, were complex and cumbersome.

The current standard used with most fax machines is called Group 3. Group 3 fax machines allow adjustable resolution selection on the documents that are being sent. Since sending time is linked to scanning time, and it is in turn linked to resolution, this feature permits an image of a rough correspondence to be sent quickly. Transmission times per page for Group 3 machines range from around 30 secs to over 1 min, and resolution quality is adequate for typescript but not for newsprint.

There is some controversy over whether the next major change in fax technology will be widespread adoption of the Group 4 international standard, which has been in existence since 1984. Designed to work with digital telephone networks, Group 4 machines offer faster transmission and higher resolutions. When using Group 4 machines, a page can be sent in as little as four seconds; a maximum resolution of 400 dots per inch (DPI) can be achieved, which is about 40% better quality output than is available from the standard 300 DPI laser printers (Wexler, 1989). The disadvantages of Group 4 technology lie in the more complicated handshake (connection and disconnection procedure) and in the fact that Group 4 signals do not travel well over satellite links. Therefore, while some manufacturers are committed to promoting Group 4, others are promoting an enhanced Group 3 standard.

The trend towards integrating current technologies seems set to continue with fax technology fully integrated with the telephone and the PC. One such system installed at the Australian Securities Commission has already been described in Chapter 3, (pp. 82–83). The addition of a fax card to a PC allows the dispatch and receipt of facsimile messages. Facsimile is also used increasingly in the document delivery systems on which libraries and other clients depend, such as the Uncover system offered by the Colorado Association of Research Libraries (CARL). The contents of current serials in a wide range of disciplines are listed on-line, and the full text of requested articles is scanned and transmitted by fax to subscribers all over the world on request by input of a valid charge card number. As in all digital systems, the seams between different applications continue to grow more difficult to discern and, for the user, such discernment becomes increasingly irrelevant. Some distinctions can, however, usefully be drawn between the LAN environment so far discussed and that of wide area networks (WANs).

5.3.3 Wide Area Networks

The success of facsimile transmission has amply demonstrated the utility of the switched telephone network for data communication. But the reliable and affordable communication of amounts of data large enough to constitute resource sharing among computers required a different solution. This was found in packet switching, a facility originally developed through the Advanced Research Projects Agency (ARPA) of the United States Department of Defense in the ARPANET Project, which was begun in 1968. Black (1987) distinguishes packet switching from message switching and explains, "Packet switching is so named because user data (for example, messages) are broken down into smaller pieces. These pieces, or packets, have protocol information placed around them and are routed through the network as independent entities" (p. 175). In comparing packet switching to message switching, Black goes on to point out that in packet switching more switches allow the network load to be distributed to multiple switching sites. Thus, alternate routing arrangements can be made around failed or busy nodes and channels. Instead of requiring either a dial-up or a leased line connection, the user of a packet-switched network can access it at a local node, attract costs that are related to the amount of data transmitted and independent of the distance involved, and enjoy communication of high reliability in which the data transmitted are virtually error-free.

Packet switching is probably the technology that has done most to allow the development of WANs, the communication links that connect computers at remote locations, whether in the building next door or all over the world. One main difference between a WAN and a LAN is the level of sophistication of the hardware involved in the communication process. Often WANs are made up of different types of computers or may even be used to connect a series of LANs. When dissimilar computers or multiple LANs are connected, it is often necessary to install intelligent pieces of hardware that act as traffic cops to keep information flowing smoothly. These pieces of hardware are sometimes called bridges or routers, and the computers or LANs they connect are referred to as nodes on the network. As one might expect, this higher level of sophistication also means that the costs involved with WANs are significantly higher than for LANs.

In a discussion about a network, or computers that are networked, there is reference to their ability to share data. One way to share data is to physically transfer the data from one place to another on the network, such as copying a file from a floppy disk to the hard disk on a personal computer. A file can be copied from one computer, through the network, to the computer on the other end. This function is sometimes called file transfer. The least sophisticated type is used by organizations to send large amounts of data to a central location at a specific time interval. Quarterly sales reports can be sent over the WAN to the home office, and then combined to prepare aggregate financial reports. Some companies have daily transfer of data. One advantage to this type of operation is that only one person at the home office needs to be trained to create and analyze the reports, rather than having to hire people in each location to perform the analysis. Another advantage is the reduction in resource needs. If the analysis requires a sophisticated computer or costly software, it is only necessary to purchase one of these systems and keep it at the central location, thus allowing the data collection to be performed at the remote sites by less costly systems.

Another way to share data is a little less intuitive and involves running a software application on one machine from the keyboard of another computer located elsewhere on the network. This sets up a link between the two machines and is called remote log-in. This concept of logging in to a distant computer is nothing new—mainframe computers have used the idea for years—but having the capability to do it over thousands of miles of network is a relatively new capability. A straightforward remote application takes all instructions and executes them on the remote machine, while a distributed processing application completes some of the programming tasks on the local computer and sends only the necessary data via the network to the remote computer. Both types of remote processing are now becoming much more feasible due to the high speeds attainable over the networks. One example of a remote database application is being used by the Italian government to automate the toll collection process on the country's busy highway system. Sensing devices at the toll booths read credit card data sent out by a radio device on the drivers windshield visor, and transmits the billing information to a central computer via a fiber distributed data interface link (Caswell, 1990).

WANs first started with the military and then incorporated connections with universities and research institutions in the ARPANET Project already mentioned. They now include applications in business, industry, and medicine. Sharing data through WANs has been an attractive technology in the business world for a number of reasons. First, the utility of interorganizational communications possible through WANs is appealing. Network mail, for example, allows quick and inexpensive communications among employees. Broadcasting mail to a whole group of employees can facilitate the distribution of company information. For large companies, another attractive feature of WANs is the ability to have employees in distant locations work on the same project. Keeping one copy of the project documents in a central location that all can access promotes efficiency and eliminates redundancy. Central location may also lessen the possibility of incompatible updates, which come about when different users work from different versions of a document, each thinking that they have the latest version. Another benefit from networking can be reduced software costs by buying one networked copy of a software package to run on one machine on the network and allowing users access rather that buying individual copies for all the machines. The motivation for connectivity is high, and the WAN is quickly becoming the vehicle through which application of a host of developing technologies is possible.

Voice transmission, sometimes called voice mail is one of them. This is a new technology that allows voice data to be recorded, transmitted, and stored via digital means. Using a special converter to change the analog sound into digital information, the data can be sent out over a WAN in much the same manner as electronic mail, which is discussed in some detail in section 5.3.4. A larger amount of data is needed to transmit sound than transmit text. For an adequate conversational quality sound, it currently requires about 100 kilobytes of data for one minute of voice (Derfler, 1990). When compared to the 2 kilobytes required to store the amount of data a person could read in a minute, this storage requirement does add up. Another issue related to networking is the increased transfer loads that are put on the WAN with voice transfer. If, for example, the volume of mail that currently travels daily on the Internet were to be suddenly converted into audio data, the network speed would suffer dramatically.

High-quality sound is also available via digital transmission. Again, the higher the quality of sound, the more data are required to represent it, and the more space needed to store it. Networks could be used to access large music databases, allowing users the superb listening quality found with digital CD players. Clearly, transmission speed and therefore capacity is the crucial variable in network performance.

5.3.3.1 WAN Performance

Prior to a discussion of the different types of WANs and their components, it is important to define this critical performance issue by which they are all judged—transmission speed, defined in terms of bits per second (bps). The key to the success of WANs is the high transmission speeds attainable. There are two basic reasons why high speeds are desirable. The application software that makes use of the network potential tends to be "real time" programs. Sometimes called interactive applications, these programs operate while the user waits, and quick response time is mandatory. A prime example of a real time application is the automated teller machines (ATMs) provided by banks that have become so popular. Another reason that high speeds are necessary for WANs has to do with reducing traffic jams on the network. WANs are made to support many users at the same time, and each user is transmitting and receiving data specific to her or his application. There is a threshold at which the number of users gets so high that the performance of the network suffers, creating a kind of electronic traffic jam. If the potential network transmission speed is higher to begin with, each user's own chunk of data gets through the network much quicker, therefore freeing up "space" for the next user.

The speed of the WAN is linked to the current state of the art of the technology. As with many other technologies, today's WANs operate much faster than just a few years ago. This increase in speed and power is expected to accelerate, and it is interesting to note the psychological phenomenon by which any given user will always be able to eagerly incorporate a newer, faster technology, provided it has the same (or very similar) interface as the old one. The same user, if asked to return to a previous slower system, will find the regression highly painful!

5.3.3.2 Protocols

The two major components of a high-speed WAN are the protocol and the media. The media are the actual pathways that the protocol travels on, and in WANs they include the actual "wire" that connects the machines as well as all the intelligent switching hardware mentioned earlier. The protocol can be thought of as the electronic language used within the network. As with most emerging technologies, there are numbers of different protocols based primarily on the development and marketing of the companies that provide them. To draw a simple analogy, the media resemble the railway line, the messages the trains, and the protocols the signals.

The network protocol defines the format in which data are sent through the media. Compared to the media, the protocol has a smaller impact in overall speed and performance of the network. As mentioned in relation to packet-switched networks, data are sent out on the network in chunks of information called packets, and the protocol is wrapped around each packet with special identifying information that insures the proper packet arrives at its intended location. This is a bit like the postal service system, with the addressed envelopes acting as the protocol and the letters inside them as the data in the packet.

Just as with current trends in computer software systems, network protocols are divided into proprietary versus open systems. One widespread proprietary protocol is Decnet, developed by DEC. Its large user base exists because it is the standard protocol used on all of DEC's computers. DEC ranks number two worldwide behind IBM in computer and information services sales (Kelly, 1990). An example of an open system protocol that has become the worldwide standard because of its performance as well as its availability is Transmission Control Protocol/Internet Protocol (TCP/IP). It was developed jointly by researchers who worked at a handful of universities and maintained the ARPANET (Hedrick, 1987).

As TCP/IP emerged as a de facto standard, the companies offering proprietary protocols realized that they needed to support TCP/IP in order for their WANs to communicate globally. The Digital Equipment Corporation provides this by adding another layer to the information packet. The data that are wrapped in Decnet protocol are wrapped again with the TCP/IP commands when the packet needs to go outside the Decnet system. This works, but all the "unwrapping" of the extra protocol results in a speed degradation. Again, open systems and standardization tend to promote efficiency and compatibility.

An emerging standard for future WAN applications is the open systems interconnection (OSI). This protocol is actually a combination of seven protocol attributes that allows for much more efficient data transmission. Depending on the task at hand, just the protocol layer necessary is used to put the data on the network. Since protocols are mostly independent of media, OSI could exist as a continuing standard no matter what the next generation of media holds in store.

Continuing work is being conducted on protocols. For example, two lines of development are being pursued in order to provide standard means by which to access remote, full text information servers. These are wide area information servers (WAIS), started as a project among Thinking Machines Inc., Apple Computers, Dow Jones & Company, KPMG Peat Marwick, and the Rosebud Server System, which operates on an internal network at Apple Computer. The overall goals of these protocols are to provide "a single interface to a wide variety of information sources, and offer a good platform on which to explore the design of interfaces for information retrieval." (Kahle *et al.,* 1992, p. 125).

5.3.3.3 Media

Significant speed gains for WANs are made possible through developments in the actual media. By increasing (in technical terms) the electrical resistance in these "wires," transmission speed is being constantly raised. The current standard network media (sometimes called the physical network) is called Ethernet. It started out as a relatively thick (1/2-in. diameter) cable and was mainly used to link large-scale computers together. The second generation of Ethernet was called "thin wire Ethernet" and uses wire that resembles round coaxial antenna wire to make the connection. The most recent advance in Ethernet was the introduction of "twisted pair Ethernet," which uses standard telephone wire and modular jacks to make connections. Each of these new developments has allowed simplified connection to the WAN as well as reduced hardware cost.

All three of the forms of Ethernet have the same transmission speed, which is 10 million bps. This in itself is a very substantial difference from the 2400 bps transmission rate that is a common rate of operation of the modem, which modulates and demodulates signals over telephone networks used for telecommunication. If, for example, the text of the Bible was to be transmitted, it would only take 3.6 sec to pass by on an Ethernet network compared to the 4.2 hr the modem would require! This is the theoretical maximum speed attainable, and does not allow for periods of heavy use on the network when traffic jams could occur or for loss in speed due to protocol overhead. Even with this qualification, it is understandable that speed is one of the prime reasons that Ethernet has become such an attractive media for networks.

Another medium that has gained quite a bit of popularity (mostly in the LAN market) is called Token Ring. Popularized by IBM, Token Ring systems have one design feature that many users felt was better than the Ethernet media. If one machine (or node) on a Token Ring network malfunctioned, the rest of the network would still be able to communicate. If a node on an Ethernet network went down, every node further out on that specific segment of wire would also go down. One offset with the Token Ring topology is that in order to ensure this kind of integrity for the remainder of the nodes on the network, a more extensive wiring plan must be installed. Token Ring has always been a considerably slower media than Ethernet, but in August 1990 Token Ring products were introduced that provide data transfer rates of 12 million bps, which is a slightly higher speed than Ethernet. Competition in this field continues to drive innovation.

The new medium of fiber optic cable—formally called fiber distributed data interface (FDDI)—offers further advantages to networks, in terms of speed and security. As its name implies FDDI is made up of fiber strands rather than copper wire. With fiber technology significant increases in performance are possible because of two qualities. Fiber strands are much smaller than any copper wire, so more fiber can be bundled into what we think of as a cable. In addition to this increase in capacity that fiber provides, electrical data travel over fiber at a much higher rate than on conventional cable. Data transmission speed on FDDI is 100 million bps, which is ten times faster than on Ethernet. To return to the example of the Bible, with FDDI it would pass by in only 0.36 seconds! FDDI will be the first media to use the new seven layer protocol called OSI that was mentioned above, which seems certain to make it the industry standard in the 1990s. An added benefit of the FDDI is higher security of the media. It is almost impossible to cut into a fiber link without the network administrator being alerted. This is a major issue when the WAN is owned by a company or agency that deals in highly sensitive data.

Some analysts believe that even the line speeds now in prospect will still not be fast enough. According to a spokesman for a Washington based communication consulting firm, the required speed for animated 3-D graphics applications used over a network is about 148 million bps—anything less will cause the moving object to appear jerky (Caswell, 1990). Already there are exotic, highly proprietary networks that perform at extraordinary speeds. One such example is the 800 million bps Ultranet. These systems combine proprietary protocol and media and are used only on very expensive large computer applications. Naturally, they carry very high price tags. As with all new technologies, however, we see prices that originally start out high begin to drop as the user base increases and the demand for the products gets to the place where large-scale production and sales develop. For example, in 1990 the new FDDI networks were available with an average price tag per node (or computer) of about $10,000. It is estimated, however, that this price will decline until, in 1995, the average price should be about $1000 (Caswell, 1990).

Any of the media that have been discussed can be installed specifically for a given company or organization. For example, in a company occupying seven large buildings, spread out over 200 acres, it would be a costly but feasible job to link all the buildings with FDDI (or Ethernet or Token-Ring). In practice, this is the scenario for the majority of WANs in use today—each building would contain numbers of LANs all linked up to the WAN. But what would happen if the company was spread out over several states? At the present time there are two options, each involving using someone else's network lines. The first option would be to hook up with data services provided by the telephone provider. The other option would be to gain access to one of the several public networks that link institutions (mostly colleges and research locations) from around the world. In the ordinary sense of the word, however, both these alternatives represent public networks, and that seems an appropriate heading under which to pursue the discussion of networking and telecommunications.

5.3.4 Public Networks

Telephone lines have been used to carry computer data for quite a few years, getting their start with the advent of the modem. The modem must translate the digital signals from the computer to analog signals, which are then sent down the telephone wire. Analog technology was developed originally with the idea of transmitting voice data only. Suffice it to say that analog signals are slow and outdated, but they still are entirely adequate for voice telephone transmission. Analog transmission standards are currently quite acceptable for carrying on a two-party telephone call between two cities, or even for periodic transfer of computer data via a 2400-baud modem. There are even newer modem standards, such as one called V.32, which allow data to be transmitted over the analog phone lines at a rate of 19,200 bps (Shandle, 1990).

However, when it comes to data transmission needs for large organizations, complicated multilocation conference telephone calls, or any of the new telephone services, a more sophisticated digital environment is essential. The telephone companies have been aware of this fact for some years now, and have been converting a large portion of analog to new digital equipment. New installations of telephone services have the digital capability built right in from the beginning. This digital equipment allows for a high amount of flexibility in determining what kind of information goes out over the phone lines, the speed at which it travels, and what services can be offered to the users.

There are two main ways phone companies offer sophisticated data transmission services to the public. The first, which has been available for a number of years, is for the customer to rent a line that specifically connects the two distant locations that are intended to be in the WAN. Often called leased lines or dedicated lines, these high quality lines are paid for on a flat-rate basis, with longer distance connections costing more than closer ones. Although some lines of this type were available using analog equipment, recent implementations take advantage of the speed and efficiency of digital technology. Two common types of leased lines being used today are called T1 and T3 lines. T1 lines transfer data at a rate of 1.5 million bps and T3 lines operate at 45 million bps. Again, the Bible comparison shows that on the T1 line it would pass by in 24 sec, and on a T3 line would fly by in less than 1 sec. T1 lines have been utilized successfully for a number of years now, but the T3 successor, with its faster speeds, is attracting users who need this speed. One example is the upgrading of the NSFNET, the United States national data network funded by the National Science Foundation, from T1 to T3 lines in 1992. Since the cost of dedicated lines is so high, this technology has primarily been used to connect large mainframe computers to each other. It would not be a feasible way to connect two personal computers, or even to connect a PC to a mainframe. As prices of the technology come down, however, use of these T1 and T3 lines will become a way to create a WAN by connecting a large LAN (consisting of many PCs) to a distant location.

The second way that phone companies offer data services is through an emerging digital standard called integrated services digital network (ISDN), some of the capabilities of which have already been mentioned in Chapter 3 (p. 83). By converting equipment to digital format the phone companies discovered that a phone jack is not limited to sending just voice. ISDN installations allow computer data as well as voice data to travel down the same wiring. And, since video data are sent via similar mechanisms to those used for computer text data, ISDN holds the potential to send audio and video images as well. There are a number of formats for ISDN, but the one with the most potential (which will be the most expensive offering) is called primary rate interface (PRI) and operates at the same speed as the T1 leased lines.

ISDN offers two major advantages over the leased line approach—

flexible format and expandability. The flexibility is that the ISDN line can be used for different purposes at different times. A discussion could be proceeding simultaneously with an associate while both are referring to financial charts created and sent out on a PC. At another time the line could be hooked into an eight-station conference call and have level 4 fax machines delivering high resolution documents at the rate of one page every four seconds. And, since ISDN jacks will become as common as the phone jacks now in offices, an organization could change locations or expand their operations without the need to rewire all the data devices. The first coast-to-coast border-to-border ISDN call in the United States was placed in November 1992, and deployment projections forecast that more than half of the anticipated 114.9 million regional company access lines will be ISDN-capable by the end of 1994 (Shandle, 1992).

A second major way to link remote sites for high-speed data transmission is via a public network, which is not controlled by a telephone company. Major parts of these networks are linked by T1 lines provided by a telephone company, but they are differentiated mainly because of their origin and administration. Several of these networks have developed over the last seven years. Research institutions and universities began establishing networks to provide links that would allow colleagues to communicate efficiently. The E-mail system developed that enabled a person to send documents to another user. Institutions shared costs to link to each other and maintain the hardware required to manage the network.

A large public network that is used primarily to route mail worldwide is BITNET, a network based on linking mainframe computers at distant sites with users logging into these computers to read and respond to their mail. BITNET is based on a "store and forward" type of design. This means that a mail message will travel from one mainframe computer to the next until it reaches its destination. This also means that if one of these mainframe computers is not operating correctly, or the program that does the mail "forwarding" isn't running, the mail just sits at the interim location. Despite these periodic inconveniences, BITNET has grown quite successfully, and is comprised of over 3000 institutions from all over the United States, Japan, and Australia, with a companion network called EARN that links hundreds of Western European institutions (Lynch, 1990).

E-mail applications are common in LANs, WANs, and public networks. Their utility is obvious and increases with the number of addresses that can be reached. Although many different E-mail programs exist for different types of computers, they have certain key features in common. These include facilities for composing the letter, reading incoming mail, responding to a letter, saving the letters (incoming and outgoing) for future reference, sending copies of a letter to another person, and easy broadcasting of a letter to any specified group of people. Advanced features differ depending on the system being used. One such feature allows an automatic response to incoming mail, which can be used to let the sender know that a person is away on vacation for a specified time, and will respond after a certain date. The most evident advantage of E-mail is timeliness—when used on the Internet, mail delivery takes a few minutes at most. Another advantage is that with E-mail there is always an electronic record of a communication, which can be filed away or included in other communication easily. As with all technologies, the effects of electronic communication are not confined to technological changes, and on pages 238–239 mention is made of some of the second-order effects of electronic mail on behavior in organizations and in society generally.

Interconnecting different types of E-mail systems has provided some technical challenges. The two areas of compatibility problems involve the addressing scheme used to send the mail and the formatting of the components. The address of a computer is a unique identifying piece of data that is similar to a postal address. Network addressing is a complex issue, made difficult because of the different protocols used on the various networks. The other problem with compatibility arises with the format when the mail is sent. One system might require that the first entry in the document be the sender's identifying information (name), whereas another system might use it for the date that the correspondence was sent. Here as so often in discussion of applications of information technology, the importance of standards is obvious as is the significant contribution of the voluntary committees of the national and international organizations who work on them. Two standards, known as X.400 and X.500, have evolved, which make possible seamless interconnectivity throughout E-mail networks.

These are standards of the International Consultative Committee on Telegraphy and Telephony. Usually referred to by its French initials, CCITT, it is part of the International Telecommunications Union, a treaty organization formed in 1865, which is now part of the complex of United Nations organizations. CCITT's notable achievements go back at least to the X.25 standard for data interchange agreed upon in 1976. The opinion of a contemporary observer, Cotton (1981) has been justified. He pointed out that until X.25 there were no standards and no way of placing international data calls, and he commented that "if anyone were going to award the standard of the year award for 1976, it would have to go to X.25, since it is really going to lead to true international compatibility and full world-wide interconnection between the national packet carriers" (p. 7).

A remarkable web of standardizing activity spreads into and out from CCITT and the International Standards Organization (ISO) through national standards bodies, (such as American National Standards Institute

[ANSI]), to national telecommunications bodies, some commercial enterprises, (such as AT&T), and to government bodies (such as the National Bureau of Standards), and again to professional associations (such as the Institution of Electrical and Electronic Engineers [IEEE]). Clear explanation of the roles and relationships of the many organizations concerned in the making of telecommunications standards is given by Black (1987).

Standards are important throughout the most widespread public network in North America—the Internet, which is comprised of over 2000 institutions, each connected to nearby institutions via regional networks, and which is itself part of the global network of computer networks that is confusingly also known as the Internet. The United States regional networks are ultimately connected to the nationwide high-speed network called the NSFNET, operating at 45 million bps via T3 lines since mid-1992. The Internet offers complex mail facilities and has additional features, including the ability to log-in to a computer thousands of miles away and run programs or transfer large amounts of data quickly. By mid-1992 the Internet had established itself as a global facility. In its first 15 months, it spread to 28 countries, linking thousands of organizations on probably more than one million computers, which has already been mentioned in Chapter 3 (pp. 120–121). Less than one year later, in early 1993, Internet connections existed in 44 countries. Particularly impressive in the Internet is the large pool of networked resources and services available, including the on-line public catalogs (OPACs) of many libraries, bulletin boards, discussion lists, and database services (Lynch and Preston, 1990). Catalogs and directories of all kinds may be consulted through the Telnet function on the Internet. Files may be transferred from any computer to any other through use of the file transfer protocol (FTP). Much of this data, which includes text files, data files, and especially software, may be downloaded without formality from anonymous FTP sites. Textbooks on the Internet have begun to appear; Krol (1992) is probably the most comprehensive so far.

Costs for the Internet are split between governmental agencies and the large research institutions using the network. A few commercial organizations have also joined by paying an annual fee. At this time, there is no charge for connect time, which means that, after a user has the physical hardware bought and paid for, no extra fees are charged for the amount of time spent accessing the network.

In the United States the notion that the National Research and Education Network (NREN) must serve all the people is embedded in public law, and many interest groups have already made submissions on which advice to the Congress has been based (United States Office of Science and Technology Policy, 1992). Public debate has already begun in the United States on who will pay for, own, and control the NREN. Debate on the future of the Internet is nowhere more lively than on the newsgroups on the Internet itself. Major issues of national information policy are of course involved. In the United States as in other countries, what constitutes equitable public access to this public network and the ways in which such access is to be ensured, are matters of important political debate.

Appreciation is also urged here of the connection between a nation's, indeed a world's, network access and the capacity to innovate. Experience evoked in the study of creativity as well as that of innovation also suggests that tightly controlled access limited to those users who can pay the going commercial rate and who have defined tasks to achieve may be counterproductive. The political philosophy that has prevailed so far in the development of the global Internet may best be described as a democratic meritocracy, in which Krol (1992) has discerned two guiding principles: individualism is honored and fostered; and, the network is good and must be protected. Whether these values can be preserved in a future in which network traffic is highly likely to be dominated by commercial usage will be an important determinant of just how innovative the Internet itself will remain.

5.4 Harnessing Information Technology for Use

Not all networking applications and products have been as readily accepted as the Internet and the fax machine. Acceptance of others has been slow and the reasons are usually related to human rather than technological factors. Again similar technologies and even systems that are identical in technical characteristics do not succeed equally in different environments. In other words, as the evidence adduced in Chapter 1 has already suggested, the technology does not determine its own success. Rather, the technology has to be appropriately harnessed to the needs of groups and individuals, and those needs are shaped by all the factors—economic, social, political, and psychological—which operate to influence human behavior. Consideration of the relationships between technology and human behavior can lay a basis for discussion of concepts and techniques by which the needs for information can be assessed and appropriate information systems and services provided. This section therefore proceeds under the subheadings: technology and human behavior; systems analysis; management information systems and decision support systems (MIS and DSS); and information resource management (IRM).

5.4.1 Technology and Human Behavior

Not all applications of information technology prove equally acceptable. Teleconferencing is an example of an information technology that has yet to deliver in accordance with its apparent benefits. Technically it is an ideal application for a WAN. Such systems typically include an audio portion, a graphics display to transmit computer-generated charts and graphs, a live video portion to show the participants, and an optional high-speed level 4 fax portion to allow quick document transfer. By linking together two or more locations, an organization can conduct meetings or training sessions. Companies have been attracted to teleconferencing in the hope that it can promote better communications among different parts of an organization and lead to better decision making as well as reduced travel budgets for employees.

In general, despite marked technological advances, these benefits have not been widely delivered, although there have been many improvements. Early teleconferencing systems required separate, dedicated lines for each function of the process, so to obtain voice, data, and video would require three links. With the emergence of ISDN, systems now can transmit all the data through one link. This is an important step in the development of the technology. The rates charged by the telephone carriers will come down, since only one line is required. In order to achieve this feat, the data sent through the line are now compressed. Video images require huge amounts of data to be sent—if the system is too slow the figures appear to move in a jerky, unnatural manner. By use of a device known as a coder-decoder (codec) at both ends of line, the signals are compressed (coded) at the sending end, sent through the WAN, then uncompressed (decoded) at the receiving end where they are shown at their full speed.

Teleconferencing technology originated at AT & T in 1964 with an invention called a "picture phone," and the technology has been described as at that time interesting but a bit premature (Walsh, 1989). It has also been less charitably described as "the Bell Laboratories Picture Phone fiasco of the late 1960s" in a report on the relative merits of public and private enterprise in the development of the NREN (Markoff, 1993, p. F6). The British Post Office also had less than brilliant success with the picture phone, which it launched in the mid-1980s, and Japanese companies also introduced a similar product in that period which was not successful. In 1992, AT & T introduced a "videophone," a $1500 unit that includes a small color screen and can plug into a regular wall jack. Despite television commercials and print advertisements in magazines, it was reported in early 1993 that only 4000 of these second-generation models had been sold (Lazzareschi, 1993). In the minds of individual subscribers at least, picture phone and videophone seem to be associated not with enhancement of communication but with invasion of personal privacy. So the new technology in this case is perceived not as adding to, but rather as detracting from the immense convenience of the voice-only telephone, which has achieved universal coverage through an extensive international network, which enables two-way easy quick communication between two or among several people in conference calls, and which simultaneously permits all parties to the call to do other things unseen. Mobile phones have found ready market acceptance; miniaturized phones in wrist watches and pocket appliances seem likely to do so. That there has been considerable resistance in the United States to the addition of a caller identification facility to telephones suggests that callers are also reluctant to give this lesser clue to their whereabouts than a picture would (Gleick, 1993).

In the early 1980s when high-speed networks came into existence, teleconferencing started to re-emerge as a communication idea. Both the T1 phone lines and ISDN offer the speeds necessary to transmit the large amount of data required for teleconferencing, so systems have become more available (Booker, 1989). As with all information technology, equipment manufacturers are moving towards standardization to allow dissimilar machines to communicate with each other. Most of the teleconferencing currently used is intra-organizational, meaning that communication is basically between departments or groups within one organization. In this scenario, standardization is less important because one company will tend to purchase equipment from only one vendor. However, with the reduced rates for transmission and lowering of cost for the equipment, teleconferencing is very likely to be used to set up meetings with client companies, interview prospective job applicants, and tap into training organizations for on-site training. To realize this potential the industry is agreeing on a basic CCITT standard for teleconferencing transmission called the H.261 *Video codec for audiovisual services.*

As teleconferencing equipment prices fall, the main thing that companies interested in using the technology look for is high transmission quality. But even in these technical requirements the order of importance is not readily predictable. Though the motion video portion of teleconferencing is technologically the most challenging, users claim that the order of importance of the components starts with good audio, then good graphics, and finally good video. Since most of the information that is going to be conveyed during a conference will usually be verbal, the call for good audio makes sense. It may also be argued that using an ordinary telephone (or perhaps a speaker phone) backed up by a separate fax line may in many cases be equally effective and cheaper.

In the early 1980s, installation of a custom teleconferencing system required a large studio installation and cost in the neighborhood of $500,000 to build. By 1990 prices for higher quality systems that are portable and can be set up wherever the meeting is to take place cost about $30,000 (Walsh, 1989). But too often other attributes have been lost in this transition, besides bulky and expensive equipment. What have often been too readily overlooked are the production values—the esthetic sense of form, (which for example arranges cameras and positions monitors so that people in separate locations feel as if they have eye contact) as well as techniques such as good lighting, and, perhaps the factor least considered, the need for a producer, who, as well as taking the chair for the meeting, has control over the camera in each location. High production values have been absorbed by all of us as consumers of television and film as mass media. Our expectations of these media may in fact be contrasted with the tolerance of poorly presented data and technical malfunction on ad hoc communication facilities like the Internet. Teleconferencing represents one of the quickly advancing areas of WAN use, and the relevance of the computer conference to the sharing and dissemination of innovative ideas and practices is obvious when audio, visual, and graphic inputs are of such quality that participants are unaware of them. Before the technology can serve this or any other purposes effectively, however, attention to production details is needed. As individuals and as work groups, participants have to feel satisfied about their opportunities to contribute to the discussion and about the number and the quality of the decisions reached. The technology will otherwise be avoided rather than embraced. Like all other information systems and services, as in face-to-face meetings for example, teleconferences need to be managed, that is planned, produced, and directed, with due regard for the principles of human communication and the range of human preferences.

More insights into the interaction of technology and human behavior have emerged in studies of the effects of working in organizations that are rich in electronic information. Sproull and Kiesler (1991), for example, in summarizing what has been learned about working with electronic text, distinguish between first- and second-level effects. "First-level effects of communication technology are the anticipated ones—the planned efficiency gains or productivity gains that justify an investment in new technology." On the other hand, "Second-level effects from communication technologies come about primarily because new communication technology leads people to pay attention to different things, have contact with different people, and depend on one another differently" (p. 4). Thus this technology changes the way work occurs and is thought about, not just how much work is done.

Awareness of the nature of these changes can help managers improve effectiveness of their organizations. For example, experiments on brainstorming in groups have shown that people can be inhibited in creativity and productivity by having to listen to other people's ideas. New decision support conference rooms have been created in which group members meet initially but before face-to-face discussion, they simultaneously and anonymously contribute to an electronic pool of ideas, which is made the basis of the face-to-face discussion. According to Sproull and Kiesler (1991), "This technique can leverage both the productivity of individual work and the motivating properties of group interaction" (p. 59).

Leveraging individual productivity and motivating groups present particular challenges to those lower in organizational hierarchies, that is, to those with least power. To some extent, all users of information technology have been under the control of the technology because computer systems have been largely specialist- or designer-driven rather than user-driven. This situation has resulted in numerous problems for the user, such as in the complexity of system interfaces and the need to learn complex command languages. This situation is changing at least to the extent that more consideration is being given to the user in the design of the technology-based systems. But problems persist. Many times the intended users have been resistant to change to a new technology. There have been frustrations and anxieties, sometimes refered to as technostress, which have resulted because of fears, frustrations, physiological demands, and social and psychological difficulties with the new systems. The case study data presented by Zuboff (1988), in a chapter entitled "Office technology as exile and integration," makes very clear, especially in clerical workers' before and after drawings of their perceptions of themselves at work, how dehumanizing badly designed and managed information-technology-based systems can be.

In the desire to implement "good" systems, more and more attention has been placed on the impact of technologies on the worker. The attention focuses on three components: (1) the physiological and psychomotor, or the external interface of the human with the machine and the psychological issues that arise therefrom; (2) the psychological, or the attitude (affective level interface) of the individual towards the machine, and the internal interface (cognitive level interface) of the human with the machine; and (3) the psychosocial, or the effect of technology on the individual within a work group and the effect on the organization.

So far most of the attention has been given to the first issue set out above, the physiological. For example, new computer hardware incorporates many positive ergonomic design aspects. Concern with minimizing visual fatigue has resulted in the development of screens that have less glare and have more user control over color and contrast. It has also been recognized that particular attention should be given to incorporating positive ergonomic designs for those individuals who spend a major portion of their work time at display terminals. Individual ergonomic differences are taken into consideration in such matters as the design of workstations.

A similar focus must be placed on the internal interactions at the affective level, that is, the personal reaction to the technology, and on the cognitive level, that is, the intellectual effort required to use a technology. The basic assumption has been that the interfaces between the individual and the technology should be as user-friendly as possible and require a minimum of human information processing. Discussions and research have focused on methods to improve the interactions on both the affective and cognitive levels—to discover the reasons for failures in human–machine interactions, how to design better systems, the way to reduce the effort for the input operator, searcher, or user of work-enhancement software, and the means of producing increased and improved results in technology interactions.

Various strategies have been employed in search of improvement, such as the use of orientation and training programs to overcome computer phobia. But research in a variety of areas is also being pursued with the view towards incorporating positive findings into interaction strategies. This research has included study of the impact of different screen display formats on user performance; the ability of front-end processors and AI systems to assist in the translation of human logic into machine logic; the application of mental models to the design of interactive systems; the use of individual cognitive differences in choosing the type of interactive session; and the use of bilateral brain specialialization, or the consideration of designs that specialize in word and number (left brain) or visual information (right brain).

Specifically, many new designs have benefited from the following: attempts to minimize the amount of knowledge the user has to bring to the system through the use of menus; easy to remember commands, help functions, iconic or graphic displays, interactive questioning; developments in training, such as on-line tutorials, and supporting training materials in a variety of media, including print, simulation, computer-based training (CBT), and interactive videodisk; and the incorporation into the interaction with the technology of positive learning components, such as attention-getting mechanisms, motivators, advanced organizers, prompts and cues, and feedback.

The amount of attention given to the psychological problems associated with human-machine interactions should not be allowed to obscure the positive forces at work. Some individuals find involvement with such systems to be motivational and find excitement, challenges, and rewards in doing something new. Automation can provide opportunities for job variety and job enrichment and higher-order problem solving. Such opportunities are motivational in themselves and create a higher level of satisfaction in the worker (adapted from Kazlauskas, 1988).

Technology not only has an impact on individual workers but also on work groups. The power of the work group in determining behavior in organizations has been well established since the studies by Elton Mayo at the Hawthorne plant of the Western Electric Company in the 1930s (Mayo, 1949). Frequently, the development of a new automated system requires redesign of jobs and changes in the work flow. The impact of such changes affects all levels of individuals in an organization but is particularly acute at the nonmanagerial levels.

Training begun early and conducted as a genuine form of information exchange can be an excellent method to lessen at least those problems likely to impede the flow of first-level efficiency effects to the organization. Unfortunately, such training frequently lags behind system implementation, even though there is consensus in theory that training programs that are specific to a new technology are essential. But there should also be programs that concentrate on affective-level training for those individuals who do not have "positive" reactions to change and to the use of new technologies. Good training should be the beginning of a positive attitude in employees—an attitude that correctly portrays the capabilities and limitations of technologies and their role in the organization (Kazlauskas, 1988). There is also some evidence that a source of expertise should reside in the organization. A study of twelve organizations indicated that the concept of a resident expert can lead to a more effective information system. The same study also confirmed that software for users should come equipped with state-of-the-art help features, which can assist to reduce the need for training personnel and decrease the learning time to make users productive (Nath, 1989).

It has been widely recognized that organizations best realize benefits from new technology when they make complementary changes in organization and management. This is not to suggest, however, that changes are necessarily in the same direction in all organizations. New information technology has prompted some managers to gain more control of information exchange, forbid extracurricular messages, and improve security in surveillance of message files. The same technology has prompted other managers to set out to achieve a learning organization, a flexible internally motivated continuously learning work force with strong participation in problem solving and dispersal of responsibility. Sproull and Kiesler (1991) conclude that "these two sets of objectives are contradictory but together make a point: computer-based communication allows people to work somewhat more efficiently, but the realized benefits depend ultimately on the policies, designs, and vision of people who want to organize work in new ways" (p. 175). Again, the importance of innovative management becomes obvious if the benefits of information technology are to be realized.

The best sociological work to date suggests that optimization of the benefits of information technology occurs in organizations where the sharing of information is allowed to transform relationships among individuals and work groups and to empower all members—in other words, where members feel that they own and are therefore responsible for the system. To represent the converse of this situation Zuboff (1988) returns to the image of Jeremy Bentham's eighteenth century Panopticon, an architectural design in which all inmates, whether prisoners or factory workers, may be seen by supervisors but are themselves prevented from seeing either supervisors or co-workers, let alone the whole organization.

The growing trend towards end-user systems, discussed more fully in section 5.4 of this chapter, demands more attention to the human factor, in terms of software development, workspace design, as well as in the much broader field of organizational culture.

There are several methods, sometimes referred to as soft technologies, which can be used to assist managers in measuring both the needs for and the effectiveness of information systems and services in their organizations. The beginning of some of the techniques embedded in these methods, such as cost accounting, predates the use of computers. But all have been extended to cope with computerized systems. Systems analysis, originally developed in the defense sector, soon proved useful to examine the cost-effectiveness of the computer alternative (and other alternatives), as well as in effective integration of the computer into the organization. Through the use of systems analysis, there came an enhanced understanding of the information needs, uses, and flow in organizations.

The development of management information systems (MIS) and decision support systems (DSS), already mentioned in Chapter 3 (pp. 93–94), has built on the understanding of information in the organization. The more recent concept of information resource management (IRM) also "conceptually rests on an open systems notion of organizational and environmental interconnectiveness and interdependence to achieve organizational goals" (Caudle and Levitan, 1989, p. 302). Use of these soft technologies could go a long way to redressing the complaint by Sproull and Kiesler (1991), which investigation in many organizations would bear out, that "people justify most new technologies a priori by their first-level efficiency gains. Indicative of problems with these justifications are studies discovering that once new technologies have been installed in the name of efficiency gains, often no one keeps figures on their actual costs or the cost savings that are supposed to derive from them" (p. 4).

5.4.2 Systems Analysis and Costing

Systems analysis can be helpful in assisting the integration of technology into the organization. It can help provide a detailed understanding of application needs and assist, for example, in determining the flow of information between departments, how various departments interact with an existing information system, which information might be unique to a department, and how departments use such information for decision making. As another example, this determination of information flow could also be a prelude to developing an MIS or DSS for an organization. Such background information is essential in order to make an informed decision regarding systems selection. By following a logical approach to technology selection and design, the manager has a better chance for success in implementing this choice in the most cost-effective manner.

In Chapter 2 a system was defined as a group of interdependent elements working together to accomplish a common purpose. In that chapter, a macroview was provided of the concept "system." This section discusses a system from a microperspective, namely in terms of a business or industrial enterprise, a governmental agency, a library, an information center. Specifically, this systems view has a management and technology orientation—systems in the context of an organizational entity. The interdependent elements in this organizational entity are referred to as subsystems and can include, for example, personnel, computers, equipment, policies and procedures, and materials. In turn, each of these subsystems is composed of groups of interdependent elements, which in turn could also be further subdivided into elements referred to as modules.

In order to accomplish the purpose of the system or subsystem, the components and the activities associated with the components can be structured in a variety of ways. The goal is to design the most feasible, suitable, and acceptable structure. This structure may be a manual system or a sophisticated computer-based information system. Normally, the entire spectrum of options that fit within established constraints is available for consideration. Systems analysis denotes the utilization of a number of management techniques to accomplish this. The person utilizing systems analysis has the technical capability for analyzing a problem—the analyst seeks to understand the problem by examining its parts, the interrelationship of the parts to the rest of the system, and to the external environment. Through this process, the analyst comes to understand what is going on and from this understanding designs a new system.

There are numerous guides, or models, which an individual can use in attempting to determine what is the best structure and the best way to accomplish a goal or to resolve a problem. These models can provide the necessary framework for conducting a systems analysis study. Table 5.1 represents a seven-step version of the systems analysis process with representative tasks associated with each step. But the task does not stop at implementation. A system requires constant review and, in turn, modifica-

Table 5.1
Systems Analysis Process Model

1. Preliminary analysis
isolating the problem(s)
understanding the constraints
determining user needs
understanding the organization
operational review
determining goals and objectives
outlining the system requirements
specifying objectives
specifying benefits
developing a management plan for the study
2. Input/output analysis
analysis of present forms, files, etc.
translation to input requirements
output requirements
3. Processing analysis
task analysis
procedural flow
determination of interactions
flowcharting
4. Alternatives review
cost-benefit study
cost-effectiveness study
5. Selection
6. Systems design
forms design
input screen design
output and reports design
user cordial interactions
7. Implementation and management
documentation
system monitor and feedback
system evaluation
8. Review
feedback to step 1

tion and change when deemed necessary, which is why step 8, review and the feedback loop to step 1 appear in Table 5.1.

Costing is an essential ingredient in a systems study. As noted in Table 5.1 this is a technique used at the stage of evaluation and selection from among alternatives. As Cortez and Kazlauskas (1986) point out, "the costing process requires identification of input and output measures. Input measures—contributors to programs and products—can be identified as resources, income, revenue, costs, etc. Output measures are benefits, profits, or products. As a decision-making tool, costing techniques make use of the organization's goals in examining the relative merits of alternatives in terms of their input and output value" (p. 21).

Various costing techniques exist, but the two most common are cost-benefit analysis and cost-effectiveness analysis. Cost-benefit analysis provides a comparison of inputs (costs) and outputs (benefits) in monetary terms. Inputs are more readily generated and include direct costs (such as hardware purchase price), indirect costs (overhead), fixed costs (such as building rental), and variable costs (such as supplies that are dependent on the volume of use of a technology). In cost-benefit studies, outputs are specified in monetary terms. Examples include the amount of money saved by the use of a new technology in an operation and the measures of increased productivity. Generating output measures is the more difficult task in a cost-benefit study since it requires the translation of sometimes intangible factors into costs. In cost-effectiveness analysis, output elements are not translated solely into monetary terms, but rather provided as performance indicators, such as system reliability, user satisfaction, and speed of service. In cost-effectiveness studies it is important to perform the analysis in terms of level of performance with constant level of input, and costs with constant level of performance. (Cortez and Kazlauskas, 1986). The difficulties of applying such studies to information services have already been discussed in Chapter 3 (pp. 134–135), but the fewer the elements in an operation that lend themselves to reliable measurement, the more important it may be to maintain awareness of acceptable techniques and to collect relevant quantitative evidence, or, in other words, to maintain effective management information systems.

5.4.3 Management Information Systems and Decision Support Systems

There has been much attention placed on the development of particular types of information system in organizations, known as management information systems (MIS) and decision support systems (DSS).

An MIS provides data on an organization's internal operations and business environment, primarily through providing recent and historical business transaction data. The developed information system may be at the departmental level, such as marketing, or at the firm or organization level, such as budgeting. Examples of such data and reports that could be provided could include total sales in volume and dollars; unit costs; production costs; advertising costs; sales costs; managerial costs; and R & D costs.

An example of a budgeting-level MIS system is the Revenue Center

Management System at the University of Southern California. This system provides a decentralized approach to academic and financial management. Like most budgeting systems, it emphasizes the annual development of spending plans but is expanded to include all costs of academic programs, including benefits, space, and services. The system is based on various assumptions, including the fact that if revenue centers exceed the bottom line their surplus is carried forward for future academic program planning; the reverse also holds true in that deficits become obligations against future revenues. Twenty percent of the centers' revenues plus unrestricted income are allocated back to the academic centers as different percent amounts to equalize low-cost and high-cost schools, to provide resources for new academic programs, and as a reward mechanism for academic success. Obviously, such a system requires a sophisticated MIS to provide planning data and to assist in monitoring the status of ongoing revenues and expenditures (University of Southern California, 1992b). The computerized budget development systems (BDS) is the tool which assists in this effort. "The BDS creates detailed payroll lines and account level budgets for the University's new fiscal year. It is a bridge between the budgeting forcasting and planning process conducted by the Office of Budget and Planning and the activation of the budget and payroll for the new fiscal year" (University of Southern California, 1992a, p. I-2).

MIS is linked historically to the old data-processing department; personnel in this department used to be responsible for MIS design, development, and report generation. But new demands on the development of MIS have occured with the change towards the use of PCs and LANs. In fact, the trend in MIS is to give users within the organization the tools to design applications and reports themselves. This is in keeping with the trend towards end-user computing. And now, MIS personnel may be responsible for many other technical applications, including LANs, word processing, and satellite communications. In many organizations other individuals are now involved in the broader concept of MIS, such as archivists, records managers, and librarians. Kesner (1988) describes this much broader perspective and includes in his discussion the need for all these groups to work in concert. His view is that the developing technologies will meld the responsibilities of these professions and will require a different individual, one who has a much more broadly based information perspective. This concept is further discussed in section 5.4.4 of this chapter (p. 248), dealing with information resource management.

A decision support system (DSS) has been defined as a "coherent system of computer-based technologies used by managers as an aid to their decision making in semistructured decision tasks" (Bennett, 1983, p. 10).

Further refinement is added to this definition by Sprague and Carlson (1982) who claim that DSS are aimed at underspecified problems, combine the use of models and analytical techniques, are designed to be used by non-computer specialists interactively, emphasize flexibility, and accomodate the time approach of the user. A DSS allows for *ad hoc* data extraction, processing, analysis, consolidation and reduction, as well as decision modeling systems. It allows the user to consider "what if" alternatives and is based on the automation of qualitative techniques. A DSS expands on the MIS concept to provide predefined data aggregation and reporting capabilities. In basic terms, a DSS supports strategic planning, whereas an MIS does not.

DSS provide support to all levels within the organization: support for top management strategic planning; middle management operation control; and front-line support functions (Mentzer and Gomes, 1988). Although a DSS normally is broadly based in that data from throughout the firm is used, it should be noted that all data from the organization need not be integrated into a DSS. A DSS can be used to assist in the management of a component of the organization, such as marketing, where it can be used as a planning and early warning system and as a diagnostic tool for marketing activities (Meredith, 1988).

Examples of DSS models could include the following, which would be appropriate to an R & D project: index models that would provide probability-weighted benefit-to-cost ratio for project comparisons; portfolio models that would allocate funding from projects based on expected profit; decision theory models; risk analysis; and use of numerical scoring models to evaluate qualitative and quantitative characteristics of various projects (Link and Tassey, 1987).

The growth of DSS has been based on increasing power and capability of computers. Further growth is predicated on the trend towards distributed processing and end-user computing, whereby executives have the computing capability at their desk or workspace. This sort of capability is fostering the development of executive information systems (EIS), where the executive participates in the selection of the problems and the selection, design, and use of the communication or computer tool (Boone, 1991). An additional impact on DSS will be the growth of expert systems with the resulting creation of knowledge bases of decision making. Increased knowledge of human factors is also at work in improving these systems. For example, the preference of top executives for terminal operation by use of a remote control device has been noted. Thus the executive feels in control, in contrast to the apparent subservience to the system of the user seated at a terminal.

5.4.4 Information Resource Management

A management perspective that has been under development for a number of years is that of information resource management (IRM). This grew out of developments in the United States at the federal level, specifically the Paperwork Reduction Act of 1980, which recognized the concept of IRM and provided for specific IRM requirements, such as the designation of a senior IRM official in each federal agency. Further federal directives were outlined directly or indirectly in various Office of Management and Budget Circulars (Andriole, 1985; Caudle and Levitan, 1989). In IRM the view of information is that of a resource comparable to the financial resources of an organization and, as such, is due equivalent management attention. Overall managerial responsibility is provided for the processing and use of information resources. This typically results in control by a single manager over such areas as data processing, telecommunications, information systems development, office automation, audiovisual media, libraries, printing and publication, records management, and archives.

A similar development has occured in the nongovernmental sector, where the position designated as chief information officer (CIO) has emerged. This position is a logical extension of the IRM concept to the private sector.

IRM is an attempt to provide an integrating mechanism for the productive combination of technology, information policy and organizational strategy, which has already been discussed in Chapter 3 (pp. 111–112).

5.5 Trends

Emerging out of the scientific and technological advances over the last number of years are several wide reaching trends. First to be discussed are those that Poppel and Goldstein (1987) describe as "infotrends." This term includes content, interoperability, disintermediation, globalization, and convergence. A second set of trends clusters in the interdependent concepts of technological entropy, the development of technostress, and the industry shift towards relying on information service providers, which is frequently referred to as outsourcing. The development of information-related standards is discussed as a continuing trend. And lastly, the trend towards end-user computing and the resultant need for training and user-friendly systems is presented. Many of these trends are themselves the results of innovations in technology and in the attitudes and expectations of users of information systems and services. All the trends are to be regarded as, if not underpinnings to innovation, at least important characteristics of the technological and social environments within which innovations will be launched and will sink or swim.

5.5.1 Infotrends

Poppel and Goldstein (1987) acknowledge that indeed there have been and will continue to be rapid technological advances. But such technological advances in themselves are not what they define as an infotrend. Instead, their view is that there are five distinct trends that are driving the supply and use of information technologies.

They also stress the importance of content because "well crafted content endures far longer than particular media" (Poppel and Goldstein, 1987, p. 4). This infotrend can be observed in various examples of the migration of content, such as the transition of manual indexes and abstracts to on-line databases, and on to CD-ROMs. Another example is the printed encyclopedia of which content is clearly more significant than medium since it is now even available on a portable Data Discman™ as previously mentioned. Film is another example of the migration of content. Film is now broadcast and available on videotape and interactive video. Interactive video allows the use of film in nonlinear sequences and thus an entire new realm of use of the same content has emerged, specifically in using film in interactive training, learning, and entertainment. The new observation is that the message is transcending the medium, a contrary observation to that made by Marshall McLuhan, where the medium is the message (McLuhan, 1962). Poppel and Goldstein (1987) also state that the "same technologies churning the media are encouraging the creation and distribution of new content" (p. 4). A prime example is the creation of new interactive training and learning materials, such as *Teaching, Learning & Technology—A planning guide,* which is an Apple Corporation, Inc., product. This interactive product provides a step-by-step process by which a school team can plan a new curriculum, technology integration, or a staff development program. The interactive package provides instruction in planning, as well as containing useful resources, such as video clips of successful programs, audio clips of advice from colleagues, a bibliography, and text-based resource materials. The product provides content in a multimedia approach that can be used for a variety of purposes and in different learning settings (Apple Computer Inc., 1992).

Another infotrend is *interoperability,* or the "ability of two or more parties, machine or human, to make a perfect exchange of content" (Poppel and Goldstein, 1987, p. 5). A prime example is that of the telephone, which provides, in most instances, international connections that yield voice quality indistinguishable from that experienced in local calls. And this connection is technologically transparent to the user—the user need not know about the specific technologies that are employed. The trend is readily visible in many other information systems: in multimedia systems, for example, which combine text, color graphics, sound and motion; in LANs and WANs; and in national and international networks, such as the Internet.

A tangible example of interoperability is provided by the sophisticated workstation whereby a user interacts with the system, with information, and with other users. The core of such a system is a knowledge work support architecture that consists of a range of sources of information, including work-group files, personal files, document image files, company databases, navigation aids, utilities for interworking (that is, exchanging information with other people), and a toolkit of utilities and applications. The interoperability concept indicates that to be successful, the system must provide tools for accessing and manipulating data that end-users can master; that provide the ability to merge information from various sources; and have decoupled end-user activity from the operational system (Gunton, 1989).

Tunneling through the Internet using a tool such as Gopher is an illustration of the beginning of this concept of interoperability. Gopher allows one to select from menu resources throughout the world, to interact with the resource in a screen-oriented, menu-driven approach, and to move data from the server with the resource to your computer (Krol, 1992). These data then could be merged with existing, client-owned data using a word-processing or database management package.

Disintermediation is the infotrend whereby the number of intermediary stages between buyer and seller, user and producer, is minimized (Poppel and Goldstein, 1987). This concept holds true within the organization where introduction of an information system can eliminate the need for an intermediary, and this is usually the middle manager. Modern information technologies can eliminate layers of staff. Staff can be reduced through minimizing handoffs, that is, one person will complete a task rather than processing the task through several individuals. Layers within an organization that consolidate and send on information can also be eliminated. Technological determinists claim that information systems will shape organizational structure and not vice versa (How future information-based firms will cut fat, 1990). While this is arguable, there is widespread acknowledgement in the management literature that information systems and organizational structure are closely interrelated (see Chapter 3, pp. 92–93).

It should be noted that disintermediation is occurring in all sectors, including private business and industry, the service industries, and government. Specific examples of information-technology-based applications that illustrate this are many, including E-mail and messaging systems that bypass the intermediaries of the telephone, the postal service, the secretary, and paper recording. Another example is that of shopping and purchasing through electronic services, such as Prodigy. These services eliminate the need, for example, for a sales clerk and a travel agent, at least for routine travel.

The traditional role of the teacher, and institutions such as the school and the library, are also, according to some, endangered by this infotrend. Some commentators have suggested new service roles and gone on to demonstrate that they are possible. For example, schools and public libraries may choose new roles to meet community needs, such as developing into a community activity center or independent learning center (McClure *et al.*, 1992). New service roles may, however, not always be possible, and this infotrend has the potential to bring about major changes in current job classifications, professional roles, and the employment locations of information specialists. When asked about the future of the library, Nicholas Negroponte, the Director of the Massachusetts Institute of Technology (MIT) Media Lab, replied that "the librarian can do what the computers can't [do] at least today. . . . In the future, computers may take on more of this role, becoming electronic intelligent agents" (*A glimpse at the inventors of the future at MIT's Media Lab,* 1991, p. 35). As system interfaces become increasingly capable of incorporating the insights of social scientists and information specialists into human information seeking and processing behavior, this prophecy could gain more credibility.

Globalization is a very evident trend in the information arena. For example, international companies maintain financial data via computer, and executives carry PCs with them to access this information wherever they might be. These same PCs are used internationally for E-mail and messaging systems. Burnell Roberts, Chairman and CEO of Mead Corporation, has stated that development of a network of contacts on a worldwide basis is necessary for survival, thus his corporation has created a shared database of contacts with such information as potential customers, local officials, and individuals who might provide introductions to potential clients (Boone, 1991). At Jones Day Reavis & Pogue, a major international law firm, information systems, specifically E-mail and shared databases, have been used to incorporate an acquisition into the corporate culture (Boone, 1991).

There are other elements that can be considered as part of this globalization infotrend. In many instances, there is more similarity among consumers and users at the same socioeconomic level in various countries, and with their information needs and use patterns, than with citizens at other socioeconomic levels in their own country. The distances that separate these potential consumers have no longer much relevance when information about even the most widely geographically separated market segments can quickly be collected, collated, and analyzed. As already remarked in Chapter 3, (pp. 107–108), digital data and the telecommunications networks that carry them have provided the international currency for globalization of industry and commerce.

The development of global information service companies is another example of the internationalization of information. The information industry news is replete with examples, such as USWest Communications and France Telecom, which have linked to provide a Community Link videotex gateway in the northwestern United States ('France Telecom joins forces with USWest . . . , 1991), and DataTimes and the China Daily Publications, which have entered into an agreement for DataTimes to provide electronic access to the People's Republic of China publications (DataTimes assembles Asian package, 1992).

Convergence in the digital environment has already been discussed in Chapter 3 (pp. 95–100). Inevitably, convergence is blurring distinctions between products and services, home and business use of information technology, and information and entertainment. There is a merging of competitive interests among information technology suppliers, players, and industry. Poppel and Goldstein (1987) summarize the power of the five infotrends thus:

> The interrelationship among the five infotrends is deeply rooted and mutually reinforcing. The quest for more perfect content drives interoperability. Interoperability enables disintermediation. Disintermediation leads to globalization and globalization fosters convergence. And to close the loop, convergence stimulates the IT—literacy that drives demand for content (p. 1).

5.5.2 The Interplay of Three Trends: Entropy, Technostress, and Outsourcing

The notions of technological entropy, the development of technostress, and the shift in industry and government towards relying on outsourcing to "automation service providers" are phenomena that are closely linked and have developed in an environment of rapid technological change and mounting end-user demands.

Technological entropy refers to the ever-increasing development pace that new products and technologies go through. New generations of microprocessors are appearing sooner after the advent of their predecessors; software applications with more complex features are being released after quicker development cycles, and the list of new areas of technological invention grows at a quicker and quicker pace. Granted, part of this phenomenon can be attributed to the increase in research and development dollars poured into this multibillion dollar industry, but the end result of technological entropy remains the same—each year more advances appear in the field than did during the previous year.

The trend towards the use of automation service providers is an interesting return to a way of thinking that was actually the status quo in the earlier days of the computer data processing era. At that time, data processing was a highly specialized function within an organization, requiring a host of personnel to feed and communicate with the computer systems. Being a new field, with relatively few specialists, and with the unsophisticated operating systems used by the early mainframe computers, the data-processing departments grew to become the central resource for all of an organization's computer tasks. These departments provided a service to the rest of the organization.

Then began the era of personal computers, with their relatively simple operating systems and easy-to-learn application software. In this environment, users with modest technical intelligence, a little patience, and some operation manuals could use PCs to increase work effectiveness. This Renaissance notion of self-sufficiency, among nonspecialists no longer dependent on the data-processing departments to do certain day-to-day tasks, grew with the market share. As a byproduct, PCs made it possible for the smaller scale companies to afford to use data-processing techniques, and in turn increase their productivity and efficiency. Company management recognized this shift towards PCs and rearranged computing budgets to deemphasize funding to the central data-processing departments, freeing up revenue to buy PCs. High costs for mainframe computing could be demonstrated. The availability of more powerful personal computers made this shift in priorities even more attractive.

This is where technological entropy started to impact the user and create user frustrations. It also had impact on the development scene and opened up the need for automation service providers. At the end of the 1980s the wave of technological advances in the field positioned the PC with a great deal of high-level potential. PCs manufactured in 1989 had more computing power than did the mainframe machines of a decade before. Networking, the ability to link different types of computers together, was a blossoming new industry with major financial potential. Mass storage devices grew to offer immense data storage capacity, while the cost for such devices decreased. With this attractive, growing potential that PC-based machines now provided also came the deeper level of technical understanding needed for their operation. For example, networking is a specialized subject, and making different computers communicate is a difficult, often frustrating task. In the office environment many users now depend on sharing access to files that are stored on large disk areas. The installation and administration of such systems is a task requiring technical knowledge and skill.

Although there are many examples of firms reemphasizing a data-processing center, in the beginning of the 1990s, a major emerging trend is for companies to off-load or outsource the responsibility for implementing the new technology to automation service providers. These providers, which are companies that can bring in the necessary expertise, often are taking over virtually all of the administration and management responsibilities for information systems in the organization. Often called "system integrators," these companies are actually providing similar corporate functions to those of the data processing departments that operated the large mainframe computers of years ago. This trend to a service orientation actually sums up an overall feeling in the community of computer users—users are becoming overloaded with the rush of new, more complex technology, and some are experiencing technostress.

5.5.3 Standards for Information Transfer

Several references have already been made in this chapter to standards and protocols (which are the standards governing format that control exchanges between systems in telecommunications). Industry standards tend to be established by market predominance, albeit recently more often by alliances of suppliers in competition, as in the Unix developments. A standard may also be arrived at by head-to-head competition such as that prompted by the United States Federal Communications Commission, which in 1993 had four systems in competition to be declared the high-definition television standard for this country. Reference has also been made to those standards formulated by agreement at national and at international level by standards organizations. Particular reference has been made to the CCITT standards and to the remarkable web of standardizing activity which supports communications worldwide. (see pp. 233–234).

The standards for information transfer have had to grow more complex with the increased complexity of the material to be transferred. For example, the ASCII (American Standard Code for Information Interchange) code produced by the American National Standards Institute, formulated in 1963, has been the most widely used and reliable tool for storing textual information and for transferring electronic text from one word-processing system to another. But, as a United Nations report pointed out in 1990, "Although ASCII has served users very well, the capability of modern office technology for creating well laid-out and readable documents with tables, graphs, and the like requires a more powerful tool than ASCII can provide" (United Nations Advisory Committee for the Co-ordination of Information Systems, 1990, p. 75). Interchange of databases also presents a problem, because databases consist not only of data but definitions of data and indicators of relationships between parts of the data.

The movement towards open systems and the trend to interoperability of systems have already been mentioned in this chapter (pp. 249–250). The OSI is important for bringing into being, or at least into wider use, the standards to make the open systems environment a reality. OSI application standards have been created by the International Organization for Standardization (ISO), or adapted from national standards bodies such as the American National Standards Institute. Among the activities for which OSI standards exist are file transfer, access and management (FTAM); message handling (X.400); open document architecture (ODA), and document filing and retrieval (DFR).

Many standards have been developed outside the OSI environment that are essential to achievement of its aim of seamless interconnection of systems. Group 3 and Group 4 facsimile communications (discussed on pp. 222–223) are based on CCITT standards. The importance of the standard generalized markup language (SGML) to publishing has already discussed in Chapter 3 page (pp. 98–99). Unesco has brought into being a common communications format (CCF) for the transfer of bibliographical, cataloging, and abstracting information, and ISO has a data descriptive format (DDF) for the exchange of computer-generated information that is most applicable to database files.

There are also many other standards formulated by ISO and other organizations that cover the description, numbering, microcoopying of documents of all kinds, and the terminology in which the subjects of the documents are to be described. Many of these are ISO standards, and many have been derived from the work of national standardizing bodies such as the ANSI Z.39 Committee. Some idea of the variety of topics covered by standards for the description of information and its transfer from one format to another may be gathered from *ISO Standards Handbook 1: Information Transfer* (2nd edition, Geneva, 1982). It is inevitable that the web of standards that support global exchange of data will grow thicker and that earlier strands will continue to need replacement. But there is progress that is likely to result in more sharing of standards with international agreement on matters of widespread significance. For example, in 1990 the United States Government Open Systems Interconnection Profile (GOSIP) became a compulsory specification for all new United States government telecommunications and computer systems procurement procedures. The United Kingdom, Canada, Australia, and Sweden have similar profiles. Their effect is to direct government departments to purchase only computer and communication systems that offer OSI functionality.

Progress continues too in strengthening the web of standardization woven at the level of specialized agencies in different countries. A notable example is the format originally created at the Library of Congress in 1968 for the interchange of machine-readable library cataloging data. MARC (machine readable cataloging) formats now exist for many different types of material (books, serials, maps, music, films, and archives and manuscripts) and in many different national versions (USMARC, UKMARC, AUSMARC, and so on) and even in an international version, UNIMARC, published by the International Federation of Library Associations (IFLA). Vendors of both the materials and the automated systems by which they are controlled in libraries and archives are however international.

Multiple MARC formats for materials have meant that automated systems have been burdened with extra overheads such as multiple validation tables, format-specific indexes, and format-specific display routines. Differences in national formats have often added to suppliers' costs and lessened likelihood of making sales when they have sought to export library systems. Some countries have also considered abandoning national formats. Australian libraries, for example, have decided that the ABN system and network will in the future carry records in USMARC not AUSMARC format. Other national and international bibliographical authorities seem sure to follow the decision by the Library of Congress from 1993 to integrate the seven existing USMARC bibliographic formats into a single format with unified data elements.

Thus, at macro- and microlevels, progress toward open systems continues through standardization. It would be naive to suggest that as in all global politics the most powerful countries do not set the pace. At the same time, the power of global communication in bringing about broader-based decision making is obvious in the making and adoption of standards as in other information-based activities.

5.5.4 End-User Computing

A democratizing tendency has also been detected in the trend towards end-user computing, which is well-established. Today virtually all engineers in the United States are expected to use computers in the course of their work. Surveys show that the use of computerized information systems by R & D organizations is almost equally widespread (Rossini and Porter, 1986; Rossini *et al.*, 1988). A recent study by Case and Pickett (1989) continues this investigation by surveying Fortune 500 companies. In the usable responses, the majority of individuals indicated that they use microcomputers everyday; two-thirds use a minicomputer, and almost half use a mainframe every day. Most of the computers in R & D were networked. Results indicate that indeed computer information systems and software are being used extensively in R & D. Respondents to the survey also believed that computer technologies have made an impact, including improving research and information access, statistical analysis, and time and error reduction.

There are a number of factors at play in this trend towards computerization. Indeed, computing, and specifially end-user systems, is influencing the manner in which staff, managers, and executives work. And, it is important to reinforce the points already made, in Chapter 3 and in earlier discussion in this chapter, that the transition to end-user computing is not merely a change to a faster and more efficient technology but also a power shift. The move towards this new perspective of computing requires changes in work patterns, in ways users interact with technology, users interact with information, and users interact with other users (Andriole, 1985). And at the managerial and executive level, the work product associated with this technology, namely professional analysis and decision making, is less tangible than, for example, computerizing an inventory control system. Thus, it is more difficult to analyze in terms of cost-effectiveness (Andriole, 1985). Sproull and Kiesler (1991) present the broad view of the effects of end-user computing in networks in reporting that:

> Network-based communication technology can change patterns of information control by allowing people to bypass gatekeepers and access information sources directly. Typically this results in not only a faster flow of information but also changes in the relative power of the parties in the transaction (p. 108).

This circumstance has of course particular implications for the providers of information services that will be addressed in Chapter 6, along with other aspects of the increased opportunities for innovation in information services which network technology makes possible.

Obviously we are only at the beginning of the changes that exploitation of communications as a plentiful resource will bring. Although the number of systems and applications have indeed been impressive, most of these have been primarily at the administrative level. As noted by Boone (1991), much of the business world still views computing, and end-user computing, as an advance in office administration. But her perspective is that the computer can be the central nervous system of an organization where it will be used to enhance the human intellect (Boone, 1991). This new approach towards the use of the computer is being seen in a variety of settings, such as Boone's case studies of executive computing and in Zuboff's of the effects of working with electronic text in a variety of manufacturing and service industry environments (Zuboff, 1988).

There have been barriers to the success of end-user and networked systems. Some of these barriers are technical and have included limited online help functions, no one place to locate network resources, difficulties with communication protocols and command languages in the interaction, and the overall lack of standardization (Murray, 1992). Other barriers have been erected by the reluctance of management to accept and the tendency of workers to resist administrative and structural changes.

Nevertheless, many individuals and organizations have made a smooth transition from existing systems to new, technology-based ones. Attempting to create simple dichotomies between the characteristics of individuals and organizations who are successful and those who are unsuccessful at harnessing information technology effectively has left researchers without any sure formulas. Such successful individuals and organizations have a common characteristic—they accept change. The literature of "the diffusion of innovation" has identified some of the characteristics of individuals and organizations that accept change. Among them are managers with high professional rating and short tenure and organizations where there is a new leader and where friendship exists among interacting units. In addition, technological innovations that are apt to be accepted tend to have high visibility, definable advantages over the old system, and relate to a preconceived need. This list might have been predicted from innovation theory and in particular from the work of Rogers (1983), which has already been discussed at several points in Chapter 2.

There are various micro-factors associated with success in end-user systems. First, end-user systems should incorporate positive human factors at the level of both physical and psychological comfort, such as providing screen positional and system consistency, using simplicity in screen organization, minimizing memory load requirements, allowing a variety of interaction methods (such as GUIs) to satisfy needs of different individuals, providing a structure to develop a mental model of the system, and utilizing appropriate and meaningful feedback. (Palanivel and Helander, 1991; Kazlauskas *et al.*, 1990). The importance of training in leading to the success of technology-based systems is again stressed as it has been throughout this chapter.

Much of the discussion surrounding the effective use of information technology remains at the level of debate. There is, however, wide acknowledgement that the interaction of system, work groups, and individuals is the more effective depending on the extent that participants at all levels in organizational hierarchies feel that they "own" the system, or at least those parts of it relevant to them. There is no doubt too that the technology trends discussed above make possible information system design and administrative practices that foster such ownership. The prospects for better systems in more productive organizations therefore seem bright.

References

Ambrosio, Johanna (1992). Host plans reveal wider options. *Computer World 26,* (issue 1, Jan. 6), 1, 88.

Antonoff, Michael (1990). Image capture for business. *Personal Computing* (April 27), 101–106.

Andriole, Stephen J., Ed., (1985). *The future of information processing technology.* Princeton, New Jersey, Petrocelli Books.

Apple Computer, Inc. (1992). *Who knows what the future holds for your students?* Cupertino, California, Apple Computer, Inc. (L0180LL/B).

Bennett, John. L., Ed., (1983). *Building decision support systems.* Reading Massachusetts, Addison-Wesley.

Black, Uyless (1987). *Computer networks: protocols, standards, and interfaces.* Englewood Cliffs, New Jersey, Prentice-Hall.

Blackford, John (1990). Resolving a nasty little war. *Personal Computing 14*(4), 43–44.

Booker, Ellis (1989). Andersen installs international ISDN video link. *Computerworld 23*(8), 7.

Boone, Mary E. (1991). *Leadership and the computer.* Rocklin, California, Prima Publishing.

Burnett, Kathleen (1992). Multimedia as rhizome: design issues in a networked environment. *Networking, telecommunications and the networked information revolution. Proceeedings of the ASIS 1992 Mid-Year Meeting.* Silver Spring, Maryland, American Society for Information Science, pp. 24–36.

Case, Thomas L., and John R. Pickett (1989). R & D information systems. *Research Technology Management 32*(4), 29–33.

Caswell, Stephen A. (1990). A new LAN standard lights the way. *Datamation* (May), 76–79.

Caudle, Sharon L., and Karen B. Levitan, (1989). Improving the role of information resource management in federal information policies. *In* Charles R. McClure, Peter Hernon, and Harold C. Relyea, Eds., *United States information policies: views and perspectives.* Norwood, New Jersey, Ablex Publishing Company, pp. 296–314.

Chen, Ching-chih, S. Miranda, and S. Seidel, (1988). The new concept of hyperbase and its experimentation on the *First Emperor of China* videodisc. *Microcomputers for Information Management 5,* 217–246.

Cocula, John W., and Mark Ryland, (1990). Battle of the DOS contenders. *Personal Workstation* (August), 34–48.

Cortez, Edwin M., and Edward John Kazlauskas. (1986). *Managing information systems and technologies.* New York, Neal-Schumann.

Cotton, Ira W. (1981). Network architecture. *In* Nancy Knight, Ed., *Telecommunication technologies, networking and libraries.* Washington, D.C., U.S. Government Printing Office, pp. 1–18.

DataTimes assembles Asian package (1992). *Information Today 9*(1), 1.

Derfler, Frank J. (1990). Building workgroup solutions—voice e-mail. *PC Magazine* (July), 311–329.

Eaton, N. L. (1989). *CD-ROM and other optical information systems, implementation issues for libraries.* Phoenix, Arizona, Oryx Press.

Egol, Len (1990). Workstations revolutionize plant productivity. *Chemical Engineering* (January), 171–176.

Electronic Industries Association. (1991). *Electronic market data book.* (1991 edition). Washington, DC.

Fallows, James (1993). Crash-worthy speedster: the unheralded IBM OS/2 2.0 is as versatile and fast as Windows pretends to be. *Atlantic Monthly 271* (2), 103–108.

France Telecom joins forces with US West to develop videotex gateways in the U.S. (1991). *Information Today* (November 1991), 37.

Francis, Bob (1989). The desktop dimension. *Datamation* (November 1), 28–40.

Glass, L. Brett (1990). Reeling in the data. *Byte* (May), 299–306.

Gleick, James (1993). The telephone transformed—into almost everything. *New York Times Magazine* (May 16), 26–29, 50, 53–56, 62, 64.

A glimpse at the inventors of the future at MIT's Media Lab. (1991). *Information today* (November), p. 35.

Grolier. (1992). *The New Grolier Multimedia Encyclopedia* Version 5.01. Danbury, Connecticut, Grolier, Electronic Publishing. 1 laser optical computer disk.

Gunton, Tony (1989). *Infrastructure: building a framework for corporate information handling.* New York, Prentice-Hall.

Hayes, Frank (1990). From TTY to VUI. *Byte 15*(4), 205–211.

Hedrick, Charles L. (1987). Introduction to the Internet protocol. *Rutgers University Publication* (July 3), p. 5.

Helm, Leslie (1992). A clear rethinking: competition has U.S. firms warming up to fuzzy logic. *Los Angeles Times* (Feb. 17), D1,D4.

Hendall, Robert (1992). MIDI goes mainstream. *PC Magazine 11*(6), 181–218.

Horwitch and Sakakibara (1986). The changing strategy-technology relationship in technology-based industries: a comparison of the United States and Japan. *Research on Technological innovation, Management and Policy 3,* 83–135.

How future information-based firms will cut fat (1990). *Los Angeles Times* (February 14), Section D3, 37.

Hunkin, Tim (1993). Just give me the fax. *New Scientist* (February 13), 33–37.

Kahle, Brewster, Harry Morris, Jonathan Goldman, Thomas Erickson, and John Curran, (1992). Interfaces for distributed systems in information servers. In *Networking, telecommunications and the networked information revolution: proceeding of the ASIS 1992 Mid-Year Meeting.* Silver Spring, Maryland, American Society for Information Science, 124–148.

Kazlauskas, Edward J. (1988). The psychological impact of information technologies on the information worker. In *The information profession: facing future challenges.* Washington, D.C., Special Libraries Association, pp. 53–60.

Kazlauskas, Edward J., Rich Pinder, and Judith H. Richardson, (1990). A review and exploratory analysis of instructional design strategies relevant to library and information management software. *Information Technology and Libraries 9*(2), 121–134.

Kelly, Joseph (1990). Information technology sales soar to $256B. *Datamation* (June), 40–47.

Kesner, Richard M. (1988). *Information systems: a strategic approach to planning and implementation.* Chicago, American Library Association.

Krol, Ed (1992). *The whole Internet: user's guide & catalog.* Sebastopol, California, O'Reilly and Associates.

Lazzareschi, Carla (1993). Finally, the videophone: communications era dawns, but is anyone watching? *Los Angeles Times* (February 28), D1.

Levy, S. (1984). *Hackers: heroes of the computer revolution.* Garden City, Doubleday.

Link, Albert N., and Gregory Tassey, (1987). *Strategies for technology-based competition: meeting the new global challenge.* Lexington, Massachusetts, Lexington Books.

Lohr, Steve (1993). "Mainframes aren't all that dead." *New York Times* (February 9), C1, C5.

Louderback, Jim (1993). Forget the name game: PDAs, palmtops identical. *PC Week 10*(18), 88.

Lunin, Lois F. (1990). Image information systems: young and growing. *Information Today* (June), 27–32.

Lunin, Lois F., and Clifford A. Lynch, Eds., (1991). Perspectives on imaging: advanced applications. *Journal of the American Society for Information Science 42*(8), 575–620.

Lynch, Clifford A. (1990). The growth of computer networks: a status report. *Bulletin of the American Society for Information Science* (June/July), 10–11.

Lynch, Clifford A., and Cecelia M. Preston, (1990). Internet access for information resources. *Annual Review of Information Science and Technology 25,* 263–312.

Magid, Lawrence J. (1991). "After 10 years, PCs continue to evolve." *Los Angeles Times* (August 8), D3.

Maguire, Carmel (1991). Beautiful hypertext: the Micro Gallery at the National Gallery in London. *Lasie 22*(3), 61–71.

Maguire, Carmel, Connie Wilson, and William Hood, Eds., (1991). *Image-based information and the future of academic and research libraries.* Kensington, Australia, University of New South Wales, School of Librarianship, pp. 14–17.

Marchionini, G. (1988). Hypermedia and learning: freedom and chaos. *Educational Technology 28*(11), 8–12.

Markoff, John (1993). Building the electronic superhighway. *New York Times* (January 24), F3, F6.

Martin, Thomas H. (1988). Office automation. *Annual Review of Information Science and Technology 23,* 217–235.

Mayo, Elton (1949). Hawthorne and the Western Electric Company. In *The social problems of an industrial civilization.* New York, Routledge, pp. 60–76.

McClure, Charles R., Joe Ryan, and Diana Lauterbach, (1992). The role of public libraries in the use if Internet/NREN services: preliminary findings. In *Networking, telecommunications, and the networked information revolution: proceedings of the ASIS 1992 Mid-Year Meeting.* Silver Spring, Maryland, American Society for Information Science, pp. 46–62.

McFarlan, F. Warren, and James L. McKenney, (1983). The information archipelago—governing the new world. *Harvard Business Review 61*(4), 91–99.

McFarlan, F. Warren, James L. McKenney, and Philip Pyburn, (1983). The information archipelago—plotting a course. *Harvard Business Review 61*(1), 145–156.

McGraw-Hill. (1987). *McGraw-Hill encyclopedia of science and technology* (sixth edition). New York, McGraw-Hill, *18.*

McKenney, James L., and F. Warren McFarlan, (1982). The information archipelago—maps and bridges. *Harvard Business Review 60*(5), 109–119.

McLuhan, Marshall (1962). *The Gutenberg galaxy.* Toronto, University of Toronto Press.

Mentzer, John T., and Roger Gomes, (1988). Evaluating a decision support forecasting system. *Industrial Marketing Management 18*(2), 313–323.

Meredith, Lindsay (1988). Developing and using a data base marketing system. *Industrial Marketing Management 18*(4), 245–257.

Miller, Michael J. (1992). Multimedia. *PC Magazine 11*(6), 112–123.

Murray, Arthur J. (1992). Cultivating the electronic heartland: preparing for the coming knowledge harvest. In *Networking, telecommunications, and the networked information revolu-*

tion: proceedings of the ASIS 1992 Mid-Year Meeting. Silver Spring, Maryland, American Society for Information Science, 241–252.

Nath, Ravinder (1989). Associations between user training and information systems success. *International Journal of Information Management 9,* 259–265.

National Geographic Society. (1990). *Mammals: A Multimedia Encyclopedia* Washington, D.C., National Geographic Society. 1 laser optical computer disk.

Nielsen, Jacob (1990). *Hypertext and Hypermedia*. New York, Academic Press.

O'Reilly, Richard (1993). Now in reach: quality color printing. *Los Angeles Times* (July 1), p. D3.

Palanivel, Thiagarajan, and Martin Helander, (1991). Human-factors issues in dialog design. *Advances in Computers 33,* 115–171.

Pen computer standard. (1993). *New York Times* (May 24), C3, D8.

Pollack, Andrew (1993). Mitsubishi drops mainframe computers. *New York Times* (January 12), C4.

Poppel, Harvey, and Bernard Goldstein, (1987). *Information technology: the trillion dollar opportunity*. New York, McGraw-Hill.

Project Quartet (1990). by Bill Tuck, Cliff McKnight, Marie Hayet and David Archer. London, British Library Research and Development Department, (Library and information research report 76).

Rogers, E. M. (1983). *Diffusion of innovations* (third edition). New York, Free Press.

Rogers, Michael, and Yuriko Hoshiai, (1990). Future looks fuzzy. *Newsweek* (May), 46.

Rosenberg, J. M., (1984). *Dictionary of computers, data processing and telecommunications*. New York, Wiley.

Rosenblatt, A. (1991). PCs and workstations. *IEEE Spectrum 28*(1), 32–35.

Rossini, F. A., and A. L. Porter, (1986). Who's using computers in industrial R & D and for what? *Research Management 29,* 39–44.

Rossini, F. A., A. L. Porter, C. C. Jacobs, and D. S. Abraham, (1988). Trends in computer use in R & D. *Research Technology Management 31,* 36–41.

Savage, J. A. (1990). Fuzzy logic? maybe; we're not sure. *Computer World* (January 29), 17.

Shandle, Jack (1990). Communications—a maturing market remains robust. *Electronics 63,* 62–64.

Shandle, Jack (1992). The golden splice: ISDN arrives in the U.S. *Electronic Design* (November 25), 150.

Sherman, Stratford (1993). The new computer revolution. *Fortune 127*(12), 56–80.

Sony introduces hand-held system for data retrieval. (1991). *Los Angeles Times* (September 13), D5.

Sprague, Ralph H., and Eric Carlson, (1982). *Building effective decision support systems*. Englewood Cliffs, New Jersey, Prentice-Hall.

Sproull, Lee, and Sara Kiesler (1991). *Connections: new ways of working in the networked organization*. Cambridge Massachusetts, MIT Press.

Stokes, A. V. (1985). *Concise encyclopedia of information technology* (second edition). Aldershot, Hampshire, England, Gower.

Thryft, Ann R. (1990). QIC tape drive capacities keep pace with competition. *Computer Design* (August 13), 30.

Tory, David (1990). Interview: the raging battle on the UNIX front. *Datamation* (May 1), 43–46.

United Nations Advisory Committee for the Co-ordination of Information Systems. (1990). *Management of electronic records: issues and guidelines*. Prepared by the Advisory Committee

for the Co-ordination of Information Systems (ACCIS). New York, United Nations. (ACCIS guides to United Nations information sources series—UN Sales no GV.E.89.0.15)
United States Office of Science and Technology Policy. (1992). *The National Research and Education Network Program: a report to Congress.* Washington, D.C.
University of Southern California, University Computing Services. (1991). *Academic computing at USC: 1991–92.* Los Angeles California, University of Southern California Press.
University of Southern California. (1992a). *Budget development system manual.* Los Angeles California, University of Southern California Press.
University of Southern California. (1992b). *Planning and five year budget forcasting manual.* Los Angeles California, University of Southern California Press.
Verity, John W. (1992). IBM's major triumph in minis. *Business Week* (industrial/technology edition) *3256,* 111.
Vogt, Carlton G. (1989). Office of the future: it's here. *Design News* (January 23), 130–138.
Walker, Teri C., and Richard K. Miller (1990). *Expert systems handbook.* Lilburn, Georgia, Fairmont Press.
Walsh, John (1989). Videoconferencing comes of age. *Telecommunications* (November), 47–50.
Weber, Jonathan (1993a). Adobe software could start new era in computer communications. *Los Angeles Times* (June 15), D1, D14.
Weber, Jonathan (1993b). NeXT to stop producing computers. *Los Angeles Times,* (February 10), pp. D1, D11.
Wexler, Joanie (1989). What can ISDN do for you today. *Networking Management* (September), 76–86.
Zuboff, Shoshana (1988). *In the age of the smart machine: the future of work and power.* New York, Basic Books.

6

Information Services as Supporters and Exemplars of Innovation

Innovation is centrally an organisational and managerial issue because innovations are produced within organisations that transform knowledge.
—Centre for Technology and Social Change, *Innovation for the 1990s,* p. 10.

It is impossible to seek valuable information without encountering valueless information
—Lee Sproull and Sara Kiesler, p. 170.

The first key problem in the management of innovation, then, is how to get people to pay attention—how to trigger the action thresholds of individuals to appreciate and pay attention to new ideas, needs and opportunities.
—Rosabeth M. Kanter, p. 173.

The process of innovation in libraries could be made much smoother if innovation champions knew more about actively managing implementation, from the stage of making the case for adoption through institutionalization and assessment of the new practice. Implementation skills include techniques for pursuing their roles as managers of change and orchestrating those of others in the implementation process, with special attention to the political and social issues of innovation.
—Jose-Marie Griffiths, Ronald G. Havelock, and Ellen A. Sweet, *Diffusion of Innovations in Library and Information Science: Final Report,* p. 221.

Chapter Synopsis

In this concluding chapter, we distill from earlier chapters some guidelines as to how information services can foster the information flows that are vital for an innovative organization. Arguments for the necessity of innovation apply equally to information services themselves. Principles for the design and management of such services are then drawn from four areas of inquiry: innovation as a phenomenon, organizations as information processing systems, effects of technological change, and information user behavior. Application of these principles is discussed in relation to information services in a variety of settings. Strategies for promotion of innovation within information services and within the organizations they serve are also expounded.

6.1 Innovation as a Phenomenon

6.1.1 Why all Organizations Need to Innovate

The definition of innovation adopted in this book is

> the application in any organization of ideas new to it, whether they are embodied in products, processes, services, or in the systems of management and marketing through which the organization operates.

Chapter 1 has demonstrated the economic and social importance of innovation to any organization that wishes to survive in a world in which continual and rapid change is the norm. Innovation is central to improved productivity, to restarting cycles of economic activity on an upward curve, and to the very nature of the capitalist system of enterprise. Innovation is connected to the wellsprings of human endeavor in invention and creativity.

Innovation is likely then to remain "an idea in good currency," to borrow a phrase from Schon (1971 p. 123), because it is strongly associated with economic concerns that will continue to dominate political debate and decision making for some time to come. The crucial social and political shift from the pursuit of unfettered economic development to the ideal of "sustainable" development, which involves preserving, managing, and sharing the world's resources, will require major cultural shifts involving the adoption of many new ideas into the operations of organizations. In other words, there will have to be substantial innovation, in the sense in which we have used it here, in all institutions and organizations, from governments down to small businesses like the local gas station.

On a day-to-day level, innovation is to be observed all around us. Some of it is highly publicized in advance; some is implemented and accepted without necessarily being perceived as innovation. Some is important, some trivial. Some is made necessary by major changes in political conditions, such as the collapse of the monolithic Soviet state, which sent ripple effects into virtually every aspect of human activity everywhere.

6.1.2 Why Information Services Need to Innovate

Information services are also organizations in themselves, whether they operate independently or as part of larger entities. An organization is a group with a purpose, structure, and procedures. This may serve as a reminder that information services may, like other organizations, be *ad hoc*, temporary and informal. At the other end of the scale are the permanent stores of information sources in institutions such as libraries, archives, and museums, which are turned into information resources through the application of more or less standardized procedures covering both the physical and intellectual arrangement of the materials and the conditions of access for clients. In such environments, information services tend to be heir to all the problems of bureaucratic organizations in which it is safer to keep rules and follow procedures than to innovate, which is to take risks. The larger and more established an information service is, the greater the danger that the formal and informal status and reward systems will invite conformity to rules not risk taking. The causes of the "dynamic conservatism" (another phrase from Schon, 1971), which accompanies the introduction of technological and organizational change in libraries, have never been better explained than by Markuson (1970). She places the library in a matrix bounded by its collection, its history, its parent organization, its users, and the library network (in the social as well as the technological sense).

The necessity for innovation in information services is based on principles of organization and management that apply in all organizations. Similarly, the successful implementation of innovative ideas in information services may be expected to include the four crucial factors in technological innovation identified by Brown and Karagozoglu (1989, p. 12—already quoted in Chapter 2, p. 55), namely the organizational structure, the quality of information flow, the relevant manpower flows, and the specification of key roles for innovative action. The key roles are (1) gatekeeping; (2) idea gathering; (3) project championing; (4) project management; (5) sponsorship of senior management, and (6) marketing internally as well as externally of the innovative idea, product, or service, which is an activity too likely to be overlooked if lumped into project management.

There are also more specific reasons why information services need to be innovative. Information services aim to serve organizations and individuals who are working in conditions of turbulence, brought about by obvious technological change and not so obvious changes in demographic and other social conditions. Compounding the constant need for change in information services is the fact that the information industry, which information service managers depend on for the information technology needed to improve services and contain costs, is in a seemingly permanent state of rapid and accelerating change. Proliferating technological options are accompanied by nontechnological changes—for example, those brought about by commercial decisions—that affect the cost to productivity ratios and consequently information service managers' decisions of whether to make, buy, lease, or contract out services. Compounding this again are changes in private and public sector roles in the provision of information systems and services. The whole scenario is clouded again by the widening phenomenon of public penury. Even in rich countries like the United States, calls for public spending on infrastructure far exceed the funds available. In poorer countries, burdens of national debt and global competition generally make public provision of information services a low priority. Within the private sector, too, information services everywhere (except perhaps in Japanese industry) constantly have to justify their costs in relation to benefits delivered.

In all these circumstances it is not fanciful but prudent to say that information services must adopt innovation as a policy and performance goal. The question is not whether to innovate but how. The sources of knowledge about innovation that could form the base of innovation strategies for information services have been examined in detail in this book. It is time to exploit them to harvest a set of design and management principles.

6.1.3 Major Features of Innovation as a Phenomenon

Table 6.1 distills, from the analysis completed in earlier chapters, the few major propositions that characterize innovation as a phenomenon. In accordance with the systems model of Chapter 2, the propositions have been grouped into three sets, namely those relating to

1. the management (processing) of innovation,
2. inputs to innovation, and
3. the environment for innovation.

A brief discussion of each proposition follows the table, as a reminder of the experiences and other evidence on which the propositions are based.

Proposition 1—Innovation is centrally a matter of organization, rather than of technology.

The concept of innovation as addressed in this book focuses attention on the organization as the key unit for consideration. To have an organization take up an idea, its members have to be persuaded that the idea is both useful and useable. Such persuasion is one facet of the central task of managing an organization, namely to get the organization as a whole marching in

Table 6.1
Propositions Derived from Study of Innovation as a Phenomenon

Propositions about managing innovation
1. Innovation is centrally a matter of organization, rather than of technology.
2. Invisible assets are important in realizing innovation benefits.
3. Managerial style is a more important determinant of the effects of technological innovations on an organization than the technology employed.

Propositions about the inputs to innovation
4. Progress from invention/discovery to application is not linear.
5. Neither science (or knowledge) push nor market pull can be categorized as the *sine qua non* of successful innovation.

Propositions about the environment for innovation
6. The more complex the system into which an innovation has to move, the more resistance it will meet.
7. Opinions differ on whether innovation is more likely to be achieved by strategy or serendipity, in small or large organizations, and in good or bad economic times.

a common direction, with some shared sense of purpose. In Chapter 1, we carefully distinguished between invention, that is, having a good idea or a good technology, and innovation, which is having that idea turned into operational or commercial practice. New technology does not constitute innovation until it is integrated into the practice of the organization.

Proposition 2—Invisible assets are important in realizing innovation benefits.

Study of Japanese management practice has increased recognition of the importance of invisible assets in innovation. The more lucrative the innovation, the quicker competitors are to enter the market and to do so without the burden of research and development (R & D) and of learning by doing accrued by the original innovator. Engineering can be reversed, patents may be worked around, but the brand name, the reputation for service, and more than anything the well trained and loyal work force are more lasting advantages. Invisible assets are strongly information-based, or as Itami (1989) says, "based on one kind of information flow or another" and are likely to be "the only source of long-term competitive edge for the firm" (pp. 37 and 40).

Invisible assets are by definition easily overlooked at all hierarchical levels in organizations. Top management may not count the invisible asset that an in-house information service represents. The information service itself may overlook the value of staff with in-depth knowledge of the organization's mission and history or of its customer base.

Proposition 3—Managerial style is a more important determinant of the effects of technological innovations on an organization than the technology employed.

Accusations of technological determinism are frequently made and sometimes justified in that technology tends to be promoted as irresistible, as well as inevitable for greater economic and social good. There seems little doubt that technological change is inherently destabilizing and will exacerbate problems of inefficiency and ineffectiveness in an organization—if nothing else it will bring them to the surface sooner.

But it is the style of management that determines the effects of the technology rather than vice versa. E-mail, for example, may be allowed by management to make organizations more open, make communications less formal, increase information flows, or may be used to tighten controls and do the opposite. Sproull and Kiesler (1991) share their vision of a networked organization as one in which "all employees participate equally in the information life of the organization, independent of their geographic, organizational, or social location" (p. 161). They also report studies that indicate that more informed workers are not necessarily more productive workers, and that people often acquire more information and more costly information than they need to do their immediate work. In their opinion "increasing employee participation by electronic communication [is to be regarded] as a capacity-building strategy with implications for long-term performance" (Sproull and Kiesler, 1991, pp. 98–99). From both the organization's and the employee's point of view, some "extraneous" knowledge can be valuable, because work tasks are often reassigned as an organization restructures; some knowledge of parts of the organization's work that have been outside one's narrow domain helps a worker fit smoothly and flexibly into a new task elsewhere. This returns us to the territory of invisible assets.

Proposition 4—Progress from invention/discovery to application is not linear.

In earlier times, and especially for a decade or two after World War II when public belief in science was unquestioning, there was also belief in innovation as a linear process, which proceeded in an orderly and inevitable fashion from basic science through to applied science and engineering and into manufacturing and distribution to eager customers. By the 1980s this linear model had been replaced by much greater appreciation of the complexities in the diffusion and lack of diffusion of apparently useful knowledge. Peter and Olson (1983) could write a plausible article to demonstrate that scientific theories are helpfully to be thought of as products that are marketed through academic distribution channels and a variety of promotional techniques. The purchase "price" (i.e., the intellectual effort that the unconvinced person has to put forth in order to take up the new idea) varies according to the degree to which the new ideas depart from established beliefs. Ideas that threaten paradigm change are much harder to sell (to the editors and referees of established journals, for example). This may serve as useful reminder that information is not free and that most of the costs involved are likely to be incurred by the user.

Proposition 5—Neither science (or knowledge) push nor market pull can be categorized as the sine qua non *of successful innovation.*

In a simpler time, Ralph Waldo Emerson is alleged to have asserted that "If a man write a better book, preach a better sermon, or build a better mousetrap than his neighbour, though he build his house in the woods, the world will make a beaten path to his door", (*Oxford Dictionary of Quotations,* 1979, p. 208). If this was ever true, it is certainly no longer true of books and sermons and very unlikely for more mundane objects like mousetraps. Lack of linearity in the progress of scientific invention to innovation does not mean that market pull, any more than knowledge or product push, can be categorized as decisive in successful innovation. The evidence on both approaches was covered in Chapter 1, section 1.3. The proposition can be interpreted to mean that in the promotion of innovation both new knowledge and market need have to be considered. This gives us a slightly deeper insight into the content of the information flow on which those seeking to promote innovation need to keep gates open.

Proposition 6—The more complex the system into which an innovation has to move, the more resistance it will meet.

There are a multitude of deterrents to innovation, some of which have always existed. There are and have always been less-costly alternatives (such as getting a cat instead of a new mousetrap) and deterrents posed by previous investment (like that in stocks of mousetraps of existing design and in the technology of their manufacture). There is also possible influence of the principle of least effort (as in decision that the mice do not eat much so why bother with a trap).

Donald Schon's (1971) phrase "dynamic conservatism" describes the plenum into which applications of new knowledge and new ideas have to move in modern complex societies. Ways of doing things and patterns of behavior are embedded in belief systems that may lie deep in our individual and group psyche. Less profoundly, an innovation may simply arrive at the wrong time—which may be at any time before, in managerial and entrepreneurial judgment, satisfactory return has been achieved on capital invested in existing plant, equipment, personnel training, and so on. Hence the so-called attacker's advantage in implementing new technology that is available to the firm that has no stake in existing technology (Foster, 1986). Dynamic conservatism may also be observed in education environments, in relation to curriculum change for example. Many a curriculum has, like the Model T Ford, outlived the needs of its market long before it is replaced. Those who seek to promote innovation in schools have to reckon seriously with the investment that has already been sunk into the existing syllabus, including the writing and trial of it and the training of teachers. Such barriers may be just as serious as those built around existing systems in business and manufacturing industry.

Proposition 7—Opinions differ on whether innovation is more likely to be achieved by strategy or serendipity, in small or large organizations, and in good or bad economic times.

Differences of opinion characterize many aspects of the study of innovation. Peter Drucker, for example, believes in "systematic innovation" that is "the purposeful and organized search for changes, and . . . the systematic analysis of the opportunities such changes might offer for economic or social innovation" (Drucker, 1985, p. 31). Michael Porter (1990) on the other hand, despite his advocacy for attention to management of innovation, says "It is striking though how often innovators are those firms that are simply looking in the right places, unencumbered by or unconcerned with conventional wisdom" (p. 48). There is also no consensus on whether innovation is more frequent and successful in large organizations or small, though the evidence suggests that size is rather a determinant of which strategy to use than a determinant of whether innovation takes place. Evidence is similarly mixed on whether innovation is more likely in good or bad economic times. If the obvious logic prevailed, major innovation would occur when money was plentiful in the good times and incremental resource-saving innovation in the bad times when money was tight. In reality either type seems as likely to occur in the bad times as the good.

6.2 Organizations as Information Processing Systems

6.2.1 Key Information Flows

A major theme of this book has been that the innovation process is best seen from an organizational perspective (Proposition 1 of Table 6.1). A second major theme has been the connection of innovation with information and with information services. The quotation from Centre for Technology and Social Change (1988, p. 10) at the opening of this chapter links these themes, by making plain that innovation is a process of transforming knowledge within an organization, from a form in which it is notional to a form in which it is embodied in new goods, services, or practices. To effect such a transformation requires the organization to function as an information processing system.

Recall from Chapter 1 that the knowledge of an organization—that is, everything that the organization knows—is much more than the information to be gathered from its files; it includes also its culture, the knowledge of its people about the contacts they use to gain information from outside, and so on. Within the organization, each person has his or her own personal stock of knowledge, and to put part of that personal knowledge into other parts of the organization requires a flow of information from one person to another. Many, repeated, and two-way are the flows required to bring about a successful innovation.

Consider for example the model of innovation derived from Roberts and Frohman (1978), which has already been used as Figure 1.4 in Chapter 1, and which was created to refer to technological innovation. The model illustrates that innovation is a multistage process. Each stage requires relevant information from various parts of the innovating organization and from outside—particularly knowledge about technology and the market—to be brought together and fed into the organization's corporate knowledge, so that the collected, assimilated knowledge can be reified into the prototype, and later the production "product." Note that the terms *technology, market,* and *product* can readily be adapted to a more general model of innovation, consistent with the wide definition adopted in this book. The definition, and the discussion in Chapters 1 and 2, emphasize that innovation is about putting ideas into practice; it is not confined to engineering technology, as some of the literature might suggest. The product might, for example, be something like a new record-keeping procedure for a government department, for which the market is the clerks, supervisors, and managers of the department, and the technology would be an array of rules, subprocedures, and perhaps computer hardware and software.

The Roberts and Frohman (1978) model is returned to here because, in addition to postulating stages of innovation, as several innovation models do, it also includes many of the key information flows. The following text steps through these flows, attempting to show where information services can contribute to them.

6.2.2 How Information Services Facilitate Information Flows for Innovation

As was noted in Chapter 2, a distinctive characteristic of innovative organizations is that they encourage and facilitate the information flows that innovation requires. Although informal flows are critical, formal sources of information are needed to complement them.

Information services are specialists in facilitating flows of formal information and often make use of the organization's informal networks to do so. An information service is defined in this book as

> a specialized organization or department of an organization, the major function of which is to capture, store, and transmit information to people, departments, or organizations outside the information service.

Information services add a variety of access points and the continuity of access, which help make information sources into information resources. As discussed in Chapter 3, the distinction between information systems and information services, when one needs to be made, may hinge on the quality and variety of the interfaces provided for clients and the adoption in an information service of a marketing approach to the design, distribution, and promotion of all products and services. Information services are peopled with information providers whose function we have described in Chapter 4 (section 4.6) as to find *already existing* information and provide it to others, adding to it varying levels of extra value, depending on the circumstance. Let us examine some of the key information flows in Figure 1.4 (p. 15), to see how information services can contribute to them.

Recognition of opportunity is the first stage of innovation in that model proposed by Roberts and Frohman (1978). The seven signals of change that suggest opportunities for innovation listed by Drucker (1985) have already been discussed in Chapter 2 (pp. 47–74). He calls them (1) the unexpected; (2) the incongruity; (3) process need; (4) changes in public perception; (5) changes in industry or market structure; (6) demographics; (7) new knowledge. As in prospecting for gold, spotting any of these signals is essentially a matter of finding and recognizing a nugget of information among the overburden of dross. As Sproull and Kiesler (1991) put it, "it is impossible to seek valuable information without encountering valueless information" (p. 170). However, as discussed in Chapter 2 (pp. 47–74), the first three of these signals would almost always be hidden in fields of information accessible only to insiders in the relevant industry, and barely touched by conventional information services, although a good sales record system should reveal glints of the "unexpected" signal if there is one. The fourth signal, changes in public perception, is hard to pick up precisely because existing players, including the trade press, are missing it. But information services can help organizations (including individual entrepreneurs) pick up the last three signals listed.

Emerging changes in industry structure often flow from changes in government regulations (very public information!) or from new technologies that are nibbling at the market of the old ones. The changes give opportunities for *new* entrants to the industry. Although the existing players are often aware of the changes, they tend to downplay them because of the investment in human and capital terms they have in the old systems. (One example is the initial lack of interest in personal computers by mainframe computer makers and by data-processing centers in large organizations). External information services, not tied to existing players in the industry but with a broad coverage, such as state and other publicly accessible research libraries, can expect to receive inquiries for detailed (public) information about the precursor signals, that is about the new rules or the new technologies and who has them.

Demographic information—a vital clue to many market opportunities for innovation—is also public information. The task of the information service is to package this information in ways that clearly bring out the aspect that the client is interested in. The technology is now available to make this easy, and should be in the repertoire of any information service likely to encounter such queries. The CD-ROM enables a vast array of census data to be stored conveniently, while, even more critically, software such as the C-DATA package developed in Australia allows the user to display in seconds maps showing the concentration of, say, families with three children under five years of age and with incomes of more than $30,000.

Providing access to "new knowledge," both scientific and nonscientific, has always been one of the goals and roles of information services. All the world's great national libraries have included and continue to collect in science, technology and the social sciences, and to make special efforts to see that new knowledge in all areas is widely available. The British Library's notable efforts in this regard have seen the National Lending Library for Science and Technology evolve into today's Document Supply Centre, which is widely used, especially through its Urgent Action Service, for electronic and conventional document delivery from all over the world. The digital revolution in information storage, described in Chapter 3, has allowed the development of an extensive commercial database industry so that even quite small and specialized information services can pull in information for clients on virtually any topic. It is, however, unlikely that the client will be able to specify precisely the information need related to an innovation opportunity. To assist this stage of the innovation process, perhaps the key role of information services is the selective dissemination of information within an organization. The interests of key individuals and work groups within the organization can be profiled and the clients notified of items of new information in the literature, including the news media and the lists of forthcoming meetings and so on, which match their interests.

In addition to providing such focused information, the information service should also aim to provide an environment that encourages browsing, which is one way to increase the likelihood that the organization will be, in Porter's (1990) phrase "simply looking in the right places, unencumbered by or unconcerned with conventional wisdom" (p. 48).

Idea formulation, the second stage in Roberts and Frohman's (1978) model, involves a fusion of the personal knowledge of the innovator with his or her perceptions and often with some brainstorming with colleagues. With a rough idea in mind, all manner of detailed questions arise before it can be articulated fully let alone put into practice.

The third stage, *problem solving,* is probably the one where most use is made of information services. It is an essential part of the role of information service managers to help clients formulate questions in the most effective manner possible. This is much easier than in stage one, because questions that arise are likely to be more precise, for example, "is there a material available that has the following properties?" Many of the questions that arise at this stage will require experiments (R & D) to answer, but the information service can save much time, effort, and money by uncovering already existing information, thus saving the clients the effort of duplicating existing work by others.

Information services can also help uncover relevant information about potential markets, using sources such as sales of existing similar products (especially those already produced by the organization) and also the demographic information referred to earlier. At this stage the key people in the innovating organization—described in Chapter 2 (section 2.3.2) as the gatekeepers, the idea generators, and the product champions—will attempt to draw on as many of the information sources as they can. Information services that strive to promote innovation will aim to make as many as possible of these sources as are conveniently accessible, since accessibility, in which ease of use is an important component, is the key factor determining whether an information source is in fact used. Possible sources, all of which are discussed in Chapter 4, include

1. internal sources of information (e.g., peers, new employees, and internally generated data and reports);
2. external sources (e.g., peers in other organizations, seminars, publications, patents, and electronic information services);

3. information providers within the organization (e.g., librarians and information professionals, competitor intelligence personnel, and marketing personnel);
4. organizations to promote innovation (e.g., industry research associations).

In *Prototyping* and *commercial development,* the fourth and fifth stages in the model, much more information has to be built into knowledge about the new product, but this information comes largely from experiments, including test marketing, rather than from already existing sources of information. Information services as such thus have little role in these stages of innovation, except that they can play a very useful role in collecting and making accessible for future reference the documentation created in these stages. In organizations where there is no information management exercised over laboratory notebooks and other records of the organization's own R & D, as well as results of outside testing and analysis of materials, and especially market research reports, the likelihood of considerable portions of the data being recreated unnecessarily at another time is high.

Technology utilization and diffusion, the sixth stage of the model, sees a different role for information services, namely spreading the news about the new product. This is also the last stage in Levitan's life cycle of information, illustrated in Figure 3.1 (p. 77). This book provides a wealth of reasons why new ideas for products, processes, services, or organizational change are not necessarily perceived on their technical merits, and why strategies for the promotion of innovation are needed. The information service should position itself to advise on strategies for dissemination of information, inside and outside the organization. In the formal literature, for example, information service managers are in a position to know which scientific journals are the most cited and which of the trade journals are most likely to get into the markets targeted. Understanding of the dissemination phenomenon can also be helpful in planning communication aspects of the organization's innovation strategies. For example, information specialists familiar with the literature on diffusion of innovation know that efforts to protect technology by patent claims and secrecy may be counterproductive. If the organization or the inventor has no established reputation for knowledge in the area, prospective licensees and the experts to whom they turn for advice may be hard to convince of the quality of the innovation.

There is also ample evidence that not all skeptics are likely to reside outside the innovating organization. Thus the marketing of new ideas within the organization is another important part of innovation strategy. The information service is well positioned to assist in this because its mission crosses organizational boundaries. This can facilitate collection of information from all parts of the organization and present opportunities for its dissemination from a source that need not be part of traditional conflicts, such as that often to be observed among production, marketing, and sales departments.

Stepping through the model presented by Roberts and Frohman (1978) has recalled the importance of information flows in the innovation process. If the information service can associate with general knowledge of the innovation process, particular knowledge of the organization, and memory of the processes by which innovation has succeeded and failed, then the information service will be in a position to make unique contribution to the organization's self-knowledge. In the frequent restructuring and realignment of ownership that is endemic in today's organizational structures, private and public, this is another challenge for the information service.

6.2.3 Some General Propositions about Organizations as Information Processing Systems

In Chapter 3 we discussed how the culture of an organization is derived from its patterns of communication or information exchange, the formal aspects of which are regulated by organizational structure. Insights have been gained from studies of organization behavior generally and particularly from attempts to design more effective systems for management information. Those judged to have most relevance to the provision of information services that promote innovation are set out as propositions in Table 6.2.

Proposition 1—There are many different modes of information gathering, analysis, and distribution in organizations and therefore many different information services.

To some extent each division or department of an organization acts as an information service for all others. Those with the least limited responsibility for information collection, analysis, and supply should not therefore assume that they are in any sense in a monopoly position. It seems reasonable, on the other hand, that those with broadest responsibilities, whether designated "library," "information center," or "information department," should seek opportunities to share their expertise in information repackaging and repurposing, as well as diffusing awareness of the information services provided by other departments throughout the organization.

Proposition 2—"News" for an organization is a first appearance of some sign of how the future is going to be, in a respect crucial to the organization. The more senior the executive, the more preoccupied he or she will be with news.

Table 6.2
Propositions Derived from the Study of Organizations as Information Processing Systems

1. There are many different modes of information gathering, analysis, and distribution in organizations and therefore many different information services.
2. "News" for an organization is a first appearance of some sign of how the future is going to be, in a respect crucial to the organization. The more senior the executive, the more preoccupied he or she will be with news.
3. Good information systems give clues about the degree of uncertainty likely in decisions based on their content, but do not burden users with information about stable features of the environment.
4. Organizations depend on formal and informal sources and channels of information and a mix of internal and external information.
5. Innovative organizations are "learning systems" in which training is very important, and even more important is the creation of a nonpunitive culture for risk-taking and risk-takers in which members are continuously learning.
6. Organizations need memory.

Definition of "news" as the first appearance of some intimation about an aspect of the future of crucial significance to the organization helps to explain the preference of senior management for "live" information sources, for people face-to-face or on telephones. It also explains why top managers, in academic institutions, government administration, as well as in corporations, are not likely to make personal use of the collections of printed materials kept in their libraries or the records of past activities in the organization's archives. Easy and transparent access to such information sources may however be very important for their administrative assistants and others who provide some of the live information on which management bases decisions.

Proposition 3—Good information systems give clues about the degree of uncertainty likely in decisions based on their content, but do not burden users with information about stable features of the environment.

The second part of this proposition may be seen as an attempt to extend to information systems the principles of management by exception. To use a geological metaphor, it is not only which outcroppings to measure but which changes in measurement to report. The technique of the snow job is well known. Information most likely to alarm and disturb a manager may be surrounded with large quantities of routine and even boring data in the hope that it will pass unremarked. The calculation of uncertainty is by nature perilous. The halo effect of an authoritative information source should serve to remind the purveyors of that source of their obligations to flag items in which their normal standard of quality control in reporting cannot be maintained. There are also ways in which information specialists can rank the reliability of sources based on reputation and on past performance in the area of the organization's interests and expertise. (A technique that librarians have long found effective in the evaluation of encyclopedias and other reference books is to peruse the articles on topics with which they are themselves most familiar.) Responsibility for monitoring the quality of sources is another element in the mission of an information service.

Proposition 4—Organizations depend on formal and informal sources and channels of information and a mix of internal and external information.

Informal sources are by definition easy to access and as such preferred by information users, as will be discussed in the propositions arising from studies of user behavior. But formal sources are also essential backup to any but the most ephemeral information, because of the distortions inevitable in the informal communication of information, interesting as such changes may be. Obviously, too, without good sources for both formal and informal information, important content in one or the other is likely to be missed. The boundaries between external and internal information are so easily crossed that distinction becomes impossible. Information may only be inside because someone brought it from outside. More likely still is that inside information is based in part on reports and perceptions of conditions outside. Not to have eyes and ears outside would be foolish, and often formal information services can help in systematic scanning of aspects of the outside environment.

Proposition 5—Innovative organizations are "learning systems" in which training is very important, and even more important is the creation of a nonpunitive culture for risk-taking and risk-takers in which members are continuously learning.

Coming at it from the angle of a student of the future of work in an age of electronics, Zuboff (1988) sees the effective organization as "a learning institution" (p. 395) and learning as an activity that is neither over before one enters the workplace nor preserved for a managerial group. "The behaviors that define learning and the behaviors that define being productive are one and the same. Learning is not something that requires time out from being engaged in productive activity; learning is the heart of productive activity. To put it simply, learning is the new form of labor" (p. 395). In this scenario the relevance is obvious of information services within the organization that can provide ready access to the formal and informal sources of learning that lie both outside and inside the organization.

Proposition 6—Organizations need memory.

Both the concept of continuous learning and that of the management of information as a resource point out the need for the organization to have a good memory. The content of a good corporate memory will include knowledge of the organization's history. Some of this is embedded in its files and archives. Some is in its oral history and traditions and not a little in its longer-serving staff. Excessive reverence for history can frustrate change and thwart would-be innovators. One of the authors has had the experience as a consultant where careful documentation in flow charts of the loops of duplication and the delays involved in a complex library acquisition and cataloging system created pride in the complexities rather than appreciation of the absurdities and the need for change. Perhaps the lesson is that the memory to be preserved is of why and what was done by whom and when, rather than excessive documentation of how it was done. As well as making sure that statutory requirements for the preservation of records are observed, for example for retention of documents and files that will become public archives, the information service can be charged with responsibility for preservation of sources for the history of the enterprise or agency that it serves.

Lest this proposition sound like some plea for antiquarian reverence for the past, the very present dangers of loss of organizational memory need to be emphasized. Kletz (1993) cites the 1987 fire on an escalator at King's Cross Underground Station in London as a good example of corporate failure to remember. As he comments: "Organizations have no memory; only people have memories and they move on . . . Problems of all sorts, not just accidents, will recur less often if we publicize, discuss and record the actions taken in the past, remind people of them from time to time, [and] do not make changes unless we know why the procedure or equipment was introduced" (p. 25).

6.2.4 Effects of Technological Change on Information Services

Technological change has been associated with some fairly consistent changes in organizations. Arguments about the extent to which technological change determines or is determined by organizational conditions are likely to remain pervasive and unresolved. Differences of opinion about the effect of technology on employment and productivity were discussed in Chapter 1 (section 1.5) and are not pursued here. There is no doubt, however, that information technology has not, of itself, brought about a new age of openness and information sharing. March (1988) has pointed out that "information is not innocent" (p. 387). We would add that neither is it necessarily guilty, but that the use to which it is put is for the most part political, that is, related to the distribution of power in organizations. There are, however, some features of the effects of technology generally and of information technology particularly that affect the way in which information services can be useful in organizations. These are expressed as propositions derived from study of technological change in Table 6.3.

Proposition 1—Instability caused by technological change calls for constant review of buy, make, and lease decisions in organizations.

Decreasing costs of computing and increasing facility for storing and accessing digital information remotely from the site on which it is to be used have been important elements in the formation of the new industry of information brokerage. Downsizing, especially in public enterprise, and the consequent increase of willingness of management to contract services out have been other crucial influences. The constant changes in cost to productivity ratios, brought about by technological changes, keep changing the cost-effectiveness of providing information services from within an organization, or hiring or buying them from outside. The frequency with which managers face these decisions may be judged from the recent appearance of a book devoted to the subject of outsourcing of information services (Woodsworth and Williams, 1993). In the United States, impetus was given to the contracting out of information services in 1983 when the federal Office of Management and Budget included library services among the functions that could be supplied by the private sector. This led many information specialists, including many who had formerly been employed in the libraries and information centers of federal agencies to form or join firms that offered to provide library services to those agencies. Many of these firms appear to have been undercapitalized and their proprietors overworked. These are characteristics typical of small businesses in the service

Table 6.3
Propositions Derived from the Study of the Effects of Technological Change

1. Instability caused by technological change calls for constant review of buy, make, and lease decisions in organizations.
2. Technological change emphasizes the importance of information content.
3. Interoperability of systems, disintermediation, globalization, and convergence are all simultaneously causes and effects of adoption of information technology and are all increasing the pressures on individuals and organizations for more effective information management.
4. Information technology induces organizational amnesia and academic ahistoricism.

sector, many of which do not succeed and which face competition not only from larger businesses, which can wait longer for a profit, but from other small businesses whose willingness to cut prices may be outside their ability to recover costs. In the information services sector, information brokers have also to face competition from large libraries in universities and research organizations that offer to provide fee-based services to external clients as a byproduct of their normal operations. The history of the information brokerage business has yet to be written, but commercial information brokerage has obviously sharpened debate on whether and which of the information services offered by libraries should be free and which for a fee, as well as demonstrated the possibility of a movement from just-in-case to just-in-time approaches to the provision of information resources and services.

Proposition 2—Technological change emphasizes the importance of information content.

In Chapter 3 the components of information were recognized as content, form, and context. Technological change makes very easy the transfer of information from one format or medium to another and also obliterates traces of such transfers. In this environment the quality of the original content and presentation becomes ever more important. Thus editorial responsibility is increased at the source since error not detected then will probably never be corrected in all the environments that it will enter electronically. As always, content and form remain inseparable in effect. Not only is attention needed to the authority of the text and to careful proofreading. The design of content for presentation has to be appropriate to the medium. Thus information design and redesign are important aspects of the work of information services.

Proposition 3—Interoperability of systems, disintermediation, globalization, and convergence are all simultaneously causes and effects of adoption of information technology and are all increasing the pressures on individuals and organizations for more effective information management.

Interoperability makes information systems transparent to the user. Links between systems and the channels between those links have been rendered invisible and irrelevant to the user. Not only are there no interventions from human operators on international telephone connections these days, there are seldom echoes or crackles. Because the clarity is at odds with the perception of the caller's remoteness, "Where are you?" has possibly replaced "What time is it there?" as the most frequent opening question in global conversations. Disintermediation, the reduction of steps between buyer and seller, user and producer, is an associated trend. The combined effect of interoperability and disintermediation in the information environment is to bring more information more directly, more accurately, and with less delay to users. Respite can no longer be sought in requests for clarification of garbled messages or in pleas of failure to receive messages at all over faulty communication lines. The need for satisfactory filters for individuals and for organizations has never been more pressing. The concept of information overload may be vague, but cognitive science recognizes its existence, and the consequences are readily detected in human systems, wherein, for example, messages are received but overlooked in subsequent decisions and actions. There is also the anxiety induced in individuals about the amount of information that crosses their desks to which they cannot attend. The consequences in the needs for information services to provide effective filters are obvious. Globalization of enterprise, systems, and services exacerbates not only the amount of information available and of potential relevance to organizations but also the number and complexity of sources and services from which access to such information may be bought or leased. Convergence, the effects of which have been explored at some depth in Chapter 3, ensures that not only will there be similar information content available from several sources, the content will be available in different formats (for example on-line database, CD-ROM, paper, microform) with different features designed to add value (for example, menus, indexes, digests, graphic interfaces, and so on). Separating the valuable from the valueless in this deluge of data becomes an ever more pressing necessity in all information-rich environments.

Proposition 4—Information technology induces organizational amnesia and academic ahistoricism.

The need for organizational memory has already been discussed as Proposition 6 in Table 6.2. Though it may seem paradoxical, in the midst of the facilities provided by information technology for the creation, manipulation, storage and retrieval of information, organizations may be more than ever subject to amnesia. Some of the complexities of electronic versions of text and their fate in organizations have been discussed in Chapter 3 (section 3.2.4). Earlier versions of documents may be deleted from the system so that the stages a policy went through in development and the decision points in its formulation may simply disappear. A change of computer system may have led to decisions that conversion of all existing files was unnecessary. Decisions on which files to abandon and why may be among those for which the rationale has also been obliterated in later transactions. The high potential of information technology to contribute to loss of memory of a nation's history may be detected also in the controversy about the tapes of presidential electronic mail and the rights and responsibilities of the Archivist of the United States in relation to them (*Doing Bush a favor: Did the*

U.S. Archivist trade his signature for a job?, 1993). The causes of ahistoricism are probably easier to understand. Among the main culprits are students writing term papers, whose notion of when the history of a topic begins coincides with the time coverage of the computerized information retrieval systems available to them, whether these are on-line public access catalogs in libraries or any other databases available to them, through commercially operated on-line services or CD-ROM products. Some of the reasons why such ahistoricism is unlikely to be confined to student members of the population emerge in the findings of research on information-user behavior discussed in the following section.

6.2.5 Information-User Behavior

Study of the behavior of information users has been carried out from a number of disciplinary bases for more than fifty years. Combination of insights from user studies in information science and in psychology and sociology suggests the propositions about user behavior that are set out in Table 6.4.

Proposition 1—Accessibility is the most important determinant of choice of an information source.

Accessibility has repeatedly been demonstrated in empirical studies to be the most important determinant of choice of an information source—more important than any other property, including the perceived quality of information carried. There are of course many aspects of accessibility. There are practical, measurable aspects, such as physical proximity, travel time, and response time. There are also psychological aspects, such as the perceived intellectual level required to access the source, and the consonance of the ambience and style of client management of the source with personal or corporate style. In fact, accessibility may be judged to have something to do with shared ideology at the corporate as well as personal level.

Table 6.4
Propositions Derived from the Study of Information-User Behavior

1. Accessibility is the most important determinant of choice of an information source.
2. Variety is needed in the responses of information services.
3. There is natural widespread ignorance about information sources and information services.
4. There is need for alleviation of anxiety about information "out there."
5. People prefer to feel in control.

Proposition 2—Variety is needed in the responses of information services.

Studies of information need have documented the variety of approaches that people take in seeking information. Expression of this variety of approaches has to be drastically attenuated to fit the relatively few standardized and stylized entrances usually offered by formal information services. In building a model for the design of subject access in on-line catalogs based on user needs and behavior, Bates (1986) applied Ashby's Law of Requisite Variety. Ashby's Law states that if a system is to function successfully, it must generate as much variety in its responses to the environment as the environment generates as inputs to the system. In applying this law to information retrieval systems, Bates proposes a model that would transform access to information by helping the user enter the system, get oriented, and generate the necessary variety.

Proposition 3—There is natural widespread ignorance about information sources and information services.

Another persistent and consistent finding of user studies has been that information services are generally underused in two ways: they are used by only a fraction of the population for whom they are potentially useful, and those who use them use only a fraction of the services available from them. When confronted with these facts the traditional response of publicly supported libraries and those in educational institutions generally has been to embark on the "library and bibliographical instruction" of users. This movement has been swept up in the broader stream of information literacy, which is discussed in more detail on pages 294–295.

Proposition 4—There is need for alleviation of anxiety about information "out there."

Empirical studies have verified the existence of widespread anxiety about keeping up with new information. The fact that this anxiety is most frequently reported among scientists, engineers, and managers of high technology enterprise is probably an artifact of the populations chosen for study rather than a total reflection of reality. Reduction of this anxiety is a worthy goal for any information service. One approach would be to lower the nonmonetary aspects of the price of access to new information including the reduction of noise in the form of unwanted information (see Chapter 3, p. 125). This is the approach which has been employed for many years in selective dissemination of information (SDI) systems provided by special libraries and by database vendors in a number of disciplines. A whole series of other filters of increasing sensitivity to individual need may be applied. These can range from an SDI profile for a department or work group in an organization to a digest of new material chosen with the preoccupations of a particular executive in mind and interpreted in the context of the organization's mission, plans, and projects.

Proposition 5—People prefer to feel in control.

People's preference for control is obvious in phenomena ranging from the reluctance of managers to use keyboards to communicate with computer systems to the reluctance of students and other library users to ask for assistance when they cannot find the information they want. Provision of control of computer systems by remote control devices seems a sensible alternative in the first case; in the second case, librarians and information brokers continue to work hard in personal interactions, educational programs, and in calls for better interfaces to machine systems that anticipate user problems in use.

Some of the studies of transaction logs from on-line library catalogs have indicated a propensity to give up without result and without seeking help from library staff. The obstacles to feeling in control are formidable when access to virtually every information system requires the use of a different set of commands. Despite interoperability and disintermediation, San Francisco public librarian, Dowlin (quoted in Woodsworth and Williams, 1993), would be "very surprised to see a significant percentage of the information available on databases become used directly by the consumer in the near future" (p. 108). So would we. There remain many challenges in giving information access power to the people.

6.3 Principles for the Design of Information Services

A set of principles for the design and management of information services has been formulated from the propositions set out in Tables 6.1, 6.2, 6.3, and 6.4, which were in turn distilled from the analysis of innovation and information addressed in Chapters 1 through 5. These principles are stated in general terms in Table 6.5, and some examples of their application in information services in different environments are then presented.

6.3.1 Flexibility and Multifaceting

Design principle 1—Information services need to be flexible and multifaceted.

Information technology has increased in important ways the flexibility possible in information services. Part of the basis of this new flexibility is the

Table 6.5
Principles for the Design and Management of Information Services

1. Information services need to be flexible and multifaceted.
2. No information service has a monopoly; all need to develop both competitive and collaborative strategies.
3. Intermediary roles need to be translated at the microlevel into transparent systems that empower users, and at the macrolevel to be expanded to perform training and education functions.
4. The information service needs to accept responsibility for performance of some monitoring functions and to assist gatekeepers and their relatives in the performance of others.
5. The information service must be client-centered rather than collection-centered or system-centered, continually aware of user needs, and have a marketing orientation.
6. The information service itself needs to be constantly innovating.

ability to integrate digital data from different sources so that the distinction virtually disappears between internal and external data, as does that between internal and external use and users. Obviously, the existence of more and more digital data transferred through ever-expanding networks has brought new threats to personal privacy and corporate confidentiality. In this connection, however, there are some research findings worth noticing. Comparative studies of more and less productive firms have indicated that the former are more open to external information, more likely to make greater investment in information systems and information services staff, and more prone to give encouragement to end-user use of those systems. As well as being more open to outside information, the more productive show somewhat less concern with protecting proprietary information (Koenig, 1992).

The possibilities of digital technology for enhancing the variety of approaches to or facets of an information service have yet to be fully realized. This is certainly so in the on-line database environment generally. With particular reference to the subject approach to on-line library catalogs, Bates (1989b) argues strongly for the more effective integration of the search capabilities of the computer systems with the existing indexing in bibliographical databases. As she points out, "The opportunity is available to improve the power and ease of catalog use for searchers, but to do that, more effective use of the capabilities provided by the online technology must be made" (p. 404). Bates also points out that "with more powerful searching possibilities, the searcher needs more powerful assistance" (p. 405) and that "document description must be distinguished from access" (p. 409). Her synthesis of existing research indicates that "the average likelihood that any two people will use the same term for a concept or a book, or that a searcher and an information system will use the same term for a concept, is in the range of 10 to 20 percent. The total number of terms generated by a group of people for a given topic is almost always very large" (p. 409).

In another article Bates (1989a) suggests a "berrypicking model" in which searching behavior is analogous to the choosing of the most desirable berries from different bushes. This model recognizes that typical search queries are not static but rather evolve, that searchers commonly gather information in bits and pieces instead of in one grand best retrieved set, and that searchers use a wide variety of search techniques and a wide variety of sources. Naturally both techniques and sources go well beyond bibliographic databases. This model seems to accommodate much better the techniques that people use in seeking information and not only those that information specialists have devised for "hiding" it in bibliographies, indexes, and catalogs. Our habit of using the old media as the content of the new dates at least from the invention of printing from movable type. McLuhan (1964) pointed out that "the first two centuries of printing from movable types were motivated much more by the desire to see ancient and medieval books than by the need to read and write new ones" (p. 171). Again, it is not only considerations of expense that influence suboptimization of the information service possibilities of digital media. The model of the printed page, and the needs that it imposes for brevity, neatness, and consistency in printed text and indexes inhibit exploitation of the digital world's hospitality to "mess" or rather to constant reconfiguration of data on demand to suit the "messiness" of the human mind. For "messiness" one may prefer to substitute that rich complexity of association and allusion and the multitudinous connections, which may appear random to all but the individual in whose mind they make meaning.

Many initiatives have been taken in information retrieval systems to increase flexibility of access. For several years now Dialog and other commercial database suppliers have provided access to many of their databases in both command and menu modes. This is a beginning of the provision recommended by Bates (1989b) of "two or more options to accommodate both the active explorers and the passive, "do-it-for-me" searcher" (p. 410).

Flexibility and multifaceting are also features that apply well outside the information retrieval environment as such. They apply, for example, to the variety of media available from an information service, including the variety of media in which the same information content is available. These features apply, too, in any evaluation of the number of sources from which the same information is or ought to be available in the same media. Necessary redundancy may also be argued in indexing and abstracting services, especially when the information may be used in environments so diverse that the same symbols may be said to carry different meanings in the different contexts of their use. Consider the range of meaning that the contents of a digest of new pharmacological formulations might have for pharmacologists, pharmacists, medical researchers, clinicians, medical insurance corporations, business analysts, patients, and for regulatory and policy arms of the United States federal government.

Another consideration is the need for healthy competition among information services—a topic to which attention is given in discussion of Principle 2 below.

Information services that are responsive to user demand seem inevitably to be led to greater flexibility and multifaceting. One example is Orion Express, the document delivery service offered to faculty and students by the libraries of the University of California, Los Angeles. Originally set up to cover only the serial literature, in 1993 within two years of its inauguration it had been expanded to cover the book collections as well.

One example of recognition of the need for multifaceting of an information service may be read from the statement of roles and responsibilities of the school library media specialist in the guidelines prepared jointly by the American Association of School Librarians and the Association for Educational Communications and Technology (1988). The roles of information specialist, teacher, and instructional consultant have all to be subsumed within the school library media specialist's responsibilities.

The need for flexibility and multifaceting extends to the provision of information services that go well beyond digital access and literature-based sources. The model of agricultural extension agents in working with farmers is well known and their part in diffusion of innovation in agriculture has been well documented. Several states in the United States support consulting and training firms to help bring new technology to small industry. One such is the Industrial Modernization Center in Pennsylvania. Holusha (1993) reports a typical day's work of two of the center's technical extension agents. There are also seven technology assistance centers subsidized by the National Institutes of Standards and Technology, not to mention the R & D companies attached to universities and research institutes, through which consultants can be hired and through which discoveries and inventions are promoted.

Flexibility and multifaceting are in fact properties which stream strongly through all other five design principles.

6.3.2 Competition and Collaboration

Design principle 2—No information service has a monopoly; all need to develop both competitive and collaborative strategies.

Some competition between players in the information services field is inevitable. One major source of conflict revolves around public and private sector roles in the provision of information services. As the Public Sector/Private Sector Task Force of the National Commission on Libraries and Information Science reported in 1981:

> There are basic differences in view concerning the proper role of the Federal government (or of government in general) with respect to providing information resources, products, and services. They result in conflicts between restricting and not restricting the role of government (National Commission on Libraries and Information Science, 1982, p. viii).

Another well-established field of competition is between publishers, especially publishers of scientific journals, and institutional and corporate subscribers to those journals. These arguments, which appear to be increasing in frequency, vehemence, and litigation, concern questions of copyright and when, where, and how much copying constitutes a fair use of the materials. Information technology has not caused this competition, but in some cases has exacerbated it, because it has made so much easier the making and taking of information products. In these battles on rights to use of intellectual property, information services are likely to be very much in the cross-fire. For example, the judgment handed down in 1992 in the United States District Court in American Geophysical Union v. Texaco, Inc., in which that company has been found in breach of United States copyright law, casts serious doubts on whether the library of a commercial enterprise may distribute photocopies of copyright material, whether made from items in its own collection or obtained from document delivery services, without specific permission to do so (American Geophysical Union v. Texaco, Inc., 802 F. Supp. 1 S.D.N.Y. 1992). The Copyright Clearance Center operates centralized photocopy authorization and payment systems for more than 8,500 United States and foreign publishers, but there are many publishers and publications that are not covered.

This conflict over copying is natural and deep-seated because the copyright owners (very seldom the authors) are anxious for return on capital and the researchers, consultants, and other users, as well as the librarians and other information specialists who act as their agents, are anxious to diffuse as much information with as little delay for as few dollars as possible. Suggestions have been made that universities and other major research establishments that pay authors to do the research on which the articles are based ought to publish their own journals and bypass the publishers. In particular, the suggestion is made that for diffusion of results of research supported by public funds, the facilities of the Internet should be used to distribute electronic journals.

In the Texaco judgment, Laval J. wrote that "The profit motive is the engine that ensures the progress of science" (Tropp, 1993). Adoption of this belief suggests that universities and research institutions will seek the "reassertion of intellectual property rights and expectation that faculty will generate consumable information," mentioned by Woodsworth and Williams (1993, p. 143). This suggests escalation of the war with publishers as well as an increase in innovation in the modes of scientific and scholarly communication. But whichever view prevails, competitive or collaborative, information services have to develop, within their broader buy v. lease, just-in-case v. just-in-time philosophies, copying policies that are within whatever copyright laws apply in the countries in which they operate.

As mentioned on pages 281–282, information brokers have at times complained of unfair competition from libraries in provision of information services of both the document delivery and consultancy types. No doubt there is in the following complaint from an information broker both justification and a pointer to the need, discussed as Principle 5 below, for marketing orientation in all information services: "Information brokerage/businesses market their services to specific targets such as corporate clients. Libraries on the other hand, continue to 'market' new services the same way they promote the old services—to everyone in sight" (Lois Warren in Woodsworth and Williams, 1993, pp. 43–44). Yet information brokers frequently find helpful in their business free access to large public collections of information in libraries.

There is in fact a long strong history of cooperation not only among libraries but between libraries and publishers and the book trade generally and indeed among governments of many different countries. The inclusion of library catalog entries on the verso of the title page of many United States and international imprints is the outcome of cataloging-in-publication (CIP) arrangements, which have been in place for several decades. CIP and the highly successful international standard numbering systems for books and serials (ISBN and ISSN respectively) are just two of the examples that allow Harold Billings (in Woodsworth and Williams, 1993) to say that "technology and cooperation have brought about a remarkable level of bibliographic control on virtually a world wide basis" (p. 105).

Within academic environments there is increasing realization of the need for collaboration between the library and the university computing center. One notable example is the University of Southern California. The director of the university library system (Lyman, 1992) has reported:

> The library's technology is increasingly dependent upon networks, hardware and operating systems supported by University Computing Services (UCS), and cooperative work on applications with UCS and the Center for Scholarly Technology. Ultimately it is in the University's interest for the Library and USC to share the same technical infrastructure, in order to save technology and personnel costs (p. 6).

Specific examples of cooperatively provided products at the University of Southern California are USCInfo, the campus information service. Included in this service are Homer (the on-line catalog), online periodical indexes, campus-wide information files, such as faculty and staff directories, and full-text news resources. In addition, the Center for Scholarly Technology, jointly sponsored by the library and UCS, is involved in a variety of projects, including the development and evaluation of prototype programs and facilities for a new technology-based library.

Other institutions have taken a similar approach towards cooperative endeavors. Some others, among them large universities like Stanford and small ones like the University of Canberra in Australia, have combined the library and computing center as one organizational unit.

A notable attempt to promote collaboration at national level between computer scientists and information service providers is the Coalition for Networked Information (CNI). Established in 1990 by CAUSE (formerly, College and University Systems Exchange), EDUCOM (a not-for-profit consortium of colleges, universities, and corporate associates to facilitate introduction, use, and management of information technologies), and ARL (Association for Research Libraries), CNI has a mission to promote the creation of and access to information resources in networked environments to enrich scholarship and to enhance intellectual productivity. This seems to be if not the first at least the most ambitious attempt to date to bring together those whose primary interests have been in computer science and engineering with those whose prime interest is in the content of the information and the needs of its potential users.

At the microlevel, any information service that is any good will threaten other interests in the organization. Whether a competitive or a collaborative stance is to be preferred depends on organizational factors relating to structures, roles, and politics. Attention to marketing the information service within the organization, in accordance with Principle 5, will often allow early warning of potential conflict and strengthen the possibility of converting it into collaboration.

6.3.3 Intermediary Roles

> *Design principle 3—Intermediary roles need to be translated at the microlevel into transparent systems that empower users, and at the macrolevel to be expanded to perform training and education functions.*

As Churchman (1971) pointed out in *The Design of Inquiring Systems,* science does not reside between the covers of scientific journals any more than knowledge resides on book shelves. Neither do information services consist only of collections of information-bearing materials. Hoekema points out (in Woodsworth and Williams, 1993), that

> the library is not really a collection of information. Rather it is a collection of research materials and of tools of access and interpretation of those materials. The question of what level of service libraries should offer is a question of how much of its effort and its budget should be expended on tools—including staff time—that facilitate the use of its collection: that attempt, as it were, to meet users halfway and lead them to resources that will be useful for their research goals (p. 181).

The same applies to any information service. The more numerous and sophisticated the tools of access and interpretation the better the service from the client's point of view. Tools may be of many kinds. They may represent temporary, permanent, or *ad hoc* value adding. They also differ in their usability. And again in the digital environment they have proliferated in number and in applications.

Just two examples are presented to represent the range of software available for tool-making and the tools that can be shaped from it. The two examples are hypertext and personal bibliographic systems.

Hypertext, which has already been discussed on in Chapter 5 (pp. 216–217) is a tool that can take advantage of the lack of necessity for linearity in the logic and for hierarchy in the array of concepts in digital systems. Thus, there is room for the eclectic and idiosyncratic needs of individuals. As Bates (1989) has remarked, "Hypertext approaches appear tailor-made for berrypicking searching," (p. 421) which is the more realistic model for on-line searching, which she proposed and which has been discussed on page 288. Hypertext can be used to tailor the tools which students, for example, might wish to add to interfaces to enhance access to existing information resources. There are, for example, the hypertext interfaces created by Steve Mamber and his students at University of California, Los Angeles, for indexing moving pictures on videodisc (Maguire *et al.*, 1991). Hypertext lends itself to the continuing enhancement of the interface between system and user. Another good example of this is the Science Library Catalog project. In this part of Project SEED (Science for Early Educational Development) the University of California, Los Angeles, is collaborating with the California Institute of Technology. The Science Library Catalog has been implemented in the libraries of two elementary schools in Los Angeles and in the Children's Literature Department of the Los Angeles Public Library's Central Library. Children have achieved remarkable success rates in using the highly graphical Hypercard interface, and the project continues to provide excellent opportunities for the study of children's information-seeking behavior (Borgman *et al.*, 1991; Rosenberg and Borgman, 1992).

In personal bibliographic systems, with software such as ProCite, the obstacles to keeping and exploiting bibliographic records in standardized formats can be removed so that users can store and present bibliographic references with more confidence and enjoy enhanced access to new references. There is no question that the tools available for information management have improved and will continue to do so. But the use of tools has to be learned. Education is at the heart of the intermediary roles that information service managers have to adopt, whether at the level of accustoming users to particular tools, such as hypertext interfaces to moving pictures, or teaching them how to use software, for example Hypercard or ProCite, to create their own access tools.

Such empowerment of users may take place at an individual level, and such expenditure of staff time will always have to be available in specialist environments, corporate, and government, wherein interpretation is a normal expectation of the value that an information service will add. Where information needs are less individual and resources have to be spread over many users, information services personnel will need to make tools appropriate to groups of users. At the macrolevel, however, the role of information services will be shaped more by society's rapidly evolving idea of the importance of creation of information literacy.

A National Forum on Information Literacy has been formed in the United States. It is described as an "umbrella group of national organizations committed to turning people into effective information consumers" (Breivik and Ford, 1993, p. 98). The forum's more than 60 members, most of whom are educational associations, include as well the American Library Association, the American Newspaper Publishers Association, the National Forum for Black Public Administrators, and the United States Small Business Administration.

Information literacy is a noble, even a utopian concept. The American Library Association (1989), for example, sets out the following competencies that are to be expected among the information literate. "Ultimately, information-literate people are those who have learned how to learn. They know how to learn because they know how knowledge is organized, how to find information, and how to use information in such a way that others can learn from them. They are people prepared for lifelong learning, because they can always find the information needed for any task or decision at hand" (p. 1).

If such outcomes are to be achieved by more than a fraction of the population, more attention needs to be given not only to the individual competencies of information specialists but to the elements of instructional design. That such attention is not adequate at the moment is suggested by a review of library and information management software by Kazlauskas *et al.*

(1990). These authors identify well-established learning strategies and show that they are frequently ignored in the creation of such software. Assurance of instructional design quality in information management tools may need to be added to the responsibilities of managers of information services.

6.3.4 Monitoring

Design principle 4—The information service needs to accept some responsibility for environmental monitoring functions and to assist gatekeepers and their relatives in the performance of others.

The selective dissemination of information techniques used by information services in monitoring new information and directing it to clients according to a stored profile of their interests have already been discussed (pp. 285–286). While the matching of interest profiles to those describing characteristics of new entries to a database is well established as a machine technique, compilation and adjustment of the profiles to this point demands human skills. To date, without human aid, the filtering capabilities of automated information systems remain rudimentary.

Incremental improvements are constantly being made, and no doubt advances in software and telecommunications will add up to significant improvements in automatic monitoring systems available to information services. One stream of such improvements is beginning to flow from the work being done in implementation of the NISO standard Z39.50. An implementers group is seeking to create intelligent information servers, that is, network file servers capable of providing other computers not merely with data but with information or, as Lynch (1993) puts it, "collections of data with mutually understood semantics".

At least until computers are rendered capable of regular and complex exchanges of meaning, the powers of the human intermediary in matching information to its potential users remain pre-eminent. Knowledge of the organization which the information service serves is not at all readily encoded into a machine system, let alone understood by one. Neither the politics (as Davenport *et al.*, 1992, make clear) nor the personal networks (on which Grosser, 1991, expounds) are amenable to automated processing.

The roles of gatekeepers and scouts, guards, ambassadors, and champions who are the gatekeepers' near relatives therefore remain important elements in the provision of effective information services for innovation. Knowledge of the organization served is again important in identification of people who play those roles naturally. Filtering of information to them and through them is one way in which the information service can remain alert to what is "news" for the organization and also channel items of that "news" most effectively (see pp. 277–278). Getting close to the people who have the "news" is an important step in getting to be one of them.

Identification of and the building of relationships with members of the gatekeeping family, who may reside inside and outside the organization served, contribute to the invisible assets of the information service, the importance of which to innovation has already been discussed (see p. 268).

6.3.5 Focus on Clients and Marketing

Design principle 5—The information service must be client-centered rather than collection-centered or system-centered, continually aware of user needs, and have a marketing orientation.

The necessity for any service to focus on the needs of clients is at once self-evident and very easily obscured in the structures—physical, organizational, and procedural—that are put in place in order to offer the service. When information could only be stored in symbols readable to the human eye and on media of minimal flexibility, the emphasis on collections and on the regulation of access to them was understandable. Happily, with digital codes and communications, a client-centered approach becomes far more feasible. This is not to suggest that the great collections of libraries and archival institutions are not important to the cultures they serve or that they have not in many cases served their clients well. The limitation of such collections has always been that they can offer access to so small a proportion of the information that they contain and to so small a percentage of the people who could make use of their contents.

The will to reorient information services toward focus on the client has been evident in the user studies that have been popular in library and information science for the past fifty years. Adoption of market research techniques has also assisted in planning the direction of computer-based commercial services and in the reorientation of some traditional library services. Focus groups have become commonplace in many public library systems. Baker (1991) reports on the focus-group interviews used by the Iowa City Public Library to determine how its business services could be improved. The Denver Public Library was confident enough of the technique to use focus groups of children aged 6–7 and 9–10 years and their parents to gather design requirements for the new children's library that will form part of its extensive new building (Sandilan and Walters, 1991). In a more abstract study, Moneta (1989) interviewed engineers, information professionals, and public library users in focus groups to determine the effectiveness of on-line search assistance software.

Many information services have applied the methods of strategic planning in which identification of their mission is often the single most powerful influence on the change in orientation from collections and rules of access to one focused on clients. An example is the mission statement adopted by the State Library of New South Wales in Australia. It reads: "We are creating for the community a thriving, dynamic organization, leading the New South Wales library system so that it becomes one of the world's best in collecting, conserving and communicating information" (Library Council of New South Wales, 1988, p. 1). The participative creation, endorsement, and constant reinforcement of the mission statement, for example, by having it inscribed on the reverse of the photo identification cards that staff wear at all times on duty, have proved powerful strategies for the remarkable changes wrought in that library (Stace and Dunphy, 1991). At the same time, it is also sobering to recall, from survey results reported in Chapter 4 (pp. 169–170), how often managers of information services appear unaware of the characteristics of their client population and of the use they make of the information service. Paying attention to clients and their information needs, including involving them in planning decisions, may be observed as a feature of the business strategy of the Online Computer Library Center (OCLC), which is probably the most successful and almost certainly the most innovative of initiatives in library management in the United States in this century.

6.3.6 Constant Innovation

> *Design principle 6—The information service itself needs to be constantly innovating.*

That innovation should be a goal of the information service is an obvious corollary of the arguments for innovation as a goal adduced in the first section of this chapter. All the reasons that the organization has for innovating are shared by the information service that is part of it or seeking to serve it on a contract basis of any kind. There is little in the literature about how information services become or keep on being innovative. A recent investigator has reported that with a few notable exceptions writing about innovation in libraries has been "a combination of the reporting of personal experience with exhortation" (Clayton, 1993, p. 87). One exception is a case study by Stace and Dunphy (1991) on the State Library of New South Wales in Australia, where substantial change was brought about in five years by a new management team whose strategies for change included the use of information technology as a catalyst, creation of opportunities for staff development, and encouragement and reward of risk-taking, particularly in entrepreneurial ventures.

6.4 Strategies for the Promotion of Innovation

Innovative organizations have been observed to make available "risk capital" in the form of funds or at least some slack by way of discretionary time for the would-be innovators, to give formal awards and public recognition to innovators, and to create what Kanter (1988) calls "a culture of pride," wherein there is "a self-reinforcing upward cycle—*performance stimulating pride stimulating performance* [italics in original]" which is "especially important for innovation" (pp. 181–182). Information services need both to create and to enjoy similar conditions if they are to be innovative and to promote innovation in the organizations they serve.

Von Hippel has assured us that "any functional class is a potential source of innovation under appropriate conditions" (Von Hippel, 1988, p. 4 and pp. 46–47, Chapter 2, this volume). The central questions are (1) what functional classes are the likely sources of innovation for information services? and (2) how can an information service function as a source of innovation?

6.4.1 Promotion of Innovation in Information Services

There are six functional classes that information services may expect to serve as sources of innovation. They are clients or customers; competitors; suppliers; new employees; information service staff; and the management of the organization. In addition to these, special mention needs to be made of information technology that may be used as a powerful weapon for change.

Clients and customers. Like the users of scientific instruments discussed by Von Hippel (1988), clients of information services may well have invented what ought to be their next product or service. One example was where the students wanted on-line reservations with all university libraries in Sydney as soon as they were given on-line reservation facilities to their own library collection at the University of New South Wales. A strategy that promotes innovation will therefore make sure that an information service stays closely in touch with clients and their work methods.

How? This can be achieved by use of a variety of communication methods, formal and informal, but primarily by members of the information service staff "being there," not only on committees concerned with the work and the social life of the organization, but on visits to the workplaces, and by providing easily grasped "handles" for entry to the information service. For example, names and corresponding responsibilities of information service staff should be promoted. As this advice strongly implies, the allocation of responsibility to particular people to act as contact points and primary service givers for different groups of projects within the organization is strongly recommended. Information service managers may also find helpful the identification and interrogation of lead users, which Von Hippel (1988) advises.

The principles of market research can be applied to great advantage in building an innovative information service and the application need not be daunting and require an army of consultants. Focus groups of lead users may be one strategy. Very good practical advice for any information service may also be gained from Van House *et al.* (1987, 1990). These are manuals for the application of output measures to public libraries and academic libraries, respectively. As in all market analysis, market segmentation is a useful technique. In the information service, identification of individual clients and client groups according to the amount of use of the information service and the type of services and materials most used may be much more useful in identifying gatekeepers and other potential allies than segmentation by geographical location, rank, professional specialty, and so on.

Competitors. As in all enterprise, not to identify competitors is a weakness that could leave the information service vulnerable to loss of support, even withdrawal of its warrant within an organization, or failure to renew contracts or fill its order book if it operates independently. Competition for an information service may come from alternative information services, which may be able to compete on components of price such as accessibility and use time, or from a client's ability to do without the information that the service could supply. Competitors are often best identified through the eyes of customers. This makes the self-report surveys of the type described lucidly in Van House *et al.* (1987, 1990) especially valuable. Study and sampling of the competition's "prices" can be done almost as readily in information services as in supermarkets, though publicity of the differentials is not widespread, even in advertisements from database vendors. The competitors' strengths can be copied or those parts of the field can be abandoned (maybe outsourced) to them. The competitors' weaknesses can be even more instructive, not only for indications of opportunities for ourselves but also because they may well mirror our own weaknesses, which are likely to be far less obvious to us. Another opportunity that may come from study of a competitor is the possibility for collaboration. After all, if IBM and Apple can decide that cooperation is good business, other organizations can hardly rule out collaboration as a strategy for innovation.

Suppliers. Suppliers are often sources of information about innovations in progress or in prospect among other customers, some of whom may be competitors, and the experience of all may contain interesting news. The information service will also be monitoring the innovativeness of the supplier, expecting a steady stream of incremental improvements in existing products and services. The supplier who is constantly innovating without getting previous products to work is likely to be severely dealt with by the market in the natural way of things, but the information service might want to pick up early warning of such traits in its suppliers both from its own operations and from sharing of experiences with professional colleagues.

New employees. The information service can gain useful ideas and insights for innovation from new blood in the information service and in the organization it serves. New employees have long been seen as possible sources of innovation. Much more colorfully, Schon (1971) has referred to them as "cultural travellers" who may carry "the spores of innovation on their boots" (p. 57). It is no accident that suppliers of computer-based information services often hire staff from libraries and other institutional information services. As new employees they bring valuable knowledge of the attitudes, cultures, and individuals in those institutions and therefore know how to communicate as suppliers with the colleagues they have left behind. People from different cultures, whether professional, sectoral, or ethnic, bring the possibility of new views on old problems, which may often result in innovative solutions or at least ameliorations.

Information service staff. A suggestion box full of spider webs if not spiders is not enough to gather input from information service staff. Various organizational strategies can be used, through quality circles, and more or less elaborate packages meant to bring about organization and personnel development, such as total quality management. Open E-mail discussion across ranks and different locations has proved useful in many organizations, according to Sproull and Kiesler (1991). Opportunities for contribution imply and also encourage the provision of good information about the information service to all its members. A climate of risk aversion is inevitable when bureaucratic norms prevail along with negative attitudes about the upward communication of ideas and suggestions for change. Von Hippel (1988) has pointed out that the reward system for the sales force is typically based only on sales of existing products. They are usually neither trained not encouraged to obtain information from users on new product needs, ideas, and prototype solutions. The same remarks could be applied to staff performing client service functions in most information services.

Management. The weak link for many information services is that with management. There are not necessarily any formal linkages between the information service, information service users, and management. As Broadbent (1992) points out: "Funding decisions can be made by a management process which does not take into account the views of users of a service," and "there might be no communication loop by which users provide direct input to management decisions" (p. 3). Since management is the source of resources, astute information service managers collect and condense evidence of use and testimony of users and make sure that the information service is connected to management through strong reporting lines. Top managers are also the arbiters of what is "news" within the organization; therefore the information service needs to be in management's networks, and there must be a reporting structure that is capable of getting "news" items from the information service through to management.

Information technology as catalyst. Suppliers, including purveyors of hardware, software, and automated systems generally, have been previously recognized as potentially a functional class for innovation. Information technology, however, can be used within organizations as a powerful weapon for change or for preservation of the status quo, if no organizational changes are made, in anticipation of or in reaction to its effects. There are numerous examples where information technology has been used effectively in bringing about profound change in information service. Among the first that come to mind are the revolution in access to bibliographic records brought about by the creation of standardized MARC formats by the Library of Congress; the extraordinary international bibliographic utility created by OCLC; the United States National Library of Medicine's Medline system and its effect on worldwide access to the medical literature; and the Institute for Scientific Information's range of alerting and citation services. These are just a few of the large examples of beneficial innovation; there are thousands of others, the effects of which differ markedly in scope and weight of impact. The similarity is that in all of them competent management has used information technology to transform the services available to clients.

At the level of the individual information service, the task of successfully implementing technological change implies the need for a technology strategy and a strategic change strategy. Benefits accrue from the making of both, especially when the tasks are cooperatively accomplished, for example, in the information technology groups and task forces that are a powerful inducement to learning. In well-managed information services this learning becomes the basis for more learning, in the implementation of the system and subsequent monitoring of its performance, and the learning organization moves from rhetoric to reality.

6.4.2 Promotion of Innovation by Information Services

In promoting innovation in the organizations they serve, information services could adopt two main goals: (1) enriching the external news sources available to the organization and (2) reducing the costs to clients of information by filtering out as much useless information as possible. Achievement of these goals would contribute to getting members of the organization to pay attention to new ideas, needs, and opportunities, which Kanter (1988), as quoted at the beginning of this chapter, has identified as "the first key problem in the management of innovation" (p. 173).

Many of the strategies to be adopted are implicit in those suggested for use in the information service. But an information service that aspires to be a functional source of innovation for an organization could be expected also to command *knowledge of the innovation process,* to promote *awareness of innovation achievements* in the organization, and, especially, by pursuing improvements in information systems to facilitate the *identification and evaluation of innovation opportunities.*

Knowledge of the innovation process. Von Hippel (1988) has argued that attempts to direct or enhance innovation must be based on an accurate understanding of the sources of innovation. There is now a considerable body of literature from which such knowledge may be obtained. Identification and analysis of the sources of innovation for any particular organization also require (1) access to the documentation and stories of its past; (2) familiarity with the techniques of social studies research that facilitate the study of the present; and (3) good sources of news, that is, of early intimations of what the future is likely to be for the organization.

Again as Von Hippel (1988) has pointed out, an innovator has only two routes towards capturing rents from an innovation. One is exploiting the innovation while preventing others from doing so. The other is licensing others to use the innovation-related knowledge for a fee. The ability to license others and obtain rent from them at a low risk and cost depends on the property rights in the innovation-related knowledge that can be used to protect a licensee against those who want to use it without paying. An information service should be capable of supplying, especially in smaller organizations that do not command their own resources of patent attorneys, up-to-date and reliable information on the legislative framework for the protection of industrial property and on the experience of the organization and of comparable organizations in licensing. The latter may be gathered through know-how trading among information service managers in different organizations. Von Hippel (1988) has characterized know-how trading between rivals as a general and significant mechanism that innovators can use to share (or avoid sharing) innovation-related costs and profits with rivals.

Awareness of innovation achievements. While know-how trading may also bring in awareness of innovations achieved and planned by competitors, the data collection required to document these within the organization may well serve as an important fillip to the creation of awareness of innovation opportunities in the organization. At the very least, innovation experiences may serve as additions to the store of knowledge for public relations and increase the appeal of the house organs and press releases that may have stories based on them. The difficulty in collecting them may also serve as a reminder of the difficulties that the firm faces if, for example, as is traditional, the R & D operation is charged with creation of new and improved products and processes and the marketing and sales departments are focused on keeping products just as customers expect them to be.

Identification and evaluation of innovation opportunities. This can be facilitated by an information service that brings in relevant information from external sources, for example on the opportunities that may be offered to enhance or shift the functional sources of innovation. While the opportunities available from suppliers to the organization and from users of its products and services may be much more readily observed by staff in operational departments, the information service may well take particular interest in collecting and disseminating information about government schemes. Taxation incentives, special conditions attaching to government purchases, and government-sponsored research may make some difference to the organization's evaluation of the economic rents likely to be available to it through any particular innovation. In the not-for-profit sector, the information service may usefully keep track of both government initiatives and the availability of research and other grants from foundations as well as public sources.

The principal contribution of an information service is to the quality of information flow in an organization. Contributions can be made at particular stages of innovative action as the analysis of the Roberts and Frohman (1978) model made earlier in this chapter suggests. The information service can also seek to identify and support the gatekeepers and project champions who have key roles to play in innovation. Information services prepared to participate in the less frequently acknowledged key role of marketing of new ideas, products, and services inside as well as outside the organization may find more scope and more relevance to the vital concerns of their clients.

6.5 Conclusion

In penury or prosperity there is no excuse for not innovating and studying innovation. Information service providers have unique opportunities for studying the behavior of information users. In adopting the reflective practice urged by Schon (1983), information service managers can consider the part played by clients in and their reactions to innovations in information products and services. There is also a lot more to be learned from active pursuit of research into all aspects of information processing behavior. Acknowledgment of the need and acceptance of the challenge to provide better access to information on a global scale involves not only diffusion of technology but a quantum improvement in political and managerial prowess. These, like all other endeavors that add to the store of useful human knowledge and skill, will be enhanced by the accessibility of innovative information services supporting innovative organizations.

References

American Association of School Librarians and the Association for Educational Communications and Technology. (1988). *Information power: guidelines for school library media programs.* Chicago, American Library Association: Washington D.C., Association for Educational Communications and Technology.

American Library Association (1989). *Final report of the Presidential Committee on Information Literacy.* Chicago.

Baker, Sharon L. (1991). Improving business service through the use of focus groups. *RQ 30*(3), 377–385.

Bates, Marcia J. (1986). Subject access in online catalogs: a design model. *Journal of the American Society for Information Science 37*(6), 357–376.

Bates, Marcia J. (1989a). The design of browsing and berrypicking techniques for the online search interface. *Online Review 13,* 407–424.

Bates, Marcia J. (1989b). Rethinking subject cataloging in the online environment. *Library Resources and Technical Services 33*(4), 400–412.

Borgman, Christine L., Virginia A. Walter, Jason Rosenberg, and Andrea L. Gallagher, (1991). The Science Library Catalog Project: comparison of children's searching behavior in hypertext and a keyword search system. *Proceedings of the 54th Annual Meeting of the American Society for Information Science 28,* 162–169.

Breivik, Patricia Senn, and Barbara J. Ford, (1993). Promoting learning in libraries through information literacy. *American Libraries 24,* and 101–102.

Broadbent, M. (1992). Demonstrating information service value: linking priorities, benefits and performance. (18p). Paper presented at the Australian Library and Information Association Biennial Conference, Albury, September.

Brown, Warren B., Necmi Karagozoglu, (1989). A systems model of technological innovation. *IEEE Transactions on Engineering Management 36*(1), 11–16.

Centre for Technology and Social Change, (1988). *Innovations for the 1990s: new challenges for technology policy and strategy*. Canberra, Australia, Department of Industry Technology and Commerce.

Churchman, Charles West (1971). *The design of inquiring systems: basic concepts of systems and organization*. New York, Basic Books.

Clayton, Peter (1993). The implementation of innovation: a study of academic and research libraries. Ph.D. diss., University of New South Wales, School of Information Library and Archive Studies.

Davenport, Thomas H., Robert G. Eccles, and Laurence Prusak (1992). Information politics. *Sloan Management Review* (Fall), 53–64.

Doing Bush a favor: Did the U.S. Archivist trade his signature for a job? (1993). *Time* (March 1), 171.

Drucker, Peter F. (1985). *Innovation and entrepreneurship: practice and principles*. London, Heinemann.

Foster, R. (1986). *Innovation: the attackers advantage*. London, MacMillan.

Griffiths, Jose-Marie, Ronald G. Havelock, and Ellen A. Sweet, (1986). *Diffusion of innovations in library and information science: final report*. Washington, D.C., U.S. Department of Education, Educational Resources Information Center (ERIC), (ED279350).

Grosser, Kerry (1991). Human networks in organizational information processing. *Annual Review of Information Processing and Technology 26*, 349–402.

Holusha, John (1993). Traveling high-tech agents help update small factories. *New York Times* (February 16), A1, C9.

Itami, H. (1989). Mobilising invisible assets: the key for successful corporate strategy. *In* E. Punset and G. Sweeney, Eds., *Information resources and corporate growth*. London, Pinter, pp. 36–46.

Kanter, Rosabeth Moss (1988). When a thousand flowers bloom: structural, collective, and social conditions for innovation in organization. *Research in Organizational Behavior 10*, 169–211.

Kazlauskas, Edward John, Rich Pinder, and Judith H. Richardson, (1990). A review and exploratory investigation of instructional design strategies relevant to library and information management software. *Information Technology and Libraries* (June), 121–134.

Kletz, Trevor (1993). *Lessons from disaster: how organisations have no memory and accidents recur*. London, Institute of Chemical Engineers.

Koenig, Michael (1992). The importance of information services for productivity "under-recognized" and "under-invested." *Special Libraries* (Fall), 199–210.

Library Council of New South Wales, (1988). *Annual report 1987–1988*. Sydney, Stale Library of New South Wales.

Lyman, Peter (1992). *Annual report 1991–1992 academic year: University Libraries*. Los Angeles, California, University of Southern California Press.

Lynch, Clifford (1993). Colloquium on Z39.50 delivered at the Graduate School of Library and Information Science, University of California Los Angeles, February 24.

Maguire, Carmel, Connie Wilson, and William Hood, Eds., (1991). *Image-based information and the future of academic and research libraries*. Kensington, Australia, University of New South Wales, School of Librarianship, pp. 14–17.

March, J. G. (1988). *Decisions and organizations*. Cambridge, Massachusetts, Blackwell.

Markuson, Barbara E. (1970). Overview of library systems and automation. *Datamation 16,* 60–68.

McLuhan, Marshall (1964). *Understanding media: the extensions of man.* London, Routledge and Kegan Paul.

Moneta, Aurelia (1989). User reactions to an online search assistance system. *Canadian Journal of Information Science 14*(3), 16–31.

National Commission on Libraries and Information Science. (1982). *Report to the NCLIS from the Public Sector/Private Sector Task Force.* Washington, DC, Government Printing Office.

Oxford dictionary of quotations. (third ed.). (1979). Oxford, Oxford University Press.

Peter, J. Paul, and Jerry C. Olson, (1983). Is science marketing? *Journal of Marketing 47*(4), 111–125.

Porter, Michael E. (1990). *The comparative advantage of nations.* London, Macmillan.

Roberts, E. B., and A. L. Frohman, (1978). Strategies for improving research utilization. *Technology Review 80* (5), 32–39.

Rosenberg, Jason B., and Christine L. Borgman (1992). Extending the Dewey Decimal Classification via keyword clustering: the Science Library Catalog Project. *Proceedings of the 55th Annual Meeting of the American Society for Information Science 29,* 171–184.

Sandilan, Pamela, and Suzanne Walters, (1991). A room of their own—planning the new Denver children's library. *School Library Journal 37*(2), 26–29.

Schon, Donald A. (1971). *Beyond the stable state.* New York, Random House.

Schon, Donald A. (1983). *The reflective practitioner: how professionals think in action.* New York, Basic Books.

Sproull, Lee, and Sara Kiesler, (1991). *Connections: new ways of working in the networked organization.* Cambridge, Massachusetts, MIT Press.

Stace, Doug and Dexter Dunphy, (1991). *Beyond acquisition to access.* Kensington, New South Wales, Centre for Corporate Change, Australian Graduate School of Management, University of New South Wales.

Tropp, Stephen W. (1933). Copyright: new issues and new concerns. From the meeting of the Los Angeles Chapter of the American Society for Information Science, March 11.

Van House, Nancy A., Mary Jo Lynch, Charles R. McClure, Douglas J. Zweizig, and Eleanor Jo Rodger, (1987). *Output measures for public libraries: a manual of standardized procedures.* Prepared for the Public Library Development Project (second edition). Chicago, American Library Association.

Van House, Nancy A., Beth T. Weil, and Charles R. McClure, (1990). *Measuring academic library performance: a practical approach.* Prepared for the Association of College and Research Libraries, Ad Hoc Committee on Performance Measures. Chicago, American Library Association.

Von Hippel, E. (1988). *The sources of innovation.* New York, Oxford University Press.

Woodsworth, Anne, and James F. Williams, (1993). *Managing the economics of owning, leasing and contracting out information services.* Aldershot, Hampshire, Ashgate.

Zuboff, Shoshana (1988). In the age of the smart machine: the future of work and power. New York, Basic Books.

Index

A

Abstracting services, 161
  online, *see* Databases
  see also Chemical Abstracts
Access to information
  need for assistance, 286
  opened by photocopiers, 108
  within organization, 113
  by public, 108
Accessibility, determines use of information source, 28, 275, 284
Adopters of innovations, 65, 144–145
Advisory services, new technology, 186, 289
Ahistoricism, 284
American Library Association, 89
American Productivity and Quality Center, 185
Apple (computer company), 196
Archipelago of information services, 150
Archives, 95, 100–107
  of electronic records, 101–102
  as part of corporate memory, 280
Artificial intelligence, 212–213
ASCII, 254
Australian Securities Commission, 82
Australian Taxation Office, technology strategy of, 58–59
Automobile industry, 11, 43
  Trabant, 11

B

Baby boomers, 52
Banknotes, as innovation, 44
Benefits, economic, from new technology, 181
  see also Cost-benefit analysis
Boundary riders, *see* Gatekeepers
British Library, 274
  Project Quartet, 108, 117

C

California, competitive technology program, 185–186
Capitalist system, 1, 6, 22
Carrier pigeon, 24
Catalogs, library, 118, 234, 256
  MARC standard for, 256
CD-ROM
  databases, 166
  products, 118
  uses, 118–119, 203–204
Census data, 52, 119, 274
Center for Analysis and Dissemination of Demonstrated Energy Technologies (CADDET), 183
Center for the Utilization of Federal Technology (USA), 185
Centrally planned economy, 11, 23
Channels, for information
  linked to content, 76, 103, 143
  trend to transparency of, 249–250
  see also Information sources
Chemical Abstracts, dispute with Dialog Information Services, 89–90
Chief information officers, 151, 248
Citation analysis, 127
Clients, *see* Customers
Clippings services, *see* Cuttings services

Coalition for Networked Information, 292
Colleagues, as information sources, 149, 160
  see also Peers
Commercialization, R & D outputs, 8, 13, 177
  see also Technology transfer
Communications technology, *see* Information technology; Telecommunications
Community analysis, of library clientele, 81
Competitor intelligence systems, 171–173
  databases for, 171
  sought through NASA, 177
Competitors, information services, 299
Computer hardware
  defined, 195–196
  ergonomics of, 239
  monitors, 204
  multimedia, 218
  printers, 205
  range of, 197–198
Computer languages, 211–213
  fourth generation, 212
  standards for, 115
Computer software, *see* Software
Computers
  as garbage generators, 126
  mainframe, 50, 197
  marketing incongruities in, 49, 50
  as supplement of the mind, 193
  see also Computer hardware; Information technology; Personal computers; Workstations
Conferences, as information sources, 159, 160
  teleconferencing, 236–238
Conspectus, ranking system for collections, 127
Content
  information, 21, 248–249
  linked to channel, 76, 128
  managed by channel, 103
  perspective on value, 127
  trend to migrate between media, 249, 250
Context, information, 125, 131
Convergence
  of information specialities, 96
  of information types, 100
  of products and services, 252
  of word processing and printing, 99
Copying machines, open access to information, 108
Copyright
  of databases, 86
  history of, 97
  of journals, 290
Corporate culture, 91, 122
Corporate strategy, 43, 55–60, 111
  development requires information, 175
  of information service, 297
  see also Information strategy; Management; Technology strategy
Cost-benefit analysis
  applied to information services, 133
  applied to information systems, 244–245
Cost-effectiveness of information systems, 245
CPU (Central Processing Unit), 199
Creativity, 4, 37
Cultural travellers, 300
Current awareness services, 134
Customers
  as source of innovation, 47, 298
  see also Users
Cuttings services, 161
Cycles
  Kondratiev long-wave, 5, 43
  life cycle of information production, 77
  product life cycle, 10, 45–46, 59

D

Data, distinguished from information, 20–21
Databases, online, 165–186
  access to, 274, 288
  for company intelligence, 172
  as key service, 165, 170, 274
  ownership rights, 88
  of patents, 162
  range of, 165–166
Databases, relational, 215
Databases, software (for PCs), 215
  with images, 216
Decision support systems, 93, 246–247
  see also Management information systems
Defense Technical Information Center (USA), 183
Demand growth as source of innovation, 43

Democracy and information flow dependency, 28, 87, 88
and privacy, 108
Demographics
census data, 52, 119, 274
information services, 274
as opportunity for innovation, 52, 274
Desk top publishing (DTP), 98–99, 106, 120, 214–215
Developing countries
information services in, 74
low priority of information services in, 267
technology transfer to, 20
Dialog Information Services dispute with Chemical Abstracts, 89–90
Diffusion of innovations, 6, 64–65, 258, 276, 289
see also Technology transfer
Digital environment, 95–121
and diffusion, 167
effect on archives (*q.v.*), 101–102
effect on specializations, 100
fluidity of, 105–106
and innovation, 114
and integration, 96
and management practice, 107–115
and repackaging, 102
and repurposing, 102
in telecommunications, 230–231
see also Information technology, impacts of
Digital information
fluidity of, 105–106, 206
published, 160
repackaging of, 102
Disintermediation, trend to cut out intermediaries, 250, 282
Disks, computer, 200–201
Document delivery systems, for libraries, using fax, 223
Drucker's signals, 48–54

E

Economic data, 175
Economic growth driven by innovation, 6
Economic rent, 46, 302
Economic theory, 6, 27, 83
Economics of information
as branch of economics, 27
statistical approach, 129, 132
Electronic data interchange, 100
Electronic information services, 164–168
see also Databases
Electronic journals, 98
Electronic mail
and pattern of communication, 113
on wide-area network, 225, 232–233
see also Internet
Employees
new, as information source, 149–150, 300
see also Personnel
Employment, in information sector, 25–26
End-users, computing by, 256–259
Engineers
and computers, 256
and informal sources, 149–156
Entrepreneurs, 40
intrapreneurship, 63
see also Innovators
Entropy, technological, 252–254
Ergonomics, 239
ERIC (Educational Resources Information Center), 184
Ethernet, 228
Examples of innovation
banknotes, 44
CD-ROM databases, 167
computer languages, 115, 211
computer operating systems, 207
computers, 49
Conspectus, 127
disinfectants, 179
fax, 222
flashlight, 179
Haber ammonia, 54
just-in-time (*q.v.*), 61
micro-irrigation system, 179
military airplanes, 44
motorcars, 11
mousetrap, 270
online databases, 165
Open University, 59
payment by installments, 61
penicillin, 3
personal computers (*q.v.*), 196, 200
portable computers, 202
shipping industry, 50

Examples of innovation (*continued*)
teleconferencing, 236–238
user interface for computers, 209–210
Executive
information systems, 247
see also Managers
Expert systems, 213
Externalities
from economies of scale, 88
in valuing information, 86

F

Fax, 222
use by Australian Securities Commission, 82
Feedback, 38
in innovation systems, 62–64
market as, 62
Sperry's systems, 43
see also System
Fibre optics, 229
File servers, 220
Files (paper), *see* Records management
Financial reporting, 154
Firms, new technology based, 63
see also Organizations; Small firms
Focus groups, of users, 296, 299
Forecasting, technological, 175
Freedom of Information Act, 87
Functional relationships between those connected with innovation, 46–47, 298
Fuzzy logic, 213

G

Garbage, 124
"garbage in/gospel out," 126
Gatekeepers, 17, 55, 94, 153, 155, 295
Geographic Information Systems (GIS), 116, 206
Globalization, of information services, 251, 283
GOSIP (Government Open Systems Interconnection Profile), 208, 255–256
Government information
Freedom of Information Act, 87
public access to, 88–89
public good, 87–90
for technology transfer, 176–184, 185
Government policies, *see* Policy, government
Government, role in providing information resources, 88
public good, 87–90

H

Hackers, 109
Hardware, *see* Computer hardware
Head-hunting in Silicon Valley, 149
see also Personnel
Hypertext, 216–217, 293

I

IBM (computer company),
venture unit develops PC, 63, 197
widened market for early computers, 49
Illinois, University of, Information Retrieval and Management Service, 185
Images (pictures)
comprehension of, 119
digital storage of, 96, 206
manipulation on PC, 206, 216
Implementation of innovation, 55
Incremental innovation, 46
Indexing services, 161
online, *see* Databases
Industrial Application Centers, NASA, 177
Industry policy, 9
Informal
sources of information, 144–146, 279
structure of organization, 55
Informants, dead or alive, 73
Informate, automate but with information gain, 110, 116
Information
costs incurred by user, 23, 270
defined, 19
digital (*q.v.*), 95–121
as garbage, 124
and innovation, 14, 30–31
institution-supplied, 85
as invisible assets (*q.v.*), 30, 90–91
markets for, 83–86
market-supplied, 85
overload of, 28
ownership of (*q.v.*), 86

as peculiar commodity, 27, 85, 87, 90, 124
as public good, 87–90
published versus unpublished, 107
valuable buried by valueless, 273, 278
value of (*q.v.*), 121–135
see also Information resources; Information sources
Information archipelagoes, 150, 195, 219
Information brokers, 281–282, 291
Information centers, corporate, 152
see also Information services
Information channels, *see* Channels
Information content, 21, 248–249
Information economy, 22, 24–27
information society, 22, 27–32
United States as, 24
see also Economics of information
Information explosion, 28, 124
see also Overload
Information flows
facilitated by information service (*q.v.*), 273–277
in and out of innovating organization, 14–19, 273–277
Information goods and services, 82–83
created by IT, 88, 116–121
see also Markets for information; Information services
Information handling, trends in
convergence (*q.v.*), 252
disintermediation, 250
end-user computing, 256–259
entropy, 252–254
globalization, 251
interoperability (*q.v.*), 249–250
migration of content, 249
outsourcing (*q.v.*), 254
standards (*q.v.*), 254–256
technostress (*q.v.*), 252–256
training, 258
Information literacy, 294
Information policy, 29
see also Information strategy
Information production, cycle of, 77
Information products, 82–83
Information providers (people), 186, 273
see also Information services; Information sources; Librarians
Information resource management (IRM), 90, 112, 128–129, 248
Information resource systems
Defense, 183
defined, 176
energy (CADDET), 183–184
NASA (*q.v.*), 176–182
other, 184
see also Technology transfer
Information resources
distinguished from information services (*q.v.*), 79–81
distinguished from information sources (*q.v.*), 76–79
as profitable investment, 83
provided by NASA, 182
set-up cost of, 88
Information sector, economic, 24–26, 82
Information services
advisers on diffusion of innovation, 276
advisory services, new technology, 186, 289
as bureaucracies, 266
client orientation, 296–297
compared to information resources (*q.v.*), 80–82
competitors of, 299
defined, 22
electronic, 164, *see also* Databases
facilitates innovation, 273–277
as filters, 295, 302
globalization of, 251
impact within organizations, 169, 277
includes marketing, 81, 296
as innovating organizations themselves, 266, 298–302
integrated management of, 150
internal versus external, 134
as invisible assets, 268
involvement in R & D, 170
link different parts of organization, 276, 277
low use of, 83–84, 285
marketing perspective on, 130–131
marketing unit as, 174- 175
need variety of responses, 285
noise reduction by, 125
outsourcing (*q.v.*) of, 281
performance rating of, 133–134, 177
priorities for, 134

Information services (*continued*)
principles for design of, 286–297
product orientation of, 84
as provider of selective information, 275
role in information design, 282
technology change, effects on, 30, 280–284
value of (*q.v.*), 126–135
value-adding by, 126, 129–131
within organizations, 94, 105, 115, 134–135, 150, 168–176
see also Competitor intelligence systems; Databases; Information resource systems; Libraries
Information society, 22, 27–32
Information sources
accessibility determines use, 28, 275
advisory services, 186, 289
categories of, 146–148
concept, 76–78
distinct from information resources (*q.v.*), 77
distinct from information services (*q.v.*), 79
electronic information services, 164–168
external, 144–146, 154–168
formal, 144–146, 160–168
formal versus informal, 144–146, 279
informal, 144–146, 155–159
internal, 144–146, 149–154, 168–176
internal data and reports, 150–154, 275
internal versus external, 144–146, 279
major, 147–148
marketing units as, 174
meetings, 159, 160
peers (*q.v.*), 149
personal, 144–146, 155–159
personnel (*q.v.*), 149–150
publications, 160–162
outside the organization, 154–168, 275
reliability of, 278
within the organization, 149–153, 168–176, 275
see also Competitor intelligence systems; Databases; Information resource systems; Information resources; Information sources; Journals; Marketing; Patents
Information strategy of an organization, 111, 114
Information systems
centralized versus decentralized, 151
defined here, 21, 72
defined by others, 73, 75
and human informant, 73
informal, 92
knowledge-based, 73
mechanistic, 73
not just computers, 74
organizations as, 92–95, 277–280
relation to users, 114, 135, 286
security of, 108
see also Information resource systems; Information services; Information technology
Information systems strategy, *see* Information strategy
Information technology, applications of
art gallery guide, 217
highway toll collection, 225
image manipulation, 206
paperless storage of documents, 203, 221
transport scheduling, 213
teleconferencing, 236
see also Examples of innovation
Information technology, impacts of
approach to valuing services, 126
creates new information products, 116–121
cuts out middle managers, 250, 257
effect on employment, 26, 250
effect on organizations, 107–115, 238–239, 241, 250, 257–258, 283
effects on information services, 280–284
effects on project organization, 112–113
enables new information products, 88, 301
facilitates flexible searching, 287–288
induces organizational amnesia, 283
measurement of effectiveness, 242, 257
needs to match human behavior, 235–242
physiological aspects, 239
promotes innovation, 74–75, 301
psychological aspects, 240
role in information systems, 74–75
training requirements, 114
transforming capability, 74–75, 301
users overwhelmed by new products, 252
users resist inappropriate I.T., 239

see also Computers; Digital environment; Information handling, trends in; Information systems; Personal computers
Information technology, technicalities of
computer hardware and software, 195–218
definitions, 195
networking and telecommunications, 219–235
see also Computer hardware; Computers; Personal computers; Software
Information trends, 249–252
see also Information handling, trends in
Infotrends, 249–252
Innovation,
adopters of, 65
definitions, 2–4, 5
deterrents to, 270
diffusion (*q.v.*) of, 64
future information technology environment of, 248–249
importance to any organization, 265
importance to firm, 7, 37, 58
implementation of, 55
incremental (*q.v.*), 46
in information services, 298–302
information services, role in, 273–277, 302–304
information sources to generate, 147
as learning, 67
management of, 47–60, 269
management more important than technology, 269
in marketing, 61
opportunities for, 48–54, 303
policies, national, 9
process of, 12–18, 35–67, 271, 303
promotes profit, 46
propositions concerning, 268, 278, 281, 284
requires information, 14–17, 30–31, 48, 273
research on, 39, 304
social, 3, 9, 41, 272
sources for (*q.v.*), 41–47
special organizations to promote, 184–186
stages of adoption, 144–145
strategy, 298–304
as a system, 38–40
technological (*q.v.*), 40
technology, role in, 40, 269
see also Examples of innovation; Inputs to innovation; Models of innovation; Signals of change
Innovators, 4
character independent of field, 40
need information, 48, 275
search for change, 48
Inputs to innovation, 38, 41–47
Drucker's signals (*q.v.*), 48–54
negative, 44
Inside information, 23
Institute for Scientific Information, 161, 301
Intellectual property rights
of electronic information, 87
see also Copyright; Ownership of information; Patents
Interfaces
from computer to user, 209–211, 239
in digital systems, 104
from information system to user, 73
see also User interfaces
Intermediaries
information services as, 292–295
see also Disintermediation
Internet, 120–121, 167, 234
promotes free thinking, 167, 235
transparency of, 250
Interoperability, 249, 282
see also Transparency of channels
Intrapreneurship, 63
Inventions
distinct from innovation, 3–5
as input to innovation, 41
Invisible assets, 90–91, 268
Invisible college, 155
ISDN (Integrated Services Digital Networks), 83, 231–232
I.T., *see* Information technology

J

Japan
fax use in, 222
firms consider information management essential, 132
industrial policies of, 141
journals in, 160
MITI, 9, 64, 158

Japan (*continued*)
patents disputes with USA, 159
patents engineering, 164
personal information networks in, 157
Jones, Barry (Australian politician), 29
Journals
copying of, 290
electronic (*q.v.*), 98
electronic copies of, 118
important for manufacturers, 147
as information sources, 160
Just-in-time, 61, 105, 120, 282

K

King, Donald, on value of information, 132
Know-how
personally communicated, 157
trading of, 62–63, 303
Knowledge
distinguished from information, 20–21
notional, 67
real, 67
Knowledge-based information systems, 73
Kondratiev long waves, 5, 43

L

Labor force, 24–25
LAN (Local Area Networks), 215, 219–222
Learning
curve, 45
as new form of labor, 113, 279
Less developed countries, *see* Developing countries
Librarians
numbers of, 169
school, 289
Libraries
changing role of, 107, 251
clientele of, 81
as collections of tools, 293
cuts to, 133
differ from archives, 102
impact within organizations, 169
marketing of, 130
within organizations, 169–170
relation to computing centers, 291
relation to publishers, 291
social context of, 266
special (*q.v.*), 105
see also Library of Congress; National Library of Medicine; State Library of New South Wales
Library of Congress, 256, 301
Licensing (of technology), 142
information service role in, 302
Life cycle of information production (Levitan), 77
Linear model of innovation, 8, 13, 42, 269–270
Literacy, in information use, 294
Local area networks, *see* LAN

M

Mainframe computers, 50, 197
Management
analagous to poker game, 59
of information resources, 248
of innovation, 47–60, 269
practice affected by digitization, 107–115
of projects, 112
see also Information resource management; Managers
Management information systems, 92, 93, 245–247
and informal systems, 92
Managers
don't like to use terminals, 247
don't value information services, 132, 170
of information services, 301
often ignorant of information, 91
marketing interest of, 174
perspectives on innovation, 10–12
seek "news," 93
seek opportunities for innovation, 48
view databases as key service, 165, 170
Manufacturers, information sources used by, 147, 156, 160
MARC (bibliographic formats), 256
Market pull, as source of innovation, 12, 42, 270
Market research, by information services, 299
Marketing, 43
division of organization, 152, 174–175
of information services, 81, 130
innovation in, 61
in innovation process, 60–61, 291

research, reports of, 276
top managers involved in, 174
Markets
as feedback to innovation, 62–64
structural change in, 51
Markets for information, 83–86
economies of scope in, 90
Mass media
as information services/resources, 80
selectivity of, 80
Medium and message, 249
see also Channels; Content
MEDLARS information retrieval system, 184
MEDLINE database, 184
rights to, 88
Memory
of innovations, 303
loss can cause disasters, 280
lost by poor record management, 176, 283
of organization, 95, 277, 280
Message, *see* Content; Information
Microelectronics, *see* Information technology
Military innovations, 43–44
Minicomputers, 197
see also Personal computers
Models of innovation, 13–19
fusion, 16, 18
interactive, 14, 16
linear (*q.v.*), 8, 13, 42, 269–270
Roberts multistage, 14–15, 272–277
science-push, 13
systems (*q.v.*), 17, 19, 38–39
Mooers law of information retrieval, 28
see also Accessibility
Mousetrap (as innovation), 270
Multimedia systems, 96, 119, 218

N

NASA (National Aeronautics and Space Administration)
examples of technology transfer, 179–180
as national information resource, 182
spinoffs produce economic benefits, 180–181
technology transfer by, 176–182
Technology Utilization Program, 177–178
National information policies, 29
National innovation policies, 9
National Library of Medicine, 88, 184, 301
National Science Foundation (USA), university-industry cooperation in R&D, 186
Need to know, as basis for access, 87
Networks (of computers), 167, 219–235
Internet, 120–121, 167, 234
local area (LAN, *q.v.*), 219–222
NREN, 167, 234
wide area (WAN, *q.v.*), 223–230
using public lines, 230–234
"New information order" (UNESCO), 30
New technology based firms, 63
News
selection by information service, 295
selection by mass media, 80
sought by managers, 93, 277–278
Newspapers, 161
see also Cuttings services; Mass media
Not invented here syndrome, 52
NREN (National Research and Education Network), 167, 234

O

OCLC (Online Computer Library Center), 86–87, 98, 115, 297, 301
OECD (Organization for Economic Cooperation and Development)
CADDET information system, 183
reviews of innovation policies, 9
workforce statistics, 25
Office automation, 219–221
see also Information technology, impacts of; Word processing
Office Document Architecture (ODA), 98–99
Online catalogs
client orientation of, 297
controversy on ownership of data, 86
notable innovation, 301
Online searching
needs flexible system, 287
saves money, 170
as service, 177
Online services, *see* Databases, online

Open systems (transferable computer programs), 208, 227
Open systems interconnection (OSI, networking standards), 228, 255
Open University (U.K.), 59
Operating systems (for computers), 206–208
MS-DOS, 207
multi-tasking, 207
multi-user, 207
single user, 207
UNIX, 208, 210
Windows, 210
with graphical interface, 210
Opportunities for innovation, *see* Signals of change
Optical Character Recognition (OCR), 116
Organizations
adapt to their environments, 65–66
changed by I.T., 107–115, 241, 250, 281
communication externally, 154, 276
communication paths in, 61, 113, 174
control of information flow, 241
corporate cultures of, 91
corporate strategies (*q.v.*) for, 55–60
different parts as information resources, 93, 152, 168, 276, 350
factors affecting uptake of I.T., 258
financial reporting within, 154
informal status systems in, 55
informal structures in, 94
information "islands" within, 150
information services within, 134–135
as information systems, 91, 92–95, 271–277
knowledge held by, 21, 272
as learning systems, 279
as locus of innovation, 12, 37, 267
memory of, 95, 175–176, 277, 280
not represented by individuals, 143
"organic" structure in, 51
power distribution within, 113–115, 242
promotion of innovation within, 276
records of, 100, 276
size of, effect on innovation, 45
special, to promote innovation, 184–186
structure affects innovation, 45, 51
see also Management; Teams
OSI, *see* Open Systems Interconnection
Outputs of innovation
new products, 38, 60–62
see also Examples of innovation
Outsourcing
of computer services, 254
of information sevices, 134, 281
of market research, 174
Overload
of information, 28, 124, 283
of I.T. products, 252
Ownership of information, 86–87

P

Packet switching, 223–224
Paperless office
at American Express, 221
at DEC, 203
not yet here, 97, 221–222
Paperwork Reduction Act, 248
Patents
databases, 162
disputes over, 159
as information sources, 162–164
Payment by installments (as innovation), 61
PC, *see* Personal computers
Peers, as information sources
external, 155–159
internal, 149
Penicillin, as innovation, 3
Performance indicators, for information services, 133, 181–182
Personal computers
as catalysts for innovation, 199, 200
early history of, 196–197
facilitate end-user computing, 253
fax card in, 223
hardware of, 199–202
in LAN, 219
input/output for, 204–206, 209
mass storage for, 202–204
in multimedia systems, 218
operating systems (*q.v.*) for, 206–208
portable, 202
workstations, 220–221, 250
Personnel
as cultural travellers, 300
as source of innovation, 300
transfer knowledge, 63, 149
Photocopiers, *see* Copying machines

Picture phones, 236
Pictures, *see* Images
Poker (card game), analogous to innovation, 59
Policy (government)
for information, 29
for innovation, 9
for science, 9
Politicians, impressed by innovation, 8
Portable computers, 202
Prices, as information, 22–23
Printers, for PCs, 205
Printing, historical effect on society, 96–97
Privacy
in digital environment, 117
legislation, 108
videophone raises concerns, 237
Privatization, *see* Government information
Product life cycle, 10, 45–46, 59
Product teams, 149, 153
Productivity
of firm, 6, 27, 45
linked to use of information, 287
of R&D, 132
Profit, spurs innovation, 46, 290
enhanced by information resources, 83
Project champions, 55
Project Quartet, 108, 117
Projects, management of, 56
Protocols, for wide area networks (*q.v.*), 227
see also Standards
Public good, information as, 87–90
Public sector, role in information services, 289
Publications, as information sources, 160–162
see also Journals
Publishing
affected by information technology, 106
on CD-ROM (*q.v.*), 119
on demand, 120
desk-top (*q.v.*), 98–99
private, 107
see also Copyright

R

R&D (research and development), 8, 51
cooperative between firms, 60
cooperative (government/university/industry), 186
diffusion of technology from, *see* Technology transfer
information services have little stake in, 170
information sources to support, 148, 173
link to marketing division, 61, 152, 174
precompetitive, 64, 159
productivity increases with information, 132
as source of innovation, 54
uses computers widely, 256–257
Records management, 95, 101
electronic, 176
importance of, 175–176, 276
Repackaging of information, 102
Reports, annual, 154
Resources, *see* Information resources
Rothschild, Nathan (financier), 23

S

SAPPHO project, 42
Scanners, 16, 205–206
Schools
as innovation, 51
innovation in, 271
Schumpeter, Joseph, 6
Science-push model, *see* Linear model of innovation
Scientific and technical information (STI), 183
Scientific research
as driver of innovation, 8, 13
as marketing process, 84, 269
Scouts, 253
see also Gatekeepers
Security, of information systems, 108
Selection of information, accidental, 29
Selective dissemination of information, 275, 285
SEMATECH, cooperative R&D on semiconductors, 187
Semiconductor industry, 47, 187
Sentries, 153
Serendipity
in innovation process, 141, 271
in selecting information, 29, 141
Shipping industry, 50

Signals of change, 48–54, 273–274
changes in market structure, 51–52, 274
demographics, 52, 274
incongruity, 49–50
new knowledge, 54, 274
process need, 53
public perception, 53
unexpected, 49
Size of organization, effect on innovation, 44–45
Small firms
difficulties of, 281–282
may be innovative, 45, 240
new technology based firms, 63
see also Organizations
Software
application, 213–218
computer languages (*q.v.*), 214
databases, 215
desktop publishing (*q.v.*), 214
graphics-based, 210
multimedia, 218
open systems, 208
operating systems, 206–208
unbundled, 198
for word processing (*q.v.*), 214
Sources, for information, *see also* Information sources
for general innovation, 41–47
for innovation in information services, 298–302
see also Inputs to innovation
Special libraries
closures of, 105
surveys of performance, 169–170
Spinoff (of technology), 176
benefits of, 180–181
Spreadsheets (on computer), 216
SPRINT program
for technology transfer in Europe, 187
Staff, *see* Employees
Standard Generalized Markup Langage (SGML), for publishers, 98, 99
Standards, 254–256
for computer applications, 218
for computer communications, 211, 233
for computer languages, 15
for digital documents, 98
for fax, 22
international organizations, 115, 233, 255
for library catalogs, 256
for wide-area networks, 227
see also Protocols
State Library of New South Wales, 297
Strategy, *see* Corporate strategy; Information strategy; Innovation; Technology strategy
see also Management; Organization
Supercomputers, 198
Suppliers, as sources of innovation, 47, 300
Sustainable development, requires innovation, 265
System
defined, 37
feedback in, 38
innovation process as, 38
organizational perspective, 243
see also Information systems
Systems analysts, role of, 101
Systems analysis, 242–245
Systems model of innovation, 17, 19, 38–41

T

Tape, magnetic, as computer storage medium, 202–203
Tattle-tape systems, for book control in libraries, 127
Teams, product, 149
see also Organization
Technological change
effect on industry structure, 51, 58
effect on information services, 280–284
forecasting of, 175
Technological entropy, 252–254
Technological innovation, 8, 40
Technology
general definition, 194
may dazzle buyers, 127
needs to relate to human behavior, 235
only one part of innovation, 40, 269
as strategic variable, 193
see also Information technology; Technology strategy
Technology policy, *see* Technology strategy
Technology push, as source of innovation, 12, 42
Technology strategy, of an organization, 57–60, 111, 173

Technology transfer
benefits evaluated, 180–181
components of, 142
as contact sport, 156
examples of, 179–180
mechanisms for, 148
by NASA, 176–182
see also Diffusion of innovations; Information resource systems; Spinoff
Technopoly, 123
Technostress, 239
Telecommunications
fax, 222–223
GOSIP, 208, 255–256
open systems interconnection, 228, 255
standards for, 233
for wide-area networks, 228–235
see also Networks
Teleconferencing, 236–238
see also Conferences
Telephones
transparent channels to user, 249, 282
universal use of, 237
videophones, 236
Trabant automobile, 11
Trade journals, 160
Trade secrets, 88
see also Know-how
Training
importance of, 114, 241, 258
interactive systems for, 249
by resident expert, 241
Transparency of channels, 76, 250
Trends, *see* Information handling, trends in

U

UNESCO
attempts "new information order," 30
promotes standards, 255
UNIX (operating system), 208
in local networks, 220
User interfaces (of computers), 209–211, 239
User studies, 31, 81, 117, 131–134, 161
propositions derived from, 284–286
Users
data on, 117
of digital information systems, 114
focus groups of, 296
judge value of information, (*q.v.*) 135
power of, 114
seek control of systems, 286
as sources of innovation, 54
stressed by poor information technology, 239

V

Value of information, 121–135
approached through context, 126–128
approached through technology, 126, 128
approached through user, 125, 126, 129
demonstrations of, 131–135
depends on circumstances, 121
depends on context, 125
King's evaluations, 131–132
managers' uncertainty about, 132
Value-adding, by information services, 129–131
Value chain, 53
Videophones, 236
Voice mail, 225–226

W

WAN (Wide Area Networks), 223–230
data sharing on, 224
file transfer on, 224
log-in, 225
media for, 228
performance (speed) of, 226
protocols for, 227
voice mail on, 224
War
as driver of innovation, 8, 9, 43–44
Wide-area networks, *see* WAN
see also Networks
Wire services (for news), 80
Word processing (WP)
digitizes information, 116
Relation to DTP, 98–99
software for, 214
Work groups, 240
Workforce, proportion in information, 24–25, 28
Workstations, 220–221, 250
see also Personal computers

Library and Information Science

(Continued from page ii)

Lois Swan Jones and Sarah Scott Gibson
Art Libraries and Information Services

Nancy Jones Pruett
Scientific and Technical Libraries: Functions and Management
Volume 1 and Volume 2

Peter Judge and Brenda Gerrie
Small Bibliographic Databases

Dorothy B. Lilley and Ronald W. Trice
A History of Information Sciences 1945-1985

Elaine Svenonius
The Conceptual Foundations of Descriptive Cataloging

Robert M. Losee, Jr.
The Science of Information: Measurement and Applications

Irene P. Godden
Library Technical Services: Operations and Management, Second Edition

Donald H. Kraft and Bert R. Boyce
Operations Research for Libraries and Information Agencies: Techniques for the Evaluation of Management Decision Alternatives

James Cabeceiras
The Multimedia Library: Matertials Selection and Use, Second Edition

Charles T. Meadow
Text Information Retrieval Systems

Robert M. Losee, Jr. and Karen A. Worley
Research and Evaluation for Information Professionals

Carmel Maguire, Edward J. Kazlauskas, and Anthony D. Weir
Information Services for Innovative Organizations

Karen Markey Drabenstott and Diane Vizine-Goetz
Using Subject Headings for Online Retrieval